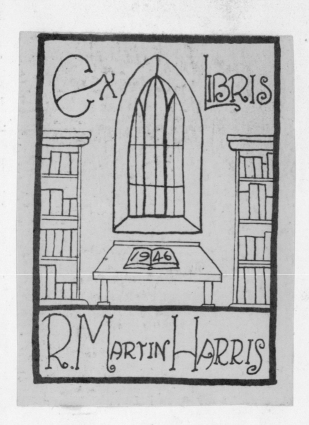

Ex Libris

1946

R. Martin Harris

SIR CHARLES SEDLEY
1639—1701

A Study in the Life and Literature
of the Restoration

BY

V. DE SOLA PINTO

M.A., D.PHIL. (OXON.)

PROFESSOR OF ENGLISH LANGUAGE AND LITERATURE IN THE
UNIVERSITY COLLEGE, SOUTHAMPTON

LONDON
CONSTABLE & COMPANY LTD
1927

PRINTED IN GREAT BRITAIN BY RICHARD CLAY & SONS, LIMITED,
BUNGAY, SUFFOLK.

TO

G. THORN DRURY, Esq., M.A., K.C.

WITHOUT WHOSE GENEROUS HELP

THIS BOOK COULD NEVER HAVE BEEN WRITTEN

CONTENTS

PART I

THE LIFE OF SIR CHARLES SEDLEY

PART II

THE WORKS OF SIR CHARLES SEDLEY

Contents

ILLUSTRATIONS

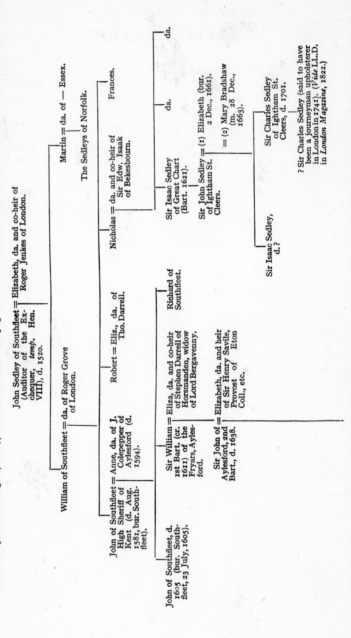

Pedigree of the Sedley Family derived from the pedigree in the British Museum (Add. MS. 33920 f. 69 b), the pedigree in the Bodleian (MS. Rawl. B, 82), a pedigree compiled by Mr. F. Darwin Swift, F.R.Hist.Soc., of Denstone College, Stafford, who kindly placed it at the disposal of the author; also from G.E.C.'s "Complete Baronetage" (IV. 187) and from MS. notes belonging to the late Col. Prideaux and now in the possession of Mr. G. Thorn Drury, K.C.

John Sedley of Southfleet = Elizabeth, da. and co-heir of
(Auditor of the Ex-   Roger Jenkes of London.
chequer, *temp.* Hen.
VIII), d. 1520.

William of Southfleet = da. of Roger Grove   Martin = da. of — Essex.
of London.

The Sedleys of Norfolk.

John of Southfleet = Anne, da. of J.   Robert = Eliz., da. of   Nicholas = da. and co-heir of   Frances.
High Sheriff of   Colepepper of   Tho. Darrell.   Sir Edw. Isaak
Kent (d. Aug.   Aylesford (d.   of Bekesbourn.
1581, bur. South-   1594).
fleet).

John of Southfleet, d.   Sir William = Eliza, da., and co-heir   Richard of   Sir Isaac Sedley   da.   da.
1605 (bur. South-   1st Bart, (cr.   of Stephen Darrell of   Southfleet.   of Great Chart
fleet, 23 July, 1605).   1611) of the   Horsmanden, widow   (Bart. 1621).
Fryars, Ayles-   of Lord Bergavenny.
ford.

Sir John of = Elizabeth, da. and heir   Sir John Sedley = (1) Elizabeth (bur.
Aylesford, 2nd   of Sir Henry Savile,   of Ightham St.   2 Dec, 1661).
Bart, d. 1638.   Provost of Eton   Cleers.   = (2) Mary Bradshaw
Coll., etc.   (m. 28 Dec,
1663).

Sir Isaac Sedley,   Sir Charles Sedley
d.?   of Ightham St.
Cleers, d. 1701.

? Sir Charles Sedley (said to have
been a journeyman upholsterer
in London in 1741). (*Vide* LL.D.
in *London Magazine*, 1822.)

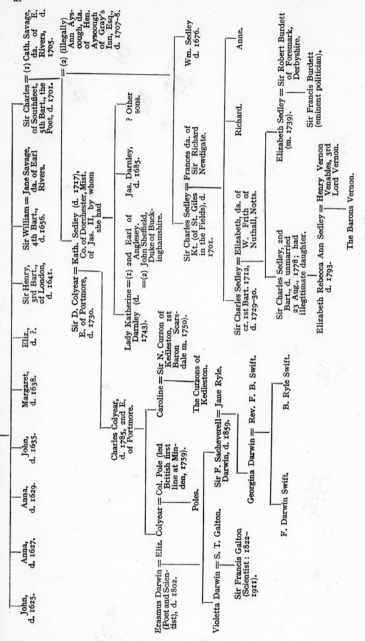

PART I

THE LIFE OF SIR CHARLES SEDLEY

"It would be a Task few Men of Modesty would undertake, viz. to Write the Life of this Person. . . ."—"Some Account of the Life of Sir Charles Sedley" by "an Eminent Hand," prefixed to the edition of 1722.

B

INTRODUCTION

SIR CHARLES SEDLEY has been badly treated by posterity both as a man and a poet. His life has been overshadowed by a single scandalous episode of his youth, and his works have been judged from faulty and dishonest editions published many years after his death. The object of the present study is to do him tardy justice by means of a detailed biography, largely derived from sources which have not been used by the authors of previous memoirs, and a critical account of his writings, based on the essential foundation of a complete and scientific bibliography. That he was the author of some of the best songs of his age and the friend of Dryden would alone be sufficient reasons for undertaking such a work. There is a further justification in the fact that he is a good representative of an interesting and widely misunderstood phase in the evolution of English society. He is typical of those Wits and Poets of the Restoration, who have hitherto been regarded merely as selfish libertines, but who are now being shown by a more careful and sympathetic study to have played an important part in building up the fine aristocratic culture of the eighteenth century. If any apology is due for the insertion of a somewhat detailed account of the career of Sir Charles's daughter, Katherine Sedley, Countess of Dorchester, in the present work, it may be pleaded that a biography of the poet without some mention of that lady would be unthinkable, while the interest attached to her own character and the extraordinary part which she played in English history demand that her doings should be recorded as fully as possible.

3

Although no detailed biography of Sir Charles Sedley has hitherto appeared, a great number of short memoirs have been published during the laſt two hundred years. Their authors have usually confined themselves to giving an account of the moſt scandalous episode of the poet's youth, and relating a few other anecdotes which have given currency to a sharply outlined portrait or rather caricature of a very wicked and witty baronet whose life was chiefly spent in debauchery and the coining of smart repartees. By co-ordinating these ſtories with other records which have hitherto been inaccessible or overlooked, I have attempted to replace this conventional piċture by one which is at once more complex and truer to life, and which may help to explain the curious faċt that the ringleader of the debauch at Oxford Kate's was also capable of the delicate beauty of such poems as "Not *Celia*, that I juſter am" and "*Phillis* is my only Joy," and the manly good sense of the Parliamentary speeches.

The earlieſt printed account of Sir Charles Sedley is that of Gerard Langbaine on p. 485 of his "Account of the English Dramatic Poets," published during the poet's lifetime (Oxford, 1691). It contains nothing but a little flattery, two quotations, from Rocheſter and Shadwell (the former of which was to be repeated *ad nauseam* by subsequent biographers) and a brief liſt and description of Sedley's plays. Charles Gildon's "The Lives and Charaċter of the English Dramatick Poets. . . . Firſt begun by Mr. Langbain, improved and continued down to this time by a careful Hand" (London, 1698), includes an even briefer notice of the same charaċter. Anthony à Wood, who knew Sedley personally, wrote a "Life" of the poet some time before his death in 1695,[1] which he did not,

---

[1] The notes which Wood made for this "Life" are to be found among his Diaries, together with other references to Sedley. They are printed in Clark's "Life and Times of Anthony à Wood," and are referred to in footnotes to the body of the present study.

however, publish in the firſt edition of his "Athenæ
Oxonienses" (Oxford, 1691), perhaps for fear of
giving offence to Sir Charles, who was ſtill alive. It
firſt appeared in the second edition (London, 1721)
and contains a detailed account of the Bow Street
affair and some amusing gossip about the trial which
followed it, besides a fairly accurate liſt of Sedley's
published works up to about 1690. Aubrey, the other
great scandalmonger of the age, unfortunately left no
life of Sedley, but only a tantalising sentence describing
his personal appearance.[1]

In 1702, the year after Sir Charles's death, his
"affinity,"[2] Captain William Ayloffe, published an
edition of his Miscellaneous Works, but his Preface to
the Reader does not throw much light on the poet's
life. In 1719 a compilation of short literary biographies,
called "Giles Jacob's Poetical Regiſter," appeared, with
a very brief notice of Sedley and a liſt of his plays.
Passing over the genealogical notes in Collins's
"Baronetage" (1720), we come to "Some Account of
Sir Charles Sedley" prefixed to the firſt volume of
the duodecimo edition of the Works published by
Samuel Briscoe in 1722. The title-page ſtates that
this "Account" is by "an Eminent Hand," and for
once this familiar ascription has a certain amount of
truth, for the "Eminent Hand" may have been that
of no less a person than Daniel Defoe.[3] Whether the
author of this memoir had any acquaintance with Sir
Charles is doubtful. The "Account" reads like a
colleƈtion of gossip, picked up at taverns and coffee-
houses. It contains few dates, a good deal of flattery,

---

[1] See p. 43.   [2] See p. 164.

[3] On the verso of the last leaf of "The Second Part of Whipping
Tom, or a Road for a Proud Lady" (Briscoe, London, 1722), there is
an advertisement of the 1722 Sedley which ends "with Memoirs of
the Author by Mr. D'Foe." I am indebted to Mr. G. Thorn Drury,
K.C., for permission to publish this fact, which he discovered and
communicated to me.

and, perhaps, a little irony. For instance, the opening
sentence, "It would be a Task few Men of Modesty
would undertake, *viz.* to Write the Life of this
Person," would appear from the context to mean that
a description of Sir Charles's dazzling "parts" was
beyond the power of an ordinary mortal. It might, however, bear another interpretation, when applied to the
hero of the Bow Street frolic. Again, "he appeared in
Publick much about the Year 1663," may be an innocent mistake as to the date of his first appearance at
Court (which was probably earlier), or it may be a sly
allusion to the Bow Street affair, a very "publick" kind
of appearance, which took place in that very year, and
to which there is no overt reference in the "Account."
Perhaps the ironical tone of this memoir gave offence.
Some copies of the 1722 edition do not contain it,
although they announce it on the title-page, so it is
possible that it was suppressed.[1] Its chief value lies
in the traditions which it preserves of Sir Charles's
relations with King Charles II, which may well be
authentic,[2] and the story of his famous remark on
the Revolution, of which it gives the earliest and
most plausible version.[3]

The so-called "Lives of the Poets of Great Britain
and Ireland, by Mr. Cibber and other Hands" (London, 1753), chiefly written by Robert Shiels,[4] contains
a notice of Sedley which has a certain interest, as the
first attempt to combine the accounts of Wood and
Defoe. Its author had, however, overlooked two important references to the poet, which had appeared in

---

[1] It is equally possible that it was not ready for publication at the
appointed time, and was only inserted in later copies. It was certainly
inserted after the rest of the book was made up, for its first leaf is
signed A2, a repetition of the signature of the first leaf of the dedication, which precedes it, and in some copies this signature is blacked
out in ink. But it is impossible to say whether it was withdrawn from
later issues, or not inserted in early ones.

[2] See pp. 54–56.   [3] See p. 174.

[4] See Sir W. Raleigh's "Six Essays on Johnson," pp. 119, 120.

John Dennis's "Original Letters" in 1721, and the
"Works and Life of The Right Honourable Charles
Earl of Halifax" in 1725. "Biographia Britannica,"
the most worthy attempt of the eighteenth century
at a Dictionary of National Biography (London,
1747–66), includes the fullest and most accurate
account of Sedley which had hitherto appeared. Its
author draws on several sources besides the memoir
by Wood and the "Account" prefixed to the edition
of 1722.

Johnson's collection of the English Poets (first
edition, 1779) contains no Life of Sedley and no
selection from his works. This exclusion seems
astonishing in a collection where such poetasters as
Stepney and Pomfret were given places. If it was
made on moral grounds, it is difficult to see why
Rochester and Dorset should have been included, but
perhaps their titles recommended them to the book-
sellers who controlled the publication, while the
memory of the Bow Street affair had surrounded
Sedley's name with a sulphurous odour which might
have alarmed their clients.[1] The Life of Dorset,

[1] Curiously enough, Johnson seems to have forgotten the Sedley
family on another occasion, recorded by Fanny Burney in her Diary
("Diary and Letters," ed. Dobson, I. 57). Speaking to Mr. Seward in
August 1778, he quoted the lines:

> "lies buried here
> So early wise, so lasting fair,
> That none, unless her years you told,
> Thought her a child or thought her old."

He prefaced the quotation with the remark, "I remember an epitaph
to the purpose, which is in—(I have quite forgot what, and also the
name it was made upon, but the rest I recollect distinctly)." The
lines are from Waller's Epitaph on the Lady Sedley (Sir Charles Sedley's
mother): see p. 27. That Johnson was well acquainted with Sedley's
career is shown by the well-known line in the "Vanity of Human
Wishes":

> "And Sedley curs'd the form which pleas'd a king."

The "form" must be that of Lady Dorchester, but "Sedley" may however, contains a full account of the Bow Street affair, and incidentally mentions the part played by Sedley on that occasion. David Erskine Baker's "A Companion to the Playhouse" (1764) and its successor "Biographia Dramatica" (1782) contain articles on Sedley, which include no new matter, but correct some of the grosser errors of former biographers. Early editions of Dr. Granger's interesting "Biographical History" (1769–74, 1775) contain a short life of Katherine Sedley, but none of her father. In Noble's enlarged edition of this work (1806) there is a short account of Sir Charles which does not add materially to our knowledge of the poet. In addition to these printed memoirs, there have survived from the eighteenth century some valuable MS. notes made by William Oldys in his interleaved copy of Langbaine (Brit. Mus. c. 28, *g*),[1] while an interesting defence of his works appeared in Dr. J. Langhorne's "Effusions of Fancy and Friendship" in 1763. It may be mentioned in passing that Oldys's notes were known to Malone, who made use of them in a footnote on Sedley on p. 63 of his "Life of Dryden," prefixed to his edition of that author's Prose Works (1800). Malone was also the first editor of Dryden to make the very important identification of Sedley with the "Lisideius" of the "Essay of Dramatic Poesy."[2]

---

refer either to the father or the daughter. It is generally taken in the latter sense, but Mrs. Jane West in a letter to the *Gentleman's Magazine* of April 1800 contended that it refers to Sir Charles. Johnson was asked the meaning of the line by Anna Seward a few months before his death; he replied: "I knew at the time I wrote the poem, but the history has since escaped my recollection" (*Gentleman's Magazine*, April 1800).

[1] These notes are reproduced in full in Appendix I, pp. 318–320.

[2] For which he was somewhat foolishly jeered at in a squib called "Essence of Malone" by George Hardinge, the judge and antiquary, writing under the name of "Minutius Felix" (London, 1800).

In 1822 a long article entitled "Memoirs of Sir Charles Sedley" was printed in the *London Magazine* (September 1822, Vol. VI. pp. 265–72). It consists of an elaborate (but not entirely correct) genealogical account of the Sedley family and a life of Sir Charles, concocted from the printed eighteenth-century memoirs and Oldys's notes, together with one tradition which had appeared in a topographical work published in 1800.[1] Its author, who signs himself LL.D., acknowledges indebtedness only to Giles Jacob and "Cibber," and concludes with the remark, that "much (more information) is not, I am satisfied, now to be obtained." A month after the appearance of LL.D.'s article, the *Gentleman's Magazine* published a most valuable note on Sedley, entitled "Fly Leaves No. IV, Sir Charles Sedley the Poet," and signed "Eu. Hood." "Hood" corrects the chief errors of LL.D., and cites some notable allusions to Sedley in seventeenth-century newspapers, as well as a description of some legal documents which throw considerable light on the poet's life. The author of this article was Joseph Haslewood, the well-known antiquary and writer on stage history (1769–1833), whose interleaved copy of "Giles Jacob's Poetical Register" (Brit. Mus. C. 45, *d*) contains MS. notes of even greater importance than those made by Oldys in the previous century. In 1855 John Heneage Jesse published his interesting "Memoirs of the Court of England during the Reign of the Stuarts." The third volume contains a memoir of Sedley based on Anthony à Wood, Cibber, the Memoir prefixed to the Edition of 1722, and Oldys's MS. notes. In the same volume there is an account of the Countess of Dorchester, in which several amusing anecdotes are preserved.

Macaulay's "History of England" (1859) was the

---

[1] Lysons's "Parishes of Middlesex, not Described in the Environs of London" (London, 1800): see p. 53.

first work to draw attention to the importance of Sedley's parliamentary career, but no biography of note appeared after Jesse's work, till the publication of the "Dictionary of National Biography" in the 'nineties. Sir A. W. Ward's article in the Dictionary is derived from the usual printed sources, but also includes certain new material which had appeared during the nineteenth century, the most notable being the numerous references in the complete edition of Pepys's Diary. No use, however, is made of the MS. notes of Oldys and Haslewood, and certain important details, such as the poet's separation from his wife, his relations with Ann Ayscough, and the place of his death, are not mentioned. Moreover, Sir A. W. Ward had, apparently, overlooked the interesting letter from Sedley to the second Earl of Chesterfield, preserved in the Earl's MS. letter book (Brit. Mus., Add. MS. 19,253) and printed, somewhat incorrectly, in his "Correspondence" (London, 1829).

The inadequate article in the Dictionary was to some extent supplemented by an interesting correspondence in *Notes and Queries* extending over some eleven years (1890–1901), when much new information concerning Sedley was contributed to that journal by the late Col. W. F. Prideaux, Mr. Gordon Goodwin and others. Prideaux was a stout defender of Sedley, and the first critic to throw real light on the bibliography of the poems. He contemplated writing a life of the poet, and collected some valuable notes for that purpose which have, since his death, passed into the hands of Mr. G. Thorn Drury, K.C., who has generously placed them at the disposal of the present writer.

Articles on Sedley by Sir Edmund Gosse in the "Encyclopædia Britannica" and other contemporary compilations merely reproduce the biographical details given by the "Dictionary of National Biography," while Mr. Charles Whibley in the "Cambridge History

of English Literature" confines himself to some
excellent critical remarks on the poems.

At the opening of the present century two German
scholars devoted some attention to Sedley. In 1904,
Edmund Plückhahn chose the "Foreign Influences"
on Sedley's comedies as the subject of a thesis for
the Doctorate of Philosophy at Rostock.[1] He prefixes a short biography to his essay, but it contains
no information beyond that which is contained in
the "Dictionary of National Biography." A learned
air is given to this work by the multitude of authorities
which are quoted in the footnotes, but as they consist
chiefly of modern English and German text-books on
English literature, they do not actually testify to
anything except the industry of the author.[2] Plückhahn's remarks on the comedies are based not on
the original editions but on the very untrustworthy
text of Briscoe's edition of the Works (1722).

In 1905 Max Lissner published a thesis for the
doctorate in the University of Leipzig. It claims to
describe "Sir Charles Sedley's Leben und Werke."[3]
The biographical section of this work is derived from

---

[1] "Die Bearbeitung ausländischer Stoffe im englischen Drama am
Ende des 17 Jahrhunderts dargelegt an Sir Charles Sedley's The
Mulberry Garden und Bellamira or the Mistress . . . von Edmund
Plückhahn aus Hamburg." 1904.

[2] An amusing instance of Dr. Plückhahn's methods is shown in his
footnote on the date of Sedley's death. After remarking, "Ueber das
Todesjahr Sedley's herrschen sehr schwankende Angaben," he quotes
different authorities for different years: for 1722, Baker's "Companion
to the Playhouse" (1764); for 1728, one modern English and two
modern German Histories of English Literature; for 1701, the "Biographia Dramatica" of 1811, Sir A. W. Ward's "History of English
Dramatic Literature," Chambers's "Cyclopædia of English Literature,"
and three less well known English and American text-books. So 1701
wins by a show of hands! Without troubling about parish registers,
Dr. Plückhahn might have glanced at the "Brief Relation" of Narcissus
Luttrell, Sedley's contemporary (which had been in print since 1857),
where he would have found the exact date.

[3] "Sir Charles Sedley's Leben und Werke . . . von Max Lissner."
Halle, 1905.

the more obvious printed sources such as the eighteenth-century memoirs, Sir A. W. Ward's article, and the references in Pepys and Macaulay. Its author had clearly never heard of the articles in the *London* and *Gentleman's Magazines*, and ſtill less of the notes of Oldys and Haslewood and the letter to Lord Cheſterfield. His critical essay is one ſtage further removed from reality than that of his compatriot, for it is founded on the 1776 *reprint* of the bad text of 1722, and this reprint seems to be the only edition which he has consulted. He is thus led to cite in support of his views poems which are probably not from Sedley's pen at all.

Finally, Mr. E. Beresford-Chancellor has published an account of Sedley's life and writings in his "Lives of the Rakes" (Philip Allan, London, 1924). Mr. Chancellor is the firſt biographer to make some use of the records of Sedley preserved in Luttrell's "Brief Relation" and the Reports of the Royal Commission on Hiſtorical Manuscripts, but he is apparently unaware that examples of Sedley's correspondence exiſt, and he has completely over-looked the events conneɔted with the poet's separation from his wife, to cite only two important omissions, whilſt he accepts such unauthenticated ſtories as the collapse of the theatre roof at the firſt performance of "Bellamira" quite uncritically.[1]

Sedley's biographers have not been impeccable, but it may be urged in their defence that it was not easy to find out much about the Reſtoration wits during the eighteenth and nineteenth centuries. There was a mass of rather unreliable gossip and a little printed correspondence. Many of the documents that are now available were then inaccessible, and very few original letters were at the disposal of the biographer. Unfortunately, Sedley has left even less

[1] See p. 147.

correspondence than his friends Rochester and Etherege. His few extant letters are included in the
present work, but most of the biography has had to
be pieced together from a variety of sources, such as
allusions in contemporary correspondence, journals,
newspapers, dedications, official records and legal
documents. For the discovery of many of these and,
above all, for their invaluable advice and assistance,
I am deeply indebted to Professor Sir Charles H.
Firth and Mr. G. Thorn Drury, K.C., who have
generously placed at my disposal the treasures of
their libraries and the still richer treasures of their
learning and experience. I wish especially to record
the fact that Mr. Thorn Drury allowed me to make
use of his interleaved and annotated copy of the 1776
edition of Sedley's Works, and gratefully to acknowledge the immense help which I have derived from
his MS. notes in that copy. I desire to express my
sincere thanks to Lord Sackville of Knole Park,
Kent, the descendant of Sedley's friend, the Earl of
Dorset, and to Sir F. Newdigate, Bart., of Arbury,
Warwickshire, for their generous permission to read
and copy the Sedley MSS. in their possession, to the
Rev. Montague Summers for lending me his important
MS. notes on Sedley's plays, to Mr. W. J. Lawrence
for some helpful advice on theatrical matters, to
Professor G. S. Gordon, Mr. D. Nichol Smith,
Mr. H. F. Brett Smith, Mr. J. Isaacs, and Mr. A. C.
Harwood, for a multitude of most useful hints and
suggestions, to Dr. H. J. Spenser, who read my
work in manuscript, to Professor R. M. Hewitt,
who read the proofs, to the many ladies and gentlemen
who sent me valuable information on the appearance
of my article entitled "Some Notes on Sir Charles
Sedley" in the *Times Literary Supplement* of November 22, 1922, and, finally, to the various officials
in Public Libraries and collections of Archives both
in England and France who have met the heavy

demands which I have made upon their patience with long-suffering kindness and courtesy. I desire to add to this lift the names of two persons who, although they have given me no direct help in the work of research, have nevertheless a very real share in whatever merits this ftudy may possess. They are those of Mr. Percy Simpson, Fellow of Oriel College, Oxon, who taught me the meaning of honeft and discerning scholarship, and the late Professor Sir Walter Raleigh, who loved the poets of the Reftoration for their wit and their gaiety and who often talked to me about them in his inspiring way during the laft years of his life. The inception of this work was indeed due to the advice and encouragement of that great English scholar and gentleman.

CHAPTER I

THE SEDLEY FAMILY, 1337–1639

"This Family (of very good Antiquity in the County of *Kent*). . ."—
Collins's "Baronetage," 1720 (I. 327).

THE Sedleys, or Sidleys,[1] of Kent were one of the
many families who emerged from their original
obscurity during the great social revolution which
changed the England of the Middle Ages into the
England of the modern world. The story of their rise,
decline and disappearance begins amid the mists of
the late Middle Ages, reaches its climax at the Court

[1] There are many spellings of the name. Here are some specimens
found by the present writer: Sedley, Sedle, Sedlye, Sedlay, Sedelay,
Sidley, Sidly, Sidlie, Sydley, Sydly, Cidley, Chidley, Sidelay and even
Chelzey. The last four, it should be added, are the versions of the
Frenchmen, Bonrépaux, Barillon and Dangeau. Malone favoured
Sidley (Dryden's Prose Works (1800), I. 64), and cites the grants of
the titles to Sir William Sidley in 1611 and to Katherine Sidley in
1687, and the dedication of the "Mulberry Garden" (1668). On the
other hand, he admits that "at a later period of his life the poet called
himself Sedley" (*i.e.* later than the "Mulberry Garden"). Haslewood
pleads as strongly for Sedley: "I have seen two original autographs of
the poet and several of his descendants and they wrote their names
indisputably *Sed*ley. In all the old Deeds from the time of Charles the 1st
the name is uniformly spelt *Sed*ley" (MS. notes to Jacob's "Poetical
Register," see Appendix I, p. 320). As the present writer has seen six
original signatures of the poet all of which are unquestionably Charles
Sedley—to say nothing of transcripts of the wills of Sir Charles and Sir
John where the same form is found—he is convinced that Haslewood
was right. Nevertheless the form Sidley (Sydley, etc.) was undoubtedly
sometimes used, and Malone was perfectly justified in deriving Dryden's "Lisideius" from it. It may have been a phonetic spelling representing a current pronunciation. In the seventeenth century the
values of the short *i* and *e* were probably not so sharply distinguished
as they are to-day.

15

of Charles II, where the poet squandered the wealth
acquired by the patience of generations, and closes in
the calm of the eighteenth century, when the Sedley
family, as though exhausted by the effort of producing
a poet and a royal mistress, sank back once more into
the comfortable and undistinguished position among
the landed gentry held by its ancestors two hundred
years before. That such an astounding meteor as Sir
Charles should have suddenly appeared in a line of
respectable squires and lawyers seems at first glance
one of the puzzles of heredity, and only explicable by
the profound remark of Don Brid'Oison, that "On
est toujours le fils de quelqu'un." A close study of the
family history, however, shows that the poet was a
true Sedley in almost every respect, and probably his
most surprising actions were merely the result of
qualities which his ancestors had possessed in a less
conspicuous form. His extravagance and his love of
letters were almost certainly inherited, while it seems
likely that the strong fundamental sanity which had
built up the fortunes of his Kentish forefathers remained at the base of his character and enabled him
to weather the storm of Restoration profligacy better
both in health and in purse than many other courtiers,
and to save for his descendants a respectable remnant
of the family property. Therefore, although the Sedleys
of the eighteenth century had lost their ancestors'
place among the magnates of Kent, it was possible for
them to retain their rank among the land-owning caste
in another part of the country, and thus, although the
male line has long been extinct, their blood has been
mingled with that of other distinguished families and
has run in the veins of eminent men of our own day.[1]

---

[1] The Sedley pedigree (see pp. x, xi) is of extraordinary interest and
might furnish material for a monograph by a student of heredity. For
some acute remarks on the subject see Professor Karl Pearson's "Life
of Sir Francis Galton" (Cambridge, 1914), I. 20, 21. Galton himself
was a direct descendant of Sir Charles Sedley: see Pedigree.

The original home of the Sedleys seems to have been the low-lying coaſt around the border of Kent and Sussex. Part of Romney Marsh was formerly called Sidley's Marsh,[1] and the name ſtill survives in the hamlet of Sidley's Green near Bexhill. In the fourteenth century a branch of the family migrated to North Kent, and built a house in the village of Scadbury, or Scotbury, near Southfleet, where, in the middle of the seventeenth century,[2] their arms and the date 1337 were ſtill visible in an old wainscot. 1337 Other Sedleys seem to have continued to live on the south coaſt, for, during the fifteenth century, the name is frequently found among those of the moſt prominent citizens of Rye and other towns in the neighbourhood.[3] The early hiſtory of the Southfleet branch has not been recorded, but it may be supposed that, like many another family of small landowners, it profited considerably by the decay of the old nobility during the fifteenth century. When we next catch sight of the Sedleys of Southfleet they are people of some importance in the fertile country to the south-weſt of London.

[1] Philipot's "Villare Cantianum or Kent Surveyed and Illustrated," London, 1659, p. 330.

[2] Philipot writes ("Villare Cantianum," p. 330): "In this mansion (Scadbery) there is a Room whose sides are covered with Wainscot, and on one of the Plates or Pains the arms of Sydley are carved in embost work . . . with the year of the Lord affixed in figures, whose date commences from 1337. And although the Structure of the House hath, like a Snail, shifted its ancient shell, yet in all its Mutations and Vicissitudes, which must certainly have very much disordered the Fabrick, when it was cast into a new mould or frame, and ravelled and discomposed the Materials: yet this Panel of Wainscot hath been like a Relique, religiously preserved to justifie not only the antiquity of the Seat but of the Family of Sydley also, which is presumed to have been resident at this place, before the above-mentioned calculation: from whom Sir *Charles Sidley* Baronet claims the original of his title to this mansion and his extraction or pedigree likewise untwisted into many Descents and now at last wound up in him."

[3] Records of the Corporations of Rye and neighbouring towns. Hist. MSS. Comm., Appendix to 5th Report, pp. 490, 491, 499, 529, 530.

c

John Sedley of Southfleet (flor. *temp.* Henry VII, Henry VIII) is the first member of the family whose personality can be recognised with any distinctness and he has a good claim to be considered its founder. He is said [1] to have been educated at Exeter College, Oxford. Afterwards he was bred to the Law, entering 1503–20 the Middle Temple on 3 July, 1503, where he was one of the Masters of the Revels elected there at Christmas 1515/16.[2] He rose high in his profession, reaching the important position of Auditor of the Exchequer to Henry VIII,[3] and he is supposed to have been employed to extract money and land from the Church. It is probable that, in common with most of Henry's tools, he profited considerably by the confiscation of the ecclesiastical property, and perhaps one of the original sources of the wealth of the Sedleys was the spoil which fell to the Auditor's share when the monasteries were dissolved.[4] Apparently he was on intimate terms with the King, for he jousted with him at Greenwich in May 1516.[5] He died in 1520, and was buried in Southfleet Church. A superb memorial brass covers his tomb, and preserves a wonderful portrait of a shrewd-featured old man and his wife, dressed in rich robes.[6] John Sedley inaugurated

[1] By LL.D. in the *London Magazine*, September 1822 (see Introduction, p. 9). There is no trace of a John Sedley, or Sydley, in the registers of Exeter College or of the University.

[2] "Middle Temple Records" (ed. Hopwood, London, 1904), I. 7, 148.

[3] Brewer's "Letters and Papers of the Reign of Henry VIII," I. 2, 1084.

[4] LL.D. states that he received the Manor of Southfleet, but this must be a mistake, as, according to Philipot ("Villare Cantianum," p. 329), this Manor was retained by the Crown till the reign of Elizabeth, who granted it to a certain William Peter of Wrettle. It was by him sold to Sir William Sedley, grandfather of the poet. However, LL.D. is doubtless right in supposing that John Sedley received grants of land from Henry VIII.

[5] Cal. State Papers Dom., 8 Henry VIII, Pt. I.

[6] Rubbing, Brit. Mus., Add. MSS. 32490, SS, 33.

in three respects the policy which his descendants were
to pursue for several generations. He married an
heiress, daughter of a London citizen; he invested his
money in purchases of land, and he made liberal
bequests to the college where he was educated at
Oxford.[1] A black-letter copy of Lydgate's "Bochas"
(perhaps Pynson's edition of 1494)[2] was among the
books which probably belonged to Sir Charles Sedley
the Poet, and it may well have been an heirloom. It
is pleasant to imagine that it was once the property
of the Auditor and that he had already a little of the
strain of poetry which was one day to produce the
songs of his descendant.

Martin, the younger of John Sedley's known sons,
migrated to Norfolk, where he also married an heiress,
and became the ancestor of the Sedleys of that county.
The elder son, William, inherited the Kentish lands,
and, following the example set by his father, married
the daughter of a London citizen. He was High
Sheriff of Kent under Edward VI,[3] and is said to
have added considerably to the estates. John, the eldest
of his three sons, succeeded his father, and was a
High Sheriff in the reign of Elizabeth.[4] Nicholas, the
youngest, married Jane, daughter of Sir Edward
Isaak of Bekesbourn, on 13 May, 1560, at St. 1560
Botolph's Church, Bishopsgate.[5] He was the ancestor
of the Sedleys of Great Chart and Ightam St. Cleers,
an important fact in the Sedley genealogy, and one
which has hitherto been overlooked.[6]

John Sedley, the Sheriff, died in 1581.[7] His eldest 1581–
child, another John Sedley, inherited the property, 1605
but died childless in 1605.[8] He was one of the
Osrics of Elizabethan England—the first of the
Sedleys to display something of the fecklessness that

---

[1] LL.D.   [2] See p. 338.
[3] "Villare Cantianum," p. 31.   [4] *Ibid.*, p. 33.
[5] St. Botolph's Marriage Register. [6] See Pedigree and p. 22.
[7] Southfleet Burial Register.   [8] *Ibid.*

appeared in many of the actions of Sir Charles and his children. Charity on a large scale was always a weakness of the family, and it seems to have come near to ruining John Sedley. Compelled "to go oversea" for debt caused by his "to lavish almes," 1601 in February 1601 he was travelling in Italy "without any man attendant." He is said to have "reade muche but not judicious," and was the first of the family to live at Aylesford, where the manor was granted to him by Elizabeth.[1] A contemporary says that he built a house there that "cost him £4000." He probably means that John Sedley spent that sum in converting the ancient priory of Aylesford into a dwelling-house.[2]

John Sedley's heir was his brother William, the most remarkable figure in the family between John Sedley the Auditor and Sir Charles the Poet. He was educated at Hart Hall and Balliol College, Oxford, where he graduated in February 1574/5, and pro-
1574/75– ceeded M.A. in July 1577.[3] Like his ancestor the
1611 Auditor, he entered the legal profession, and had a brilliant career at Lincoln's Inn, where he was Barrister-at-law in 1584 and Treasurer of the Inn in 1608.[4] He was knighted on 30 August, 1605, and created a baronet by James I on 20 August, 1611.[5] He married a titled widow, Lady Abergavenny,[6] and by her had a single son, named John.

Sir William Sedley was a person of wealth, learning and munificence, a splendid type of the English

[1] "Villare Cantianum," p. 47.
[2] The above details of John Sedley's life are from John Manningham's Diary (ed. Camden Society, 1868), pp. 20, 21, s.d., February 1601. J. P. Collier cited the passages referring to John Sedley from Manningham's MS. in his "Personal Notes concerning Old Writers" (Brit. Mus., Add. MSS. 32382, f. 124). Collier writes that they refer to Sir Charles Sedley's father. It is clear, however, from the dates that the person described by Manningham is the poet's great-uncle.
[3] "Alumni Oxonienses," p. 1356.   [4] *Ibid.*
[5] *Ibid.*   [6] Hasted's "Kent," II. 170 (ed. 1782).

gentleman of the Renaissance. His "fair Habitation" of "the Fryars" at Aylesford—probably the mansion on which his hare-brained brother had spent so much money—and his princely generosity were famous throughout the county, where he was 'painefully and expencefully ſtudious of the common good."[1] He was so highly eſteemed that in July 1616 he was 1616 included in a Commission with the Archbishop of Canterbury and the Lord Admiral to inquire into the misemployment of lands and moneys bequeathed for charitable purposes in the county of Kent.[2] Aylesford owed to him a school, a hospital and a bridge, and Oxford the Sedleian Lecture in Natural Philosophy, which ſtill preserves his name in his ancient University. He was a patron to John Owen, the ingenious Latin epigrammatiſt, who dedicated a book of his verses to him as one of his "Mæcenates,"[3] and a friend to Sir Henry Savile, one of the greateſt English scholars of the Renaissance, editor of St. Chrysoſtom, Warden of Merton and Provoſt of Eton. In the winter of 1612/13, London gossips were talking of a match 1612/13

---

[1] Philemon Holland's enlarged translation of Camden's "Britannia," London, 1610, p. 332.

[2] Cal. State Papers Dom., 1611–18, p. 387.

[3] "Epigrammatum Ioannis Owen . . . Editio Secunda Londini," 1618, 8vo. Epigrams 4, 5, 45 and 99 in Book II are addressed to Sir William. I quote Nos. 4 and 5 in Thomas Harvey's English versions (from J. Owen's "Latin Epigrams Englished . . ." 8vo., 1677):

> "To William Sedley, *Knight* and *Baronet*, &c.
>
> Thy sundry languages, thy skill i' th' Laws,
> Arts, Piety, sublime thee with applause.
> Thy counsel many, poor thy money have;
> This virtue leads the tourney to the brave;
> Live so to Christ, thy Countrey, to thy King,
> Thyself till Angels thee to glory bring.

> To John Sedley, *only Son* of *the aforenamed* William Sedley.
>
> Thou *Janus* art, but sole in name, now young;
> Thy Father emulate in deed ere long,
> Thou shalt be Janus, hard 'tis to precel
> Thy Father, if thou equal'st him, 'tis well."

between John, only son of Sir William Sedley, and Elizabeth, Sir Henry Savile's younger daughter and co-heir, and at the beginning of February there was a "great meeting" at Sir Henry's house to discuss the proposal.[1] In spite of a tempting offer from the son of a peer, Elizabeth Savile was betrothed to John Sedley in 1613 and married in the same year.[2] Sir 1619 William died in March 1619, and his estates and title were inherited by his son, John, husband of Elizabeth Savile and father of the poet.

All genealogists of the Sedley family have been confused by the fact that, contemporary with this Sir John and Elizabeth, Lady Sedley, and residing in the same county, was another Sir John Sedley, whose wife was also named Elizabeth. He was a second cousin of the Sedleys of Aylesford and Southfleet, grandson of Nicholas Sedley, the youngest son of the first William Sedley, and son of Sir Isaac Sedley, Bart., of Great Chart. This Sir John had one eye, and was "a person of violent and malicious disposition," unlike his kinsman, the poet's father, who is said to have been a man of "better quality."[3] The one-eyed Sir John belonged to the extreme wing of the Opposition to the Court during the reign of Charles I, and during the Civil War he was one of the leaders of the Kentish Roundheads. His property was at the village of Ightam St. Cleers, not many miles from his kinsman's, and, what is still more confusing, his second son, who ultimately became his heir, was called Charles. This Sir Charles Sedley of Ightam St. Cleers was the poet's third cousin and almost exact contemporary. When the poet's son, Charles, was knighted

---

[1] Cal. State Papers Dom., 1611–18, p. 69 (J. Chamberlain to Alice Carleton, 4 February 1613); State Papers, Jas. I, Vol. 72, p. 23.

[2] *Ibid.*, p. 175 (same to same, 11 March). Also p. 122 (Sir H. Savile to Carleton).

[3] Cal. State Papers Dom., 1636, p. 47. (Sir J. Rayney to Secy. Coke 2 July; same to Secy. Nicholas, 5 July.)

by William III, there were thus three Sir Charles
Sedleys living at the same time, a fact that has never
been clearly stated before and which has caused endless confusion to biographers and genealogists.[1]

Sir John Sedley of Southfleet, father of the poet,
like most of the Sedleys, was educated at Oxford,
entering Magdalen in April 1609, graduating in 1609-13
February 1611/12, and proceeding M.A. in July
1613,[2] the year of his marriage to Elizabeth Savile.
He appears to have celebrated the taking of his degree
in the ancient manner by a carouse. A learned treatise
on the wines "drunk to Sr. Sedlye late Bachelor of
Art in joy of his degree in learning," entitled "Health
in a Cup of Wine," was written (but never published)
by a certain Dr. Robert Hervie. It survives in MS.[3]
and is dedicated to Sir John's mother, Lady Abergavenny. It gives a curious description of "whyte
wyne," "pale wine, 'twixt whyt and yellow," "yellow
wyne," "mulsum," "hippocras," and other concoctions
with which young men used to ruin their digestion
in those days.

Sir John Sedley entered Lincoln's Inn on 9 June,
1610,[4] but there is no evidence that he ever practised 1610-22
as a barrister.

In 1622, William Barret dedicated to him his
edition of Underdown's translation of " Heliodorus
His Aethiopian History,"[5] and from the language
used by the translator it appears that, as befitted a
son-in-law of Sir Henry Savile, Sir John was a lover
of literature and a patron of men of letters. His town
house was in Shire Lane, the narrow and ancient
thoroughfare which ran into Fleet Street just by

---

[1] LL.D., for instance, confuses the son of the poet with his third
cousin.
[2] "Alumni Oxonienses" (Early Series), IV. 1332.
[3] Now (1924) in the possession of Messrs. P. J. and A. E. Dobell.
[4] "Lincoln's Inn Admission Register," I. 153.
[5] See Bibliography, under Barret, William.

Temple Bar, and in the reign of Charles I, he and his wife formed part of a cultivated and aristocratic circle which included Sir Henry Savile, Viscount Dorchester,[1] Secretary of State and husband of Ann Savile, Lady Sedley's sister, and Sir Anthony Welldon, a somewhat eccentric person, who had been dismissed from Court by James I for some outspoken comments on the Scottish nation,[2] and who was now a bitter opponent of the Government.

Sir John and his wife had nine children, of whom five predeceased their father.[3] The survivors were three sons, Henry, William and Charles (the last named being posthumous), and a daughter, Elizabeth. Sir John died at Mount Mascall, North Cray, Kent, not far from his ancestral property at Southfleet, 1638 on 13 August, 1638.[4] On 5 October of the previous year, when his wife was already an expectant mother, he had made a will which is still extant.[5] By it he left the bulk of his property to his wife, Sir Edward Hales, Sir Anthony Welldon, Anthony Croftes and Anthony Langston, in trust for his eldest son, Henry, to inherit on attaining the age of twenty-three. If he died childless, it was to revert to the second son, William, and, if he also died without issue, to the unborn child, if it should prove to be a son. In either case the heir was to attain the age of twenty-three before coming into his estate. If no son survived, the daughters, Elizabeth and Margaret (or whichever outlived the other), were to inherit the property on marriage, or

[1] D. N. B., s.a., Carleton, Dudley. For his intimacy with the Sedleys see Cal. State Papers. Dom. Jas. I.

[2] D. N. B., s.a., Welldon, Sir Anthony.

[3] Two Johns died in 1625 and 1635, two Annas in 1627 and 1629, and Margaret in 1638 (Southfleet Burial Register). The elder John lived long enough to be admitted to Lincoln's Inn on 29 January, 1621/2 ("Lincoln's Inn Admission Register").

[4] Cal. State Papers Dom., 1637/8, p. 598.

[5] There is a copy in Somerset House, of which I possess a transcript; see also Haslewood's notes to Jacob, note (6), Appendix I.

on attaining the age of seventeen. There was also 1638
generous provision for the younger children, in the
event of the inheritance falling to Henry. Elizabeth
was to have five thousand pounds, William twelve
thousand, and Margaret and the unborn child two
thousand five hundred each. Sir John's servants were
to have board and lodging in his house for six months
after his death, and a special provision was made for
a Mr. Rabbet, who appears to have been the tutor
of the young Sedleys, and who was also recommended
to the heir. Finally, there were liberal bequests for
educational institutions: four hundred pounds to be
laid out in lands to maintain a schoolmaster at Wymondham in Leicestershire, which formed part of the Sedley
estates, a like sum to provide a schoolmaster for Southfleet in Kent, five hundred pounds for the Postmasters
of Merton, and another five hundred for the Demies
of Magdalen College, Oxford. The whole will is in
accordance with the best traditions of the Sedley
family, and a pleasant human touch is added by a
codicil which proves that Sir John was fond of hunting. It enjoins upon the heir to keep "ten couples of
hounds att the least," and provides a rent charge of
twenty pounds a year for their maintenance. In a
second codicil, made only one day before the testator's
death, Sir John endeavours to win for his widow and
children the powerful support of Laud, Archbishop
of Canterbury, and of Mr. Secretary Windebanke,
by bequeathing a hundred pounds' worth of plate to
each, and another hundred pounds to the Archbishop
for the rebuilding of St. Paul's. At a time when it
seemed possible that Charles I might succeed in
setting up an absolute monarchy, with Laud as one
of his chief ministers, these bequests were probably
the natural precautions of a far-seeing man, who had
already appointed Anthony Welldon, a prominent
figure in the Parliamentary party, as one of his
executors. Events were to justify his actions, for,

1638 although the Archbishop and the Secretary were powerless to help Lady Sedley and her children, Sir Anthony was to prove a good friend to them when his party triumphed. No doubt the testator felt a very considerable responsibility, for the Sedley estates were extensive. At this time they probably included manors in several parts of Kent, Leicestershire, Oxfordshire and Cambridgeshire.[1] From the sums named in the will the rent roll must have been a very large one.

1639 No record exists of the exact date and place of the birth of Charles, the posthumous son and future poet. He was certainly baptised on 5 March in the year following his father's death at the ancient church of St. Clement Danes, which, before the Great Fire, stood on the site of Gibb's masterpiece in the Strand.[2] As St. Clement Danes stood at no great distance from Shire Lane, it seems highly probable that Charles Sedley was born in his father's house in that street some time in the month of March 1639.[3]

[1] Haslewood's Notes to Jacob, No. (2), Appendix I.
[2] Entry in St. Clement Danes Baptismal Register:—

1639

March Charles Sydley son of Sr John Sydley and
lady Eliza   bd. 30.

[3] Anthony à Wood, followed by most biographers, says he was born "at or near Aylesford." Wheatley, on the other hand, in his "London Past and Present" (III. 240), asserts positively that he was born in the house in Shire Lane, and, in the absence of more definite evidence, the entry in St. Clement Danes register certainly supports his view.

CHAPTER II

THE SEDLEYS DURING THE CIVIL WAR AND UNDER THE COMMONWEALTH

"Here lyes the learned *Savil's* Heir,
So early wise, and lasting fair ;
That none, except her years they told,
Thought her a Child, or thought her old."

"Epitaph on the Lady *Sidly*," by Edmund Waller, first published in the 6th edition of his Poems, 8vo, London, 1693; Part II (dated 1690), p. 43.

"Hail Sacred *Wadham !* whom the Muses Grace
And from the Rest of all the Reverend Pile
Of Noble Pallaces, design'd thy Space :
Where they in soft retreat might dwell.
They blest thy Fabrick, and said—do thou
Our Darling Sons contain."

Mrs. Aphra Behn, "To Mr. Creech (under the name of Daphnis)," Poems upon Several Occasions, 1684, p. 53.

ELIZABETH, Lady Sedley, seems to have been a woman of high spirit, of considerable intellectual attainments, and of great personal charm. Her father probably named her after his great patron, the Virgin Queen, and his choice was appropriate, for she was one of the ladies who carried into the seventeenth century something of the dignity and aristocratic culture of the Elizabethan age. Her youth was passed when the glories of that age had scarcely waned, for our first record of her dates from the year 1613, when Shakespeare, Bacon and Raleigh were still alive. It is a few words in a letter from her father, Sir Henry Savile, to his son-in-law, Dudley Carleton, then English Envoy at Venice :

27

"A match for yor sister Besse wth Sr Wm Sidleys sonne wee the parēts have cōcluded."[1]

Although the match was "concluded" by the parents and neither "Besse" nor John Sedley probably had much to say in the matter, there is every reason to suppose that its results were successful. Sir John seems to have been a man of a refined and dignified temperament, which muſt have been perfectly congenial to that of Elizabeth Savile. We know that he was a lover of books and of hunting, and so little of a politician that he had friends among the extremiſts of both parties, and we can imagine that the tranquil married life of these wealthy and cultivated people was clouded only by the death of many of their children in infancy.

1629   Lady Sedley's one extant letter, dated from Aylesford, 21 June, 1629, is addressed to her brother-in-law, Dudley Carleton, now Viscount Dorcheſter, a truſted adviser of King Charles I, and shows that she was on intimate terms with that nobleman.[2] Sir Anthony Welldon, her husband's Roundhead friend, was also among her acquaintances, and an anecdote told by Anthony à Wood proves that she was highly respected by that republican baronet. According to Wood Sir Anthony wrote his very scurrilous "Court and Character of King James I" at the beginning of the Long Parliament, and showed the manuscript to Lady Sedley, who "did lay the vileness of it so much to his door" that he resolved never to publish it.[3] From this ſtory, as well as from the fact that she named her youngeſt son after the King, it would seem that Lady

[1] State Papers Dom., Jas. I, 72, p. 122.
[2] State Papers Dom., Chas. I, 45, p. 22. See Appendix I, pp. 305–6.
[3] "Athenæ Oxonienses," ed. Bliss, II. 868. Sir Anthony's book was published after his death in London (12mo, 1651, reprinted 1811), and dedicated to The Lady Sedley(!). Sir W. Sanderson in the Preface of his "Compleat History of Mary Queen of Scotland," etc. (London, fol., 1656), says that the manuscript had been "intended by Sir A. W. for the fire," but since then it had "ſtoln to the Press out of a Ladies closet."

Sedley was one of those grave, cultivated, moderate 1629
royalists, like Falkland and Hyde, who were equally
horrified by Wentworth's "Thorough" and the proceedings of Hampden and Pym. The "sad breaking
of the Parliament" was a terrible blow for such
persons, who had always hoped for a reconciliation,
and who were now compelled to look on in help-
less terror and sorrow, while the wilder spirits on
both sides were dragging down into the dust all they
cherished most in England. For Lady Sedley the
public calamity coincided with a period of domestic
sorrow. Her husband died two years before the meeting
of the Long Parliament. On 17 April in the following 1639
year (1639), Archbishop Laud wrote to the President
of St. John's College, Oxford, recommending Sir
Henry Sedley, her eldest son, to his care, "that his
mother may see that he is entertained with more than
common respect."[1] Sir Henry was admitted to St.
John's on 14 June, and died in the following month,
three years after his father and in the midst of that
fatal summer which followed Strafford's execution.[2]
Sir Henry Savile's daughter was not, however, a
woman to be cowed by misfortunes. On 8 June, 1642, 1642
only six weeks before the King set up his standard at
Nottingham, in spite of her known royalist sympathies,
she had the courage to appear at the Bar of the House
of Commons and petition that exasperated and revolu-
tionary assembly against one of their members, a
certain Mr. John Griffith junior, who had insulted
her.[3] This John Griffith is described by Clarendon as
"a young Welshman of no parts or reputation, but for
eminent licence."[4] He had sought "with great bold-
ness" for preferment at Court, and, when rebuffed by
the King and Queen, had joined the extreme section

[1] Laud's Works (Library of Anglo-Catholic Theology), VII. 558.
[2] "Alumni Oxonienses," Early Series, IV. 1332.
[3] "Journals of the House of Commons," II. 613, 712; IV. 109, 162, 169.
[4] "Hist. of Great Rebellion" (8vo, Oxford, 1705), I. 434.

1642 of the Parliamentary party. He probably attempted to
show his zeal to his new friends by insulting an
eminent royalist lady. It is to its credit that the House
listened to Lady Sedley with respect and granted her
"Liberty to prosecute against the said Mr. Jo.
Griffiths, the younger, notwithstanding that he is a
Member of this House." His person was ordered to
be secured, and a Committee was appointed to inquire
into the affair. On 10 August he was expelled from
the House and proceedings were begun against him
before the King's Bench. He escaped to the army, but
his career would appear to have ended, after many other
escapades, in Newgate prison in 1645.

Lady Sedley and her family seem to have left the
house in Shire Lane about the time of the outbreak
of the Civil War, and in the summer of 1643 she was
living at the pleasant village of Highgate, then
separated from London by many miles of open
country.[1] The sturdiness of Charles Sedley's constitution, and, indeed, the very fact that he survived at all,
may well be due to his having spent his early childhood
in the pure air of Highgate.

During the Civil War the part of England which
was in the power of the Parliament was administered
by Committees of the two Houses. One of the most
famous of these bodies was the Committee for Advance
of Money, which usually sat at Haberdashers' Hall in
Gresham Street, under the presidency of Lord Saye and
Sele. Its business was to fill the coffers of the Parliamentary armies by means of what was actually a heavy
property tax, although it was euphemistically called
1643 a loan or "advance of money." It was supposed to be
levied on all estates impartially, but, in practice, it
naturally fell more heavily upon those persons who
were suspected of royalism. It must not, however, be

[1] In the first mention of Lady Sedley in the Accounts of the Committee for Advance of Money (State Papers Dom., Int. A. 61, f. 38) she
is described as "Lady Sedley, Highgate." The date is 8 August, 1643.

confused with the sequestration or entire or partial 1643 confiscation of the estates of "delinquents," or proved royalists, which was the business of a special Committee. Eventually, when the Parliament obtained control of the whole of England, it was enacted that the "assessments" of the Committee for the Advance of Money were to be levied only on those who had failed to take the oaths to the new Government. As Lady Sedley had probably neither the means nor the desire to show any active sympathy for the royal cause, whatever her personal opinions may have been, she was at present spared from the necessity of "compounding" with the more Draconian of the Committees. She was subjected, however, to a good deal of annoyance from the Committee for Advance of Money, although, thanks to the timely help of Sir Anthony Welldon, she and Sir William escaped more lightly than many other landowners. On 8 August, 1643, a minute of the Committee informs us she had been "assessed" to pay what was then the very large sum of £1500. She had already "lent" £375, and was now called upon to pay the remainder.[1] Two days later the Committee ordered that she was to be "respited" pending inquiries.[2] At the beginning of October, as she had not yet satisfied the authorities, she was actually "attached" or arrested, and brought to London by warrant of the Committee of Examinations.[3] While she was waiting to be examined, she was placed in the custody of the Messenger of the House of Commons. The domiciliary visit of the crop-headed Parliamentary soldiers, which probably preceded his mother's arrest, may well have been among Sedley's earliest memories, and perhaps, when he introduced such a visit many years later into his comedy "The Mulberry Garden," he was drawing

[1] State Papers Dom., Int. A. 61, f. 38.
[2] *Ibid.*, Int. A. 75, f. 44.
[3] *Ibid.*, Int. A. 2, f. 106. (Cal. of Proceedings of Committee for Advance of Money, I. 207.)

1643 upon recollections of his own childhood. How long Lady Sedley remained a prisoner is not recorded, but by 9 October Sir Anthony Welldon had come to her rescue, and, on his undertaking that "the Lady shall appear on ffriday next," she was released. She appeared on the 16th,[1] but the Committee was not 1645 sitting. On the 17th she was brought before them and ordered to pay £375 by Thursday, the 26th of the month, whereupon she was to be allowed to "make oath" as to her proportion:[2] that is, to state on oath the value of the twentieth part of her estate, which, according to the ordinance, was to be levied by the Committee. On 1 November,[3] having paid the £375, she swore before the Committee that this represented "her full twentieth, that is for the estate both reall and personall." Her original contribution of £375 was thereupon repaid to her, and henceforward she was not troubled very much concerning her own estate, which, if her figure was correct, must have been worth about £7500. As trustee for her husband, and mother of Sir William Sedley, the second surviving son, who had now succeeded to the baronetcy, she had still a good deal to endure at the hands of the Committees.

On 3 July, 1645, Sir Anthony Welldon wrote a letter to the Committee for Advance of Money on behalf of Lady Sedley and her son.[4] The letter is dated from Aylesford, and it is possible that the Sedleys and Sir Anthony were all staying on the family estate in that village. Sir Anthony says that Lady Sedley assured him that neither she nor Sir William had inhabited London "or within 20 myles" since she acquitted herself by oath at Haberdashers' Hall (on 1 November, 1643). Apparently the Committee had made some demand upon the Sedleys, on the ground

---

[1] State Papers Dom., Int. A. 2, f. 114.
[2] *Ibid.*, f. 117.
[3] *Ibid.*
[4] *Ibid.*, A. 90, f. 110. See Appendix I. pp. 306–7 .

that they were occupying a house in London. This 1645 house, which was probably the house in Shire Lane, had, according to Lady Sedley, been "a long time tennanted" (*i.e.* let to a tenant), and so she conceived herself "in noe weye concernd" with the demand of the Committee. Sir Anthony also paints a gloomy picture of the estate probably with the object of softening the hearts of the Committee towards his ward. "A plentifull fortune" had been swallowed up "in necessary payments," and Lady Sedley was "ingulphed in the usurer's books."[1] On 11 July, Sir William Sedley's case was discussed by the Committee. He appears to have been "assessed" at £1000, but in view of the facts that the "greatest part of the estate" was "under the power of the King's army," and that his guardian had paid £160 to the Court of Wards for what was under the power of the Parliament, the assessment was discharged, and it was ordered that neither Sir William nor his guardian were to be troubled any further.[2] The part of the estates "under the power of the King's army" in 1645 must have been the Leicestershire and Oxfordshire Manors, and perhaps some title-deeds or other securities, which were in the hands of the other executors, who may have been adherents of the King. The Kentish lands were certainly in the power of the Parliament, and would be protected by Sir John Sedley of Ightam St. Cleers, now a Colonel in the Parliamentary army, who, with Sir Anthony Welldon, is said to have "ruled all Kent" during the Civil War.[3] On 29 August the Committee for Sequestration of Estates, the body which dealt with the property of "malignants," or royalists, received a petition from Lady Sedley, in her quality of executrix of Sir John Sedley, and Sir William, her son. The

[1] State Papers Dom., Int. A. 90, f. 110.
[2] *Ibid.*, Int. A. 4, f. 199.
[3] "Archæologia Cantiana," II. 196, III. 197. See also "Acts and Ordinances of the Interregnum," I. *passim.*

D

1645 petition is not preserved, but it may be supposed that it was a complaint against agents of the Committee who had forcibly occupied some of the Sedley property. It was referred to Mr. Bradshaw, later to attain celebrity by becoming president of the court that tried Charles I. His report upon it seems to have been favourable, and, on 19 September, it was ordered that either the "just debt and damadges" should be paid to the petitioners, or else they were to be permitted "to enjoy" a certain Mortgage.[1]

Before the Committee came to this decision the Sedleys had left England. On 6 September, 1645, Sir William had received permission from the House of Commons to go "to France or other parts for his health and education," with his mother, a tutor (probably Mr. Rabbet), two men-servants, and three maid-servants to attend Lady Sedley.[2] In the entry in the Journals of the House which records the granting of this permission, no mention is made of Charles, but it is not improbable that he may have accompanied his mother.

If he spent two years in France at this age, it cannot be supposed that he received anything more than a very fleeting impression. However, he may well have laid the foundations of the knowledge of the French language which he certainly possessed in later years. The permission to travel granted to the Sedleys was revoked by an order to return by the 1647/48–49 10th April, 1647/8, recorded in the Journals of the House of Commons under the date of 7 February.[3]

They were prudent enough to obey the order of the Parliament. If they had failed to do so, their estates would certainly have suffered. As it was, Sir William was again summoned before the Committee for Advance of Money on 26 December, 1649, when

[1] State Papers Dom., Int. B. 1, ff. 978, 1000.
[2] Journals of House of Commons, IV. 264.
[3] *Ibid.*, V. 457.

he is described as living "at Temple Bar," which may 1647/51
mean that he was occupying his father's old house in
Shire Lane.[1] He was "assessed" at £1000, but discharged on 2 June, 1649.[2] The Committee sent for
him again on 2 January, 1650,[3] and he then proved to
their satisfaction that he was "no delinquent" (*i.e.*
that he had taken the oaths to the Commonwealth),
and, as it had been decreed that the " assessments"
were to be levied only on "delinquents," he was finally
"discharged from attendance" on the Committee.
After this it is possible to understand why John Tatham
in his dedication of his tragedy, "The Distracted
State,"[4] "To the truly Noble Sir William Sidley,
Baronet," says that Sir William had "equally balanced
his actions in these distempered times." This must be
a way of congratulating him on having been astute
enough to win the favour of the new Government
without alienating his old friends among the Cavaliers.
This dedication, it may be remarked, is the only sign
of Sir William's having taken any interest in literature.
As early as 1647 he had apparently been regarded as a
supporter of the Commonwealth, for on 3 March he
was called upon to "seize and dispose" of the goods of
Sir George Strode, a Kentish Cavalier. Lady Sedley, however, was regarded as a royalist as late as 1651. On 15
October in that year, some of her property in Lincolnshire was seized by the Parliamentary Commissioners,
and she never seems to have obtained redress.

[1] State Papers Dom., Int. A. 28, f. 17.

[2] *Ibid.*, Int. A. 71, f. 96.

[3] *Ibid.*, Int. A. 8, f. 96.

[4] 4to, London, 1651, said on the title-page to have been written in
1641. In the British Museum copy the dedication is headed "To the
truly Noble Sir John Sedley." In the Bodleian copy the dedication is
to Sir *William*. Perhaps the dedication to "Sir John" was a mere
printer's error, corrected in later copies. The editors of Tatham's
Plays in the "Dramatists of the Restoration" Series (Edinburgh, 1878)
state incorrectly in their introduction to the "Distracted State" that
the play is dedicated to "Sir Charles Sedley's grandfather," who had
been dead for many years.

c. 1650 From such records of his mother and family we can form some idea of Charles Sedley's childhood. It was passed in an age of strife and confusion, when traditional ideas and beliefs were crumbling away, and new theories were rapidly springing up and being applied with fiery haste. Clarendon comments bitterly on the kind of upbringing which even children of noble families received at this time: "All relations," he writes, "were confounded by the several sects in religion, which discountenanced all forms of reverence and respect, as relics and marks of superstition. Children asked not the blessing of their parents; nor did they concern themselves in the education of their children; but were well content that they should take any course to maintain themselves, that they might be free from that expense."[1] At that time the education of a fatherless boy, even though he belonged to a rich family, must have been peculiarly undisciplined and chaotic. "Parents," writes Clarendon, "had no authority over their children nor children any obedience or submission to their parents; but 'everyone did that which was good in his own eyes'."[2] The frequent changes of residence, the absence of Lady Sedley, while defending her own and her children's interests before the Committees and elsewhere, and, finally, the exciting continental journey, would all help to encourage idleness and pleasure-seeking, and also, in a gifted boy, to stimulate intellectual curiosity. The studies of the future poet were doubtless superintended by his mother ("the learned *Savil's* heir"), who, if we can believe Waller, was herself a poetess,[3] and by Mr. Rabbet, if that

[1] "The Life of Edward, Earl of Clarendon, etc." Oxford, 1857, I, 305.

[2] *Ibid.*

[3]
> "The muses daily found supplies
> Both from her hands and from her eyes."

(Waller's " Epitaph on the Lady *Sidly.*") This couplet may, however, refer to music.

gentleman still continued to teach the young Sedleys. *c.* 1650 Charles is said to have received "a proper foundation of grammar learning,"[1] which, in the seventeenth century, meant a very thorough grounding in Latin and perhaps some French and Greek. The cultivated and refined atmosphere in which he was brought up must, however, have had a more important influence than any formal lessons. In such a family as the Lady Sedley's there must have been much more of the love of beautiful and gracious things which is usually associated with the civilisation of the Renaissance than in most households of the seventeenth century. The tradition of the flighty great-uncle, John, and his Italian wanderings must have survived. Among Sir Charles Sedley's books was the 1559 edition of Baldassare Castiglione's "Il Cortegiano," the favourite guide of the Renaissance courtier, which may well have been brought by John Sedley from Italy. Certainly the memory of those learned friends, Sir Henry Savile and Sir William Sedley, must have counted for a great deal. It was probably from desultory readings in their great folios that Charles Sedley acquired that knowledge and love of the Latin poets that was to colour most of his writings. Moreover, there is evidence that Lady Sedley was visited by at least one distinguished living writer under the Protectorate. Edmund Waller, in his fine " Epitaph on the Lady *Sidly*" (first printed in 1690), wrote lines that prove that both he and other Cavaliers were among her friends at this time :

> "Such was this Dame in calmer days,
> Her Nation's ornament and praise.
> But when a Storm disturbed our Rest,
> The Port and Refuge of th' opprest.
> This made her fortune understood,
> And look'd on as some public good,

---

[1] The phrase is first used in the article on Sedley in "Biographia Britannica" (1747–66).

c. 1650

> So that, her Person and her State
> Exempted from the common Fate,
> In all our civil fury she
> Stood, like a Sacred Temple, free."[1]

From these verses it may be inferred that Lady Sedley made use of such influence as she possessed with the Parliamentary leaders to mitigate the sufferings of distressed Cavaliers. Also, they leave little room for doubt that Waller and other cultivated royalists often met under her roof. Their rich dresses and courtly conversation must have had a great effect on an intelligent boy. From them he would hear something of the great days of Ben Jonson and his tribe, and more of Sir John Suckling, that paragon of court poets. The Sedley household may thus be pictured as a little oasis of culture in the gloom of Puritan England. The contrast between such surroundings and the drabness of the exterior world under a Government that cut down maypoles, punished actors, and fined Sabbath-day tipplers, must have struck boys like William and Charles Sedley no less than the differences between certain of their mothers' friends —for example, the cantankerous old precisian, Sir Anthony Welldon, and the graceful and polished Waller. Such impressions found an echo years later in the characters of Sir John Everyoung and Sir Samuel Forecast in "The Mulberry Garden."

c. 1652–
55.

In the latter years of the Protectorate there was a general and very natural inclination among young men of good birth and liberal education to break through the restraints of the kill-joy Puritan Government, and indulge in the traditional pleasures of English gentlemen. The Lord Protector was known to be by no means so severe a censor as some of his associates.

---

[1] "Epitaph on the Lady *Sidly*," by Edmund Waller (6th edition of Waller's Poems, London, 8vo, 1693; Part II. (dated 1690), p. 43). Poems, ed. Thorn Drury, II. 115.

He was said to pardon conspirators, if they happened *c.* 1652–
to be poets, to love music and fine horses, and to 55
connive at private dramatic performances. Sir William
Sedley was one of the young people who began to
attempt something like a revival of the gay society of
the days of Sir John Suckling. According to Anthony à
Wood he lived "very high" in London in the time of
Oliver with his friend, Mr. Robert Dormer of Oxfordshire.[1] To "live very high" under the Commonwealth was to frequent taverns, cock-fightings, and
illicit dramatic performances at the Cock-pit at Drury
Lane, or the Red Bull in St. John's Street.[2] Wood
writes that Sir William and his friend "did ſtrive
who should outvie each other in gallantry, and in
splendid coaches." The laſt detail is significant. Cromwell had a very English weakness for fine horses
and carriages, and it was natural that young men who
were attempting to revive the gallantries of court
life should have chosen this way of amusing themselves,
as that which would leaſt offend the Government. The
"splendid coaches" in which Sir William Sedley and
Mr. Dormer drove "in the field near the Town which
they call Hide Park,"[3] were huge, clumsy Noah's
Arks on wheels, immensely wide, with unglazed
windows. Sir William Davenant muſt have been thinking of such young sparks as these when he urged on
the authorities the necessity of "divertissements," "not
only to recreate those who will too much apprehend the
absence of the adverse party, but alsoe to entertaine
a new generation of youth uningaged in the late differences, of which there is a numerous growth since the

---

[1] "Athenæ Oxonienses" (Bliss), I. lxii; "Life and Times," ed. Clarke,
II. 147.

[2] All these amusements were popular under the Commonwealth,
in spite of the ordinances against them. See "Middlesex County
Records," III. pp. 247, 248, 282.

[3] "A Character of England" (by John Evelyn, London, 1659, 12mo),
p. 54.

c. 1652–
55
warre, who should be withdrawne from licentiousnesse, gaming and discontent."[1]

1654/55
Sir William married Lady Chandos, widow of John, Lord Chandos, who died in February 1654/5.[2] This Lady Chandos was the eldest daughter of John Savage, Earl Rivers, a friend of Richard Sackville, fifth Earl of Dorset. Earl Rivers had died, ruined by his stubborn resistance to the Parliament, in 1654.[3] He left a widow and eight children, of whom the eldest, John, succeeded to the title. The marriage of Jane, the eldest daughter, widow of Lord Chandos, to Sir William Sedley took place at St. Mildred's, Poultry, on 9 October,[4] 1655. It must have been conducted before a civil magistrate, according to the law of 1652. Charles Sedley, now a lad of sixteen, was, doubtless, present at the ceremony. After his marriage, in accordance with the prudent custom of his family, Sir William made provision for the unborn children, of whom he apparently expected to be father, by means of a deed, limiting his estate to his first and other sons.[5]

1655/56
Meanwhile, Charles, like most of his ancestors, entered the University of Oxford, where he was admitted a fellow-commoner of Wadham College on 22 March, 1655/6.[6] Wadham was one of the most fashionable colleges in that regenerate Oxford of the Protectorate, which was admitted, even by Clarendon, to have "yielded a harvest of extraordinary good and sound knowledge in all parts of learning." Its Warden was the famous Dr. Wilkins, the husband of Crom-

[1] "Some Observations concerning the People of this Nation," printed from Davenant's MS. by Sir C. H. Firth in the *Historical Review*, Vol. XVIII. p. 319. The italics are mine.

[2] G. E. C., "Complete Peerage," ed. Vicary Gibbs, 1916, III. 128.

[3] "The Ancient and Noble Family of the Savages of the Ards," compiled by G. F. A(rmstrong). (London, 4to, 1888), p. 50.

[4] St. Mildred Poultry Marriage Register.

[5] See Haslewood's "Notes to Jacob," Appendix I. p. 322.

[6] Gardiner's "Registers of Wadham College," I. 213.

well's sister, who had done, perhaps, more than any
single man to renew the intellectual life of the University after the Civil War. He was especially noted as a
leader of the new school of experimental and rationalist
thinkers, which claimed to be carrying out the scientific
programme of Bacon. At his Lodge at Wadham were
held some of the first meetings of the philosophical
club that afterwards developed into the Royal Society.[1]
These scientific enthusiasts or "virtuosi," as they were
sometimes called, were inclined to discourage mysticism
and religious "enthusiasm," and to exalt the power of
human reason and profane learning. They were the
intellectual forerunners of the latitudinarians of the
Restoration and the eighteenth century. It is very
significant that several of the wits of the Restoration
Court were educated at Wadham,[2] which was the
head-quarters of the Oxford "virtuosi" under the
Protectorate. The excesses of these young men in the
reign of Charles II may be regarded as a sort of
distorted application of the experimental view of life
taught by such men as Wilkins.

The Warden is said to have been a "lustie . . . broad-
shoulder'd person, cheerful and hospitable,"[3] and
among his undergraduates, in 1655,[4] besides Charles
Sedley, was John Lovelace, afterwards Lord Lovelace,
famous later for licentiousness and Whiggism. Nevertheless, good discipline was maintained in Wadham
under the rule of Wilkins. Undergraduates had to
speak Latin within College walls, while tutors
exercised control over their pupils' finances, receiving

[1] He was the principal reviver of experimental philosophy at Oxford
(*secundum mentem domini Baconi*), where he had weekly an experimental philosophical club "which . . . was the incunabula of the
Royal Society." Aubrey (on Wilkins), "Brief Lives," ed. Clark, II. 301.

[2] Sedley (1655/6), Rochester (1659/60), Car Scroop (1664). Gardiner,
Reg. Wadham. Coll., Vol. I.

[3] Aubrey, ed. Clark, "Brief Lives," II. 301.

[4] He came up on 25 July, 1655 (Gardiner's " Registers of Wadham
College," I. 209).

1655/56 and regulating their allowances.[1] Sedley's tutor, according to the College Register, was "Mr. Pope," afterwards Dr. Walter Pope, half-brother to the Warden, and, like him, a prominent "virtuoso." This Dr. Pope is ever memorable in literary history as the author of that famous ballad beginning:

> "If I live to be old, for I find I goe down,
> Let this be my fate, in a Country town;
> May I have a warm House with a Stone at the gate,
> And a cleanly young girl, to rub my bald Pate."[2]

He was a man possessed of wide and curious learning and of a strong sense of humour, although, according to Anthony à Wood, he "lived a heathenish and epicurean life."[3] Sedley probably enjoyed his company and spent many pleasant hours listening to his "puns, proverbs and senseless digressions"[4] in the beautiful gardens of Wadham, which at that time had been recently laid out. After a period of confusion that followed the Civil War, the life of the University had been notably renewed under the Protectorate. Oliver Cromwell had been elected Chancellor in 1650 and his able friend and chaplain, John Owen, became Dean of Christ Church and Vice-Chancellor. There was a marked improvement in discipline, but, except on the religious side, the teaching remained very much what it was after Laud's great re-organisation. One reform may be noticed as especially affecting students of the type of Sedley: "Gentlemen Commoners were required to do exercises like others 'to the intent that noe person may live idlely in this University, and that Gentlemen may answere the expectation of their friends.'"[5] Like all first-year men, besides reading

1 Cf. Wells's "History of Wadham College," p. 67.

2 "The Old Man's Wish." Broadside, ?1685. See Bibliography under Pope, Walter.

3 "Athenæ Oxonienses," IV. 724 (ed. Bliss).

4 The phrase is from Thomas Wood's "An Appendix to the Life of Seth Ward in a Letter to the Author" (8vo, 1697).

5 Mallet's History of the University of Oxford, II. 391.

and writing exercises for his tutor, Sedley would have 1655/56
to attend at least four lectures a week: two by the
Praelector in Grammar and two by the Praelector in
Rhetoric, all delivered in Latin at eight o'clock in
the morning and all lasting at least three-quarters of an
hour.   He might also have attended the lectures on
Natural Philosophy founded by his grandfather Sir
William Sedley. Still more uncongenial for a young
man of Sedley's stamp would be the compulsory
attendance at sermons on Sundays (when notes had
to be taken) and catechism in Hall on Saturday
afternoons.   There was, however, a lighter side to
Puritan Oxford. We hear from Anthony à Wood
that there was a great deal of music and entertaining
in college rooms when "tarts, custards, chees cakes
or any other junkets"[1] were largely consumed.
Although the taverns were in disfavour, coffee-houses
were springing up and Arthur Tillyard had opened
one by All Souls in March 1655/6.   It may have
been at one of the new coffee-houses that Sedley met
the shy, eccentric scholar Anthony à Wood, who claims
"some acquaintance"[2] with him and his friend John
Aubrey, who was struck by Sedley's likeness to his
distinguished godfather, Sir Henry Savile, though he
thought him not "so proper a man."[3]

Charles Sedley had only been at Oxford a few weeks
when his brother, Sir William, died of an attack of
measles. His funeral was "carried" from London to
the family vault at Southfleet on 18 April, 1655/6.[4]
Thus the last bar between Charles and the title and
estates was removed, and, at an age when a young man
of spirit and intelligence naturally craves for pleasure
and excitement, he was suddenly placed in a position
to amuse himself beyond his wildest hopes. When his

[1] Anthony à Wood, "Life," I. 298.
[2] *Ibid.*, I. 477.
[3] "Aubrey's Brief Lives," ed. Clark, II. 215.
[4] Smyth's "Obituary," ed. Camden Society, p. 42.

wild doings after the Restoration are recorded in a later chapter, this fact should be kept in mind.

1656   At the end of May 1656, Sir Charles Sedley was "sick of a feaver and the meazills of which Sir William died."[1] This illness was the first of several serious maladies from which he suffered at different periods of his life. That he survived both the diseases and the remedies of contemporary physicians shows that he had an exceptionally robust constitution.

Although he took no degree, it may be supposed that he was at Oxford for about a year. On his departure he presented his college with a silver castor and a mustard pot both of which are still among the college plate.[2] When he returned to London, he must have assumed the place that his brother had held in the fashionable society of the period. This society seems to have grown more and more licentious in the latter years of the Protectorate, and consisted largely of "mad drinking lords" who used to "sweare, game, and commit all the extravagances that are insident to untamed youths."[3] Among the leaders of the rakes of the town were Philip Stanhope, second Earl of Chesterfield, and his mistress, Barbara Villiers, a dazzling beauty, afterwards to be the most voluptuous and profligate courtesan of the Restoration. Sedley was well acquainted with Chesterfield at a later date, and it is likely that their intimacy began under the Protectorate.

It was natural that, after Sir William's death, his heir should see a good deal of his brother's widow and her two sisters, Katherine and Mary Savage,[4] who were probably flighty young girls in 1656. Perhaps it is

---

[1] Hist. MSS. Comm., 5th Report, Appendix, Pt. I. 152. (A. Newport to Sir W. Leveson.)

[2] I have been allowed to see them by the kindness of the present Warden.

[3] Cf. Letter of Lady Essex to the Second Earl of Chesterfield, printed in his Correspondence (London, 1829), p. 97.

[4] "The Ancient and Noble Family of the Savages of the Ards," p. 53.

not too fanciful to find an idealised portrait of them in 1656 those two charming madcaps, Sir John Everyoung's daughters, in Sedley's comedy "The Mulberry Garden," which, as its scene is laid at the end of the Protectorate, may be supposed to embody recollections of these years. The manners of young ladies partook of the general social confusion. Clarendon notes with horror that they "conversed without any circumspection or modesty, and frequently met at taverns or common eating houses."[1] It needs no great stretch of imagination to picture Katherine and Mary Savage, like Olivia and Victoria in the play, repairing unescorted and masked[2] to the Mulberry Garden, which stood on part of the site now covered by Buckingham Palace, and which, according to Evelyn, was "the onely place of entertainment about the town for persons of the first quality to be cheated at," after Cromwell's soldiers had shut up Spring Gardens.[3] There the ladies would meet their "servants," who would entertain them with "certain trifling *Tarts, Neate's-tongues, Salacious meates,* and bad *Rhenish,*"[4] and make love to them in stilted language borrowed from the high-flown French romances which were then the latest novelty in fiction.[5] Amid such surroundings it was very natural that a match should be concluded between Sir Charles Sedley and one of the sisters of his brother's widow. As both the baronet and Katherine Savage were under twenty, it may be safely assumed their courtship was rather in the nature of a boy and girl flirtation against the pretty background of Park and Mulberry Garden than the result

---

[1] Clarendon,"Life," ed. 1857, I. 305.

[2] Like Dorothy Osborne in Spring Gardens in June 1654. See her letter to Sir W. Temple, 6 June, 1654 (ed. Parry, Everyman's Library p. 243).

[3] Evelyn's Diary (ed. Dobson), II. 71, s.d. 10 May, 1654.

[4] "A Character of England," 1659, p. 57.

[5] Sedley's library probably included the "Grand Cyrus" in the English translation of 1655, see p. 388.

1656 of any serious passion. Their intimacy was, doubtless, encouraged both by Lady Sedley (if she was still alive[1]) and the Savages, who had been ruined by the Civil War, and who must have been glad enough to marry a scantily portioned younger daughter to one of the richest baronets in Kent. The wedding took place at the church of St. Giles-in-the-Fields on 9 February, 1656/57 1656/7,[2] and, like that of Sir William, it must have been conducted before a civil magistrate. The newly married couple seem to have gone to live in Great Queen Street,[3] then a very fashionable thoroughfare running from Drury Lane to Lincoln's Inn Fields. Their house was possibly one of the fine row, built 1657 there by Inigo Jones in the reign of Charles I, which included the residence of Lord Herbert of Cherbury, and also that of Earl Rivers, Lady Sedley's brother.[4] On 21 December, 1657, about ten months after the wedding, Lady Sedley gave birth to a daughter, who, at St. Giles's Church, eight days later, was baptised by the name of Katherine.

In the following spring the Sedleys were staying on their estates in Kent, and were being watched with some vigilance by the Government. Sir Charles may have already betrayed some sympathy with the royal cause, and his marriage into a Cavalier and Roman Catholic family would be quite enough to cast suspicion

---

[1] I have been unable to find any record of the date of her death. Waller's epitaph on her was only published in the sixth edition of his Works (1693), and it is quite possible that she survived the Restoration by many years.

[2] St. Giles-in-the-Fields Marriage Register. *Gentleman's Magazine*, October 1850 (p. 366).

[3] I infer this from the letter (quoted below) from Wm. Persall to Sir W. Paston (Hist. MSS. Comm., 7th Rep., Appendix, p. 531), which gives details of Sir Charles Sedley among " our Queen Street news."

[4] Lord Herbert of Cherbury died there in 1648 (Aubrey's " Lives," ed. Clark, II. 387). Earl Rivers mentions Rivers House, his residence in Great Queen Street, in his will (Wheatley's "London Past and Present," II. 137).

on him. The fact that on 26 March, 1657/8, he had to obtain permission from the Protector's Council to leave his house in Kent to attend some legal proceedings at Maidstone shows that he was not regarded very favourably by the authorities.[1]

By May they had returned to London. On the 16th of that month the baronet and his lady were driving —perhaps in one of the coaches so dear to Sir William—through the parish of St. Martin's-in-the-Fields. They were probably returning from the fashionable "tour" of Hyde Park, and were accompanied by another coach, containing a person who was possibly identical with one of the most prodigious coxcombs of the reign of Charles II. Both coaches were stopped by an official called the "Overseer of the Poor" of the parish, who fined the single gentleman ten shillings, and the married couple twenty-five shillings, for the heinous offence of "using of their coaches on the Sabboth day at an unlawfull time,"[2] that is, during church hours. Why five shillings should have been added to the joint fine of the married couple it is difficult to imagine. That one of the offenders was a woman may have added to the sin in Puritan eyes—or perhaps the Sedleys were hardened enough to laugh at the guardians of the Sabbath's purity. Some light on the motives of these guardians is thrown by a passage in a comedy, written some years later, where a Puritan constable sighs after the lucrative office of fining wealthy Sabbath-breakers:—"Would I were an Overseer of the Poor . . . there were

---

[1] State Papers Dom., Int. I. 78, f. 553.

[2] Accounts of the Overseers of the Poor of the Parish of St. Martin's-in-the-Fields (MS. preserved in the City Hall, Westminster). Wheatley's "London Past and Present" (II. 181) states incorrectly that Sir Charles was fined "several times" for this offence. The entry quoted above is the only one referring to him in the Accounts. The single gentleman is called "Sir John Hewitt" in the entry. I strongly suspect that this is a slip for Sir George Hewitt, the notorious coxcomb and supposed original of Sir Fopling Flutter.

1657/58 somewhat to be got by that."[1] The scene between the gay young people of fashion and the kill-joy Puritan officials was typical of the age. It represents the half-absurd, half-pathetic, and wholly ineffective protest of the Saints against a generation which preferred the Park and the Mulberry Garden to the Kingdom of Heaven. The tables were soon to be turned, and, in the meantime, youth could afford to laugh and pay.

The household in Great Queen Street seems to have been equipped on a pretty lavish scale. It certainly 1658 included a number of men-servants, for at the end of September 1658, the month of Cromwell's death, we hear that two of Sir Charles Sedley's footmen had died "of the new disease."[2] From the same source we learn that among his neighbours in Great Queen Street was Lady Anne Brudenell (afterwards Countess of Shrewsbury), the dark-eyed beauty whose depravity was to cause one of the most tragic events of the reign of Charles II.

1659–60 Only a single clue to Sir Charles' movements in the last troubled months of the Commonwealth has survived. At this time prudent royalists were content to keep quiet, while different sections of the "fanaticks" weakened themselves by their dissensions, and paved the way for a peaceful Restoration. When Monk reached London in January 1659/60, one of the first acts of the Provisional Government, which was formed pending the election of a "free parliament," was, with the help of the loyal nobility and gentry, to reconstitute the Militia as a protection against the army, which was still a formidable menace to the nation. Sir Charles Sedley was one of the Commissioners appointed on 7 March, 1659,[3] to raise this force in the counties of Kent and Leicester. In spite of the fact 1660 that there might have been very grim work before them,

---

[1] John Wilson's "The Cheats" (4to, London, 1664), V. ii. p. 65.
[2] Hist. MSS. Comm., 7th Report, Appendix, p. 531. (Wm. Persall to Sir Wm. Paston, 24 September, 1658.)
[3] "Acts and Ordinances of the Interregnum," ed. Firth, II. 1433, 4.

these rustic battalions seem to have been enrolled in a 1660 holiday spirit. We are told that the "captains and other officers" were specially active in providing "very rich atire"[1] for themselves and their troops, who consisted chiefly of their tenants and farm labourers. It was the final emancipation from the Puritan gloom.

The Kentish contingent was under the command of the old Cavalier general, George Goring, Earl of Norwich, and, as one of the officers of this body, it is almost certain that Sir Charles was present at the actual landing of the monarch to whom he was to prove so congenial a companion. We may picture him setting out from Canterbury with his gaily dressed followers in the train of General Monk on the morning of 25 May, 1660, when news had been brought that the royal flotilla was in sight. At "two of the clock in the afternoone" they reached Dover, and at three that fine old ship, formerly *Naseby*, now *King Charles*, was close to the pier. Two boats put off, one containing Mr. Samuel Pepys and one of the King's favourite dogs, and the other the swarthy, black-eyed Charles II with his two brothers, the Dukes of York and Gloucester. A canopy was held over the King's head as he landed, and Monk and thousands of spectators on the beach and cliffs fell on their knees. After Charles had raised and embraced the "Lord General," he walked towards his coach. On his way he was met by Mr. Reading, the Minister of Dover, who had come with the Mayor to welcome him. The divine made a short speech and presented the King with "a large bible wth gold clasps." It would be interesting to know if Sir Charles Sedley was close enough to see the twinkle in the royal eye as his Majesty thanked Mr. Reading, and gravely assured him "it was the thing he loved above all things in the world."[2] Soon the procession started on the road

---

[1] Rugge's "Diurnall" (Brit. Mus., Add. MS. 10116, f. 95).

[2] Pepys, ed. Wheatley, I. 162. Rugge's "Diurnall," f. 98. According to Pepys it was the Mayor who gave the Bible.

E

1660 to Canterbury, where the Recorder presented the restored monarch with a golden tankard, a far more appropriate gift than the Mayor of Dover's Bible. When the King had passed two nights in the Archbishop's Palace, the cavalcade set out for London, along roads lined with booths and gay with streamers. After inspecting the Puritan army, drawn up to give him a sullen welcome on Blackheath, the King and his train reached the outskirts of the capital, where " the maids in their ornaments came to meet them, making a gallant showe." At St. George's Fields was the formal reception by the Lord Mayor, and from there, along streets hung with rich tapestry and crowded with spectators, the royal procession passed on to the ancient Palace of Whitehall. One of the gaily-dressed battalions that marched down the Strand consisted of the gentlemen of Kent, dressed in "white doublets," and among them, we may be sure, was Sir Charles Sedley of Southfleet, along with the representatives of other loyal and ancient families of the county.

CHAPTER III

THE WITS AND THEIR FROLICS

". . . lived mostly in the great city, became a debauchee, set up for a satyrical wit, a comedian, poet, and courtier of ladies and I know not what."—Anthony à Wood: "Life of Sir Charles Sedley," Athenæ Oxonienses.

"That notorious business in the balcony . . . scelus *inauditum*."—Anthony à Wood ("Life and Times," ed. Clarke, I. 476).

"Des Garnements comme Sidley."[1]—"Mémoires de Grammont," Chap X.

"Mark the friendship of the dissolute!"—Dr. Johnson (on Sedley in his Life of Dorset: "Lives of the Poets," ed. Hill, I. 303).

"He appeared in Publick much about the Year 1663."—"Some Account of the Life of Sir Charles Sedley," prefixed to the edition of 1722.

Sir Thomas Urquhart is said to have died of 1660 laughing when he heard of the Restoration. There is certainly a grim kind of humour in the way in which the exiled king was brought back to the throne of his ancestors. The large and influential body of Englishmen that actually accomplished the change was composed of elements which had nothing in common except the desire to restore the traditional political system. In every other respect their aims were ludicrously dissimilar. The Presbyterians thought that they could compel Charles II (of all people) to set up, if not the Kirk, at any rate a godly and sober administration and court. The old-fashioned royalists such as Hyde, Ormonde and Southampton wanted a complete reversion to the aristocratic and episcopal government

[1] Reading of MSS. in *Bibliothèque Nationale* and *Bibliothèque Mazarine*. Printed ed. read *Sidney;* see Ruth Clark's "Anthony Hamilton" (1921), p. 308.

51

1660 of the early seventeenth century with a revival of the
stately ceremonial life of the old court. The third
important section of the king's supporters were those
whom Clarendon describes as "young men, who had
never seen the king, and had been born and bred in
those corrupt times 'when there was no king in
Israel.'"[1] These young men, of whom Sir Charles
Sedley was certainly one, belonged to the kind of generation which often follows a great war. Utterly disgusted
with the endless discussion of questions of principle
and conscience, they had reverted to a purely pagan
attitude, and proclaimed that intellectual and sen-
suous pleasures were the only aims of a sensible man:

> Let us indulge the Joys we know
> Of Musick, Wine and Love.
> We're sure of what we find below,
> Uncertain what's above.

This hardness shocked old-fashioned observers like
Clarendon, who writes that among them "the tenderness of the bowels, which is the quintessence of justice
and compassion, the very mention of good nature was
laughed at and looked upon as the mark and character
of a fool; and a roughness of manners, or hardhearted-
ness and cruelty, was affected."[2] These were the young
men who were "uningaged in the late differences"
and who "lived high under Oliver," and it was among
them, and not among the sober Presbyterians or the
grave old-fashioned royalists, that the restored king
found his most intimate and sympathetic friends.
Charles II with his artistic and pleasure-loving nature
and his complete lack of a moral sense must indeed
have appeared to them the very incarnation of their
own spirit and many an old soldier who had poured
out blood and treasure for the Stuarts must have slunk
away in disgust at the sight of the son of the Royal
Martyr surrounded by—

[1] Clarendon, "Life," etc., ed. 1857, I. 307.
[2] Clarendon, " Life," I. 307.

"those
Whose Chins are beardless, yet their Hose
And Buttocks still wear muffs;
While the old rusty cavaleer
Retires, or dares not once appear
For want of Coin and Cuffs."[1]

We have only two definite pieces of information about
Sir Charles Sedley in the first years after the Restoration.
One is a tradition that Harefield House, Middlesex,
was burned down "by the carelessness of the witty
Sir Charles Sedley, who was amusing himself by reading
in bed" "about the year 1660."[2] Harefield House
was the property of Lady Chandos, the widow of
Sir William Sedley and sister of Sir Charles's wife,
and it was there that Milton's "Arcades" was acted
by the Countess of Derby's children about 1653.
The Sedleys probably paid a visit to Lady Chandos
soon after the Restoration, when the accident occurred.

In July 1661, Sedley was seriously ill[3] and his
death was considered imminent. However, as on more
than one other occasion, his sturdy constitution gave
the lie to the doctors. The nature of this illness has
not been recorded, but it may be conjectured that it
was caused by the enormous revels which accompanied the gorgeous and somewhat disorderly coronation of Charles II on St. George's Day, 1661. The
whole of London seems to have been more or less
intoxicated with wine and loyalty on this occasion,
and some riotous incidents occurred even on the stairs
of Westminster Hall.[4] If Pepys, a hardworking official
of moderate means, suffered a little from the effects of
the orgies of 23 April, 1661,[5] it may be readily

[1] Merrie Drollerie, 1661, reprinted Ebsworth 1875, pp. 53, 54.
[2] Lyson's "Historical Account of those Parishes of Middlesex not
included in the Environs of London" (London, 1800), p. 109. Lysons
quotes no authority for the story.
[3] Letter from Eliz. Bodvile to Lord Hatton, date ?July 1661.
Hatton Corr., ed. Camden Soc., I. 21.
[4] Pepys's Diary, ed. Wheatley, II. 23 and note *ad loc*.
[5] Pepys's Diary, ed. Wheatley, II. p. 26.

1661 imagined that a young man of wealth and leisure like Sir Charles Sedley was laid up after the "extraordinary feaſting" by which even sober John Evelyn admits that the Court celebrated the coronation of the reſtored King.

Although there is no other aćtual record of Sedley during the firſt three years after the Reſtoration, we know enough from the ſtatements in the early memoirs to be certain that about this time he became a member of the Circle of Wits, as they came to be called, with whom Charles II was accuſtomed to spend his evenings. In 1661 Ormonde told Clarendon that "the king spent moſt of his time with confident young men, who abhorred all discourse that was serious, and, in the liberty they assumed in drollery and raillery, preserved no reverence towards God or man, but laughed at all sober men, and even at religion itself."[1] Sir Charles Sedley was certainly one of these "confident young men" if we may believe Anthony à Wood and the author of the "Memoir" of 1722. The latter writes, "It happen'd by him in respećt of the King, as is said of the famous Cardinal *Richlieu, viz.* That they who recommended him to the King, thereby supplanted themselves, and afterwards envied him ; but with this Difference between the Cardinal and *Sir Charles, viz.* That the latter was never ungrateful." The meeting-place of the Wits where Charles went to hear what Clarendon ironically calls "the nightly conversation" was the house of Barbara Palmer, the King's mistress, whose contemptible husband, Roger Palmer, was created Earl of Caſtlemaine in 1662, and it is likely that it was at Lady Caſtlemaine's that Sedley firſt met the King.

The author of the "Memoir" writes that "when he had a Taſte of the Court, as the King never would part with him, so he never would part with the King; and yet two things happen'd to his Damage in it:

[1] Clarendon's "Life," I. 354, 355.

First his Estate was never the better . . . and secondly *c.* 1661 his Morals much the worse.

"The King delighted in him to an Excess, and he pleas'd his Majesty in one thing, in which he eminently differ'd from all the rest of the Wits of the Court, *viz.* That he never ask'd the King for any thing, and they were always a begging of him." This was indeed a recommendation to a king like Charles whose pockets were always empty.

The leading spirit of the "nightly congregation," as Clarendon calls it, was the brilliant, wealthy and mercurial Duke of Buckingham, Dryden's *Zimri*, who

> In the course of one revolving Moon,
> Was Chymist, Fidler, States Man, and Buffoon;
> Then all for Women, Painting, Rhiming, Drinking;
> Besides ten thousand freaks that dy'd in thinking.

Another prominent figure was Charles Sackville, Lord Buckhurst, who was about a year older than Sedley. Prior writes tactfully of this young nobleman that "coming very Young into the Possession of two plentiful Estates and in an Age when Pleasure was more in Fashion than Business, he turned his Parts rather to Books and Conversation than to Politicks."[1] Other " confident young men" were Fleetwood Shepherd, Henry Savile, Baptist May, Henry Killigrew and Sir Charles Berkeley. Anthony à Wood describes the first-named in a sentence that summarizes the whole group: " after his majesty's Restoration he retir'd to London, hang'd on the court, became a debauchee and atheist."[2]

There is no doubt that the King enjoyed Sedley's conversation, which must have often enlivened those supper parties at Lady Castlemaine's, where, to the scandal of his subjects, his Majesty was to be found every night. It was very likely on some such occasion that he "singl'd him (*i.e.* Sedley) out for the best

[1] Prior's Dedication to "Poems on Several Occasions," 8vo, 1709.
[2] "Athenæ Oxonienses," ed. Bliss, IV. 627.

c. 1661 Genius of the Age, and frequently told his Familiars that Sedley's Stile, whether in Writing or Discourse would be the Standard of the *English* Tongue." Sir Charles's criticisms were doubtless listened to attentively by the patron of Dryden and Betterton, and the King told him one day in jest that "Nature had given him a Patent to be *Apollo's* Viceroy."[1]

Round the Wits clustered a throng of their would-be imitators, the Dapper-wits, Woodcocks and Tattles, whose aping of the real "man of parts" provides such frequent subjects for contemporary comedy. These Fops, as they were called, were youths of the same class as the Wits, but who lacked the necessary mental equipment to be either tolerable writers or good companions. One of the chief joys of Sedley and his friends was the baiting or "smoking" of such cox-

1662/63 combs. In the winter of 1662/3 Sir Charles took part in such a baiting, the victim of which was the second Earl of Chesterfield, whom we have already seen among London's gay butterflies in Oliver's time. The whole affair is in the style of a "fête galante" of Watteau or Fragonard.

According to Hamilton (whose description is an exquisite diminuendo) the Earl "had a very agreeable face, a fine head of hair, an indifferent shape and a worse air," and in the pages of De Grammont's Memoirs we see him strutting like a peacock among the courtiers at Whitehall with his beautiful neglected Countess by his side. Round this beauty the gallants cluster like flies on a jar of honey, and foremost among them is the still young and handsome James, Duke of York. There is a scene in Lady Chesterfield's apartments, whither her brother Lord Arran has brought the Duke, ostensibly to borrow her fine guitar. Unfortunately the Earl happens to be there, and he is compelled to look on while Arran plays innumerable sarabands to the Duke, and Lady Chesterfield "accom-

[1] Memoir prefixed to Briscoe's edition of 1722, p. 5.

panies him with her eyes."[1] When the well-known 1662/63
incident of the green stockings[2] has confirmed Chesterfield's suspicions, he commits what, in this world of
cloud-cuckoldry, is the unforgivable sin of showing
his jealousy and hurries the lady off to his country seat
in mid-winter. Then "God only knows what a terrible
attack there was made upon his rear," and Sedley and
Buckhurst are mentioned among the Wits who
bombarded the unfortunate Earl with innumerable
lampoons.[3]

We must now turn aside from the world of pleasure
and gallantry in order to look at the more sordid
realities of the street and tavern life which lay behind
it. The Wits were something a great deal more interesting than mere courtiers. They were the inheritors
of the great traditions of the literary and Bohemian
tavern clubs of the days of Shakespeare and Ben
Jonson, which they handed on to their successors, the
circle of Addison and Steele at the beginning and that
of Johnson and Goldsmith in the middle of the
eighteenth century. The frequency of tavern scenes
in the contemporary comedy of manners, which is
largely a mirror of the life of the Wits, shows that
much of their time was spent in these places.[4] Their

[1] Hamilton's "Memoirs of Count Grammont," ed. Gordon Goodwin,
I. 175.
[2] *Ibid.*, I. 179, 180.
[3] *Ibid.*, II. 2. Rochester and Etherege are mentioned by Hamilton
as taking part in this onslaught, but this must be a mistake, as probably
neither came to Court till 1664 (see p. 68 below). The baiting of
Chesterfield can be dated by a reference in Pepys's Diary (ed. Wheatley,
II. 384).
[4] For a contemporary description of a tavern see "The Character
of a Tavern" (4to, 1675), from which I give an extract: "A Tavern
is an Academy of Debauchery, where the Devil teaches the seven
deadly sins instead of Sciences, a Tipling-School a degree above an
Ale-house, where you may be drunk with more credit and Apology,
'tis the Randevous of Gallants, the Good Fellowes' Paradice, and the
Miser's Terrour. . . . 'Tis a *Bedlam* of Wits, where men are rather
mad than *merry*, here one breaking a Jest on the *Drawer*, or perhaps a

c. 1663 favourite houses seem to have been at Charing Cross, in the neighbourhood of the Royal Mews, and in the maze of narrow streets between Drury Lane and Covent Garden. Locket's, so called from its proprietor, Adam Locket,[1] was the chief of the Charing Cross taverns. The great haunt of the Wits in the Covent Garden quarter seems to have been the Rose in Russell Street, which adjoined the Drury Lane Playhouse, and was still a fashionable house in the time of Hogarth.[2] It was kept by a Mr. Long and subsequently by his widow, and seems to have shared with Locket's the honour of being the usual dining-place of Sir Charles Sedley and his friends.[3] A special attraction, which doubtless had some share in drawing the Wits to this house, was a very pretty barmaid—"a lilly at the bar"—as one of them calls her in a letter written many years after.[4] A contemporary descrip-

---

Candlestick or *Bottle* over his Crown, there another repeating scraps of Old Plays or some Bawdy Song . . . whilst all with loud hooting and laughing confound the noise of *Fidlers* who are properly called a *Noise*, for no Musick can be heard for them."

[1] Probably founded soon after the Restoration. It was a well-known house by 1675, when Wycherley mentions it as being frequented by courtiers ("The Country Wife," IV. 3). On the other hand, it did not exist at the time of the Civil War if we may believe Dr. King's "Art of Cookery" (1709):

> "The fate of things is always in the dark;
> What Cavalier would know St. James's Park?
> For Locket's stands where gardens once did spring,
> And wild ducks quack where grasshoppers did sing."

[2] It is the scene of Plate III. of the "Rake's Progress." There was more than one tavern of this name.

[3] Cf. Etherege's "The Man of Mode" (4to, 1676, I. i.), where Etherege (Young Bellair) says, "Where do you dine?" Rochester (Dorimant) answers, "At Long's or Locket's," and Sedley (Medley) adds, "At Long's let it be." For this identification of the characters of "The Man of Mode" see below, p. 71.

[4] Sir George Etherege's "Ratisbon Letter Book," Add. MS. 11513, f. 163 (to Mr. Will Richards, 2/12 Feb., 1687/8).

tion of a barmaid helps us to visualise the "lilly." *c.* 1663
"You muſt firſt appear at the Bar, where Madam
Minks, with her Head behung with as many Toys as
their *Bush*, sits like the Goddess *Semele* (Mother of
Bacchus) under her all-commanding Canopy."[1] Near
the Rose in Russell Street was the "great Coffee-
house" kept by William Urwin, and usually known
as Will's. We learn from Pepys[2] that by the winter
of 1663/4 it was already a well-known meeting-
place of the Wits, and it was there that Dryden
was to hold his court in later years. The taverns
were frequently cook-shops or reſtaurants, and there
was often a daily ordinary. Conversation and manners
were remarkably free, and the greateſt nobles
in England might be seen choosing pieces off the
spit, cheek by jowl with members of the humbleſt
classes.[3] Riotous conduct was naturally common in
places where unlimited supplies of liquor could be
obtained at all hours. The scene of the moſt famous
of all the drunken frolics of the Wits was a tavern
called the Cock in Bow Street, a turning off Russell
Street. The Cock was kept by a woman called Oxford
Kate,[4] and, like many of the Covent Garden taverns,
was probably a house of no very good reputation.
The escapade which took place there was sufficiently
foolish and disguſting, and furnishes an effective
contraſt to Hamilton's rose-tinted picture. However,
it is surely absurd to speak of the wild pranks of some
hot-headed youths in their cups as though they were
monſtrous sins, and, taking into consideration the
general softening of manners, the affair is perhaps

---

[1] "Character of a Tavern," 1675, p. 3.
[2] Pepys's Diary (ed. Wheatley), IV. 33.
[3] Cf. "Mémoires et Observations Faites par un Voyageur en
Angleterre à La Haye, 1698" (by H. M. de V. Henry Misson de
Valbourg), pp. 241, 242.
[4] It is called "Oxford Kate's" by Shadwell in "The Sullen Lovers"
(4to, 1668), V. i.

c. 1663 comparable to the more reckless "rags" of modern students, having, like them, an element of humour that only the stiffest-grained Puritan could fail to notice.

    This was the second scene of aristocratic debauchery which scandalised the graver citizens of Westminster in 1663 the spring of 1663. The first had been enacted at an entertainment given by the young Earl of Oxford[1] in honour of General Monk, now Duke of Albemarle, on 12 May.[2] According to a letter of De Comminges, the French Ambassador, "all the young men of quality" were present, and we may be sure that Lord Buckhurst and Sir Charles Sedley were among them. The banquet was followed by a revel which ended in a violent quarrel, during which periwigs were pulled off and swords were drawn. When the combatants had been separated, some of them accompanied the Duke to his lodgings in Whitehall Palace, where they continued drinking till nightfall, and, after having been provided with supper by their new host, carried on the bout till the small hours of the morning, "each man being resolved to drink his neighbour under the table." The Duke, who had the strongest head of all present, hit on an excellent device for getting rid of his uninvited guests. He handed to each gentleman a goblet (*un hanap*) of such a size that the whole company was rendered senseless for many hours—with the exception of the host, who calmly left them to their

[1] This was Aubrey de Vere, the twentieth and last Earl (1626–1703), described by Macaulay as "a man of loose morals, but of inoffensive temperament and courtly manners."

[2] Letter from De Comminges to Lionne printed in Wheatley's "Pepysiana," App. IX. p. 292. De Comminges' letter is dated "15 mai." He says that the Earl of Oxford's party had taken place three days before. Pepys, who gives a less detailed account of the affair, says (on the 15 May) that "it happened two days ago." Perhaps the divergence is accounted for by the fact that the revel started in the afternoon and ended the following morning (Pepys's Diary, ed. Wheatley, III. 122). Pepys's comment is, "To such a degree of madness is the nobility of this age come."

fate and went off to attend a debate at the House of 1663 Lords.

On 16 June,[1] about a month after this Rabelaisian feast, passers-by in Bow Street, Covent Garden, were treated to a spectacle which must have convinced the more puritanical that London would soon share the fate of Sodom and Gomorrah.[2] Three young men of fashion, having doubtless dined very well and being "all inflam'd with strong liquors," appeared on the balcony of the Cock Tavern. They were Sir Charles Sedley, Lord Buckhurst, and Sir Thomas Ogle, Knight, of Pinchbeck, Lincolnshire (destined to become a highly respectable Governor of Chelsea College, where he died in 1702).[3] The trio stripped themselves stark naked,[4] and Sedley, after performing

[1] According to the Rev. C. N. Sutton's "Historical Notes of Withiam," etc. (1902), Withiam Church in Sussex was burnt down on this date. Now Anthony à Wood states emphatically that the fire took place on the same day as the Bow Street affair. It was certainly an extraordinary coincidence that the church which contained the tombs of the Sackville family should have been mysteriously burnt in a great storm on the very day on which the young heir was taking part in a drunken and blasphemous orgy. Doubtless the superstitious made the most of such an opportunity.

[2] This account of the affair is pieced together from Pepys's Diary (ed. Wheatley), III. 191; Anthony à Wood's "Life and Times," ed. Clark, I. 476–7, II. 335–6, and "Athenæ Oxonienses" (ed. Bliss), IV. 731; Johnson's Life of Dorset ("Lives of the Poets," ed. Hill, I. 303); Siderfin's Reports, I. 168; Keble's Reports, I. 620, and Col. Prideaux's letter to *Notes and Queries*, 9th Series, Vol. VIII. p. 151. Pepys heard of the frolic and the trial from Mr. Batten on 1 July, 1663.

[3] Le Neve's "Knights" (Harl. Soc.), p. 93; Luttrell's "Brief Relation," V. 212.

[4] Wood says in his Diary ("Life and Times," II. 335): "They all (I am sure Sedley) . . . stripped themselves naked." Pepys only mentions Sedley as having "shown his nakedness." Was this a tribute to the "State of Nature" which may have been the theme of part of the sermon? It is interesting to compare Rochester's remark to Burnet that he and his friends "in their Frolicks they would have chosen sometimes to go naked if they had not feared the people" (Burnet's "Life and Death of Rochester," 6th ed., 1724, p. 28). It seems, however, to have been a common practice among seventeenth-century revellers to divest themselves of all or part of their clothes. Judge

1663 certain disgusting pranks[1] (which Pepys and Anthony
à Wood relate in plain English), preached a kind of
mock sermon,[2] probably in ribald imitation of a
Puritan divine, to a large crowd of over "1000 persons," who had assembled outside the tavern. It is a
pity that there was no stenographer present to take
down this remarkable discourse for the benefit of
posterity. Its main drift is said by one contemporary[3]
to have been "blasphemy" and by another[4] "abusing
of scripture." Leaving theology, the orator turned to
medicine, and imitating the harangues of the itinerant
quacks, who at that time were a common sight in the
streets of London, began to enlarge upon the merits
of "such a powder as should make all the women
of the town run after him."[5] The crowd, which
probably contained a large Puritan element, greeted

Jeffreys and his cronies "stripped into their shirts" at a wild debauch
at Alderman Duncomb's, according to Reresby ("Memoirs," ed. Ivatt,
p. 282), and Etherege and his friends danced stark naked at Ratisbon
according to his horrified secretary ("Ratisbon Letter-Book," *ad fin.*).

[1] It may be remarked that the full details of the pranks played by
Sedley prior to the "sermon" are not printed by Wheatley. They
may be seen in the Rev. Mynors Bright's complete transcription in
the Library of Magdalene College, Cambridge, which I have been
allowed to examine by the courtesy of the Librarian.

[2] Note that Etherege's "Medley" in "The Man of Mode" (4to,
1676, Act V. sc. i.), who is probably a portrait of Sedley, used to get
"rhetorically drunk." The phrase may well be a reminiscence of this
scene.

[3] Anthony à Wood.

[4] Pepys.

[5] The idea of masquerading as an itinerant quack always had a
fascination for the Restoration gallants. Perhaps they owed the notion
to Ben Jonson's "Volpone," Act II. sc. i. Buckingham is supposed to
have adopted the disguise of a "Jack Pudding" in order to visit London
under the Protectorate, and to have erected a stage at Charing Cross,
where he sang ballads and threw into the coach of his sister a bundle
of important letters (see Lady Burghclere's "Life of Buckingham," p.
28). Later, Rochester disguised himself as a German doctor "and
practised on Tower Hill under the name of 'Alexander Bendo.'" A
Speech "To all Gentlemen and Ladies and others, whether of City,
Town or Country," supposed to have been delivered by him in this

Sedley's sermon with showers of ſtones. The orator 1663
and his friends replied by flinging down bottles,[1]
but were finally driven to take shelter in the
tavern, while the mob expressed their disapproba-
tion of atheism and drunkenness by breaking the
windows.

The Puritans or "fanaticks" naturally took full
advantage of such an incident in order to caſt dis-
credit on the Court. They are said to have "aggravated
it to the utmoſt" by making it "the moſt scandalous
thing in nature, and nothing more reproachful to
religion than that," and the scandal was so great that
even Charles II's Government could not neglect it.
Sedley, as the chief culprit,[2] was summoned to appear
before Sir Robert Foſter,[3] Lord Chief Juſtice of the
King's Bench, an old-fashioned, high-minded Cavalier
of the school of Ormonde and Clarendon, to whom
such escapades were especially odious as caſting dis-
credit on the whole party. The case came on before
the end of June,[4] and, from the gossip heard by Pepys

---

character, is printed in several editions of his works. Perhaps he took
some hints from Sedley's oration.

[1] This detail is from Keble's note on the case (Reports 13–17,
Charles II, p. 620). The bottles were not *empty:* see Appendix I,
pp. 308–9.

[2] Wood says that the "company" were summoned before the Lord
Chief Justice. Legal proceedings, however, seem to have been taken
only against Sedley. Col. W. F. Prideaux' comment is worth quoting:
"His (Sedley's) fate compared with Buckhurst's exemplifies the common saying that one man may steal a horse while another is hanged
for looking over the hedge. Johnson in his 'Life of Dorset' quotes
Rochester's remark, 'I know not how it is, but Lord Buckhurst may
do what he will yet is never in the wrong. Poor Sedley, on the other
hand, was never in the right.' " (Letter in *Notes and Queries,* 9th Series,
Vol. VIII. pp. 157, 158, August 24, 1901.)

[3] Wood says incorrectly that Sir Robert Hyde tried Sedley. Hyde
did not succeed Foster at the King's Bench till the latter's death in
October 1663.

[4] Pepys heard of both frolic and trial on 1 July, so the trial must
have been soon after the "misdemeanours."

1663 and Anthony à Wood and the quaint jargon of Siderfin's Reports, we can form some idea of what took place.

It may be supposed that the court was filled with courtiers on the day of the trial. The reading of the indictment, which gave a detailed account of the affair, must have given considerable amusement to an audience who knew quite well that the men who were being charged with having broken "the King's Peace" were intimate friends of the King himself. The case had a certain amount of technical interest to lawyers, as none of Sedley's actions was strictly punishable by law[1] at that time. Cases of immorality and indecency had formerly been tried by the Star Chamber, which inherited these functions from the old ecclesiastical courts. The Star Chamber had been abolished for ever by the Long Parliament, and it was not clear which, if any, tribunal had jurisdiction in the cases which it had formerly tried. Sedley alone apparently of the three offenders was charged with "several misdemeanours against the King's Peace," though Buckhurst also seems to have been in court. Sir Robert Foster told the baronet from the bench that "as the Star Chamber no longer existed, this Court was now Custos Morum of the King's subjects, and it was high time to Punish such profane Actions committed against all decency." He also said that "it was for him and such wicked wretches as he was that God's anger and judgments hang over us," and "called him sirrah many times." Being told that Buckhurst was in court, he asked "if it was that Buck-

---

[1] "There being no law against him for it," Pepys (ed. Wheatley, III. 192). "Henry Fielding quoted Sedley's case as a precedent in his Charge to the Grand Jury . . . held for the City and Liberty of Westminster . . . 29 June, 1749" (Works, ed. Murphy, 1806, X. 170).

For a modern view of the legal aspect of the case see Judge Parry's "What the Judge Thought" (Fisher Unwin, 1922, p. 845).

hurst who was lately charged with robbery,[1] and 1663 when he answered Yes, he asked whether he had so soon forgot his deliverance at that time, and that it would have more become him to have been at his prayers begging God's forgiveness than now running into such courses again." The Lord Chief Justice asked Sedley if he had read "a book called the Compleat Gentleman," referring to Henry Peacham's well-known work (first published 1622, reprinted 1634 and 1661).[2] Sedley replied irrelevantly (but perhaps not wholly untruly) that "set aside his lordship, he had read more books than himself."[3] He was asked if he would stand his trial at the Bar, but took the sensible course of confessing the indictment and throwing himself on the mercy of the court. Judgment was then passed that, "as he was of a very ancient Family of the County of Kent, and as his Estate was encumbered (since the Court did not intend his ruin but reform), he should be fined 2000 marks, imprisoned for a week without Bail and bound over for good behaviour for three years."[4] His parting shot at Old

[1] Buckhurst with Edward Sackville, his brother, Sir Henry Belasyse and others mortally wounded an innocent tanner near Waltham's Cross in February 1661/2. They are said to have mistaken him for a robber and to have taken money from his pockets under the impression that it was stolen property. They were apprehended on a charge of robbery and murder, but the Grand Jury only found a Bill for manslaughter, and they were apparently acquitted (Pepys's Diary, ed. Wheatley, II. 193 and note). It must have been to this affair that Sir Robert Foster was alluding.

[2] Perhaps Sir Robert Foster was thinking of the following passage: "Above all, learn betimes to avoid excessive drinking, than which there is no one Vice more common and reigning, and ill beseeming a Gentleman, which if grown to a habit is hardly left, remembring that hereby you become not fit for any thing, having your reason degraded, your body distempered, your soul hazarded, your esteem and reputation abased, while you sit taking your unwholsome healths—*ut iam vertigine tectum Ambulet,* & geminis exsurgat mensa lucernis.*" ("The Compleat Gentleman," by Henry Peacham, 1661, 4to, p. 271.)

[3] See the list of some books probably in Sir Charles Sedley's library, Appendix II, pp. 324 *seq.*

[4] Judge Parry in "What the Judge Thought" says incorrectly that

F

1663 Father Antic the Law was amusing but unfortunately unquotable.[1]

The week spent by Sir Charles in prison could have certainly involved no great hardship. In those days, if a prisoner had sufficient money to pay the rent of a room and the perquisites of the gaolers, he could live in far greater comfort than could the miserable wretches who herded on the "common side."[2] The imposition of the fine of two thousand marks had a curious sequel. Sedley is said to have asked young Harry Killigrew (who had married Mary Savage, Lady Sedley's sister),[3] a Groom of the King's Bedchamber, and another gentleman to beg the King for a remission of the fine. The story goes that Killigrew and the other courtier begged the money from King Charles and then refused to pay Sedley "twopence" of it.[4] Whatever truth there may be in this tale, it is certain that Sedley paid one thousand marks (£333 6s. 8d.), which, like all fines in those days, actually went into the King's Privy Purse. A minute among the State Papers[5] shows that this sum was not paid till July 1664, and was then granted to

---

Sedley was fined "two thousand marks *or in the alternative* seven days." Siderfin's report of the case (Appendix I, pp. 307–8) shows clearly that the fine was *an addition*, and not an alternative to the sentence of imprisonment. Keble's report of the case gives "one year" as the period for which Sedley was bound over to keep the peace.

[1] It may be found in Wood's "Life of Sedley" ("Athenæ Oxonienses," IV. 731).

[2] See "The History of Thomas Ellwood," the Quaker, written by himself, for a vivid picture of the interior of Restoration prisons.

[3] "The Ancient and Noble Family of the Savages of the Ards," by G. F. A(rmstrong), 1888, p. 53. This Henry or Harry Killigrew was the son of Thomas Killigrew and his wife Cecilia Crofts, and was born in 1637. He was Groom of the Bedchamber both to the Duke of York and to the King, and succeeded his father as Master of the Revels.

[4] See Anthony à Wood, "Life and Times," ed. Clark ("Athenæ Oxonienses," IV. 331).

[5] See Appendix I, p. 309.

"George Hamilton, Esquire." This George Hamilton 1664
must be the famous Anthony's brother, formerly page
to King Charles and one of his most intimate friends.
It would seem that the King exercised his prerogative
of mercy in order to reduce the fine by one-half.

About a year after the Bow Street affair, the heroes
of that episode made the acquaintance of two young
men who had recently come to Court and who proved
notable accessions to the circle of Wits. John Wilmot,
Earl of Rochester, son of one of the loyalest servants
of Charles I, at this date a thin-faced, precocious boy
of sixteen, had just made the Grand Tour with his
Scottish tutor, Dr. Balfour. On his return he was
presented to the King, who took him into high favour
and made him a Gentleman of the Bedchamber.[1] 1664/65
Buckhurst was one of his colleagues in this office,
and it was, doubtless, through that nobleman that he
made the acquaintance of Sir Charles Sedley. The
corruption of his naturally modest character, which
the good Bishop Burnet deplores, was probably due
in some measure to his new friends. The other new
member of the fraternity that assembled at the Rose
and Will's was a fair man of about thirty with a pale,
handsome, debauched face.[2] His name was George
Etherege, and his acquaintance with the Wits seems
to have originated in the extraordinary success of his
lively comedy, "The Comical Revenge, or Love in a
Tub," produced at the Duke's Theatre in 1664/5.[3]
He received the nicknames of Gentle George and
Easy Etherege, and his vivacious and witty con-

---

[1] D. N. B., s.a. J. Wilmot, Earl of Rochester.

[2] Oldys's Notes to Langbaine (Brit. Mus., c. 28, 9, 1, p. 137): ["Sir
George] was a fair man but spoilt his face with drinking."

[3] Pepys saw it on 4 January, 1664/5 (Wheatley, IV. 325), but he
does not say that this was the first performance. That Etherege became
acquainted with Buckhurst (and hence doubtless with Sedley) through
this play is proved by his own statement in the dedication (4to, 1664)
to Buckhurst. "The Writing of it (the play) was a means to make me
known to your Lordship."

c. 1664/65 versation must have delighted his friends. Sedley, now a short, plump, round-faced youth with merry black eyes, a slightly aquiline nose and full voluptuous lips,[1] was known among these young sparks as "Little Sid." He was especially noted for the magnificence of his lace neckcloths and for his ready wit, which usually took the form of absurd similes which convulsed his hearers with laughter.[2] Many years later a certain "old Mrs. Partridge" told Oldys, the eighteenth-century antiquarian,[3] a tale about Sir Charles's neck-cloths which probably refers to this "very merry laughing, dancing, drinking" decade that followed the Restoration. Sedley's friends, knowing his weakness, are said to have proposed one of those frolics where every drinker had to throw into the fire a certain article of their dress, and thus compelled him to sacrifice a gorgeous cravat of point d'Espagne or point de Venice. The Baronet took a heartless revenge. When he was next in the same company, he arranged to have a tooth drawer in attendance, and, having proposed a toast of the same nature, called in the dentist and made him draw a rotten tooth which had been troubling him for some time. The rest of the company, in spite of "tears and oaths," had to follow his example, while the proposer of the toast coolly remarked, "Patience, gentlemen, Patience, you know —you promised I should have frolick too." Such stories as these are merely tantalising fragments of the great legend of the Restoration Court. Like many other legends it has never been embodied in an epic. Hamilton's delightful book is too slight to deserve that title, though it might perhaps have been applied to

[1] See Oldys's Notes to Langbaine (No. 1), Appendix I, p. 318. Cf. also the Knole Park portrait.

[2] I deduce this from Mulgrave's "Little Sid for Simile renowned" ("Essay on Satyr," see p. 145 below). "Little Sid" must have been his usual nickname, as it is also used in the anonymous lampoon called "The Ladies' March" (Brit. Mus., Harl. MS. 7137, f. 31, see p. 140).

[3] See Oldys's notes (No. 6), Appendix I, p. 319.

those Memoirs of Rocheſter which perished in the *c.* 1664/65
flames.[1] The four central figures were Rocheſter,
Buckhurſt, Sedley and Etherege. Burnet in his
Hiſtory[2] gives a thumbnail sketch of three of them.
"Lord Dorset" (*i.e.* Buckhurſt), he writes, "was a
generous, good-natured and modeſt man . . . so
much oppressed with phlegm that till he was a little
heated with wine he scarce ever spoke, but was upon
that exaltation a very lively man. Never was so much
ill-nature in a pen as his, joined with so much good-
nature as is in himself, even to success. . . . He is
bountiful to run himself into difficulties and charitable
to a fault, for he commonly gives all he has about
him, when he meets an objeſt that moves him. But
he was so lazy that, though the King seemed to court
him for a favourite, he would not give himself the
trouble that belonged to that poſt." Rocheſter "was
naturally modeſt, till the Court corrupted him. His
wit had in it a peculiar brightness to which none
could ever arrive. He gave himself up to all sorts of
extravagance, and to the wildeſt frolics that a wanton
wit could devise. . . . He would have gone about
the ſtreets as a beggar and made love as a porter.
He set up a ſtage as an Italian mountebank. He was
for some years always drunk and was ever doing
some mischief." Sedley "had a more sudden and
copious wit which furnished a perpetual run of discourse; but it was not so correſt as Lord Dorset's or
so sparkling as Lord Rocheſter's."

Fortunately there is another source of information
concerning the Wits besides the gossip of the eighteenth century and Burnet's meagre notes. They were
all partly conscious that their lives were the ſtuff
of which legends are made, and, having a genuine
literary gift, tried themselves in plays and verses to

[1] D. N. B., s.a. John Wilmot, Earl of Rochester.
[2] Burnet's "History of My Own Time," ed. Osmund Airy, 1897,
I. 476, 477.

*c.*1664/65 express the spirit of the society in which they lived. Etherege, after several attempts, achieved a certain measure of success in this very difficult task. His comedy, "The Man of Mode, or Sir Fopling Flutter"[1] (4to, 1676), is almost certainly neither more nor less than a series of scenes from the lives of Rochester, Sedley and the author, recollected from the early years of the Restoration Court. By substituting real names for the fictitious ones in "Gentle George's" comedy,[2] it is possible to obtain an excellent idea of the daily life and conversation of the Wits. The first scene is incomparably vivid. We are in Rochester's dressing-room, probably about midday. The Earl is in gown and slippers awaiting the ministrations of his valet. Hearing "Foggy Nan," the Orange-Woman, chattering below, he sends his man Handy to fetch her up and amuses himself by listening to her racy gossip while he samples one of her peaches. She is telling him about a beautiful young lady who is lodging at her house, when Sedley bursts in and the following dialogue takes place.

[1] Congreve drew the inspiration of much of his exquisite art from Etherege's masterpiece, and hence, at second hand, from the lives of the Wits.

[2] See Oldys's Notes to Langbaine (Brit. Mus., C. 28, 9, 1, p. 187). Note to Life of Sir G. Etherege : "The Characters in this play were all from Real Persons or most of them, as Sr. Fopling, Beau Hewit, Dorimant, Lord Rochester and even the shoemaker that got vast trade by this representation of him. Himself he has also set forth under the Character of Young Bevil (*sic*) or Medley." Oldys must be mistaken about "Medley," for it can hardly be doubted, merely from the resemblance of the names, that a portrait of Sedley was intended. This identification is confirmed by the phrase "rhetorically drunk" applied to Medley, which must refer to the affair at the Cock Tavern. M. E. D. Forgues in his article on Rochester in *La Revue des Deux Mondes*, August, September, 1857, identifies "Medley" with Sedley. Finally, cf. Aubrey's remark that "Shakespeare's comoedies will remaine witt as long as the English tongue is understood, for that he handles *mores hominum*. Now our present writers reflect so much upon *particular persons* and *coxcombeities*, that twenty years hence they will not be understood." ("Short Lives," ed. Clark, II. 227.)

SEDLEY: *Rochester*, my Life, my Joy, my darling *c.*1664/65 Sin; how doſt thou?

ORANGE-WOMAN: Lord, what a filthy trick these Men have got of kissing one another (*She spits*).

SEDLEY: Why do you suffer this Cart-load of Scandal to come so near you, and make your Neighbours think you are so improvident to need a Baw'd?

ORANGE-WOMAN: Good, now we shall have it, you did but want him to help you: come, pay me for my Fruit.

SEDLEY: ... You are an Insignificant Brandy Bottle.

ROCHESTER: Nay, there you wrong her, three Quarts of Canary is her Business.

ORANGE-WOMAN: What you please, Gentlemen.

ROCHESTER: To him, give him as good as he brings.

ORANGE-WOMAN: Hang him, there is not such a Heathen in the Town again, except it be the Shoomaker without.

SEDLEY: I shall see you hold up your Hand at the Bar next Sessions for Murder, Huswife: that Shoomaker can take his Oath you are in Fee with the Doctors to sell Green Fruit to the Gentry, that Crudities may Breed Diseases.

The conversation turns again on the beauty about whom the Orange-Woman was gossiping when Sedley came in. Sir Charles is acquainted with the lady and describes her in an exquisite sentence:

"What alteration a Twelve-month may have bred in her I know not, but a year ago she was the beautifulleſt Creature I ever saw; a fine easie clean Shape, light brown Hair in abundance; her Features Regular, her Complexion clear and lively, large wanton Eyes, but above all a mouth that has made me Kiss it a Thousand times in Imagination, teeth white and even, And pretty pouting Lips, with a little moiſture ever hanging on them like the Province Rose fresh on the *c.*1664/65 Bank, e'er the morning Sun has quite drawn up the Dew."[1]

If this is a fair specimen of Sedley's conversational style, it is easy to understand why the King called him "Apollo's Viceroy," and the last phrase is probably one of the "similes" for which he was renowned.

The Earl and the Baronet are soon joined by Etherege. The new-comer is greeted as "a good third man," and the important question whether the company shall dine at Long's (the Rose) or Locket's discussed, and decided in favour of the latter. As Rochester's coach is not yet ready, they sally forth in sedan chairs to Charing Cross. In the afternoon we find Sedley paying a visit to two ladies of fashion.[2] A page arrives in advance to ask if the intrusion "will be troublesome." On the contrary they are both delighted, for Sedley is popular among the ladies on account of his good-nature and amusing conversation. "He's a very pleasant man," says Emilia. "He's a very necessary man among us Women," replies her aunt, Lady Townley. "He's not scandalous i' the least, perpetually contriving to bring good Company together, and always ready to stop Up at a gap at Ombre; then he knows all the little news o' the Town." The niece is equally charmed with the Baronet's conversation: "I love to hear him talk o' the Intrigues, let 'em Be never so dull in themselves, he'll make 'em pleasant i' the Relation." Later we are given a glimpse of the nature of the Intrigues which Sir Charles related so admirably: "Y' have an exact Account from the Great Lady i' the Box down to the little Orange Wench," he says to Emilia after regaling her with a choice morsel of Court gossip.

While Sir Charles is visiting Lady Townley and her niece, Rochester has "looked in at the Play,"

[1] "The Man of Mode" (4to, 1676), I. i. pp. 3, 4.
[2] *Ibid.*, II. i. p. 20.

probably at the King's House at Drury Lane, where *c.*1664/65 Mrs. Gwynne is doubtless acting in a new piece by Mr. Dryden. In the cool of the evening the two friends are found walking in the "Mail" (or as we now say the "Mall"),[1] the fine avenue on the north side of St. James's Park, which Charles II had planted with trees shortly after the Restoration. It is the hour of the fashionable promenade, and the twilit alleys are crowded with the fine ladies and women of the town in "Sky, and Pink, and Flame-coloured Taffetas,"[2] with gallants in periwigs and scented gloves, and drunken bullies singing catches as they reel from group to group. In the evening we find the three Wits dancing at the lodgings of some ladies of their acquaintance. Rochester slips off early to an assignation, but Sedley and Etherege stay on till midnight, drinking with their host, a bluff old gentleman of the "true Elizabeth breeding," and singing a merry chorus in praise of "the Pleasures of Love and the Joys of Good Wine." Finally, in the small hours of the morning, the whole company, escorted by fiddlers and carrying torches, repair to Rochester's lodgings in order to serenade the Earl. It is interesting to have this last reminiscence of Gentle George confirmed by a letter dated 4 February, 1664, which records that Sir Charles had recently taken part in a surprise visit of this kind in the company of the young Duke of Richmond and Lennox and his Grace's fiddlers.[3]

---

[1] "The Man of Mode" (4to, 1676), II. iii. Cf. also the following passage from Mrs. Behn's "Sir Patient Fancy" for the hour of the fashionable promenade. "Lodwick" is describing the day of a fashionable lady "Beginning at Eight, from which down to Twelve you ought to imploy in dressing, till Two at Dinner, till five in visits, till Seven at the Play, till Nine i' the Park" (etc.). (Works, ed. M. Summers, IV. 22.)

[2] Etherege's "She Wou'd if She Cou'd," III. ii. (Works, 8vo, 1704, p. 126).

[3] Hist. MSS. Comm., Appendix to 6th Report, p. 364. (Sir R. Paston to his Wife, 6 February, 1664.)

1664/65   The background of this life of pleasure and gallantry
was the comparatively new part of the town which
had sprung up in the first half of the seventeenth
century on what had formerly been the open country
between London and Westminster. In the early years
c. 1664- of the reign of Charles II, it was a maze of narrow
66   streets of gabled wooden houses, bounded on the
north by Holborn and the Oxford Road and on the
south by the Strand. Beyond Holborn there was only
a single row of houses, and a breeze from the north
would bring the fresh airs of the fields into Drury
Lane and Covent Garden.[1] In Sedley's comedy, "The
Mulberry Garden," Olivia and Victoria tell their
father that they are going to drive "either up into
the City or towards the Park," and thus show that
they are living in the new fashionable district. The
young sparks drove and rode round the Ring or Tour
of Hyde Park, still well outside the town, where
Sir Charles must have appeared in even greater
splendour than that which his brother had formerly
flaunted in the eyes of the Puritans,[2] and, like Ned
Estridge in "The Mulberry Garden," he probably
galloped round it many a time for a wager on
horseback. For pedestrians the favourite promenades
were the Mall or Mail, where we have already seen
Rochester and Sedley, and the New Exchange, an
Arcade off the Strand, noted for pretty glove mer-
chants and perfumers and Herringman's well-known
bookshop.

When the Wits were not driving round the Ring
or buying gloves for their mistresses in the New Exchange, they spent much of their time in the playing

---

[1] See Newcourt and Faithorne's Map ("An Exact Delineation of
the Cities of London and Westminster . . . by Richard Newcourt,
W. Faithorne Sculpsit, 1658, engraved from the original by G. Larman,
London, 1857").

[2] "Medley" in "The Man of Mode" (II. ii.) is said to "Understand an Equipage the best of any Man in Town."

of outdoor games. Pall Mall, a robuſt anceſtor of *c.* 1664–
the modern croquet, was played before the Civil War 66
on the site of the ſtreet that now bears its name.
After the Reſtoration, when houses had been built
in the old "Pall" Mall, a new Mail or Mall was laid
out in St. James's Park, where both the King and his
brother often played.[1] Bowling was as fashionable as
in the days of Sir John Suckling, and there was an
alley in Whitehall where Pepys saw "lords and ladies"
bowling on a fine summer day in 1662.[2] Sedley's
favourite game appears to have been tennis;[3] not the
degenerate lawn tennis of the moderns, but the ancient
and strenuous game played in a covered court with a
penthouse. There was a tennis court of this kind in
Whitehall, and Charles II was an excellent player.
Indoor games of cards and dice were equally popular,
now that the shadow of Puritanism was removed.
The moſt fashionable card game was the newly introduced Basset, upon which Gentle George wrote some
pretty *vers-de-société:*

> "Let Equipage and Dress Despair
> Since *Basset* has come in;
> For nothing can oblige the Fair
> Like Mony and Morine."[4]

It is ſtrange to be reminded that in the city where
the Wits were dancing, drinking and writing verses
on Celia and the game of Basset, John Milton was
sitting in darkness, meditating "Paradise Loſt."
Once we almoſt seem to hear the voices of Little Sid,
Gentle George and the Lords Buckhurſt and Rocheſter

---

[1] Pepys, ed. Wheatley, II. 1.

[2] *Ibid.*, II. 88.

[3] Cf. the following passage in Etherege's "Ratisbon Letter-Book,"
f. 154 (Sir G. E. to Mr. Guy, 19 December, 1687): "I bungle away
now & then a morning at Tenis, here is a pretty carré Court and
players so exactly seiz'd for Sr. C. that were he here, he wou'd live in
it." The "carré" court is the smaller variety of tennis court. Cf. this
allusion with the nickname *"little* Sid."

[4] Works (8vo, 1704), p. 287.

c. 1664 interrupting that solemn vision of Hell which the poet breaks off to speak of

> "Luxurious cities where the noyse
> Of riot ascends above their loftiest Tow'rs
> And injury and outrage : and when Night
> Darkens the streets, then wander forth the Sons
> Of Belial flown with insolence and wine."

For Milton the young sparks of Whitehall and Drury Lane were only "Sons of Belial." Yet the laughter of the diners at the Cock and the Rose and very audacity of their frolics were perhaps helping to keep alive a part of England which was as valuable as the ſtrength and ſteadfaſtness of the Puritan.

CHAPTER IV

THE WITS AS MEN OF LETTERS

" *B-st* and *Sydley*, with two or three more
   Translators of *Pompey*, dispute in their claim,
But *Apollo* made them be turn'd out of door,
   And bid them be gone like Fools as they came.

" My old Friend, *Mr. Waller*, what make you there,
   Among those young Fellows that spoil the *French* plays?
           The Session of the Poets to the
                tune of " Cook Lawrel."
                ("Poems on State Affairs,"
                1697, I., 221).

". . . A Wit is like a running Horse, good for no earthly thing beside;
when did you ever know any of 'em well with a great Man, or so much
as taken down to a Lord's house a Buck-hunting? They can drink, some
of 'em; but then they talk of Philosophy, History, Poetry, as if they
came into company to study; this stuff the Devil would not hear."—
"A True Widow," Act III (4to, 1679, p. 43).

IT has been said that a libertine's heart is trampled
by pleasures as a playground is trampled by schoolboys
till nothing green will grow there. Fortunately there
is abundant evidence that Sedley, Rochester and their
friends were not libertines of this kind. It is fair to these
idle and debauched young scamps to emphasise the
fact that they were also men of real culture who
preserved much of that love of elegance and grace
which had descended to them from the courtiers of the
Renaissance, and which they were to hand on to their
more civilised successors, the gentlemen of the eighteenth century. Not only were they all writers of
distinction and friends and patrons of men of letters,

but they were also enthusiastic and widely read students of literature, thoroughly appreciating the cynical grace of Latin poetry, the full-blooded drama of Elizabethan England,[1] and the elegant prose and verse of contemporary France. It has, indeed, been implied by one of the most distinguished historians of Restoration literature that the literary interests of Charles II's courtiers were merely due to a prevailing fashion, and that their culture was only a courtly veneer that covered the "unbridled and shameless debauchery of their lives."[2] That there is an element of truth in this diagnosis will be denied by nobody who has made it his business to read the quantities of inferior plays and feeble lyrics written by the gallants of the Restoration Court. But it is unjust to confuse the few real Wits, men of genuine talent and taste (who would probably have gained an important

---

[1] The numerous revivals of the plays of Shakespeare, Jonson, Fletcher and Webster testify to this. Dennis writes of the "Merry Wives of Windsor" that "the late Duke of Buckingham, my Lord Normandy (*sic*), my Lord Dorset, my late Lord Rochester, Sir Charles Sidley, Dr. Frazer, Mr. Savil, Mr. Buckley were in Love with the Beauties of this Comedy." (Preface to "The Comical Gallant," 4to, 1702.)

[2] Beljame, "Le Public et Les Hommes de Lettres en Angleterre au dix-huitième Siècle" (Hachette, 1897). "Pour la littérature tout le monde en fit. On ne fut pas un galant sans être un bel esprit: les deux mots devinrent synonymes. Les hommes le plus à la mode, les courtizans les plus brillants, le comte de Rochester, Sir Charles Sedley, Villiers duc de Buckingham, le comte de Mulgrave, Sir Car Scroop, Edmund Waller Esquire, Lord Buckhurst, le duc et la duchesse de Newcastle furent des lettrés, des critiques, des auteurs . . . (p. 10). Au surplus, toutes ces grâces, toutes ces poétiques mièvreries ne sont qu'un faux semblant. Grattez le gentil-homme élégant d'alors, vous trouvez vite le débauché débridé et sans vergogne; il en est de même dans cette poésie: son marivaudage est tout de surface; si elle s'étudie à composer de petits vers tendres et langoureux, elle aime surtout à faire appel aux sens à exciter les désirs et, dans cet office, elle ne redoute pas le mot vif, cru au besoin" (p. 12). To support the last statement Beljame quotes Rochester's playful lines on Sedley's poetry, for the significance of which see Part II. p. 284.

place in English literature if, like Dryden and Shadwell, they had been compelled to write for a living), with the numerous host of fine gentlemen who dashed off one or two insipid songs to Chloe or Phyllis or furnished a spicy prologue to a friend's play, and who, had they lived at the Court of George IV instead of that of Charles II, would probably never have written a line. Sedley was called by one of his earliest biographers "a man of wit and pleasure,"[1] and the title belongs equally to Etherege, Rochester and Buckhurst. If they were libertines, they were also artists, and like all true artists were essentially sincere. "They writ like themselves,"[2] says an author of the early eighteenth century of Sedley and his friends, and there was something not wholly bad in the composition of men who were capable of the grace of Sedley's best lyrics, the indignation of Rochester's satires, and the gaiety of Etherege's comedies. To form a just estimate of Sir Charles's character we must set against the lurid scene at the Cock Tavern the record of his literary career and friendships, which is, on the whole, an honourable one.

As early as the winter of 1662/3 several young men 1662/63 of fashion made their formal entry into the world of letters under the ægis of the elegant Mr. Waller. They were Sir Charles Sedley, whom, as we have seen, Waller had probably known from his boyhood, Lord Buckhurst, Sir Edward Filmer, son of the ultra-royalist author of "Patriarca," and Sidney Godolphin, who was to achieve quite a different kind of fame from that of the companions of his youth.[3] To these young

---

[1] Oldys's Note to Langbaine, No. 4 (Appendix I, p. 319).

[2] Henry Felton's "A Dissertation on the Reading of the Classics," 12mo, 1715, p. 65. The passage is worthy of quotation: "Sir Robert Howard, Sir Charles Sidley, Sir John Denham, Mr. Waller, Sir George Etherage, and I may add Mr. Walsh, writ like themselves; their Learning and Quality adorn each other, and you read their Education as Gentlemen, as well as Scholars, in their Compositions."

[3] "Letters of Orinda to Poliarchus" (1705), p. 112, 10 January, 1662/3.

1662/63 men Waller doubtless gave a glowing description of the poet-courtiers of the days of Charles I, and, above all, of his friend Sir John Suckling, now the almost legendary type of a literary dandy. It is pleasant to picture this company assembling under the trees in the "Mail" and walking to Waller's new house in the pretty suburban road running north from St. James's Palace, since named St. James's Street. The conversation would naturally turn on the theatre, and especially, as all things French were in vogue, on the classical drama of France, now in the heyday of its triumph. Could the French riming tragedies be naturalised in England? It was resolved to answer this question by producing a joint translation of some of the plays of the great Corneille in English riming verse. The first to be chosen was "La Mort de Pompée," a piece which had been staged in France nearly twenty years before. Each gentleman made himself responsible for an act, the first being allotted to Waller and the last to Buckhurst. The results, which were not unpleasing, were probably handed round in manu-

---

"I long to hear what becomes of the other Translation of Pompey and what Opinion the Town and Court have of it; I have laid out several ways to get a Copy, but cannot yet procure one except only of the first Act that was done by Mr. Waller. Sir Edward Filmer did one, Sir Charles Sedley another, and my Lord Buckhurst another; but who the fifth I cannot learn." " Biographia Dramatica," s.a. "Pompey the Great," gives the Earl of Dorset, "Sir Charles Sedley and Mr. Godolphin" as the translators (ed. 1812, II, 172). Sidney Godolphin (1645–1712) was later to become a well-known statesman. He was made a Page of Honour to the King on 29 September, 1662. It is curious to notice that his relative, also named Sidney Godolphin (1610–43), had been known in the circle of Suckling by the same nickname ("Little Sid") as that which was given to Sedley at Charles II's Court (see Suckling's "Session of the Poets"). This early Sidney Godolphin was a poet of some merit. The D. N. B. attributes to him (and not to the future statesman) the share in "Pompey"; but it is surely impossible that he had anything to do with it, as he died in 1643.

script at Court, where they would meet with the hearty 1662/63
approval of the King, who was an ardent admirer of
the French drama. Copies seem to have been in
circulation as early as the second week in January
1662/3,[1] and by that time it is very likely the play
had been acted at the private theatre called the Cockpit
in Whitehall Palace.[2] These proceedings caused
considerable perturbation to a young lady called
Katherine Phillips, who, although only twenty-two
years old, was already an aspirant to literary fame. She
herself had produced an excellent translation of the
same play, and was rather alarmed at being challenged
by such fashionable rivals. Probably in December
1663/4 the work of the "Confederate translators," as 1663/64
Katherine contemptuously calls them, was acted for
the first time in public by Sir William Davenant's
company at the Duke's House or "Opera" in Lincoln's
Inn Fields. Mrs. Phillips—or, to give her the name by
which she was known in literary circles, the Matchless
Orinda—describes the performance in a letter to Lady
Temple dated 22 January, 1663/4.[3] To judge from
this letter it was not a great success. The actors were
dressed in "English habits" without even the very
half-hearted attempt at Roman costumes which it was
customary to make in Restoration theatres. Cæsar,

[1] "Letters from Orinda to Poliarchus," 1705, p. 112, s.d. 10 January
1662/3. See above.

[2] The 1664 edition has epilogues both "to the King" and "the
Duchess" "At St. James."

[3] "Life and Letters of Martha Giffard," by J. G. Longe (George
Allen, 1911), pp. 39, 40, where Orinda's letter is printed. It is dated
22 January, 1664 (*i.e.* 1663/4), and she says that "Pompey" was
followed by ' Harry the 8th" (probably an adaptation of Shakespeare's
play by Davenant). Now Pepys mentions that this "Harry the 8th"
was being acted on 10 and 22 December, 1663/4, and he saw it
himself on 1 January, so it is probable that "Pompey" was produced
about Christmas time. Pepys specially notes the "shows and pro-
cessions" in "Harry the 8th." Doubtless "Pompey" seemed very bare
after such magnificence.

G

1663/64 who was very likely the great Thomas Betterton himself, appeared with "a feather and a ſtaff" and was hissed off the ſtage. The "citizens' wives"—they would naturally form a large part of the audience of the Lincoln's Inn House—are said to have been chiefly responsible for this disaſter, and it may well be imagined that, having been brought up on the buſtling, highly-coloured old English drama, they found that

> "The French convey their Arguments too much
> In Dialogue; their Speeches are too long,"[1]

especially when the speeches were unrelieved by any speſtacular splendour.

1664   Early in 1664, "Pompey the Great, a Tragedy as it is aſted by the Servants of His Highness the Duke of York, translated out of the French by certain Persons of Honour," was printed in a neat quarto and sold by Henry Herringham, the fashionable bookseller, at his shop at the Sign of the Blew Anchor in the Lower Walk of the New Exchange. Sedley's share in this translation was probably his firſt printed work. The "Persons of Quality" who had tried their hand at "Pompey" probably translated "Heraclius"[2] as their next contribution towards a complete English Corneille. "Heraclius" appears to have been acted, but was never published.[3] Perhaps the translators were discouraged by the cold reception of "Pompey," which is recorded on its title page, where they felicitously

---

[1] Sir W. Davenant, "The Play House to be Lett," Act I.

[2] See Orinda's letter in Longe's "Life of Lady Giffard," quoted above.

[3] Lodowick Carlell published a translation of "Heraclius Emperor of the East" in 1664 (4to). In his "Advertizement," he writes that his translation was rejected by the actors in favour of another presumably by the "confederate translators" (see Orinda's letter quoted above, note 2): *"Another Translation formerly design'd (after this seem'd to be accepted of) was perfected and acted, this not return'd to me until the very day."* Pepys saw this play at the Duke's House on 8 March 1663/4.

quote Horace's complaint that "now even among the 1664 knights all pleasure has fled from the ear to the fickle eyes and to vain pomps."

As Sedley's career was closely connected with the drama for many years after the production of "Pompey," it is necessary at this point to glance at the condition of the English theatre during his youth. From the closing of the theatres in 1642[1] till the 1642-60 Restoration, public performances had been forbidden by law. Nevertheless, the actors often crept back to their old haunts—the Red Bull or the Cockpit—and acted scenes from Shakespeare and other dramatists to spellbound audiences, until a file of Puritan musketeers removed them to the Gate-house.[2] Probably Sir William Sedley, whose interest in the drama is shown by Tatham's dedication, and his brother Charles had frequented these illicit performances, and they may also have taken part in the amateur theatricals with which young people of quality sometimes amused themselves under the Protectorate.[3] The Restoration of the King was bound to mean the restoration of the theatre, which was essentially a royalist institution. Already, when Monk was ruling in London, and everyone knew that the King's return was imminent, John Rhodes, a bookseller, who had once been wardrobe-keeper to King Charles I's old actors at the Blackfriars theatre, applied for and obtained a licence from the General to give public performances.[4] He

---

[1] On 2 September, 1642, plays were forbidden "during these times of humiliation." They were altogether suppressed by an Ordinance of 22 October, 1647, and a still stricter decree was issued on 11 February, 1648.

[2] Cf. Whitelocke's "Memorials," 30 December, 1649. "Some Stage-Players in St. John's Street were apprehended by Troopers, their Clothes taken away, and themselves carryd to Prison." Also Middlesex County Records, III. 279-80, where similar cases are recorded in May 1659.

[3] Cf. the "Letters of Dorothy Osborne," ed. E.A. Parry, 1903, p. 270.

[4] Lowe's "Life of Betterton" (1891), p. 60.

1642-60 "opened" at the old theatre called the Cockpit in Drury Lane, possibly before the King reached London. This Drury Lane "Cockpit" (not to be confused with the King's private theatre in Whitehall Palace of the same name) was one of the old "private" houses of the days before the Civil War, which, unlike the "public" theatres (such as the Globe and the Fortune), had roofed auditoria and were lit by candles. It was probably here that (according to Pepys) the Dukes of York and 1660 Gloucester saw Jonson's "Silent Woman" in June 1660,[1] and it is very likely that Sir Charles Sedley was among the first patrons of Rhodes's venture. The Cockpit was not left alone in the field for long. Two other companies were soon playing at the old Red Bull, a "public" or partly unroofed theatre in St. John's Street, Clerkenwell, and at a "private" house in Salisbury Court, Strand. The Red Bull company consisted of old players who had survived from the pre-Commonwealth theatre, and probably included such excellent actors as Michael Mohun and Charles Hart,[2] but against these veterans Rhodes was able to pit a certain Thomas Betterton, still unknown to fame, but destined to become the greatest actor of the Restoration theatre. From the Restoration to November 1660 the theatrical world was in a state of confusion and anarchy complicated by the constant interference of Sir Henry Herbert, Charles I's old Master of the Revels, who, having survived the Civil War and the Commonwealth, attempted to re-assert his authority over the players in order to extract what profit he could from the revived theatre. Some kind of order was restored by the erection of two companies under royal patent, their managers being Sir William Davenant and Thomas Killigrew (father to Lady Sedley's

---

[1] Pepys's Diary, ed. Wheatley, I. 173.
[2] Downes's "Roscius Anglicanus" (8vo, 1708), p. 1; Lowe's "Life of Betterton" (1886), p. 62.

brother-in-law). These two men were both admirably 1660
fitted for the work of carrying on and strengthening
the theatrical tradition. They were keen students of the
latest foreign improvements in the production of plays,
and it is to them that the form of the modern theatre
owes in a large measure its origin. Killigrew's company
was called the King's Servants. It was composed chiefly
of the old Red Bull actors, and acted at first in a
Gibbon's tennis court in Vere Street, Clare Market.
Davenant's company (known as the Duke of York's)
was composed mainly of the younger actors like
Betterton, and played at first at the Salisbury Court
House, but at the end of May 1661[1] moved to a new
theatre in Portugal Row on the south side of Lincoln's
Inn Fields. Here Davenant introduced some important
innovations, such as the regular use of movable
scenery.[2] The new theatre was called the "Opera,"
probably on account of Davenant's reputation for
musical dramas. It was at this "Opera" in Lincoln's
Inn Fields that "Pompey the Great" was produced,
and it was here that Mr. Samuel Pepys, Clerk of the
Acts to the Admiralty, caught his first glimpse of Sir
Charles Sedley. Already, on 1 July, 1663, he had
heard with pious horror (not perhaps unmingled with
prurient pleasure) from his friend Mr. Batten "of the
late triall of Sir Charles Sidley" and of the scandalous
proceedings in Bow Street. Since then, doubtless, he
eagerly awaited an opportunity of seeing the hero of
that episode in the flesh, and when, on the afternoon
of 4 October, 1664,[3] he found himself sitting next to 1664
the famous Wit at the theatre in Lincoln's Inn Fields,
we can well imagine that he strained his ears to catch

[1] Pepys's Diary, ed. Wheatley, II. 62, s.d. 2 June, 1661. "Home . . .
and went to Sir William Davenant's Opera, this being the fourth day
it hath begun."
[2] Cf. Lowe's "Life of Betterton," p. 73.
[3] Pepys's Diary (ed. Wheatley), IV. 258.

1664 all the wicked (but delightful) things which were likely to fall from his lips. It is possible to picture the malodorous, dark little theatre, lit only by candles guttering from chandeliers that hung from the roof,[1] with its stage still jutting well forward into the auditorium, and beneath it on the green-covered benches[2] of the pit, Sir Charles Sedley and his friends in rich suits, with swords and lace ruffles and huge flaxen periwigs which they occasionally "careen" with a pocket-comb. Doubtless they are well warmed by the good wines of the Rose or Locket's, and make a great hubbub, talking, laughing and fooling with the orange-girls, whose usual station is in this part of the house.[3] Pepys, also handsomely dressed, with a middle-class precision that contrasts with the easy negligence of his aristocratic neighbours, listens cautiously, treasuring up the pearls of their wit to retail to his gossips. On the stage a riming "heroic" play by Lord Orrery is in progress. Pepys, however, pays less attention to the actors than to Sir Charles's criticisms, which he says were those of "a very witty man," Sedley taking "notice of the dullness of the poet and the badness of the action, and that most pertinently." The effect of such remarks, made in a perfectly audible voice, must have been more than a little disconcerting to the actors.[4] Unfortunately, Pepys has recorded only

---

[1] Lowe's "Life of Betterton," p. 54.

[2] Misson's "Mémoires et Observations," p. 64. "La Parterre est en Amphitheatre, rempli de bancs sans dossiers, garnis et couverts d'une étofe verte."

[3] "*Several young Coxcombs fool with the Orange-Women.*" Stage direction in the playhouse scene in Shadwell's "A True Widow" (4to, 1679), Act IV. p. 49.

[4] Cf. with this incident the following speech of Sparkish, Wycherley's fop in "The Country Wife": "Gad, I go to a Play as to a Country-treat; I carry my own wine to one, and my own wit to t'other, or else I'm sure I shou'd not be merry at either; And the reason why we are so often louder than the Players is, because we think we speak more wit,

one of Sir Charles's observations, which was provoked 1664
by a situation of the kind which were so dear to
"heroic" dramatists. An ardent lover resolves to rescue
his rival and then surrender his mistress to him :

> "Ile save my Rivall and make her confesse
> That I deserve while he do but possesse,"[1]

declaims Betterton in the part of the magnanimous
Clorimon on the stage. "Why what Pox," breaks
in Sir Charles's voice from the pit, "would he have
him have more, or what is there to be had more of a
woman than the possessing her?" This outburst

---

and so become the Poet's Rivals in his audience." ("The Country
Wife," 4to, 1675, III. ii. p. 38.)

[1] This play was not published till 1702 (4to), when it appeared under
the name of "Altemira, A Tragedy," having apparently been recently
revived. Pepys incorrectly says that the lines which provoked Sedley's
contempt are spoken by "Lucidor" (in the printed edition "Lycidor").
Actually (unless Orrery altered the names of the characters) they occur
in a speech of Clorimon in Act III. The situation is as follows: Lycidor,
a rebel general, having been captured, has been sentenced to death.
Clorimon, the general who has captured him, is in love with Altemira,
Lycidor's mistress. She intercedes with the conqueror for her lover,
and Clorimon resolves to obtain a reprieve from the King. The lines
in the 1702 edition are slightly different from Pepys's version. They run
as follows:

> "I'll save my Rival, and make her Confess
> 'Tis *I* Deserve what he does but Possess."

The part of Clorimon was taken by Betterton, according to the cast
printed in the 1702 edition, which probably refers to the original
production. It is curious to notice that the play incurred the displeasure
of the Wits, for it contains what seems a kind of clumsy attempt to win
their approval. In the midst of a very "heroic" atmosphere of Love
and War, we are shown in Act II. a drinking scene in "a Sutler's Tent,"
where various gallants toast their mistresses in a cynical strain which
contrasts strangely with the magnanimous sentiments expressed in the
speeches of the chief characters. It should be mentioned that "Altemira" was, according to the introduction to the 1702 edition (signed
by Francis Manning), left unfinished by Orrery at his death and
revised by "a Gentleman, who is universally esteemed an Ornament
to Learning."

1664 scarcely seems to us to merit the epithet "witty," but it is a natural enough protest of flesh, blood and common sense against the dehumanised absurdities of the "heroic" style. It represents fairly accurately the almost aggressive reaction of the Wits against the idealism of the pre-Commonwealth theatre, of which the "heroic" dramas were a belated and exaggerated expression.

1663 In May 1663, about a month before Sedley's oration at the Cock, the King's company, under the command of Tom Killigrew, had, like their rivals, changed the scene of their operations. Leaving the old Salisbury Court (or Whitefriars) theatre, they were now installed in a fine new house in Drury Lane.[1] Here, for the first time apparently, the orchestra was placed in something like its modern position in front of and below the stage. Associated with Killigrew, and probably to a large extent financing his enterprise, was the well-known busybody, poetaster and would-be Admirable Crichton, Sir Robert Howard, and it may well have been through Killigrew, who was connected by marriage with the Sedleys, that Sir Charles made the acquaintance of Howard's brother-in-law, John Dryden, who had now for some time been writing plays for the King's company. About this time the great poet was courting the society of the Wits with the object of gaining something of the easy grace of their conversational style,[2] and it is not improbable

[1] See Lowe's "Life of Betterton" (1891), p. 100; Pepys's Diary (ed. Wheatley), II. 115 (s.d. 8 May, 1663).

[2] Cf. "Satyr to his Muse." By the Author of "Absolom and Achitophel." London, 1682, pp. 1 and 2:

> "I from that Fatal hour new hopes Pursu'd,
> Set up for Wit and Aukwardly was Lewd,
> Drunk 'gainst my Stomach, 'gainst my Conscience Swore";

also Rochester's "Allusion to Horace" (Antwerpen, ed. p. 42):

> "D—— in vain tried this nice way of wit,
> For he to be a taring Blade thought fit."

that he firft met Sedley behind the scenes at Killigrew's theatre. Our firft definite knowledge of their acquaintance is, however, dated from a river excursion in which they both took part in the summer of 1665, and which was to be immortalised by Dryden in the nobleft prose work of the age.[1] It was a fine afternoon in that terrible sultry June when the Plague was at its height in London, and in every ftreet houses were to be seen with the "tragical mark" of the red cross indicating that they contained infeſted persons. This national calamity was complicated by a naval war with Holland, and during the day news had circulated that the fleet under the Duke of York had sailed out to give battle to the Dutch Admiral. The fashionable taverns and coffee-houses were emptied of their usual after-dinner occupants, who had heard the rumbling of diftant cannon, and sallied forth in what they imagined to be the direćtion of the bombardment, in order to get an inkling of the result of the battle which was probably being fought at no great diftance from the mouth of the Thames. Among these adventurous spirits were four gentlemen who had perhaps dined together at the Rose. Two were young sparks in the twenties, dressed in the height of fashion, the third a rather older man with an officious, buftling air, and the fourth a plainly-dressed person about thirty years of age and very deferential to his companions. They were the Lord Buckhurft, Sir Charles Sedley, Sir Robert Howard and Mr. John Dryden. Taking a barge, provided by one of Sedley's servants, they shot the rapids under old London Bridge with its houses and

[1] Dryden's "Essay of Dramatick Poesie" (4to, 1668). The present writer considers that it bears all the marks of being founded on reminiscences of real events. The identification of the four interlocutors, Eugenius, Lisideius, Crites and Neander, was originally made by Malone in his edition of Dryden's Prose Works (1800), and has since then been generally accepted.

1665 towers, where the heads of the regicides were still decaying on their pikes, and were rowed down-stream towards Greenwich through the crowded shipping which fear of the Dutch fleet had drawn into the Thames. When they arrived at the lower reaches, at that date bordered by trees and fields, they told the watermen to row softly, and strained their ears to catch the sound of the guns, which they heard "like the noise of distant thunder or like swallows in a chimney." Before long they noticed that the sound was receding from them, and Buckhurst, breaking the silence, congratulated his companions on what he considered to be "a happy omen of the nation's victory." In the course of the conversation which followed, Howard made a joking reference to the numerous bad panegyrics which would be called forth by a victory and the host of equally bad elegies which would fill the book-shops if the Duke should be killed. Hence arose, by an easy transition, a discussion of the question of the merits of contemporary poets compared on the one hand with "the ancients," and on the other with the men of "the last age" (or the period preceding the Civil War). Buckhurst championed the moderns, while Howard, to whom the part of a *laudator temporis acti* was congenial, undertook the defence both of the classics and of the older English writers. Sir Robert suggested that the comparison should be limited to the drama, and Buckhurst consented, with the reservation that, while he was convinced that the English drama is superior to that of the ancients, he considered the plays of the last age (that of Shakespeare, of Jonson) far superior to the drama of the Restoration. The latter judgment seems commonplace enough now but was sufficiently bold and original in 1665. Buckhurst consoled himself for the inferiority of the contemporary theatre with the thought that "in the epic or lyric way" the older English writers were being easily

out-diftanced by the poets of the reign of Charles II, 1665
and in support of this view (which with regard to the
"epic way" was more accurate than he imagined),[1]
cited the names of Suckling, the idol of the Wits
(who surely belonged to "the laft age"), of Waller
and of Denham. The company agreed that the discussion could not proceed further till an adequate
definition of a good play were forthcoming, and they
paid Sedley the compliment of asking him to provide
such a definition. After some "modeft denials" he gave
what he called "a rude notion": "A juft and lively
image of human nature representing its passions and
humours for the delight and inftruction of mankind."

This definition, which, despite its slightly too
general charaĉter, ftill seems excellent,[2] was adopted
by the whole company, and, after they had told the
watermen to turn the barge and row softly back through
the cool of the evening, Howard and Buckhurft began
an argument in which the former rather pompously
defended "insolent Greece and haughty Rome," while
the latter wittily pointed out the weakness of the
ancient drama,[3] dwelling especially on its inability
to treat the subjeĉt of love. When this dispute had
been ended by general consent in Buckhurft's favour,
Sedley and Dryden took up the cudgels—this time on
behalf of the respeĉtive claims of the English and
French theatres. Sedley made out a ftrong case for the
latter, laying special ftress on the neatness of the French
ftage-craft, and acutely analysing some of the obvious
weaknesses of the romantic drama. At the same time
he referred in terms of warm admiration to Beaumont

---

[1] "Paradise Lost" did not appear till 1667, and Milton was almost
unknown as a poet in 1665.

[2] It might serve equally for the ideal novel, but critics of the
Restoration nearly always thought in terms of the stage.

[3] Which, it must be remembered, was mainly known to the speakers
through Seneca and the Latin comedians.

1665 and Fletcher and Ben Jonson. It is interesting also to find him citing the "Eunuch of Terence," a play which more than twenty years later he was to adapt brilliantly for the English stage. Dryden's reply was an eloquent but moderate defence of the English tradition, concluding with magnificent "characters" of Shakespeare, Jonson, and Beaumont and Fletcher, and an "examen" or analysis of the "Silent Woman." The rest of the evening was occupied by a hot dispute between Dryden and Howard, who, true to his character of a Sir Positive Atall, could not long remain silent. The subject was the vexed question of the comparative merits of blank verse and riming couplets as a vehicle of dramatic expression. During this discussion it is permissible to imagine that the attention of the two younger members of the company wandered. Perhaps their conversation turned on the reigning beauties of Whitehall and Drury Lane or some equally unacademic subject. When the barge had reached Somerset Stairs, Buckhurst had to call several times to the poets, who were so absorbed that they did not notice that they had reached their destination. The four friends, unwilling to separate, stood and gazed awhile at the river, which the full moon was flooding with light. Then, passing through a crowd of French refugees who were merrily dancing in the open air, they walked across the Strand to the Piazza of Covent Garden, whence Dryden and Howard repaired to their lodgings and Sedley and Buckhurst to "some pleasant appointment," probably at the Rose or the Cock.

For many years after this meeting, Dryden apparently continued to be intimate with Sir Charles Sedley. In 1673 he published a record of their friendship[1] which forms a significant contrast to the scene in Bow Street. He compares Sir Charles to Tibullus for his

---

[1] Dedication of "The Assignation, or Love in a Nunnery," to "My Most Honour'd Friend Sir Charles Sedley, Baronet" (4to, 1673).

"Candour, his Wealth" and "his way of Living," and 1665 applies to him the beautiful lines which Horace addressed to that amiable Roman knight. After praising the "innocent and inoffensive Pleasure," the "eruditam voluptatem" of the ancient poets, he describes his meetings with Sedley and the other Wits as follows :

"We have, like them, our Genial Nights; where our discourse is neither too serious, nor too light; but always pleasant, and for the moſt part inſtruċtive : the raillery neither too sharp upon the present, nor too censorious on the absent; and the Cups only such as will raise the Conversation of the Night, without diſturbing the business of the Morrow." These frugal and polite banquets, where the talk was doubtless of Shakespeare and Corneille, of Terence and of Horace, surely deserve to be remembered as much as the debauches which Sir Charles Sedley's biographers have described in so much detail. Dryden, proteſting againſt contemporary scandal-mongers, seems to anticipate the "ignorant and ridiculous Descriptions" of a later age. "Such Wits as they describe," he continues to Sedley, "I have never been so unfortunate to meet in your Company : but have often heard much better Reasoning at your Table than I have encounter'd in their Books. The Wits, they describe, are the Fops we banish: for Blasphemy and Atheism, if they were neither Sin nor Ill Manners, are Subjeċts so very common and worn so Thredbare that people who have sence avoid them for fear of being suspeċted to have none."

According to a curious but by no means improbable ſtory, Dryden owed to the Wits something more important than the graceful conversational ſtyle which he admired so much. If this tradition be true, it was aċtually the friends of Nell Gwynne and Old Rowley, who firſt showed "Paradise Loſt" to the future author

1665 of "Absalom and Achitophel." The tale is told as follows
by Jonathan Richardson, the eighteenth-century
painter and critic —"*Dr. T. Robinson* told me that it
was my *L. Dorset* that made *P. Lost* firſt taken notice
of: that he light upon it by Chance in Little Brittain,
& reading a few lines was so pleas'd with it that he
bought it for a Trifle, for it was then but waſte Paper
& when He came home read it many times over, &
sent it to *Dryden* to know his opinion of it. *Dryden*
had never seen it before, but brought it back to Him,
& told Him *that Poet had cutt us all out.* This was yᵉ
4ᵗᵒ Ed. & abᵗ 2 years after yᵉ firſt Publication of yᵉ
work. & My *Lᵈ Dorset* told it himself to Dʳ Robinson
at that Time at yᵉ Grecian Coffee House."[1] Dr. Tancred
Robinson was an elderly London physician in 1734,
when Richardson's book was published. The ſtory,
which Dorset told him at the Grecian Coffee House,
a great haunt of men of letters in the reigns of
William III and Anne, has the ring of truth. Masson,
in his "Life of Milton," imagines Buckhurſt and
Sedley visiting the blind old republican at his house
in Bunhill Fields. It is pleasant to picture such a
meeting between the courtiers and the Puritan. It
would be ſtill pleasanter to know that the conversation
of his visitors convinced Milton that good manners
and polite learning were not confined to the serious-

[1] MS. note by Jonathan Richardson on p. cxix of annotated copy
of "Remarks on Milton's Paradise Lost by J. Richardson Father and
Son," London, 8vo, 1734, in the London Library. In the printed
text Richardson states that the story was told to Robinson by "Fleet
Shephard," *i.e.* Fleetwood Shepherd, the friend of Dorset and Sedley,
but he prefixes to the MS. note the words: "This is a former account
that I wrote down as soon as I came home," so it would seem that
the account given in the note is more likely to be the true one. In
the printed text the version of Dryden's remark is as follows: "This
Man (says *Dryden*) Cuts us All Out and the Ancients too." The "Lᵈ
Dorset" of Richardson's note was, of course, the later title of Lord
Buckhurst. I am allowed to reproduce Richardson's MS. note by kind
permission of the Librarian of the London Library.

minded, and that the "Sons of Belial," besides 1665
indulging in

> "Court Amours,
> Mixt dance or wanton Mask or Midnight Bal,"

also found time to read the best ancient and modern
authors and were as capable of appreciating great
poetry as his friends, Andrew Marvell and Cyriack
Skinner.

CHAPTER V

"Sidley indeed and Rochester might write
For their own credit and their friends delight,
Showing how farr they cou'd ye rest outdoe
As in their fortunes, so their writings too."
                              Stowe MSS. 969, f. 67.

"*Sidley* indeed may be content with Fame,
Nor care should an ill-judging Audience damn:
But *Settle*, and the Rest, that write for Pence,
Whose whole Estate's an ounce, or two of Brains,
Should a thin House on the third day appear,
Must starve, or live in Tatters all the year."
                    Oldham: "A Satyr" (Works, 1694, p. 175).

"But let no alien S-dl-y interpose
To lard with wit thy hungry *Epsom* prose."
            Dryden (To Shadwell) in "MacFlecknoe" (1682).

"There go divers with him, but especially the Lord Buckhurst and
Sir Ch. Sidly, who will lead the muses and the graces such a dance as
may instruct and civilise fair France."—Mr. Henshaw to Sir R. Paston,
July 16, 1670 (Hist. MSS. Comm., 6th Report, Appendix, p. 367).

WHEN Dryden's Melantha cried, "How charming
is the *French* ayr! and what an étourdy bête is one of
our untravel'd Islanders,"[1] she was only expressing
the general opinion of the Restoration Court. There
were several causes for the attraction towards France
felt by young Englishmen of quality in the later
decades of the seventeenth century, which was, in some
ways, not unlike the "anglomanie" of the young French
aristocrats of a later age. The King had not only passed

[1] "Marriage à la Mode," II. i. (4to, 1673, p. 16).

much of his youth in France, but was half-French by descent and especially attached to his French relatives. Many of the exiled Cavaliers had spent years in Paris and other French towns during "the late troubles," and, after the Restoration, many Frenchmen, banished for religious or political reasons, came to live in England. This increased intercourse between the two nations coincided exactly with a time when the Latin element in the English character was asserting itself more strongly than ever before. Nowhere is this fact more clearly reflected than in the literature of the age. Obscure magnificence and "the fairy way of writing," which may be supposed to represent the Teutonic and Celtic strains in the English blood, disappear almost entirely for a while, and, in their place, alike in verse and prose, Roman logic and good sense reign supreme. The men who were reading and writing verse like Dryden's and prose like Locke's were in a peculiarly favourable position to appreciate the qualities of the countrymen of Racine and Pascal. Finally, the French nation was really at this time entering into one of the most remarkable phases in its history, and it was perfectly natural that Englishmen should feel a keen interest in that monarchy of Louis XIV which, with all its faults, was in many ways the most civilised institution in Europe. The relations of the Wits (who represent the intellectual element in the English aristocracy of the period) with France are therefore of very great interest to the student of literary and social history. That they all visited France and were influenced by French life and literature is a commonplace of the text-books. The actual details of this connection are not, however, so well known.

Sedley, as we have seen, probably visited Paris at the age of seven. There is no record of his having crossed the Channel again till 25 November, 1665, on which date a laconic minute among the State Papers informs us of the granting of a "Pass for Sir Charles

H

1665 Sydley Bt. into france."[1] That bare statement is the only trace of this journey that survives, but it is possible to build some fascinating conjectures upon it. A man of twenty-six, with a natural bent towards Latin culture, must have been profoundly influenced by a near view of a society which had attained to a degree of external splendour and intellectual eminence capable of dazzling the most prejudiced Briton. The Paris that Sir Charles Sedley visited in 1665—it may be assumed that he went to the capital—was the city of Louis XIV, of Madame de Sévigné, of Madame de Lafayette, of Bussy de Rabutin, of Corneille in his decline, of Molière at the zenith of his glory, of Racine in the flush of his first success. "Alexandre," the second tragedy of the last author, was produced at the Hôtel de Bourgogne on 4 December, 1665, before a brilliant audience, which included the King's brother, the Duke of Orléans, and his wife, "Madame Henriette d'Angle-terre," the favourite sister of Charles II. If Sedley left England on 25 November (the date on which his pass was granted), he may easily have arrived in Paris in time for this performance. It is probable that he hastened to pay his respects to "Madame," who was the protectress of the English in Paris, and to whom he may have been presented when she visited her brother at Whitehall in 1661. He may have attended the State performance of "Alexandre" in her train, and it is pleasant to imagine him comparing the theatre of Molière with Drury Lane and Lincoln's Inn Fields, and noting details of foreign stage-craft for the benefit of his friends, Tom Killigrew and Sir William Dave-nant. On the eve of Twelfth Night, 1666, the Duke and Duchess of Orléans gave a magnificent entertainment at the Palais Royal. Among the guests was le Roi Soleil himself, who is said to have been dressed in a suit of violet cloth covered with pearls and diamonds. The King was received "in the great gallery filled with

[1] Cal. State Papers Dom., Chas. II. Ent. Book XXII. p. 316.

dazzling lights which were reflected in numerous 1665 mirrors, a great luxury at that period," and we are told that one of the objects of this display was to impress "several foreigners who were in Paris at that time and before whom the King was pleased to exhibit the magnificence of his Court."[1] It is highly probable that these "foreigners" included a group of Charles II's courtiers, and among them Sir Charles Sedley. Part of the entertainment consisted of a performance of Molière's "Le Médecin Malgré Lui" by the author's troupe, who were now the King's comedians, and Sedley, if he was present, must have envied a Court that could command the services of such a dramatist.

War was declared between England and France on 1 February, 1665, but it was a very half-hearted affair, at any rate so far as the Governments of the two countries were concerned. The French King allowed English subjects who were in France at the time to stay on for three months after the declaration of war, and Lord Hollis, our Ambassador in Paris, was permitted to remain. No doubt this decree was generously interpreted, and it is not impossible that Sedley was still in Paris in June 1666, when he may have had the honour of assisting at the "première" 1666 of the greatest of all French comedies, "Le Misanthrope." 64840

By February 1666/7 Sir Charles was certainly back in England, for on the 18th of that month Pepys 1666/67 saw him at the theatre[2]—this time at a performance of "The Maid's Tragedy" at the King's House in Drury Lane. Apparently the diarist was again sitting close to the Baronet, for he was "vexed all the while" by his conversation with "two talking ladies," "he (Sir Charles) being a stranger." In spite of the fact that

---

[1] "Henriette Anne d'Angleterre par le Comte de Baillon," Paris, 1886, pp. 254–5.
[2] Pepys's Diary (ed. Wheatley), VI. pp. 185, 186.

1666/67 he could not hear much of the play, Pepys has to admit that he was "pleased to hear their discourse," which, to judge from his description, must have been very amusing. One of the ladies kept her mask on "all the play," and "being exceedingly witty as ever I heard woman, did talk most pleasantly with him, but was, I believe, a virtuous woman and of quality."[1] Sedley tried to discover the identity of the fair unknown, but she refused to tell him her name, "yet did give him many pleasing hints of her knowledge of him, by that means setting his brains at work to find out who she was, and did give him leave to use all means to find out who she was, but pulling off her mask. He was mighty witty and she also making sport with him very inoffensively, that a more pleasant rencontre I never heard." The "pleasant rencontre" probably prevented many people besides Pepys from hearing the actors, but they were occasionally reminded that a play was in progress by "Sir Charles Sedley's exceptions against the words and pronouncing," which Pepys considered "very pretty." It is not unlikely that some verses included in the collected editions of Sedley's works (but first printed anonymously in 1672),[2] under the title, "On falling in Love with a Stranger at the Play," are connected with this episode. It would certainly have been an exquisite sequel to the "rencontre" for the masked beauty to have received the next morning a copy of verses beginning:

> "Fair *Amarallis* on the Stage whil'st you
> Beheld a feigned love, you gave a true;
> I like a Coward in the Amorous War,
> Came only to look on, yet got a Scar. . . ."

---

[1] Prof. Allardyce Nicoll, in his "Restoration Drama" (p. 15), says that these ladies were "of doubtful propriety even though Pepys tends to believe they are virtuous and of quality." I cannot see why he should cast any doubt on Pepys's statement.

[2] "A Collection of Poems," printed for Hobert Kemp, 1672 (Pt. II. p. 1).

In the same year (1667) Sedley seems to have been 1667
intimate with a lady who was less cultivated than her
Grace of Richmond, but probably her superior in wit
and beauty. Pretty Nell Gwynne, the incarnation of
the free Bohemian spirit, had for some time been
delighting the patrons of the King's House by her
piquant acting. Sprung from the dregs of the popu-
lation and brought up, by her own admission, in a
brothel,[1] this astonishing girl succeeded not only in
becoming a brilliant comic actress at the theatre,
where she started her career by selling oranges in the
pit, but also in captivating one of the most gifted
young noblemen in England. Exactly when Lord
Buckhurst succeeded the actor, Charles Hart, as her
acknowledged lover is unknown, but we can be
pretty sure that his lordship was often accompanied by
his bosom friend, Sir Charles Sedley, in his visits
to Nelly's lodgings in Drury Lane.[2] On 13 July, 1667,[3]
Pepys heard from Mr. Pierce that Lord Buckhurst
"hath got Nell away from the King's House . . . and
gives her a £100 a year, so she hath sent her part to
the house and will act no more." The next day
(Sunday, 14 July) Pepys[4] took his wife by coach to
Epsom Wells and thence to Epsom village, where they
bespoke dinner at the King's Head. There, apparently
from local gossip, they heard that Lord Buckhurst,
Nelly, and Sir Charles Sedley were lodging next door,
where they "keep merry house." "Poor girl, I pity
her, but more the loss of her at the King's House,"
adds the diarist with a quaint mixture of cant and
ingenuousness. The place where the trio lodged is said
by local tradition to have been a two-storied building
with bow-windows which still stands next door to the
King's Head Inn.[5] With Sedley's wit and Nelly's

[1] Pepys's Diary (ed. Wheatley), VII. 172.
[2] Pepys's Diary (ed. Wheatley).
[3] *Ibid.*, VII. 20.   [4] *Ibid.*, p. 22.
[5] It is now the "Nell Gwynne Restaurant." The interior has been
entirely modernised.

1667 laughter, and abundance of good wine, the evenings muſt have passed merrily, while plenty of diversion was doubtless provided during the daytime by the "sprucer sort of citizens," the Fribbles and Biskets of Shadwell's comedy, who brought their wives to drink the waters and were eased of their guineas by the swarms of London sharps and bullies who haunted the place. One afternoon Sir Charles deserted his friends for more respeétable company. On 5 Auguſt, 1667, he appears to have ridden over to the Durdans, Lord Berkely's fine country seat, about a mile from Epsom. Among the gueſts was a pious old lady, Mary Rich, Countess of Warwick. Sir Charles seems to have behaved in a perfeétly decent manner, but the Countess, who had perhaps heard of the Bow Street sermon, was in an agony of apprehension leſt the very air breathed by such a monſter should sully her purity. The entry in her diary[1] which records her meeting with Sir Charles is worthy of quotation:

> *Aug.* 5, 1667.—Went with Lady Robartes and her lord to Durdans to see my lord who was there. At dinner that day dined Sir Henry [*sic*] Sedley,[2] which was much trouble for me to see him leſt he should be profane. But it pleased God to reſtrain him; yet the knowledge I had how profane a person he is much troubled me to be in his company. . . .

It is unfortunate that we cannot supplement this note with the description of the Countess that Sir Charles

[1] Printed in "Mary Rich, Countess of Warwick," by Charlotte Fell-Smith (London, 1901), p. 195.

[2] Obviously a slip for "Sir Charles," as Miss Fell-Smith points out in a footnote, where she comments on the diversity between Sir Charles's temperament and that of Lady Warwick, but does not cite the passage from Pepys which proves that Sedley was in Epsom in July, and which conclusively identifies Lady Warwick's "Sir Henry" with Sir Charles. She also states incorrectly that the real Sir Henry died in 1656 (see p. 29).

Sedley probably gave to Nelly and Buckhurſt on his 1667 return to the "merry house." That Sedley's reputation for profanity and general wickedness was widely eſtablished about this time, even among less saintly persons than Lady Warwick, is shown by two chance allusions in Pepys's Diary. On 2 July, 1667,[1] Pepys's cousin, Roger, told him an aſtounding and altogether incredible piece of scandal concerning Archbishop Sheldon, the narrow, haughty, but virtuous and upright Primate of England. There is not a shadow of doubt that it is the mere gossip of persons who "hate to acknowledge that others are better than themselves,"[2] but it is intereſting to find that Sedley is selected as a suitable hero for the tale. "My cozen Roger told us as a thing certain that the Archbishop of Canterbury that now is do keep a wench, and that he is as very a wencher as can be; and tells us that it is publicly known that Sir Charles Sidley had got away one of the Archbishop's wenches from him, and the Archbishop sent to him to let him know that she was his kinswoman, and did wonder that he should offer any dishonour to one related to him. To which Sir Charles Sidley is said to answer: 'a Pox take his Grace! pray tell his Grace that I believe he finds himself too old and is afraid I shall outdo him among his girls and spoil his trade.' But he makes no doubt that the Archbishop is a wencher and known to be so, which is one of the moſt aſtonishing things I have heard of."

Again, on 16 November, Mr. Gregory, wishing to give Pepys a thoroughly bad character of Lord Vaughan, told him that he was "one of the lewdeſt fellows of the age, worse than Sir Charles Sidley."[3] Perhaps the character of the Wicked Baronet, so dear to the imagination of the British public in the eighteenth and nineteenth centuries, originated in these

[1] Diary (ed. Wheatley), VII. 48.
[2] The phrase is from Wheatley's footnote.
[3] Pepys's Diary (ed. Wheatley), VII. 199.

1667 times, and its prototype may have been none other than Sir Charles.

The news that the Dutch fleet was in the Medway on 23 July, 1667, probably did not disturb the merry party at Epsom. As Sedley was still there in August, it does not seem as if his duties as an officer in the Kentish militia weighed very heavily on him, even when there was an imminent danger of invasion. He was probably occupied with the more serious business of writing a comedy. The gossips of the London 1667/68 theatres were discussing this work in January 1667/8. On the 11th of that month, Pepys heard of it from his friend Mrs. Knipp or Knepp, a popular actress at the King's House, where she was a colleague of Nelly.[1] She told him that the title of Sedley's play was "The Wandering Ladys," that it was shortly coming upon the stage, and that it "will be most pleasant." There can be no doubt that Mrs. Knipp was referring to the play which was afterwards called "The Mulberry Garden." The subject of "Wandering Ladys" seems to have been very popular among dramatists about this time. Perhaps it was suggested by the bold frolics of the Maids of Honour, who, imitating the Court gallants, had sometimes sallied forth from Whitehall in disguise.[2] George Etherege, Sedley's friend, was probably at work on a comedy on a very similar theme at this very time, and it can hardly be doubted that there was some kind of friendly rivalry between the two Wits. In spite of Gentle George's proverbial laziness, on this occasion he was first in the field, and his delightful play "She Wou'd if She Cou'd" was produced at the King's House on 6 February, 1667/8. Buckhurst and Sedley were in the pit with the author at the first performance,[3] and they

---

[1] She acted with Nelly in the "Maiden Queen," "Tyrannic Love," and other plays.

[2] Pepys's Diary (ed. Wheatley), IV. 359, V. 324.

[3] *Ibid.*

were accompanied by his Grace of Buckingham, who, 1667/68
only a fortnight before, had fought his notorious
duel with the Earl of Shrewsbury at Barn Elms.

By 7 May preparations for the production of
Sedley's play seem to have started in earnest. On that
day Pepys called for his friend Mrs. Knipp, at the
King's House in Drury Lane, and drove her to her
lodgings, where Bannister, the musician, taught her
the setting which he had composed for the exquisite
song in Act III. of "The Mulberry Garden":

> "*Ah*, Cloris! *that I now could sit*
> *As unconcern'd as when . . .*"

We may infer from this circumstance that she was
already cast for the part of Victoria. Bannister's tune
has not survived, but it is interesting to know that
Pepys dismissed it contemptuously as "a slight, silly,
short ayre."[1] On 18 May the long-expected "Mulberry
Garden," as it was finally christened, was at last
produced at Drury Lane. Sedley's reputation for wit
(and also for profanity) drew immense crowds to the
King's play-house for the first performance. Pepys,
in his anxiety to obtain a seat (there were no reserved
places in those days), arrived at midday with three
lady friends, and found the doors still closed. When
the diarist and his friends were able to enter, they
discovered "many people already come in by private
ways to the pit." These were, doubtless, the dramatist's
numerous acquaintances, who were provided with
what is now called "paper."

The prospect of waiting dinnerless till the end of the
play at five or six o'clock did not appeal to Pepys, so,
having hired a boy to keep his place, he very ungallantly
left the ladies and slipped out to the Rose, where he
dined heartily off a breast of mutton. He returned in
time to see the King and Queen come in "with all the
Court; and the house infinitely full." Let us glance

[1] Pepys's Diary (ed. Wheatley), VIII. 7.

1667/68 round the theatre on this momentous occasion. The ſtage, at present empty, runs well forward into the auditorium, covering part of the area corresponding to the position of the modern ſtalls. It has no footlights, and the only illumination is provided by wax candles in branches hanging from the roof. The floor of the house round three sides of the ſtage is occupied by the pit, and here on benches without backs loll a great crowd of Beaux and Wits in large flaxen periwigs[1] and rich suits, among whom can be recognised the author of the play, with his allies, Buckhurſt, Etherege, Rocheſter, Savile, Fleetwood Shepherd and the Duke of Buckingham. In the pit too, with their backs to the ſtage, stand the Orange-girls, with their baskets of "Hesperian Fruit"[2] on their arms, under the command of their famous and very efficient leader, "Orange Moll."[3] The firſt tier, corresponding to the modern dress circle, but probably much lower down and very close to the pit, is composed entirely of boxes. The largeſt is in the centre, and is at present occupied by the swarthy King, "Old Rowley" himself, with his black moustache and twinkling eyes. Beside him sits his much-wronged wife, the sallow Katherine of Braganza, with her Maids of Honour. The other boxes are filled chiefly with fashionable ladies, blazing with jewels. Among them, we may be certain, is the lovely Frances Stuart, now Duchess of Richmond and Lennox, to whom Sedley showed the play when "it was in loose sheets,"[4] and to whom he dedicated it. The next gallery is occupied by less respeĉtable ladies in vizard masks and tawdry finery with their bullies. Still higher, in the "gods," ſtand the lackeys in their brilliant liveries, who make nearly as much noise as

---

[1] "You men with bright rose-noble Hair": Davenant's Ballad Epilogue to "The Man's the Master" (4to, 1669).

[2] Rochester: "A Panegyrick on Nelly" (Works, 8vo, 1709, p. 100).

[3] Pepys's Diary (ed. Wheatley), VII. *passim*.

[4] Dedication of "The Mulberry Garden" (4to, 1668).

their masters in the pit. After the orchestra, consisting 1667/68
of "nine or ten fiddles," sitting just below the stage,
has executed a few ballad-tunes[1] the curtains are drawn
and the long-expected comedy commences. In spite of
Mrs. Knipp's vivacity, the audience does not warm to
the play. None of the witticisms elicits a trace of a smile
from the King, and we may be sure that most of the
Court regulated their countenances by their master's.
Perhaps the loyal Etherege and some of the other Wits
attempted to applaud, but the general opinion of the
house was undoubtedly expressed by Pepys, who considered that "though there was, here and there, a pretty
saying, and that not very many neither, yet the whole of
the play had nothing extraordinary in it at all, neither
of language nor design."[2] The poorness of the music,
on which Pepys specially remarks, may have contributed to this cool reception. It is to be hoped that the
poet consoled himself afterwards by entertaining his
friends to a merry supper at the Rose. It is probable
that subsequent performances were more successful,
for "The Mulberry Garden" had what was considered
a long run in those days. Pepys went to see it again
on 20 May, but could not "be reconciled to it, but find
only here and there an independent sentence of wit, and
that is all." It was still being acted on 29 June, when
Pepys went a third time, accompanied by his wife.[3]

If Sedley was disappointed at the reception of his
first original play, he had the consolation of making
a new and lifelong friend in this spring of 1668.
Thomas Shadwell, a Norfolk gentleman with a coarse,
jolly character and a great zest for life and literature,
had probably been admitted to the circle that met at
the Rose and Will's on the success of his brilliant
social satire, "The Sullen Lovers," produced at the

---

[1] Lowe's "Life of Betterton," p. 27.
[2] For analysis and criticism of "The Mulberry Garden," see pp.
247–63.
[3] Pepys's Diary (ed. Wheatley), VIII. 58.

1667/68 Duke's house in May. Sedley seems to have been on specially intimate terms with Shadwell from the first.[1] The hearty and rather plebeian temperament of honest Tom must have provided a healthy antidote to the rather foppish and affected conversation of such companions as Etherege, and Sir Charles was doubtless drawn to him by the element of downright good sense and realism in his own character. There is abundant evidence that Sedley gave Shadwell considerable help in his writings, and the flashes of wit that lighten up the scenes of some of his best comedies are, no doubt, often due to the Baronet's pen.[2]

1668   Anthony à Wood's statement that, after the affair at the Cock Tavern, Sedley "took up and grew very serious" is, unfortunately, belied by the records of certain events which took place in the autumn of 1668, when the Wits indulged in some frolics that rivalled their escapades of 1663. Buckingham was now supreme at Court,[3] and he and his friends, Sedley and Buckhurst, appear to have been constantly in the King's company. They went with his Majesty on a royal progress which he made through the eastern counties at the end of September.[4] The party seem to have

---

[1] Cf. Shadwell's statement in the dedication of the "Tenth Satyr of Juvenal," etc. (8vo, 1687), to Sedley, that he had lived "from his youth" in Sir Charles's company.

[2] It may be as well to summarise some of this evidence. Firstly, Shadwell himself admits in the dedication of his "True Widow" to Sedley that the Baronet had given the play "the honour of his correction and alteration." Secondly, Dryden implies in a mordant couplet in "MacFlecknoe" that Sedley had a hand in "Epsom Wells":

> "But let no alien S-dl-y interpose
> To lard with wit thy hungry *Epsom* prose."

Thirdly, Oldys in his MS. Notes to Langbaine says, "I have heard that Dorset, Sedley and others of those idle Wits would write whole Scenes for him" (see Appendix I, p. 320).

[3] "The Duke of Buckingham is now all in all": Pepys, 23 October, 1666 (Wheatley, VIII. 129).

[4] Cal. State Papers Dom., Chas. II, Nov. 1667–Sept. 1668, pp. 600, 606.

visited the little town of Thetford in Norfolk, where 1668
Charles II conducted himself in a way which must
have caused grave misgivings to Cavaliers of the old
school, accustomed as they were by now to his
Majesty's frailties. The King, Sedley and Buckhurst,
having probably dined well together, sent for the
fiddlers of the town, and made them "sing them all
the bawdy songs they could think of," while the
company, doubtless, joined in the choruses.[1] By 8
October the Court was at Saxham Parva, the beautiful
seat of William, Baron Crofts, near Bury St. Edmunds,
the "native sweets" of which had been daintily hymned
by Carew many years before.

One night Lord Arlington, Secretary of State for
Foreign Affairs, arrived with despatches for the King.
The effects of an evening spent with Sedley and
Buckhurst, however, seem to have been too much
for his Majesty, and he was unable to see the Minister.[2]
The next day the Duke of York reproved Bab May,
the well-known courtier, who seems to have been one

[1] Pepys's Diary (ed. Wheatley), VIII. 129. Pepys told the story on
23 October, but is obviously referring to events which had happened
some time before. The Calendar of State Papers informs us that the
King was going on a progress on 23 September, and on the 28th we
learn from the same source that "the Court is removing to Audley
End" (references in Note 4, p. 108). We may thus suppose that the
visit to Thetford took place during this progress. The royal party were
at Harwich on 3 October, and at Saxham near Bury on the 7th. From
a letter from Captain Taylor to Pepys dated 8 October (summarised
on p. 9 of Cal. State Papers Dom., Chas. II, 1668–9) it appears that
the royal party included, besides Buckingham and his friends, the Earl
of Oxford, the Duke of Monmouth and the Duke of York.

[2] Pepys's Diary (ed. Wheatley), VIII. 130; see also Cal. State
Papers Dom., Chas. II, 1668–9, p. 8, where a letter from Arlington
from Bury stated that he "could not see the King at Saxham, nor until
to-day, *by reason of the uncertainty of his motions.*" Compare the words
which I have italicised with Pepys's less courtly but probably truer
explanation. ". . . the King was drunk at Saxham with Sidley and
Buckhurst the night my Lord Arlington came thither, and would not
give him audience or could not: which is true, for it was the night
that I was there, and saw the King go up to his chamber and was told
that the King had been drinking."

1668 of the prime movers of this debauch, and who, according to James, was the cause of "the King's giving himself up to these gentlemen, to the neglecting of Lord Arlington." Bab May's answer gives us a startling glimpse of the liberties which "Old Rowley" allowed his favourites: "By God, there was no man in England that had heads to lose durst do what they do, every day, with the King," which, as Pepys devoutly added, was "a sign of a mad world. God bless us out of it."

From Saxham the Court went to Audley End, the King's house near Newmarket, and Sedley, it may be supposed, was one of the party who hunted and attended race-meetings with the King during October. A letter from the Earl of Thomond shows how Charles II and his friends passed their time.

"The King is highly pleased with all his Newmarket recreations; up by candle-light this morning and yesterday morning hunting the hare; in the afternoon he hawks and courses with greyhounds; to Harwich to-morrow and Monday here again. The Cup will be ridden for next week before the Queen."[1]

1668/69 Hard drinking and hard riding were the chief diversions at Newmarket that autumn, and the former did not, apparently, cease when the Court returned to Whitehall on 17 October.[2] Some time between that date and the 23rd, there occurred a kind of repetition of the Bow Street frolic.[3] There does not seem to have been any speech-making on this occasion, but Sedley and Buckhurst again endeavoured to appear publicly in the "state of nature." They are said to have run up and down the streets in their shirts, to have fought the watch, and, finally, to have been beaten and "clapped up" by a constable. On this occasion Lord Chief Justice Keeling played a less manly part than his

[1] Cal. State Papers Dom., Chas. II, 1668/9, p. 3.

[2] *Ibid.*, p. 23.

[3] Pepys heard this story with much other gossip from Mr. Pierce on 23 October, 1668. This is the only evidence on which it rests.

predecessor, Sir Robert Foster, and, apparently at the 1668/69 command of the King himself, instead of punishing the disturbers of the peace, he actually admonished and imprisoned the constable for daring to interfere with the pleasures of the royal favourites! If this account of the affair be true, Pepys was justified in his comment that "it was a horrid shame."

Early in the following year we hear of Sedley in connection with an incident which is hardly more creditable to him than the drunken frolics of 1663 and 1668, although on this occasion it must be admitted that he acted under a good deal of provocation. Like most of the tales in which he figures, the story of this affair is shrouded in a good deal of mystery,[1] but the following seem to have been roughly the facts. Edward Kynaston was a handsome young actor who originally belonged to Betterton's company, but who, after the issue of the patents to Killigrew and Davenant, was transferred to the King's house. He was especially noted for his success in female parts (which were still sometimes acted by youths after the Restoration), and was a great pet of the fine ladies, who used to drive him round the "tour" of Hyde Park in his stage

---

[1] The authorities are Pepys's Diary (ed. Wheatley), VIII. 217; Oldys's Notes to Langbaine, No. (1) (see Appendix I, p. 318); Genest's "Some Account of the English Stage," I. 80, 81, 93. Genest connects the affair with the beating of Sir Samuel Forecast, who is mistaken for Sir John Everyoung on account of his fine clothes, in the "Mulberry Garden." "It was," he says, "perhaps meant by Sidley as a hint to Kynaston. Kynaston was, however, far from taking the hint and he seems to have proceeded to greater liberties with Sir Charles." Although there is no evidence for this except Genest's bare word, it is by no means improbable that Kynaston had been aping Sedley for some time, and that the poet either introduced the caning incident into his play as a warning to the actor, or else took a hint from it when he wanted to punish him. I see no reason to suppose (as Lord Braybrooke does in his note on the passage in Pepys) that the beating referred to by Oldys may have been different from that recorded by Pepys. Oldys merely says that the reason for the beating was that Kynaston dressed like Sedley; Pepys says that he acted a part in "The Heyresse" "in abuse" of Sir Charles. The divergence is not very great.

1668/69 clothes.[1] This young man bore a strong resemblance to Sedley, and did all he could to heighten it by dressing like him. He seems to have gone so far as to have appeared on the stage in clothes that exactly resembled those of Sir Charles, and to have acted a part which was intended to ridicule the Baronet in a play called "The Heyresse,"[2] by the Duke of Newcastle. After a performance of this piece, probably on the last day in January 1668/9, Kynaston was imprudent enough to take a stroll in St. James's Park in the "laced clothes" in which he had impersonated Sedley on the stage. An insult of this kind was not to be borne lightly by a Restoration gentleman. Sedley replied, as any other man of his class and age would have done, by having recourse to what Rochester called "Black Will and a cudgel." His manner of administering chastisement was not, however, without humour. He hired a ruffian[3] whom he ordered to waylay Kynaston in the Park, pretend to mistake him for Sedley, by whom he was to feign to have been insulted, and to give the unfortunate actor a sound thrashing. Sedley's emissary carried out his instructions so thoroughly that poor Kynaston was unable to appear at Drury Lane the next day, being "mightily bruised, and forced to keep his bed." On the 2nd he was still too indisposed to appear on the stage, and Pepys heard his colleague, Beeston, read his part. According to Pepys, the King, who always took a keen interest in his "servants," was exceedingly angry with Sedley, but the latter is said to have disclaimed all knowledge of the affair. By 9 February, Kynaston was well enough to appear in Fletcher's "Island Princess," and was probably cured for ever of masquerading as a baronet.[4]

---

[1] See Cibber's "Apology," ed. Lowe, I. 119–21.

[2] No play of this name by the Duke of Newcastle has survived. It may be remarked that the word "Heir" was formerly used for "Heiress," and this was the title of a play by Thomas May (1620).

[3] Pepys says "two or three."   [4] Pepys, VIII. 223.

In 1670 Sedley seems to have paid another visit 1670 to Louis XIV's Court, under more magnificent circumstances than those of 1665. In April, Madame Henriette was sent by her brother-in-law, the French King, to negotiate a secret treaty with Charles II. The whole Court (including the Duke's company of players) went down to Dover to meet her, and Charles II, with that boyish impetuosity which was one of his most attractive qualities, sailed out in an open boat to welcome his beloved sister at sea. We may be sure that Sedley was among the courtiers who dazzled the worthy citizens of Dover and Canterbury (whither the Court removed after Madame's arrival) for a few weeks. The entertainments provided for the fair ambassadress included a performance of "The Sullen Lovers," the comedy of Sedley's friend, Tom Shadwell, which is said to have delighted "Madame."[1]

The death of Henriette on 30 June, shortly after her return to France, gave rise to the usual stories of poison, which followed the death of every celebrated person in those days. Charles II betrayed more genuine feeling on this occasion than he had perhaps ever shown in his life, and Louis, in order to clear himself from all suspicions, ordered a post-mortem examination to be made. He also hastened to send the Maréchal de Bellefonds, one of his most distinguished courtiers, on an embassy of condolence to the Court of St. James. The Duke of Buckingham, probably at his own request, was selected as the chief of an English mission, the ostensible object of which was merely to repay the compliments conveyed by de Bellefonds. Buckingham was, however, secretly empowered to conclude the famous "traité simulé" by which Louis and Charles deceived the Duke and the party in England which, though stoutly Protestant and constitutional, was not averse from an alliance with France. This mock

---

[1] Downe's "Roscius Anglicanus" (8vo, 1708), p. 29.

I

1670 treaty was a version of the secret pact concluded between Charles II and Madame at Dover, from which the most offensive clauses (such as that by which Charles agreed to declare himself a "Papist") were omitted. Buckingham, in spite of some opposition from the Duke of York,[1] set out about 20 July,[2] accompanied by Buckhurst, Sedley and a small train "without anything of greatnes." The rest of the party, which included Samuel Butler, the witty author of "Hudibras," Dr. Sprat, that mercurial divine who collaborated with Buckingham in "The Rehearsal," and Joe Haines, the famous comic actor, followed at a short distance. Never perhaps before or since has such an amazing diplomatic mission left the shores of this country.

Louis XIV gave them a magnificent reception. An apartment in the Palace of St. Germain-en-Laye was set aside for the Duke, and a table was provided for him at the King's expense, "furnished with the same

---

[1] "Correspondance d'Angleterre" (Quai d'Orsay Archives), tom. 98, f. 76. Colbert writes on 20 July, "Le Voyage du Duc du Bouquinkam est resolu. Mr. le Duc d'York fait neansmoins encore ce qu'il peut pour l'empescher."

[2] Hist. MSS. Comm., 5th Report, Appendix I, p. 652. Sir A. Fraser, to Lord High Commissioner of Scotland: "Whythall 23 July [1670]. . . . The Duk of Bugingham, with the Lord Buckhurst, Sir Ch. Sidley, Mr. Stanly, James Porter, and 4 seruants sets out Moonday at night, without traine, coach or anything of greatnes: his abood fortnight only. They discourse variously of his journy and because I know not, I will say nothing of it." Cf. Colbert writing of 24 July (tom. 98, f. 80): "Je pourray vous rendre compte beaucoup plus tost que le Duc de Bouquinkam n'arrivera a Paris." This implies that Buckingham had already gone by the 24th and confirms Fraser's statement. The Embassy had been planned as early as the 16th, when it was already decided that Buckhurst and Sedley should accompany the Duke: Hist. MSS. Comm. 6th Report, Appendix, p. 367. Mr. Henshaw to Sir R. Paston, 16 July 1670: "The Duke of Buckingham is to go compliment the French King; there go divers with him, but especially the Lord Buckhurst and Sir Ch. Sidly, who will lead the muses and the graces such a dance as may instruct and civilise fair France. . . ."

dishes and the same quantity as his owne."[1] On 16 1670
August the Englishmen were shown a review of what
were considered the finest troops in Europe. On the
20th poor Madame, whom the French Court soon
forgot, was solemnly buried at St. Denis, the sepulchre
of the French kings. On the 23rd the whole party were
superbly entertained at Versailles. The exquisite canal
in the park (still one of the loveliest things in France)
had then been newly sunk, and a Watteau-like mimic
battle was arranged on the waters in honour of the
visitors. A "great ship" was attacked by small boats
"deckt with Pennants and Streamers," one of which
contained the King and Queen, while the others were
"manned" by the beauties of the Court. There was much
music from kettle-drums, trumpets and a band of
violins, but "no firing because the ladies should not be
discomposed." It may easily be imagined that a man
of Sedley's tastes would thoroughly appreciate the
charm of this entertainment, which seems to have
embodied the spirit of French civilisation at one of its
most wonderful moments. After the naval action, a
light collation of "fruits and sweetmeats wth some fish"
was served, and it must be added with regret that
his Grace of Buckingham partook so lavishly of the
fruit that he was indisposed for some days after.[2]
Later in the evening the whole party were conducted
to an illuminated grotto, where an orchestra of "40
violins, 2 flutes, 2 voyces of Women" performed, and
"a Pastorale" (the title of which has not survived) was
acted. It is interesting to note that this is one of the very
few occasions when English men of letters are recorded
to have been present at a play in France during the
classic age of French drama. On 3 September the
"Duke's gentlemen," a term which may have included

---

[1] State Papers, France. Francis Vernon (secretary to Lord Montague),
20 August, 1670.
[2] *Ibid.*, 27 August, 1670.

1670 Buckhurſt, Sedley and Sprat, departed.[1] Buckingham himself lingered on for ten days, and before leaving was presented with a diamond-hilted sword by the French King.[2] He brought back to England[3] a young Breton lady with a pretty "baby face," called Louise de Kéroualle, who had formerly been a Maid of Honour to Madame Henriette, and who had already attraćted the attention of the King of England when she visited Dover with her miſtress in April. Under the title of the Duchess of Portsmouth she was deſtined to become at once the moſt powerful and the moſt unpopular of the miſtresses of Charles II.

Sedley's intimacy with Buckingham seems to have been especially close about this time. In the spring 1671 of 1671,[4] handsome young William Wycherley took the town by ſtorm with his firſt comedy, "Love in a Wood, or St. James's Park," produced at the King's house in Drury Lane. Like Etherege and Shadwell before him, he was at once admitted into the circle of Wits. The tale of how he made the acquaintance of the Duchess of Cleveland (formerly Lady Caſtlemaine) is well known. He soon became her acknowledged lover, much to the indignation of her cousin, Buckingham, who had previously held that position in more or less friendly rivalry with his royal maſter. Wycherley, alarmed at making such a powerful enemy, is said to have applied to Rocheſter and Sedley to help him to make his peace with the Duke. How they performed

[1] State Papers, France. Francis Vernon, 3 September, 1670.

[2] The Dispatches of William Perwich, ed. Royal Historical Society, 1903, p. 110.

[3] Or rather he brought her as far as Dieppe and left her there, having promised to send a yacht to fetch her. As he characteristically forgot all about her, the damsel was marooned for ten days at the seaport, till Colbert, the French Ambassador in London, exerted himself on her behalf. See Burghclere's "Life of Buckingham," p. 230. Also Perwich's Dispatches, p. 111.

[4] See W. C. Ward's introduction to Wycherley's plays in the Mermaid series.

this task is best told in the words of John Dennis, who 1671
may have heard the story from Wycherley himself:

"He (Mr. Wycherley) applied himself therefore to
Wilmot, Lord Rochester, and to Sir *Charles Sedley*,
and entreated them to remonstrate to the Duke of
Buckingham the Mischief he was about to do to one
who had not the Honour to be known to him, and
who had never offended him. Upon their opening the
Matter to the Duke, he cry'd out immediately *that he
did not blame* Wycherley, *he only accused his Cousin.*

"*Ay, but,* they reply'd, *by rendering him suspected of
such an Intrigue, you are about to ruine him, that is, your
Grace is about to ruine a Man with whose Conversation
you would be pleas'd above all things.* Upon this
Occasion they said so much of the shining Qualities
of Mr. *Wycherley* and of the Charms of his Conversation, that the Duke, who is as much in love
with Wit as with his Kinswoman, was impatient till
he should be brought to sup with him, which was in two
or three Nights. After Supper Mr. *Wycherley*, who was
then in the height of his Vigor both of Body and of
Mind, thought himself obliged to exert himself, and
the Duke was charm'd to that degree that he cry'd
out in a Transport, 'By G——, *my Cousin was in
the right of it*'; and from that very Moment made a
Friend of a Man whom he believ'd to be his happy
Rival."[1]

We catch another glimpse of Sedley in Buckingham's company in August. A Mr. Brockenden, writing
to Sir Robert Paston on the 19th, tells how he had
seen "last night" the Duke "with the Count[ess] of
Shrewsbury, Sir C. Sydley and James Porter with him
in the coach," driving to Holland House, which it was
rumoured that his Grace was going to buy.[2] Holland

---

[1] "Original Letters," etc., by John Dennis (8vo, 1721), Vol. I.
pp. 218-19.

[2] Hist. MSS. Comm., 6th Report, Appendix, p. 369 *b*. (Mr. Brockenden to Sir R. Paston, 20 August, 1671.)

1671 House was a famous mansion at Kensington, the property of the Earls of Holland. It appears to have been let at this time to the Earl of Anglesey, and Buckingham made several visits with a view to taking it.[1]

The Countess of Shrewsbury was the fascinating but depraved Anne Brudenell, for whom Buckingham had deserted his unfortunate wife, and who lived with the Duke after he had killed her husband, the Earl of Shrewsbury, in 1668.

In December "The Rehearsal," Buckingham's long-expected skit on Davenant, Dryden, Sir Robert Howard and the whole tribe of "heroic" dramatists, was produced at Drury Lane. We may be sure that Sir Charles Sedley was among the brilliant audience which applauded Lacy's acting on the first night. His name is connected with the play by the author of the "Life of Jo. Hayns" (8vo, 1701), who records that the gentlemen who especially delighted in that actor's impersonation of Bayes (he took the part when Lacy was ill) were "the Earl of R[ochester], Lord B[uckhurst], and Sir Charles S[edley]."[2]

The date of the production of "The Rehearsal" perhaps marks the full and joyous maturity of the society of Wits, which now included some of the most brilliant writers in England. Rochester's famous lines (perhaps written about this time) preserve the names of its chief members, and express exactly the aristocratic disdain for public opinion which characterised their lives and writings:

1 "We hear that the Duke of Buckingham is to take Holland House of the Earl of Ang. He has been there three nights successively." (Mr. Brockenden to Sir R. Paston; see above.)

2 "The Life of the Famous Comedian, Jo. Hayns," etc. (London, 4to, 1701), p. 5. The text gives only the initials of Hayns' admirers: "The Earl of R., Lord B., Sir *Charles S.*" The full names "Earl of Rochester, Ld Buckhurst, Sir Charles Sedley" are written in the margin of the Brit. Mus. copy in a contemporary hand (Brit. Mus. 641, *e.*, 18(1)).

"I loathe the Rabble, 'tis enough for me   1671
If SEDLEY, SHADWEL, SHEPPARD, WICHERLEY,
GODOLPHIN, BUTLER, BUCKHURST, BUCKINGHAM,
And some few more, whom I omit to name,
Approve my Sense, I count their Censure Fame."[1]

It is interesting to find a very different kind of person from Buckingham and his friends among Sedley's acquaintances at this time. Sir William Joyner, a devout Roman Catholic, of whom Hearne[2] writes that "he was one of the most retired men I have known," published his single tragedy, "The Roman Empress," in 1671. This work, which had been performed with success at the King's house, is dedicated by the author to Sir Charles Sedley in the most complimentary terms. He ascribes to him an "elevated wit," "rich fancy," and "subtile judgment," "which qualities concur in you in so high a perfection that there is no free noble soul which denyes you herein the just tribute of preference." It is surely incredible that the man to whom a grave and pious person like Joyner could address such words was the mere rakehell of the eighteenth and nineteenth-century biographers.

[1] These lines are from Rochester's "Imitation of the Tenth Satire of the First Book of Horace," originally printed in the "Antwerpen" edition (8vo, ?1680), where they appear in the following form:

"I loathe the Rabble, 'tis enough for me
If S——, S——, W——,
G——, B——, B——, B——,
And some few more whom I omit to name,
Approve my sense, I count their Censure Fame."

The lines quoted in the text with the names in full are from "The Works of the Right Honourable the Earls of Rochester and Roscommon, etc." (8vo, 1709,) p. 22.

[2] Quoted in D. N. B., s.a. Sir William Joyner.

CHAPTER VI

"Our Arcadia is in Hyde Park and the Mulberry Garden; our nymphs are modishly attired, and our love-sick swains are powdered beaux."— A. H. Bullen (Preface to " Musa Proterva," 1889).

1657　THERE were several reasons why Sir Charles Sedley's marriage, though doubtless considered a good match for both bride and bridegroom, was likely to end in disaster. That Katherine Savage was a Roman Catholic, while the Sedleys were all Anglicans, was sufficient at least to endanger the prospects of domestic peace in an age when the Roman Catholic religion was regarded with fanatical hatred by most Protestants; while Sir Charles's leaning towards free-thought, or rationalism (as illustrated by the oration at the Cock), would hardly improve matters, since a deist or infidel of the seventeenth century was likely to regard Catholicism as merely a debased form of the prevailing "superstition."

Moreover, as the combined ages of the young couple in 1657 probably fell short of forty, it may be supposed that their mutual affection was as transitory as most of the passions of very early youth. The shortness of the interval which divided the marriage of Sir William with the eldest daughter of Earl Rivers from that of Sir Charles with her sister, suggests that the latter was a business arrangement concluded between the two families in order to renew the bond broken by the death of the elder baronet. Perhaps Elizabeth, Lady Sedley, arranged the match on the old principle of marrying sons early in order to prevent the sowing of wild oats.

No precaution could have been more futile on the eve 1657 of the great sowing of wild oats that followed the Restoration. A premature and unwise marriage, probably engineered by well-meaning but short-sighted relatives, may thus be added to the causes that have been already suggested for the wild life led by Sir Charles in the 'sixties. The fact that poor Lady Katherine presented her husband with a single daughter in place of the son and heir which every English baronet desires, would increase the chances of discord, while the final solvent of this unfortunate union was probably a strain of eccentricity in the Savage family,[1] which in Lady Katherine developed into actual madness.

The early years of the married life of the Sedleys 1658 seem to have passed peaceably enough, and, as we hear of Sir Charles and his lady driving together in his coach on 17 May, 1658,[2] it is to be hoped that, by then, no cloud had appeared on the matrimonial horizon. There is no further record of Lady Katherine Sedley's married life except the statements that she "had been far from an exemplary Catholic"—which may imply that, like her husband, she took part in the orgy of riotous living that followed the Restoration—and that "after a few years of married life (she) lost her reason and had to be placed under the care of a Catholic Physician skilled in this kind of malady."[3] If she became insane soon after the Restoration, her condition may have been either a cause or a result of her husband's way of living. A mad wife certainly might drive a man "aux tavernes et aux filles," but a husband whose conduct resembled that of Sir Charles in the years 1663

---

[1] The third Earl Rivers, her brother, was a miser and was robbed by his son (afterwards the fourth Earl), who was called "Tyburn Dick" (see D. N. B., s.a. Savage, Richard, fourth Earl Rivers).

[2] See p. 47.

[3] These statements are from the narrative of Father Bede of St. Simon Stock, quoted in Father B. Zimmerman's "Carmel in England," p. 236; see below, p. 122.

1658 and 1668 might equally have deranged the mind of a highly-strung and sensitive woman with a hereditary tendency towards eccentricity. The "Catholic Physician" is said to have treated Lady Sedley's "malady" according to the barbarous contemporary practice, with drugs which, she pathetically complained, "would impair her health." The condition of this unhappy lady sitting alone in the house in Great Queen Street is a melancholy pendant to the merry meetings at Locket's and the Rose. She is entitled to a place among the pathetic company of the wronged ladies of the Restoration, which includes Queen Katherine and the Duchess of Buckingham; though, in justice to Sir Charles Sedley, it must be admitted that there is no evidence that he ever treated his wife with the barbarity that Buckingham displayed in his dealings with his unfortunate lady.

Lady Sedley's mania took the form of a fixed idea that she was a queen. She is said to have insisted on being addressed as "Your Majesty," and to have shown "extreme vanity." This hallucination may have been the effect of brooding over the parallel between her fate and that of Katherine of Braganza, and the similarity between the conduct of their respective husbands. The fact that the Christian names of the Sedleys were identical with those of Charles II and his 1665–72 consort probably strengthened the delusion.

At some time between 1665 and 1672,[1] Sir Charles

---

[1] The following details are from the translation of an Italian manuscript by Father Bede of St. Simon Stock contained in Father B. Zimmerman's "Carmel in England" (Burns and Oates, London, 1899), pp. 235–8. No indication of the exact date of Father Bede's visit to Lady Sedley is given, but it is stated that the MS. describes events which took place between 1665 and 1672, when the Father was Vicar Provincial. As the description of Lady Sedley's case occurs in the latter part of the narrative, it may be supposed that it was nearer the latter date than the former when Father Bede met her, and this fits in with the fact that Sir Charles's second "marriage" took place in April 1672; see below, p. 129.

was enabled to get rid of his unfortunate wife. During 1665-72 these years a certain Carmelite friar, called Father Bede of St. Simon Stock (his secular name was Walter Joseph Travers), was in London. He was the head of a Roman Catholic mission in England in the reign of Charles II, and was a rather important person in that curious "Papiſt" underworld which, in spite of a brutal persecution, continued to exiſt and even to proselytise in Reſtoration London. He had been inſtrumental in the conversion of Lord Castlemaine, the contemptible husband of the King's miſtress, and was often consulted by Roman Catholic ladies. He was asked to visit Lady Sedley, whom he describes as "the wife of a moſt eccentric English nobleman with a revenue of twenty thousand scudi."[1] Lady Sedley gave the prieſt "a moſt kind welcome," and complained a good deal to him about her treatment and surroundings. It ſtruck him that "she spoke with great reverence of the Lady Abbess of Ghent, who at that time was in London colleɕting funds for her abbey." This Lady Abbess was a certain Dame Mary Knatchbull, the head of a society of English Benediɕtine nuns at Ghent, who, according to Father Bede, had "burdened themselves with debt to such an extent" by certain building operations that they "knew not where to turn for help." Dame Knatchbull had been kind to Charles II during his exile, and had already made one visit to England to colleɕt money in 1661, when the King gave her £3000.[2] A decade later his Majeſty probably had no money to spare, and the Abbess had to fall back on the generosity of private persons. Father Bede seems to have regarded Lady Sedley's condition as a heaven-sent opportunity to repair the fortunes of Dame Knatchbull's nunnery. He "went

[1] About £4000 in English money.
[2] Gillow's "Bibliographical Dictionary of the English Catholics," IV. 65. Dame Knatchbull belonged to an old Kentish family, members of which were probably acquainted with the Sedleys.

1665-72 ſtraight to the Abbess," and returned with her to Lady Sedley, whom they "found in tears" because, as she explained, "she could not possibly leave England." The next day Father Bede visited her again, and "the conversation turned chiefly on the Abbess." Finally, she sent the Father to her husband with "a message to the effeét that she was willing to go to Ghent." Sir Charles, as we can easily imagine, was "well pleased." He accompanied Father Bede "back to Lady Sedley"— it appears that husband and wife were living apart—to make "some further arrangements." Then the whole party proceeded to the abode of the Abbess, where it was decided that the afflicted lady was to live at the nunnery at Ghent on "a pension of four hundred pounds to be paid by the family." "The family," it would appear, meant Sir Charles.

As Lady Sedley desired to leave England immediately, it was necessary to provide her with an escort. Her husband does not seem to have volunteered his services, and the Abbess refused to take charge of her, so the task of conduéting "the patient" to the seaport fell to the good-natured Father Bede. Before they departed, Sir Charles told the Father that the wife "wore jewels to the value of four thousand scudi" (£800), and asked him "to obtain them if possible." How far he was juſtified in making this requeſt it is impossible to say. If the jewels were heirlooms of the Sedley family, it seems right that they should have been reſtored to its representative on the dissolution of the marriage, which was, in faét, taking place. Father Bede, who was probably as ignorant of the rights of the case as the present writer, hit on an excellent device. During the journey he did all he could to persuade Lady Sedley to give up the jewels, but met with an obſtinate refusal. When they arrived near the sea, however, she consented to let him take charge of them. He divided them into two equal portions, one of which he kept for Sir Charles, while he reserved the other for

the lady, to whom he restored it "later on." The 1665–72
jewels included "a gold watch studded with diamonds."
Father Bede adds ingenuously that "nothing whatever
remained in my hands."

The rest of Lady Sedley's history can be briefly
told. She entered the convent at Ghent, where she was
visited a year later by Father Bede. Her first question
was about the jewels. The Father replied "that her
husband kept them for her Majesty," because she
insisted on being addressed in that style. She answered 1672–
in dreadful excitement, "I shall have the gates of the 1705
town closed and you shall go to prison." She then left
the room. After a while a message came to bid Father
Bede stay, and presently "her Majesty" returned very
much calmed down, and said quite cheerfully, "Sir,
the cause for which I came hither no longer exists, and
I am quite willing to return to England." The Father,
in his own words, "politely declined the honour of
accompanying 'her Majesty,'" and left Ghent quietly.
He adds: "Many other incidents occurred in regard
to that case," but unfortunately does not relate them.
Lady Sedley's pension, which was paid regularly,
helped the Abbess to clear off the debts of the community, and according to Father Bede proved "a great
help towards establishing the present prosperous state
of the abbey." This pension seems to have been reduced
later—probably when the finances of the abbey were
stabilised—to £200.[1] Lady Sedley outlived her husband,
and died at Ghent on 1 July, 1705.[2]

Very little definite information survives concerning 1660–72
the numerous temporary "flames" with which Sir
Charles consoled himself for the loss of his wife's
society. Like the other Wits, he doubtless began to
"fawn on those little insignificant Creatures, the
Players,"[3] soon after the innovation of employing
actresses was introduced, and his special connection

[1] "Carmel in England," p. 235 n.   [2] *Ibid.*
[3] "The Man of Mode," II. ii.

1660-72 with the theatre would give him ready access to the tiring-room, where good looks, witty conversation, and, above all, a plentiful supply of guineas easily overcame the very fragile defences which guarded the virtue of its fair occupants. It is probable, though not absolutely proved, that he had a liaison with that lively actress, Mrs. Knipp or Knep. As we have seen, she knew all about the approaching production of "The Mulberry Garden" in January 1667/8, and was, apparently, cast for the chief female part in Sedley's comedy. From these circumstances it is natural to suppose that she was acquainted with the author. A transcript of one of Sedley's love-poems in a contemporary hand in the Bodleian furnishes a conclusive proof of this intimacy. The poem, which, in the printed versions, is headed "To Celia," is here introduced by the words "To Mrs. Mary Napp."[1] Mrs. Knipp's name is actually spelt "Napp" in the printed cast of Lord Orrery's "The Black Prince" (fol. 1669), so there is no doubt that Sedley's poem is addressed to her. It is very interesting to find that Mrs. Mary Knipp, or Napp, seems to have been a close ally of Nell Gwynne. They nearly always acted together,[2] and it was very natural that when Lord Buckhurst was Nelly's lover, her friend Mary Knipp should be the mistress of Sir Charles Sedley, his lordship's inseparable companion. Mrs. Knipp also bestowed her favours on Mr. Samuel Pepys, as readers of the Diary are aware. She had a surly "jealous-looking" husband who, according to Pepys, was "a kind of jockey." Her life seems to have been far from happy, and there are records of her having been arrested twice; on 12 February, 1667/8, and 23 April,

---

[1] It is the poem beginning "As in those Nations where they yet adore" (Kemp's Collection, p. 43, Miscellaneous Works, 1702, p. 51). The Bodleian transcript is in a MS. book of contemporary verse (West. MS. Eng. Poet., *e*, 4).

[2] Knipp acted Asteria to Nell's Florimel in the "Maiden Queen," and Nakar to her St. Catherine in "Tyrannic Love." They sang the prologue to Howard's "Duke of Lerma" together.

1668,[1] about a fortnight before she told Pepys about 1660–72 Sedley's new play.

Sedley had another connection with a pretty actress 1668 named "Pegg" at the King's house. Pepys, calling at Drury Lane on 7 May, 1668,[2] saw (and kissed) this lady, apparently behind the scenes. He roundly declares that she "was Sir Charles Sidly's mistress," and adds emphatically, "a mighty pretty woman and seems, but is not, modest." It is evident that "Pegg" is a Christian name,[3] and the only actress at the King's house whose Christian name is known to be Margaret is the famous Mrs. Hughes,[4] afterward Prince Rupert's mistress. Lord Braybrooke, in his edition of Pepys's Diary, identified her with "Pegg." The chief difficulty is that Pepys describes her as "newly come," a description which could hardly be applied to Margaret Hughes, who was one of the very first English actresses and had been with the King's company since 1663. There 1668–76 are, of course, many actresses whose Christian names are unknown. A Mrs. James probably joined the Theatre Royal company in the spring of 1668. If it could be shown that her Christian name was Margaret, she might be identical with Pepys's "Pegg." On the other hand, a satire written on Sedley some years later refers to him as "the Apostolick Bard of Mother Hewes,"[5] but it is not clear if this "Mother Hewes" refers to the actress. It may be remarked that an actress

---

[1] Warrants cited in Allardyce Nicoll's "Restoration Drama," p. 287 n.

[2] Pepys's Diary (ed. Wheatley), VIII. 7.

[3] Peter Cunningham, in a letter to *Notes and Queries* (24 November, 1849), suggested that Pepys's "Pegg" was a surname and stood for Katherine Pegge, a lady who had a child by Charles II. Lord Braybrooke, replying in *Notes and Queries*, 26 January, 1850, pointed out that Katherine Pegge was in her fortieth year in 1668 and that there is no record of her ever having been on the stage.

[4] Margaret Hughes was certainly called "Peg Hughes" in one of Tom Brown's "Letters from the Dead to the Living," Works (12mo, 1719), II. 241.

[5] See below, p. 166.

1668-76 called Mrs. Hughes, who was, perhaps, identical with Prince Rupert's mistress, acted the minor part of Charmion in Sedley's tragedy of "Antony and Cleopatra" in 1676. Oldys records the fact that Sir Charles had "two naturall daughters named L. and E. Charlot." According to the same authority he settled part of his estate on them.[1]

1670 At an unknown date—probably about 1670—Sir Charles met a young lady called Ann Ayscough, whose influence changed the whole course of his life. She was a daughter of Henry Ayscough, a Yorkshire gentleman of an old family, who was imprisoned in the Fleet for many years, and who seems to have been always in rather needy circumstances.[2] One of his daughters, Frances, married a Joseph Ayloffe, a distinguished barrister of Gray's Inn and grandson of Sir William Ayloffe, an Essex baronet.[3] As Sedley seems to have been well acquainted both with Joseph Ayloffe and his son, Captain William Ayloffe, in later years, it is probable that he originally met Ann Ayscough, the sister of Mrs. Ayloffe, at her brother-in-law's house. It would be perfectly natural for a libertine like Sir Charles to make love to the barrister's pretty sister-in-law, and, from an extremely interesting poem (printed among Sedley's works), it seems that he actually started by treating the affair as one of his usual temporary "flames," but met his match in the lady, whose beauty and character so captivated him that he consented to make her the head of his household, and, in

---

[1] Oldys, Notes to Langbaine, Note No. 2. See Appendix I, p. 318.

[2] There is a minute concerning a petition from Henry Ayscough, a prisoner in the Fleet, to Cromwell, preserved in the Bodleian (Rawl. MS. A, 37, f. 711). In the Cal. State Papers Dom., Chas. II, 1661-2, p. 420, there is a record of a petition of Henry Ayscough to the King for £300 lent to his Majesty, "with recommendation of the petitioners on account of their condition." He still seems to have been in the Fleet in 1660 and 1661, for two petitions from him bearing these dates and written from that prison are calendared in Hist. MSS. Comm., 7th Report, Appendix, pp. 115*b*, 144*b*.

[3] Morant's "Essex," p. 71.

every sense except a legal one, his wife. The opening 1670
verses describe the change in the Baronet's intentions
(which originally appear to have been far from
honourable):

> "*Cloris*, I justly am betray'd
> By a design my self had laid;
> Like an old Rook, whom in his cheat
> A run of Fortune does defeat,
> I thought at first with a small sum
> Of love thy heap to overcome;
> Presuming on thy want of art,
> Thy gentle and unpractis'd heart."

The poem ends with a reference to the fact that their
author was already married:

> "My hand, alas, is no more mine
> Else it had long ago been thine.
> My heart I give thee, and we call
> No man unjust who parts with all.
> What a priest says moves not the mind,
> Souls are by love, not words, combin'd."[1]

It is very significant that in the version of this poem
published by Ann Ayscough's nephew, Captain
William Ayloffe, after Sedley's death, the last two
lines are omitted, perhaps by the editor out of deference
to his aunt, or possibly by Sir Charles himself, because
of the change in his attitude towards religion since the
days of his anti-biblical harangue at the Cock.

In April 1672,[2] Sedley, who had perhaps recently 1672

---

[1] Kemp's Collection, I. 21.

[2] MS. note in a Pedigree of the Sedley family in book of MS. Kentish
Pedigrees (Bodl., Rawl. MS. B, 82, *f.*). "Sir Charles Sydley 4th Baronett
of Southfleet marryd Lady Cath. Savage da: of —— E. Rivers & *sent
her to a monastery & marryd Ms —— Ayscough da of —— in Aprill
1672.*" The italicised words are added in a different handwriting from
that of the rest of the pedigree. Cf. Cokayne's "Baronetage" (s.a. Sir
Charles Sedley): "By Catherine Ayscough of Yorkshire (with whom he
is said to have celebrated a marriage during his wife's lifetime) he had a
natural son. . . ." The name "Catherine" in Cokayne seems to be a
mistake perhaps arising from the fact that the writer had just mentioned
Catherine, Lady Rivers, and her daughter Catherine, Lady Sedley.

K

1672 sent his legal wife to the nunnery at Ghent, went through a form of marriage with Ann Ayscough. This "wedding" was, of course, quite illegal,[1] but it was easy to bribe a needy "Levite" in the seventeenth century to perform the ceremony without asking any awkward questions. It was probably soon after this "marriage" that Ann Ayscough presented Sir Charles with a son, who was named Charles after his father and was known by the name of Sedley as though born in lawful wedlock.[2] A second son, named William (probably in memory of the gay Sir William who died before the Restoration), died in infancy and was buried in 1672-76 October 1676, in Southfleet church,[3] where his name is entered in the burial register as "Wilhelmus filius Caroli Sedley militis et Baronett," a formula probably devised by the vicar or parish clerk to satisfy his own scruples against calling an illegitimate child by the family name, and, at the same time, to avoid offending the Lord of the Manor.

It is fairly certain that the reformation of Sir Charles's manners which began about this date was due chiefly to Ann Ayscough's influence. He seems to have withdrawn from the brilliant but profligate circle of Buckingham and the Countess of Shrewsbury, of

---

Other authorities call her Ann (*e.g.* the deed quoted by Haslewood: see Appendix I. p. 322), and the entry recording her death in Southfleet Parish Register (see p. 234).

[1] Not only was it illegal, but Sedley was liable to a prosecution under an Act of James I which made bigamy an offence punishable by death. He would have been exempt from the penalty if he had obtained a divorce "a mensa et thoro" from the ecclesiastical courts, although his second marriage would still have been illegal. There is, however, no record of his having obtained the ecclesiastical divorce among the case papers of these courts preserved in the Public Record Office.

[2] The younger Sir Charles Sedley was knighted by William III in 1688/9 (see p. 203), when he is said to have been a minor. He married in 1695, when it may be supposed that he was over twenty-one. Hence he was probably born before 1674.

[3] Southfleet Parish Register, 10 October, 1676. This entry is the only one in Latin among many relating to the Sedley family.

which he was a prominent member in 1670 and 1671, 1672–76 and to have passed his time in comparative retirement for many years. It is significant that Mrs. Ayscough insisted on a religious "marriage" in order to regularise her situation as much as possible, and it appears that her family accepted her union with Sedley as perfectly honourable. For a moment, perhaps, she suspected that Sir Charles would revert to the habits of his youth. Some charming lines survive in which he replies to such suspicions:

> "Fear not, my Dear, a flame can never die,
> That is once kindled by so bright an eye,
>
> .   .   .   .   .   .
>
> For though thy Beauty first allured my sight,
> Yet now I look on it but as the light
> That led me to the treasury of thy mind."

There can be little doubt that these verses are addressed to the same person as the poem to "Cloris" cited above, and they confirm the supposition that Sir Charles was at first attracted merely by the lady's external qualities, but later found that she had more enduring charms.

Perhaps Ann Ayscough helped to re-establish the financial as well as the moral reputation of her " husband." His expenditure must have been enormous in the first riotous decade after the Restoration. At the beginning of February 1672, two months before his second marriage, he was actually arrested, probably at the instance of some irate creditor.[1] He was driving in his coach "near the Old Exchange" in the City, when a certain constable called Daniel Axton, or Ackson, forced him to descend, carried off the coach and horses to "the Greene Yard" (or City Pound) in Lower Whitecross Street (a place where "stray or offending horses, cattle and carriages were taken and impounded"), while the Baronet, his coachman and other servants were haled to the Compter, the City prison for debtors in Southwark. Having somehow obtained his release, Sir Charles complained of his arrest from his seat in

[1] House of Commons Journals, IX. 251, 256, 264.

1672 the House of Commons on 8 February, informing the House that he had been arrested "though the constable was informed and did know that he was a member of the House." The Commons ordered their Serjeant-at-Arms to apprehend the constable for his breach of the privilege of Parliament, and referred the matter to the Committee of Privileges. On 25 February, Ackson (whose Christian name had now become "Samuell") petitioned the House, doubtless asking them to consider circumstances that extenuated his offence. On 7 March it was ordered that he should be released from custody provided that he paid "his Fees." Before he was allowed to depart, Sir Charles Sedley had the satisfaction of seeing him kneel at the bar of the House while the Speaker reprimanded him for daring to lay hands on a member of Parliament.

1673 By 5 July, 1673, Sir Charles had put his affairs sufficiently in order to be accepted as a good "surety" for a certain Edmond Ashton, Receiver of Hearth-money for the County of Lancashire.[1] On 21 June, 1675, he raised £4120 by mortgage on his lands, probably with the object of paying off outstanding debts.[2]

When Ann Ayscough became the recognised head of Sir Charles Sedley's household, she must have taken charge of Katherine, the fourteen-year-old daughter of Lady Sedley. If this young person had already begun to display the qualities for which she was afterwards celebrated, it may be supposed that there was little love lost between her and the woman whose very presence in her father's house must have seemed an insult to the memory of her unfortunate mother. Katherine was a dark, thin girl, with bold, sparkling eyes. She was no beauty, but she had a real gift for conversation, and especially for satire, which she doubtless inherited from her father. Her childhood must have been neglected and stormy, passed as it was in a household in which the master spent his nights at

[1] Cal. Treasury Papers, IV. (1672–5), p. 367.
[2] Haslewood's Notes to Jacob, Note No. 10 (Appendix I. p. 322).

G. Kneller, pinxit.   J. Smith, exc.

The Countess of Dorchester.

Emery Walker, ph. sc.

the Cock or the Rose, while the mistress was the mad 1673
"patient" of a "Catholic physician." Such an upbringing was appropriately rounded off by her introduction
at a very early age into the most dissolute society in
Europe. These were the days when the three sultanas,
Portsmouth, Cleveland and Mazarin, reigned at Whitehall in a voluptuous setting that was probably unequalled
in contemporary Europe, while the merry odalisque,
Nelly, enlivened, though by no means completed, the
royal harem. The qualities of a saint would have been
necessary in order to escape the contamination of such
an atmosphere, and qualities of this kind were not
likely to be found in a daughter of Sir Charles Sedley.
Mr. John Evelyn, whom she visited with other young
ladies of quality when she was only fifteen (on 13 June,
1673), summed her up—at that tender age—as "none
of the most virtuous but a witt."[1] This description
might have served as her epitaph. A few days after
Katherine Sedley's visit to Evelyn, Mary of Modena
landed at Dover and was married to James, Duke of
York. It appears to have been in the circle of this
beautiful princess that the daughter of Sir Charles
Sedley made her first appearance at Court.

In the years immediately following his separation
from his wife and the reconstitution of his household,
Sir Charles Sedley was engaged in the composition
of a tragedy. Probably he consoled himself during his
retirement from the society of the Wits by turning to
his books. The result of his studies was a heroic play on
the subject of Antony and Cleopatra, which to-day seems
the most worthless of his writings. It had, however, a
very good reception on the stage, when produced at
the Duke's Theatre in Lincoln's Inn Fields in February
1676/7, where it was still being acted in March.[2] 1676/77
An elaborate musical setting by Jeremiah Clarke[3]

---

[1] Evelyn's Diary, ed. Dobson, II. 358.
[2] Hist. MSS. Comm., 12th Report, Appendix IX. (Duke of Beaufort's
MSS.), p. 66. (Marquis of Worcester to Marchioness, 17 March, 1676.)
[3] See D. N. B., s.a. Clarke, Jeremiah.

1676/77 must have contributed greatly to its success. John Dryden was probably one of the audience, and the performance may well have suggested to him the idea of writing a tragedy on the same subject. It is at least remarkable that his "All for Love" was produced in the following year, and, of course, drove Sedley's piece from the stage for ever. Eleven months before the performance of "Antony and Cleopatra," a very different and, to a modern taste, far more attractive play, Sir George Etherege's masterpiece, "The Man of Mode, or Sir Fopling Flutter," was staged, as its hero would have said, with great éclat, by the Duke's company at their magnificent new theatre in Dorset Gardens. The new Duchess of York, to whom the comedy was dedicated, was present with her husband at the first performance, and it is very likely that the witty Dorinda, as Mrs. Sedley[1] was nicknamed, was in their train. Doubtless she recognised her father in the pit, for we may be sure that "little Sid" came out of his retirement to do honour to the triumph of "Gentle George," especially when we recollect that the play was a perfect incarnation of the spirit of the whole group of Wits.

1676/77   In the winter of 1676/7, Mrs. Katherine Sedley seems to have been already a well-known figure at Court. Towards the end of January, the Duchess of York gave a ball at Whitehall, during which a violent quarrel broke out between "Dorinda" and Sir Car Scroop, a witty young member of her father's circle who had written the prologue to "The Man of Mode." The origin of the quarrel seems to have been an exchange of extremely scurrilous verses. One of these lampoons, which was attributed to Sir Car, insinuated that Katherine was "as mad as her mother and as vicious as her father." The victim of this attack repaid its reputed author with a maidenly effusion hinting

---

[1] The title "Mrs." is used throughout the present work in the seventeenth-century manner to denote the unmarried woman.

very broadly at his relations with a certain Mrs. 1676/77 Fraser, a wealthy young heiress, daughter of Sir Alexander Fraser, the King's Scottish physician. It was notorious that Sir Car was courting this young lady, whose charms—and expectations—were doing great execution at Court, and Mrs. Sedley, doubtless glad of an opportunity to revenge herself simultaneously on an enemy and a rival, suggested that the professional attendance of Mrs. Fraser's father would soon be necessary both for his daughter and her prospective husband.[1]

Sir Car Scroop was not the only author who ventured to satirise Mrs. Sedley. Charles Sackville, formerly Lord Buckhurst and now Earl of Dorset, her father's old friend and playmate, wrote a series of dainty little pasquils on "Dorinda" at various stages in her career. The earliest probably refers to her first appearance at Court.[2]

> "*Dorinda's* sparkling Wit, and Eyes,
>   Uniting cast too fierce a Light,
> Which blazes high but quickly dyes,
>   Pains not the Heart but hurts the Sight.
>
> Love is a calmer, gentler Joy,
>   Smooth are his looks, and soft his pace;
> Her *Cupid* is a Black-Guard Boy[3]
>   That runs his Link full in your face."

In the spring of 1677 there was serious talk of a 1677 marriage between Katherine Sedley and her distant

[1] Hist. MSS. Comm., 12th Report, Appendix, Part V. Vol. II. p. 37. (Letters from Lady Chaworth to Lord Roos, 30 January, 1676/7.)

[2] The version given here is found on p. 94 of "A New Miscellany of Original Poems," etc., London, 1701 (Gildon's *Miscellany*). The last word in the fourth line in Gildon's version is "Eyes," which is obviously a misprint for "Sight" (the reading of all later editions of Dorset's poems).

[3] This must be a very early use of the adjective "blackguard" in something like the modern sense (earliest in N. E. D. in this sense is 1683). The Black-Guard was a troop of "idle dirty boys that lie about the Horse Guards and the Mews and Ride horses to water (commonly called the Black guard)." (News-letter cited by Lady A. E. N. Newdigate in "Cavalier and Puritan," p. 86.)

1677 relative, the handsome Jack Churchill, a Colonel of His Majesty's Foot Guards. This brilliant young man was already engaged to a beautiful but penniless Maid of Honour called Sarah Jennings, but his parents, Sir Winston and Lady Churchill, endeavoured to make him break with her and marry the daughter of the wealthy Sir Charles Sedley.[1] Churchill yielded at first to his parents, and the match was nearly concluded when Mrs. Jennings wrote her treacherous lover a letter that worked upon his feelings to such an extent that, in spite of his well-known avarice, he resolved to abandon Katherine and her fortune and marry for love. Henry Savile, Sedley's friend, seems to have acted as intermediary between the Churchills and the Sedleys in the delicate business of breaking off the engagement.[2]

Having failed to secure the Colonel, "Dorinda" attempted to obtain an official position in the royal household. A vacancy among the Queen's Maids of Honour was caused by the marriage of one of their number, Mrs. Howard, in November 1677, and Katherine applied for the place. She failed to obtain it, and, when rejected, is said to have "scorned" it. A contemporary implies that her haughtiness was already well known by expressing surprise that she ever deigned "to look so low as to think of itt."[3] On 27

---

[1] Wolseley's "Marlborough," II. 186–8.

[2] A letter of his to this effect is quoted in Wolseley's "Marlborough" (I. 189). It is dated 8/18 May, 1677, so it may be supposed that Churchill and Katherine Sedley were engaged in the winter or early spring of 1676/7. Sarah Jennings wrote on one of Churchill's letters many years later: "This letter was writ when I was angry at something his father and mother had made a disagreeable noise in the town about, when they had a mind to make him marry a shocking creature for money." The "shocking creature" was Katherine Sedley. It is interesting to speculate whether she would have made as successful a Duchess of Marlborough as her rival. She was quite as clever and quite as haughty, and she possessed far more wit and humour than Sarah.

[3] Hist. MSS. Comm., 12th Report, Appendix, Part V. Vol. II. pp. 42, 43. (Lady Chaworth to Lord Roos, 22 November, and 11 December, 1677.)

December[1] it was rumoured that she was going to 1677 marry "the widdower Sir Hungerford." This gentleman was Sir Edward Hungerford, the builder of Hungerford Market on the site of the present Charing Cross Station. He was twenty-six years older than Katherine and had already been married twice.[2] Mrs. Sedley's portion was estimated at this time at £6000, with £4000 at her father's death.[3] Hence it would appear that she was no longer the sole heir of Sir Charles, and that he had already resolved to bequeath a large part of his estate to his son by Ann Ayscough.

It must have been at the beginning of 1678 that a 1678 person of far more exalted rank than Colonel Jack Churchill or "Sir Hungerford" yielded to the charms of "Dorinda's sparkling wit and eyes." It was probably about this time that she became a Maid of Honour to Mary of Modena,[4] and attracted the attention of James, Duke of York. The vices of this prince have been described as a caricature of those of his brother. While Charles, at any rate, had the excuse that his mistresses were among the most beautiful women of the age, James made his intrigues appear in the most sordid light by selecting as his favourites the plainest damsels of the Court. Lady Denham and Lady Bellasis, it is true, were handsome women; but Arabella Churchill and Katherine Sedley were notoriously plain. Katherine, speaking of herself and the rest of the Duke's harem, said: "We are none of us handsome, and if we had wit,

---

[1] Hist. MSS. Comm., 12th Report, Appendix, Part V. Vol. II. p. 44 (same to same, 27 December, 1677).

[2] His first wife, Jane, daughter of Sir John Hele, died in 1664. The second was a Jane Culme, who died in 1674. (D. N. B., s.a. Sir Edward Hungerford.)

[3] Hist. MSS. Comm., 12th Report, Appendix, Part V. Vol. II. p. 44.

[4] "Mrs. Sidley" appears in the 12th edition of Chamberlayne's "Anglia Notitia" (1679, p. 206) among the Duchess's "Maids of Honour." She is not mentioned in the 7th edition (1677). I have not seen the 8th, 9th, 10th or 11th editions.

1678 he has not enough to discover it,"[1] while Charles II said his confessor imposed his mistresses on James by way of penance.[2]

Katherine Sedley seems to have awakened in her ducal lover a far stronger passion than any of her predecessors, whose influence had been very transitory. His feelings towards her would appear to have been the most passionate of which his cold, narrow character was capable. It is difficult to explain why an elderly roué, who was now a devout and even bigoted Roman Catholic, should have fallen violently in love with a young lady who had no claim to be considered a beauty, but who was the possessor of a biting and irreverent wit which she loved to exercise on the very objects which James held most sacred. There is a sense, indeed, in which the pair were admirably suited to each other. Katherine possessed exactly the qualities which were most painfully lacking in her lover; a strong understanding, good-nature, and an acute sense of humour. It may be conjectured that, if anybody could have brought him back to the Church of England and the hearts of his future subjects, it was the daughter of his brother's boon companion, and it is at least probable that, if she had been his wife, he might have retained his crown for himself and his descendants. It was "Dorinda's" tragedy that, herself the child of a

---

[1] There are many versions of this witticism. The above is from G. E. C.'s "Complete Peerage" (ed. Vicary Gibbs), IV. 407 n., where it is quoted from Lord Orford, IV. 319. It seems to have inspired the following lines by the Earl of Dorset, first published in Gildon's "New Miscellany" (8vo, 1701, p. 94):

> "*Sylvia*, methinks you are unfit
>   For your great Lord's embrace;
> For tho' we all allow you Wit,
>   We can't a handsome Face.
>
> Then where's the Pleasure, where's the Good,
>   Of spending Time and Cost?
> For if your Wit be'n't understood,
>   Your Keeper's Bliss is lost."

[2] G. E. C., "Peerage" (ed. Vicary Gibbs), IV. 407 n.

marriage of expediency, she was destined to find her 1678
only road to happiness and the salvation of her lover
barred by a union similar to that which gave her birth.

While the Duke was making love to her, Mrs.
Sedley appears to have been taking music lessons from
Henry Bowman, a well-known contemporary composer.
A book of songs with her book-plate and the date 1678[1]
is preserved in the British Museum. It appears to be
in Bowman's writing, and includes a number of
religious pieces in Latin and some drinking songs,
among which is her father's Bacchanalian verses
beginning:

> "Drinke about till the day finde us,
> These are pleasures which endure."[2]

Doubtless she sang the Latin anthems to her pious
lover and the drinking songs to her jovial father. On
4 March, 1679, Charles II was forced to send his 1679
brother to the Continent on account of the fury of
public opinion against his religion and politics. Before
his departure, it was known at Whitehall that Katherine
Sedley had become a mother.[3] The child was a girl,
and was baptised by the name Katherine. James
appears to have acknowledged his paternity at once,

[1] Brit. Mus., Add. MS. 30, 382. The date 1678 is written very faintly
in pencil on the book-plate, which is the family coat-of-arms, with the
printed inscription, "Katherine Sedley, sole daughter and heyre of
Sr Charles Sedley of Southfleet Baronet."

[2] Works, 1702, p. 44. The leaf of the music-book containing the first
stanzas (pp. 89, 90) is torn out: p. 91 contains the last lines from
"Joyning thus our mirth & Beauty."

[3] Peter Le Neve's MS. Diary in the possession of Mr. G. Thorn
Drury, s.d. "Mars 7, Veneris 1678/9." "I heard that the only daughter
and heir of Sir Charles Sedley baronet being reputed a Maid was
brought to bed of a child and layd it to ye D. of York, before he went
beyond the seas; which together with the thought of departing out
of England made his Dutchess very melancholy." A contemporary
satirist (possibly Dorset) celebrated the event in the following couplet:

> "Poor Sidley's Fall, ev'n her own Sex deplore,
> Who with so small Temptation turn'd thy whore."

A Faithful Catalogue of our Most Eminent Ninnies (Harl. MS. 7319,
f. 473).

1679 and the title "Lady" and the surname "Darnley" were conferred on the child by letters patent. Nevertheless, it is not certain that he was the real father of the child. Colonel James Grahame, or Grahme, second son of Sir George Grahame of Netherby, Bart., and Keeper of the Privy Purse to the Duke of York, was known to be very intimate with Mrs. Sedley, and a striking likeness was afterwards observed between Katherine Darnley and Grahame's legitimate daughter, the Countess of Berkshire and Suffolk. According to Horace Walpole, Katherine Sedley used to say to her daughter: "You need not be so proud, for you are not the King's but old Graham's daughter," while Grahame himself remarked concerning the Countess of Berkshire and Katherine Darnley: "Well, well, kings are great men, they make free with whom they please. All I can say is that I am sure the same man begot these two women."[1]

Sir Charles Sedley is said to have been "greatly shocked"[2] when he heard of his daughter's seduction, though he could hardly have expected any other result from the training which she had received. He probably decided at this time to leave the bulk of his estate to Ann Ayscough's son, and it is also possible that his grievance against the Duke of York helped to drive him into the ranks of the Whig or "Country Party," of which his friend the Earl of Dorset was a prominent member.

[1] Horace Walpole's Letters, ed. Toynbee, I. 332 n.

[2] Cibber's *Lives of the Poets* (1753). "Biographia Britannica," s.a. Sedley (1747–66). Lampoons of the grossest kind were written on Katherine's relations with the Duke. The following is a specimen from "The Ladies March," a MS. satire on the ladies of the Court:

> "Lo thy Daughter, little Sid,
> She who lately slip'd her Kid,
> Sure a hopefull 'twill be
> Soaked in Pox and Popery."
> (Harl. MS. 7317, f. 31.)

CHAPTER VII

THE END OF THE SOCIETY OF WITS

" Oh, Dog and Partridge, thou hast cause to mourn;
Thy Darling Son is from thy Bosom torn;
Sidley is gone and never will return.
. . . .
Lesse were thy joys and expectations crost
In Strephon's Death, then now when Sidleys lost."
Charles Montague: MS. Satire on Sir C. Sedley
(Add. MS. 28,644).

" Witty Dorchester next, like a Queen took her place,
And brag'd she a Monarch subdu'd to her Arms.
If Jove in a Shower does court my embrace
Can Adonis deny to submit to my charms?"
" The Session of Ladies" (Harl. MS. 7319, f. 564).

"And Sedley curs'd the form that pleas'd a king."
Dr. Johnson: "The Vanity of Human Wishes."

THE laſt records of the Society of Wits before death,
repentance and exile put an end to its joyous exiſtence
belong to the years 1678–80. In the former year its
chief members paid a graceful aƈt of homage to a
negleƈted and unhappy genius. On leaving Oxford,
John Oldham, the son of a dissenting miniſter, had been
prevented by his religious opinions and independent
spirit from taking orders, then the usual resource of
impecunious men of letters who had no vocation for
the drama. Inſtead, he became an usher at Croydon
Grammar School in 1674, and it was probably while 1674
occupying that poſt that he wrote his earlieſt poems.[1]
Some of these verses seem to have circulated in manuscript, and to have come to the notice of Sir Charles

[1] Probably not the mordant "Satyrs on the Jesuits" (which are said
in the first edition to have been written in 1679). The earliest poems
which are dated in the Collected Edition of 1703 (8vo) belong to the
years 1676, '77 and '78.

Sedley and his friends. The powerful "Ode upon Ben Jonson"[1] and the amusing "Dithyrambick" or Drunkard's Speech[2] would probably make a special appeal to such judges. One day in 1678,[3] Rochester, Sedley, and Dorset are said to have driven over to Croydon School to pay a surprise visit to the young poet. The headmaster received them under the mistaken impression that these dazzling figures had left Whitehall in order to visit him. When he was undeceived, he was considerably surprised that his usher should have had such attractions for the great. Whether any material gain came to Oldham from this visit is not recorded. In the same year (1678) he became tutor to the grandsons of Sir Edward Thurland, the judge. It is not unlikely that it was through the Wits that Oldham was introduced to Dryden, who mourned the death of this Marcellus of Restoration Satire in a burst of unusually moving and majestic music.

Oldham was not the only aspirant to literary fame who received help from the Wits about this time. Another of their protégés was destined to attain to a far greater celebrity. This was Matthew Prior, the nephew of the landlord of the Rummer Tavern at Charing Cross, where Dorset found him one day translating Horace.[4] His exquisite art was in many ways a continuation and development of Sedley's lyrical vein, and it can scarcely be doubted that Sir Charles as well as his friend Dorset was among his early patrons.[5]

In March 1678/9, Sir Charles was probably present at the production of "A True Widow," an excellent comedy by his friend Shadwell, staged at the fine

Margin notes: 1678 · 1678/79

---

[1] Dated 1678 in the edition of 1703.

[2] Dated 1677 in the edition of 1703.

[3] Memoir prefixed to "The Works of Mr. John Oldham: Together with his Remains," etc., 2 vols. in 8vo, 1770: Vol. I. p. v.

[4] Voltaire," Lettres Philosophiques," Lettre XXII, "Sur M. Pope et quelques autres poètes fameux."

[5] Bickley's "Life of Matthew Prior" (Pitman), London, 1914, p. 11. That Prior knew Sedley well is proved by the reference in his "Session of the Poets" quoted on p. 283.

theatre in Dorset Garden. The quarto edition of the 1678/79
play (1679) is dedicated to the Baronet in an epistle in
which the author frankly admits that his work has "had
the benefit" of Sir Charles's "correction and alteration." The same epistle gives a glimpse of the merry
evenings which Sedley must have often spent in Shadwell's company about this time. According to the
dramatist, he was heard "to speak more wit at a supper
than all my adversaries with their heads joined together can write in a year." Another interesting personal note in this epistle tells us that Shadwell had
received many "obligations" and "favours" from
Sedley. Probably the author of "A True Widow," who
admittedly lived by his pen, ate many a hearty meal and
drank many a pint of wine at Sir Charles's expense, nor
is it likely that he was above accepting a timely offering
of guineas in the intervals between his precarious earn-
ings at the theatres. Dryden, it may be noticed, wrote
the Prologue to "A True Widow" and must have been
friendly with both Shadwell and Sedley at this time.
There must have been some good talk at the Rose when
Sir Charles supped there with the authors of "All for
Love" and "Epsom Wells." A dramatic collaboration
of the old Elizabethan type between the three might
have produced very interesting results, for each had
literary qualities that the others lacked. A play which
combined Dryden's brilliant artistry with Sedley's wit
and distinction and Shadwell's full-blooded realism
would surely have held no mean place in English
literature. It is sad to remember the bitter feud which
was to break out a few months later and render such a
collaboration impossible for ever so far as Dryden and
Shadwell were concerned.

The twilight was now drawing in on the original
company of Wits. Etherege, indeed, remained true to
the spirit of the fraternity, and was to preserve the
character of a Restoration gentleman to the end, but
the diplomatic missions which form such an incongruous close to his career took him frequently away

1678/79 from London. Rocheſter, whose conſtitution had been wrecked by his wild life, had "bin at the gates of death" in April 1678, and was "so penitent that he said he would be an exsample of penitence to the whole world."[1] Buckhurſt, now Earl of Dorset and Middlesex, was happily married, and Sedley, under the influence of Ann Ayscough, was faſt becoming a respeċtable charaċter. In 1679 the whole fraternity were savagely attacked by John Sheffield, Earl of Mulgrave, in a scurrilous lampoon entitled "An Essay Upon Satyr." Mulgrave, a man with hardly a tinċture of real wit or literary talent, had been a sort of hanger-on of the group, and had quarrelled violently with Rocheſter. His squib, which was circulated in 1679 in manuscript, was printed 1679–80 anonymously in 1680,[2] and was attributed to Dryden, whom Rocheſter had treated very badly. Although the evidence is not very clear, it seems that the Earl revenged himself for the supposed insult by means of the famous Rose Alley Ambuscade, in which Dryden was waylaid and cudgelled by some ruffians in an alley off the Strand. There is no evidence that Sedley had any conneċtion with this outrage, and it is to be hoped that his friendship with the Laureate was not interrupted by the publication of the poem, which was commonly attributed to Dryden. Certainly he would have been juſtified in feeling resentment—not againſt Dryden, but againſt Mulgrave. His "charaċter" in the Essay runs as follows :

> "And little *Sid-y* for *Simile* renown'd,
> Pleasure has always sought, but never found:
> Tho' all his Thoughts on Wine and Women fall,
> His are so bad sure he ne're thinks at all.

---

[1] Hist. MSS. Comm., 12th Report, Appendix V. Pt. II. p. 50. (Lady Chaworth to Lord Roos, 23 April, 1678.)

[2] Term Catalogues, ed. Arber, I. 385. I have never seen the edition of 1680. According to the half-title of the poem in The Works of John Sheffield, Earl of Mulgrave," etc. (8vo, 1723), it was written in 1675. Rochester wrote to Savile in November 1679, that it was then circulating in manuscript (letter quoted in Scott's "Life of Dryden," ed. 1821, p. 203).

The Flesh he lives upon is rank and strong, 1679–80
His Meat and Mistresses are kept too long;
But sure we all mistake this Pious man,
Who mortifies his Person all he can:
What we uncharitably take for Sin,
Are only Rules of this old *Capuchin*,[1]
For never Hermit under grave pretence
Has liv'd so contrary to common sense;
And 'tis a miracle we may suppose,
No nastiness offends his skilful Nose;
Which from all stink can with peculiar Art,
Extract Perfume, and Essence, from a F—t;
Expecting Supper is his great delight,
He toils all day but to be drunk at night:
Then o'er his Cups this night-bird chirping sits,
Till he takes *Hewet* and *Jack Hall* for wits."[2]

What we know of Sedley enables us to annotate this
brutal passage. The ſtatement that his "miſtresses are
kept too long" is certainly a reference to his conneƈtion
with Miss Ayscough, with whom he had now lived for
seven years, which muſt have seemed a miracle of con-
ſtancy to Mulgrave. The comment on Sedley's "piety"
is doubtless a sneer at the reformation in his manners
which was now in progress. Of the two persons mentioned in the laſt line as the Baronet's drinking companions, "Hewet" is probably Sir John Hewitt, prince
of Reſtoration coxcombs and the alleged original of

[1] Cf. "Satyr to His Muse." By the Author of "Absalom and
Achitophel." . . . (London, 1682. 4to) p. 5.
   "*Adriel* to please, call *Rochester* a Fool,
    Sidley a Capuchin, and sharp *Dorset* Dull."

[2] This is the text printed in "The Fourth and Last Collection of
Poems, Satyrs, Songs, etc. (4to, 1689) and is, I believe, the earliest
extant printed version. In the Term Catalogues for 1680 an octavo
edition of "An Essay upon Satyr or a Poem on the Times. . . .
Printed for T. Dring in *Fleet Street*" is entered, but no copy seems
to be now extant. It was reprinted in the "Poems on State Affairs"
of 1697 (I. 195) with practically no variants. A widely differing
version appeared in the Quarto Edition of Sheffield's Works of 1725.
There can be little doubt that "*Sid-y*" refers to Sedley. In the Brit.
Mus. copy it is filled up as "*Sidley*" in MS., and the couplet quoted
above from "Satyr to His Muse" is a strong support of this interpretation, although it should be mentioned that in some copies of the
"Poems on State Affairs" the name is expanded in MS. to "Sidney."

L

1680 Etherege's Sir Fopling Flutter. The allusion to "Jack
Hall" is more obscure. A Puritan poet of some merit
called John Hall died in 1656,[1] and a Dr. John Hall
became Bishop of Bristol in 1691,[2] but it is hardly
likely that Mulgrave refers to either of these persons.
It is more tempting to suppose that "Hall" is a printer's
error for "Howe," and that the person referred to is
Jack Howe, the dissolute scribbler and politician,
notorious for his violent speeches in the Parliaments of
William III. Howe is said to have been "an amorous
spark of the Court" in his young days, and to have
written some savage lampoons.[3] His character would
fit in very well with the sense of this context.

In the following winter there occurred an accident
which seems to have contributed a good deal towards
Sir Charles's conversion, though it nearly cut short the
career of the convert. One day in the early part of
January, Sedley, Etherege, Fleetwood Shepherd and
others were warming themselves with some setts of
their favourite tennis in a Court in Peter Street, Clare
Market,[4] when the roof of the building collapsed and
buried the whole company in its ruins. Both Etherege
and Sedley were severely hurt, the latter receiving such
serious injuries to the skull that he was at first supposed
to be dead. The newspapers published notices to this
effect,[5] one adding a short but significant eulogy.[6] The
news reached Anthony à Wood at Oxford very rapidly,
and he entered the incident in his Diary on 13 January,

[1] D. N. B., s.a. John Hall.
[2] Luttrell's "Brief Relation," II. 246.
[3] D. N. B., s.a. John Howe, Macaulay's "History of England," ed.
Firth, III. 1336.
[4] Clare Market lay between Lincoln's Inn Fields and the Strand.
Peter Street was sometimes called Denzell Street after Denzell Hollis,
Lord Clare (Wheatley's "London Past and Present").
[5] "True Domestic Intelligence," 16 January, 1679/80; "The True
News, or Mercurius Anglicus," January 14/17, 1679/80. See also
"Hatton, Correspondence," ed. Camden Soc., I. 216.
[6] "True News," etc. January 14/17. "A Person of ancient descent
and no less admired for his wit and admirable parts."

adding the following amazing note: "he (Sedley) died a 1680 week later; he left his estate to his natural son and £10,000 to his owne daughter."[1] It may be noticed that the provision made for Katherine according to Wood tallies exactly with the sum mentioned by Lady Chaworth when she wrote to Lord Roos that Mrs. Sedley was engaged to "Sir Hungerford" in 1677.

Sir Charles was not dead, and the newspapers had to publish disclaimers,[2] while Wood scored out the news of the Baronet's death in his Diary, and added the quaint note, "alive again quære." The resurrection was signalised characteristically by a witticism. Sir Fleetwood Shepherd, perhaps when visiting the invalid after the accident, remarked that "there was so much fire in his (Sedley's) play that it blew up poet, house and all." Sedley replied, "No, the play was so heavy that it broke down the house and buried the poet in the ruins."[3]

[1] Anthony à Wood's "Life and Times," etc., ed. A. Clarke, II. 477.
[2] "True Domestic Intelligence," 20 January 1679/80; "True News, or Mercurius Anglicus," 1721 January, 1679/80.
[3] I follow Haslewood in restoring this witticism to its proper context. It was originally related by the author of "Some Account of Sir Charles Sedley" prefixed to the 1722 edition (see p. 5). He lays the scene in "the theatre" and makes the occasion of the witticism the collapse of the roof of the theatre at a performance of Sedley's "Bellamira." The anecdote has been repeated in subsequent memoirs in this form. However, as there is no record of the collapse of the roof of any English theatre during Sir Charles's lifetime, and as such an event would certainly have attracted attention, it is certain that the tale in the form in which it appears in the 1722 edition is apocryphal. On the other hand, as we know that Sedley was actually injured by the collapse of a roof—not of a theatre but of a tennis court—it seems extremely probable that the witticism, if genuine, was uttered on that occasion. The author of the "Account" probably picked up the anecdote at a tavern or coffee-house, and was either misled by his informant or deliberately embellished it. It may be noticed that the word "play," both in Sir Fleetwood's remark and Sir Charles's rejoinder, is taken to mean "comedy." It could, however, be understood perfectly well in the sense of "game" (viz. tennis). See J. Haslewood's pseudonymous article on Sedley in the *Gentleman's Magazine* of 1822 (cf. p. 9) and his MS. notes on Jacob's "Poetical Register," Appendix I, pp. 320–23.

1680   The serious illness which, doubtless, followed this accident seems to have had a very natural result of turning Sir Charles's thoughts towards religion, and it may be conjectured that the good Dr. Burnet, then engaged in his famous reclamation of Rochester, did not fail to improve the occasion by visiting the penitent.[1] Rochester died at Adderbury on 26 July, 1680, in the odour of sanctity, and, if Sedley had sufficiently recovered, it may be supposed that he was present at his friend's death-bed, and was deeply influenced by his conversion. The carnival of the Restoration was, indeed, at an end when the prince of the lewd Wits turned to Burnet for consolation, and died an exemplary Christian.

It is to be hoped that Sir Charles's health and newly-discovered conscience allowed him to attend the first performance of John Crowne's vigorous tragedy, entitled "The First Part of Henry VI, or the Murder of the Duke of Gloucester," produced at the Duke's 1681 House in September 1681. The first edition of this play[2] is dedicated to Sedley in a long epistle of a very "True Blue" and anti-Catholic character. This epistle contains the following passage, which furnishes definite proof that Sedley had recently joined the Whigs—or, as they loved to call themselves, the party of liberty and property :—"It would be foolish to lash out into unnecessary praises of a Wit that has so long been the delight and ornament of the Nation and is now become the Defence of what is very dear to it, Truth, Liberty, and Property." The tragedy itself is deeply tinged with

---

[1] Cf. Montague's MS. satire on Sedley's conversion (see pp. 166–68 below and Appendix I, pp. 311–14):

"Sidley He started once and did return again,
But now his ears are bored by his own pen.
When the old tennis court fell on his back,
Tho his soul fluttered and the Goose cryed Quak,
Devotion by compulsion is but short . . ."

[2] 4to, London, 1681.

anti-"papist" feeling, as the following typical passage 1681 shows:

> " *Enter* Cardinal *with three* Murderers.
>
> *Card.* So you have all sworn at the holy Altars;
> Now have a care, don't let your Consciences
> Fool you, to flinch with fear e'er it is done,
> Or to repent and tell when 'tis done;
> If so you are doubly Damned.
>
> 1*st Murd.*   I warrant your Grace.
>
> *Card.* Believe your Priests, and not your Consciences,
> For Priests are to direct your Consciences;
> Your consciences are silly, false, corrupt."[1]

That Sedley should have consented to patronise such a work is in itself strong evidence that he was now a supporter of the ultra-Protestant party.

On 5 August, 1682, occurs one of the few references to Sedley in the contemporary press. On this date, Curtis's *Protestant Mercury*, one of the crop of short-lived Whig newspapers which flourished at the time of the Exclusion Bill, printed the following advertisement:

> " Tobias Floyd, a middle-sized man, a black bushy hair; the two middle fingers of both his hands are a little shorter than usual, and a little lame in one of his legs at present: was ffootman to Sir Charles Sedley and is ran away from his master with 19 guinneys and a mixt green cloth coat, lined with scarlet shag, spotted with black : whoever apprehends him or gives such Intelligence of him to Sir Charles Sedley at his house in Bloomesberry Square, whereby he may be apprehended, shall have 40*s.* reward."

Whether Tobias was ever apprehended and whether Sir Charles ever recovered his "19 guinneys" and "mixt green cloth coat" are historical problems which are not likely to be solved. However, apart from Tobias

---

[1] " Henry VI, The First Part," etc., Act IV. (4to, 1681).

1681 and his shortcomings, the advertisement contains two points of interest to a biographer of Sir Charles Sedley. The first is its appearance in a journal of very strong Whig tendencies, which helps to confirm the conjecture that Sedley had definitely joined the opposition to the Court. Secondly, it gives us the interesting information that Sedley was now living in Bloomsbury Square. The exact date of his removal from Great Queen Street is not recorded, but it may be suspected that, after the departure of Lady Sedley, he was not particularly anxious to remain in the neighbourhood of the Savages. It has already been observed that, at the time of Father Bede's visit, husband and wife seem to have been living apart, and it may be supposed that after the "marriage" of April 1672, Sir Charles definitely installed himself with Ann Ayscough in Bloomsbury Square, where he continued to live until just before the end of his life.

In the reign of Charles II people of quality were just beginning to leave the neighbourhood of the Strand and Whitehall, and to live in what were then the suburbs. The oldest of the London squares, St. James's Square and Bloomsbury Square, were originally part of this new suburban development. Bloomsbury Square was at first called Southampton Square after its original owner, the Earl of Southampton, who, according to Evelyn, was engaged in the winter of 1663/4[1] in building "a noble square or Piazza, a little town," in Bloomsbury. One side was occupied by his own mansion, which Evelyn considered "too low," but which "had some noble rooms, a pretty cedar Chapel and a naked garden to the North." This square or piazza was regarded by Londoners with considerable pride, and foreign visitors, like the Grand Duke Cosmo of Florence, were carried to see it as one of the lions of the metropolis. To judge from a print of the early eighteenth century,[2] it must indeed have been a pleasant

[1] Evelyn, Diary, ed. Dobson, II. 223.
[2] Reproduced in Macaulay's "History of England," ed. Firth, I. 345.

place. The centre was occupied by a noble stretch of 1681
turf with intersecting diagonal pathways, but, unlike
a modern London square, without a single tree. On
three sides were neat terraces of houses, each built
round an interior courtyard like the older houses in
Paris to-day. Two of these terraces were called Alling-
ton (?Arlington) Row and Seymour Row, doubtless
after Lord Arlington and Sir Edward Seymour, who
probably lived in them or leased them. On the north
side was the long, low structure of Southampton House,
and, over its chimneys and the trees that surrounded it,
the two green hills of Hampstead and Highgate could
be clearly seen. Indeed, there were no houses beyond
the single row which extended on either side of Southampton House, the gardens of which looked on to the
open fields, whence the fresh country airs must have
been wafted through the windows of the houses in the
square. No record survives to inform us of the exact
position of Sir Charles Sedley's house. He had some
distinguished neighbours, among whom were Richard
Baxter, the gentle and learned Nonconformist divine,
and the second Earl of Chesterfield, whom he had long
ago lampooned, when the Duke of York was pursuing
the pretty Countess. That Chesterfield bore no rancour,
and that any coolness caused by Sedley's squibs had
long been forgotten, is proved by an interesting letter
written by Sir Charles to the Earl in August 1682. It 1682
is the earliest extant specimen of Sedley's correspondence, and its racy, gossiping style makes us regret that
so few of his letters survive.[1] On 29 November, 1679,
Chesterfield had been appointed " Warden and Lord
Chief Justice in Eyre on this side of the Trent." At the

[1] We owe the survival of this letter to the meticulous care with
which Chesterfield kept copies of his correspondence. A letter-book,
which is not in his own hand, is now in the British Museum (Add. MS.
19,253). Sedley's letter is on ff. 121*b* and 122. Chesterfield's Correspondence was printed very incorrectly in 1820 under the title of "The
Letters of Philip Earl of Chesterfield." I have printed the text of the
British Museum MS.

1682 time when he received this letter he had, apparently, been recently in London, and had offered Sir Charles a buck, which the Baronet had refused. Sir Charles now writes to ask whether the offer still stands good.

" From Sir Charles Sedley,
1682.

" My Lord,
" When your Lordship was last in town you made mee an offer of some venison, which I did not then lay hold off, having no occation, nejther was it then in season, but now I would thank you for a Buck, tho the town is so empty that with all my bowling, Tennis, drinking and other generall acquaintance, I shall have much adoe to find company for a Pasty: besides the distinction of Whigg and Tory doth much add to the present desolation, they are in my opinion (at least the violent part on both sides) much of the same stuff at bottom since they are so easily converted one to another, I mean self interest; for instance the Lord Sunderland upon the Dutches of Portsmouth's arrivall is recejved at Court: the Lord Anglesey was voted a Libellour and his book against the Duke of Ormond a libell at the Councill: so tis thought he will be three Quarters Whigg. The Lord Vaughan is this week to be Marryd to the Lady Ann savile notwithstanding he voted her father an enemy to King and country last Sessions. Tho wee are not blest with Poets that can write us comedys equall to the auntients, I beleive never was any age so comicale as this, and a Laugher where ever he turns himself will have occation to hold his sides : Madam de Soyssons is arrived whom the lord Crafes were he alive would call Madame de Soyxante, for she is ten years older than her sister Mazarin, but whether our Court will have her a beauty, a Mis, a Wit or a pollitition, is not yet known.

" Ruinous play is grown the only divertion at 1682 Windsor, and a man without a thousand Guineys to venture, is an Asse, and on the contrary, as it has ever been the Custome of people of Quality that had infirmities, to introduce fashions that might hide them, soe they now cover up their want of sence and conversation with extravagant play. some considerable removes are to be made at Court, but what they are your Lordship can not but know before mee, so I will not trouble you with my conjectures. I could wish England were not so large, that it might fall within my diocess to visit your Lordship, for I know no man I would speak more freely to, nor more willing hear then your Lordship. being without compliment or any regard to the common close of a letter your very

" Obedient servant."

Sir Charles seems to have received his buck, to judge from the Earl's reply, which runs as follows :

" SR,
" You can not oblige mee more than by commanding anything that is within my power and I hope you will never doubt of my readyness to serve you. I have written to my secretaire to prepare a warrant which shall be sent you by the first oportunity and I shall be glad of any occation to assure you of my respects. As to the newse you mention, it may well seem strange to one who lives in the Country, since it is the wonder of the Towne, but I have long thought this Kingdom the Iland of uncertainty, though I am sure no change can make me more or less than I am,

Sr,

Your, &c."

It is pleasant to learn from Sir Charles's letter that he had sufficiently recovered, both in body and in

1682 spirits, to consort again with his "bowling, Tennis, drinking and other generall acquaintance." The "newse" which he relates for the Earl's diversion throws some interesting sidelights on contemporary history, and helps us to date the letter. The "Lord Sunderland" is the crafty and fickle Robert Spencer, second Earl of Sunderland, who supported the Bill to exclude James, Duke of York, from the succession to the throne. All through that stormy period he acted in close conjunction with Louise de Kér[oualle, Duchess of Portsmouth, the King's mistress, who, at first, also intrigued on behalf of the Whigs. Sunderland's name was struck off the list of Privy Councillors in February 1681, and he was not formally restored to favour till 28 August, 1682, when the Duchess of Portsmouth succeeded in persuading the King to allow him to kiss his hand.[1] It must be to this reconciliation that Sedley refers, and it is thus almost certain that the letter was written about the end of August. "Lord Anglesey" is Arthur Annesley, first Earl, an old Roundhead peer who fought for the Parliament in Ireland during the Civil War. He had supported the Restoration, and held office under Charles II. The book mentioned by Sedley is his "Letter from a Person of Honour in the Countrey,"[2] containing his "Animadversions" upon the Earl of Castlehaven's Memoirs. This pamphlet contains passages which reflect both on Ormonde's administration of Ireland and on Charles I. Charles II was deeply offended, and, on 8 August, Anglesey was called upon to resign his office of Lord Privy Seal.[3] Lord Vaughan, afterwards Earl of Carberry, is the person to whom Pepys had compared Sedley as "one of the lewdest fellows of the age." He was a friend and patron of Dryden, who dedicated his comedy "Limberham" to him in 1678. His second

---

[1] D. N. B., s.a. Robert Spencer, Earl of Sunderland.
[2] See Bibliography under Annesley, Arthur, first Earl of Anglesey.
[3] D. N. B., s.a. Arthur Annesley, first Earl of Anglesey.

marriage to Ann Savile, daughter of the great Marquis 1682
of Halifax, to which Sedley here refers, took place in
August 1681.[1] Halifax had actively opposed the Exclu-
sion Bill, and the Whig House of Commons in 1680
had addressed the King to remove him from his
Council and presence for ever. Madame de Soissons is
the beautiful Olympe Mancini, niece of Cardinal
Mazarin, and sister of the Duchesse de Mazarin. Her
husband, the Comte de Soissons, had been Ambassador
Extraordinary from Louis XIV at the coronation of
Charles II. Her brilliant and sensational career at
Louis XIV's Court was cut short by the revelations of
La Voisin in the notorious "drame des poisons," when
she was accused of having plotted to poison her rival,
Louise de la Vallière. In 1679 she was given the choice
of going to the Bastille or leaving France. She chose
the latter alternative and retired to Brussels. According
to her latest English biographer,[2] she is said to have
visited "Hamburg and other parts of Western Ger-
many." Neither this author nor her French biographers[3]
mention a visit to England. Sir Charles Sedley's statement is, however, confirmed by Narcissus Luttrell,
who on 27 July, 1682, notes that "the dutchesse of
Soissons, sister of the dutchesse of Mazarine, is daily
expected here."[4] The nickname, "Madame de Soyxante," is unfair to Olympe. She was only forty-three
in 1682. The "lord Crafes" is Sedley's spelling of Lord
Crofts, his merry old drinking companion at Saxham
Parva in 1668.[5]

There are few records of Sir Charles Sedley in the
last years of the reign of Charles II. This is natural
when it is remembered that after Shaftesbury's flight
and death, and the complete triumph of the Court,

[1] D. N. B., s.a. Robert Spencer, second Earl of Sunderland.
[2] H. Noel Williams, "Five Fair Sisters," London (Hutchinson), 1906.
[3] *E.g.* "Nouvelle Biographie Générale," Firmin Didot, Paris, 1865.
[4] Luttrell's "Brief Relation," I. 209.
[5] See p. 109.

1682 persons who had shown Whig or Exclusionist sympathies found it wise to keep quiet. Sir Charles was
probably protected by the influence of his daughter
over the Duke of York, but his intimacy with members
of the party opposed to the Court must have been well
1680–84 known. In 1684 he contributed to a miscellany edited
by Dryden, and it is pleasant to deduce from this fact
that political differences had not interfered with his
friendship with the great poet. Meanwhile, Katherine
Sedley continued to strengthen her empire over the
pious James, much to the chagrin of his beautiful young
wife. In 1680,[1] Dorset had again lampooned her in
verses that satirise her fading natural charms and her
love of finery :

> "Tell me, Dorinda, why so gay,
>   Why such embroid'ry, fringe, and lace?
> Can any dresses find a way,
> To stop th' approaches of decay,
>   And mend a ruin'd face?
>
> Wilt thou still sparkle in the box,
>   Still ogle in the ring?
> Canst thou forget thy age and pox?
> Can all that shines on shells and rocks
>   Make thee a fine young Thing?
>
> So have I seen in larder dark
>   Of veal a lucid loin;
> Replete with many a brilliant spark,
> As wise philosophers remark,
>   At once both stink and shine."[2]

As Maid of Honour to the Duchess of York,
Dorinda had formerly lived in Whitehall Palace, but,
since her liaison with the Duke, she had established
herself in "a little apartment in sight of the Court."
During the last years of Charles II she had become

[1] This date occurs in the half-title of the poem in all the printed
copies.
[2] Poems by the Earl of Dorset, "Works of the Minor Poets," 8vo,
London, 1749, I. 131.

very intimate with Louise de Kéroualle, Duchess of
Portsmouth, and had been a great favourite with the
King, whom she often met in the Duchess's apart-
ments, and who took a keen delight in her wit.[1] In
September 1684 she bore a second child to the Duke of 1684
York.[2] It was a boy and received the names of James
Darnley.

In the following winter a momentous change came
over Whitehall. One Sunday evening at the end of
January 1684/5, John Evelyn saw King Charles II for 1684/85
the laſt time "in that glorious gallery," surrounded by
the dissolute and voluptuous courtiers among whom
Sir Charles Sedley had squandered so much of his time
and money. Six days later the King was dead and "all
was in the duſt."[3] Probably, like moſt Englishmen,
Sedley mourned sincerely for the dead King, whose
temperament had much in common with his own, while
the accession of the gloomy, prieſt-ridden James
muſt have filled him with apprehension.

The High Sheriff of Kent proclaimed King James
with great pomp at Bromley on 10 February. Sedley,
as one of the chief landowners in the county, was
probably present at this ceremony, and drank the new
King's health "in a flint glass of a yard long"[4]—with
some mental reservations. James had already made a
great show of purifying the Court from the loose living
for which it had been notorious under his brother.
Yielding to his wife and the prieſts, he sent a message
to Katherine Sedley a few days after his brother's
death to the following effeſt: "reflecting upon the

---

[1] Barillon, 7 February, 1686 (see Appendix II).

[2] See p. 159, note 1. Was it Katherine's second child? Dangeau,
the French diarist, states on 27 March, 1686 (N.S.), that King James
had *two* sons by the Countess of Dorchester, "at present being educated
in Paris " (Journal, Firmin Didot, Paris, 1854, I. 303–4). There is
no other trace, as far as I know, of these other sons, so perhaps Dangeau
was mistaken.

[3] Evelyn's Diary, ed. Dobson, III. 145.

[4] *Ibid.*

1684/85 frailty of mankind by the example of his brother, he has resolved to lead another kind of life, and therefore if she should either go out of England or retire privately in the country she should be competently provided for, but that he would see her no more."[1] Katherine was so sure of her hold over her lover that she seems to have refused to listen to these suggestions. Her very slight personal charms, which, so far as can be judged from contemporary portraits, consisted chiefly of finely modelled arms and bust, had by now nearly completely disappeared, and she is said to have become very thin at the time of James's accession.[2] Her wit and intellect, however, seem to have been unimpaired. As an attempt to compromise the divergence between his suggestion that she should go into exile and her determination to stay at Court, James bought her a fine house in St. James's Square, for which he is said to have paid ten thousand pounds, doubtless in the hope that she might be induced to spend her time there instead of flaunting her finery in the eyes of the scandalised Catholics at Whitehall. The finest sculptors and painters in London are said to have been employed to adorn this mansion, and, in addition, Mrs. Sedley received a large pension out of the Privy Purse.[3] In spite of these bribes, she continued to appear at Court, though for three months James kept his promise to his wife by abstaining from visiting her in private. At the end of this period temptation proved too strong for the pupil of the Jesuits, and it became known at Court that Chiffinch's secret room, which had seen such strange sights in the reign of Charles II, was now being used again, this time by King James and the daughter of Sir Charles Sedley. It is possible that the King may have felt some remorse on the death of

[1] Hist. MSS. Comm., Ormonde MSS., N.S., VII. 323. (Sir C. Wyche to D. of Ormonde, 7 February, 1684/5.)

[2] Barillon, 7 February, 1686 (see Appendix III, p. 355).

[3] *Ibid.*

Katherine's son, James Darnley, which took place on 1684/85
23 April, the day of his father's coronation.[1] The death
of this child was one of several ominous incidents which
occurred on that day, and which were afterwards
remembered by the superstitious.

The King's confidants in his relations with Mrs.   1685
Sedley were Colonel Grahame of Kendal, the Keeper
of the Privy Purse, and a "Mrs. Bocky,"[2] usually
known at Court as Mrs. Sophy. Grahame,[3] it will be
remembered, was an old friend of Katherine, and very
probably the King's successful rival. Far more powerful
persons than these are said to have encouraged the
meetings between the King and his mistress. The
Protestant section of the Ministry, headed by Lawrence Hyde, now Earl of Rochester and Lord Treasurer,
was seriously alarmed at the growing influence of the
extreme Catholic party. Remembering how Louis XIV
had used Louise de Kéroualle, they formed the design
of employing Katherine Sedley as an instrument to
counteract the designs of the Jesuits. The choice was a
clever one, for Katherine loved to exercise her wit at the
expense of the priests, while the King's love for her
was almost as strong a passion as his ardour for the
Church. Macaulay in a well-known passage[4] has described the extraordinary spectacle of the pious Earl
and Countess of Rochester and the high-minded Duke
of Ormond acting as panders in order to serve what
they conceived to be the interests of their religion.
Lady Rochester seems to have gone so far as to have

[1] Burnet, "Original Memoirs," ed. Foxcroft, p. 150. Also unofficial
Register of Westminster Abbey, "1685, April 26, *A male child buried
in Henry 7th Chapel, in the middle, between the stalls.*" On an examination of the royal vaults in 1868, a coffin plate was found with the
following inscription: "James Darnley naturall son to King James ye
second Departed this life the 22 April 1685 Aged about eight
Months."

[2] So Barillon calls her. See Appendix III, p. 353.

[3] Barillon, 3 January, 1686 (see Appendix III, p. 353).

[4] "History of England," ed. Firth, II. 726.

1685 attempted to divert the Queen's suspicions of Katherine by the ignoble expedient of "insinuating" that the King's real favourite was Mrs. Grafton, one of the Maids of Honour, and thus causing this perfectly innocent girl to lose the confidence of her mistress.

It must be admitted that, according to her lights, Katherine worked hard for the Protestant cause. In the months when it was almost as dangerous to criticise the Government as in the reign of Henry VIII, she told the King to his face what many of his subjects were thinking, but what nobody dared to whisper. In one of these outspoken conversations, she made the prophetic remark to her lover that Arundel and Tyrconnel would lose him his crown. It was the very completeness of her triumph in her battle with the Queen and the priests that was to be the cause of her downfall. The King, in a fit of fondness, and doubtless acting on a momentary impulse to emulate his brother, determined to create his mistress a Countess in her own right. This resolution was probably taken in the middle of January 1685/86 1685/6.[1] The titles chosen were Countess of Dorchester and Baroness Darlington. The news threw the Court into an uproar, and it was commonly rumoured that the new Countess was going to be installed in the magnificent apartments formerly occupied by the Duchess of Portsmouth, and would henceforth occupy the almost official position that Louise de Kéroualle had held under Charles II.

James probably expected that, after a little murmuring, his wife would accept the presence of the new Countess at Court, as her predecessor had accepted that of the Duchess of Portsmouth. But Mary of Modena was a very different person from Katherine of Braganza. On 19 January, when the patent of Mrs. Sedley's title passed the Great Seal, John Evelyn was

---

[1] Barillon, 3 January, 1686. (Barillon uses the New Style. According to the Julian Calendar still in use in England, his letter would be dated 14 January, 1685/6.)

standing close to the royal table, and noticed that the 1685/86
Queen "ate scarcely a morsel nor spake one word to the
King."[1] According to Burnet,[2] when the Queen heard
the news (of Katherine's title) "she gave order to bring
all the priests, that were admitted to a particular confidence, to her closet. And, when she had them about
her, she sent to desire the King to come and speak to
her. When he came, he was surprised to see such a
company about her, but much more when they fell
on their knees before him. And the Queen broke out
into a bitter mourning for this new honour, which they
expected would be followed with the setting her up
openly as mistress. The Queen was then in an ill habit
of body, and had an illness that as was thought would
end in a consumption. And it was believed that her
sickness was of such a nature, that it gave a very
melancholy presage that, if she should live, she should
have no children. The priests said to the King that a
blemish in his life blasted their designs; and the more it
appeared, and the longer it continued, the more in-
effectual all their endeavours would be. The King was
so much moved with this, and was out of countenance
for what he had done. But to quiet them all he promised them he would see the lady no more, and pretended he gave her this title in order to be breaking
with her more decently." These assurances failed to
convince the Queen, and she told her husband that if
the new Countess came to Court she would not receive
her, and, unless she was really sent out of England, she
herself would retire to a convent.   James, who could
never understand why anyone should oppose his
desires, was genuinely surprised at this outburst, which,
in his sublime conceit, he attributed "to her great love
for himself."

The Catholic faction at Court, headed by the unscrupulous Sunderland, now came to the rescue of the

[1] Diary, ed. Dobson, III. 197, s.d. 19 January, 1685/6.
[2] Burnet's "History of His Own Time" (ed. Oxford, 1833), II. 120.

M

1685/86 Queen and the priests. James listened to Father
Gifford with respect when he admonished him for his
conduct, but when Sunderland, Tyrconnel, Dover and
Arundel presumed to add their voices to the priest's, he
told them very shrewdly that he had taken what Father
Gifford said kindly, as he recognised that he was doing
his duty as a priest, but for their parts this was the first
time he took them for divines, and was sure they spoke
"not out of religion, but some private piques, and bid
them for the future not concerne themselves with things
that did noe way relate to them."[1] The "private
piques" are, of course, an obvious reference to the
jealousy shown by Sunderland and his friends toward
the Hydes. Father Petre, the Jesuit priest, made a far
more effective protest, pointing out that the whole
Catholic world would be scandalised at the spectacle of
a prince, who professed to be a champion of the faith,
preferring an ugly, middle-aged, Protestant mistress to
a beautiful young Catholic wife.

James bowed before the storm, and, in accordance
with the tradition of his family, consented to sacrifice his
favourite. The Queen's demands were that the new
Countess should be dismissed from Court and sent
away either to the country or out of England. But to
dislodge a person of Katherine's strength of character
was no easy matter. She made the King promise that
he would never consent to be separated from her
without granting her a parting interview. It was,
perhaps, the memory of this promise (which was
probably broken) that caused James to treat her
with unusual patience. Her conduct was certainly
impudent to the last degree. At first she flatly refused to move, and posed as a Protestant martyr
oppressed by the Jesuits. Middleton, one of the most
honourable men among James's ministers, was sent to
inform her that a yacht was ready to take her to Holland.

---

[1] Belvoir MS., quoted by A. Fea in "James II and his Wives"
(Methuen, London, 1908), p. 139.

Katherine replied in the language of a defender of 1685/86
constitutional rights, and invoked Magna Charta to
support her contention that, as a British subject, she
could not be deported without her own consent. Her
resistance was so determined that it was whispered at
Court that she received secret encouragement from the
King. By January 28 she had consented to leave the Court
and move into her luxurious lodgings in St. James's
Square.¹ Her last resource was a real or pretended illness
and miscarriage. France and Flanders were suggested
as possible retreats, but she said that her friend the
Duchesse de Mazarin had warned her never to go to a
country where there were convents, and that she would
prefer death to being shut up among nuns.   Doubtless
she was thinking of her unfortunate mother, who was at
that very moment confined in a Flemish cloister.
Finally, she proposed Ireland, but demanded at the same
time that if Holland were chosen, she should be permitted to visit the Princess of Orange! She probably
chose Ireland because part of the lands granted to her
by the King were situated in that country. She is also
said to have been friendly with a certain Lady W——
who lived there, and to have desired to settle with her.²
After a long delay she finally departed about the
middle of February 1685/6.³ Some letters written by
her while she was in Ireland survive. They provide good
examples of her wit and her original orthography, but
are not complimentary to the land of her exile.⁴

It was rumoured as early as April 6, 1686, that Mrs. 1686
Sedley was going to return from Ireland. Her house in
St. James's Square was said to be "furnishing very fine"

¹ Marquis of Downshire's MSS., Hist. MSS. Comm., 1924 (Dr. Owen
Wynne to Sir W. Trumbull), p. 109.
² *Ibid.*, p. 117.
³ *Ibid.*, p. 122. News-letters dated 18 February: "The Countess of
Dorchester hath begun the journey into Ireland."
⁴ They are printed and annotated in Appendix III of the present
study: "Some Documents illustrative of the Life of Katherine Sedley,
Countess of Dorchester" (pp. 345–52).

1686 on this date, and a pew in the new St. Anne's church had been taken for her.[1] She actually returned to England on 14 November, 1687.[2] She is said to have coolly appeared at Court on her return as if nothing had happened.

It was probably soon after her return that she purchased Ham House, Weybridge, from the widow of the sixth Duke of Norfolk. Here James is said to have visited her from time to time, though she never regained her old influence over him.[3]

While his daughter was waging her war of wit against the priests, Sir Charles Sedley seems to have continued to live the pleasant, leisurely life of a wealthy patron of literature. Soon after King James's accession, he and his friend Dorset were struck[4] by the Latin and English verses in a collection published by graduates and other members of the University of Cambridge to lament the death of King Charles and to congratulate his successor.[5] It may be noticed that this book contains "a Pindaric Ode" by William Ayloffe, Ann Ayscough's nephew, and perhaps it was this young man who brought the collection to Sedley's notice. Several other youths, who were destined to obtain celebrity, had contributed verses. There is a Latin epigram by Matthew Prior, who had been enabled by Dorset's generosity to go to St. John's College. But the best English verses

---

1 "Ellis Correspondence," II. 92.

2 "Clarendon Correspondence," ed. Singer, I. 544, 552. Some contemporaries were very sceptical about the journey to Ireland. Dr. Owen Wynne wrote to Sir W. Trumbull on 14 June, 1686: "As for C. D. [Lady Dorchester] I am unable to answer you. The party vanished hence of a good while and we took it for granted would appear next in Ireland. But I am apt to think another course was steered, first Northward to see some relatives, then back hither or not far off" (Marquis of Downshire's MSS., Hist. MSS. Comm., 1924, p. 184).

3 D. N. B., s.a. Katherine Sedley, Countess of Dorchester.

4 "Works and Life of C. Montague, late Earl of Halifax," etc. London (Curll), 1715.

5 "Moestissimæ ac Lætissimæ Cantabrigiensis affectus Decedente Caroli II Succedente Jacobe II, etc., Cantabrigiæ," 1684/5, 4to (see General Bibliography under "Cambridge").

in the book are unquestionably the vigorous heroic 1686 couplets by Charles Montague, a young graduate and fellow of Trinity, containing, among the usual flattery, some really musical lines such as the following, which compare the dead King's career to a river:

> "But oh! he ebbs; the smiling waves decay
> (For ever, lovely stream, for ever, stay);
> To the black Sea his silent course does bend,
> Where the best streams, the longest rivers end."

Sedley and Dorset were so impressed with this young poet's performance that they invited him and his friend, George Stepney (also of Trinity), to come to London, and enter the literary society of the capital under their patronage. Stepney refused the offer "out of his love for a retir'd life," but Montague accepted and thus laid the foundations of his brilliant public career. It is pleasant to imagine that Sedley visited his talented young friends at Cambridge, and renewed in their company the memories of his own undergraduate days in "another place."

On 25 March, 1686, Sir Charles was again seriously ill.[1] His condition was so serious that he was actually reported to have died on 13 April in a contemporary news-letter.[2] Apparently this illness completed the "conversion," the first signs of which had begun to appear about seven years before. Sir Charles seems to have gone so far as to have written an effusion in defence of the doctrines of the Church, which, unfortunately, has not been preserved. The spectacle of the orator who had "abused the scriptures" on the balcony of the Cock Tavern coming forward as a defender of Christianity was certainly tempting for a satirical wit. Young Charles Montague nearly yielded to the temptation of holding his patron up to public ridicule by means of a

[1] Add. MS. 2869. "25 March, 1686: Sir Charles Sedley is very ill and some think he will scarcely wether his disease." This note on a small scrap of paper is in an unknown hand.

[2] Marquis of Downshire's MSS., Hist. MSS. Comm., 1924, p. 150.

1686 satire in verse on his "conversion." Perhaps his conscience prevented him from finishing and publishing it.
The draft remains in his handwriting in a small manuscript book in the British Museum, and has never hitherto been printed.[1] It provides some interesting information concerning Sedley's conversion. The following
lines leave no room for doubt that the convert had
written some kind of a defence of Trinitarian theology.

Knight
"Prodigious *Man* that among Husks and swine   10
   Couldst learn the Mysterys of ye sacred Trine
Could fathom mysterys and turn Divine
[And in the sacred Trinitys Defence][2]

[Defys at Arms Reason and Common sense]
Has drawn his Pen and thrown his Gantlet down   15
To his forsaken Bretheren of the Town
To all that dare the Trinity disown

.   .   .   .   .

Commence a Doctor reeking from ye stews   20
The Apostolick Bard of Mother Hewes

.   .   .   .   .

valiant
So our Great Sidley who has triumphed long   25
  us   our
Kil'd [men] wth Satyr and [their] wives wth Song
Hew'd down the Monstrous Fopperys of men
On the High Altar Dedicates his Pen
Dos Club his Talent to the Churches stock   30
And in the Quire displays the Comick sock."

Line 21 gives the impression that the Baronet's
Apologia was in verse, which is strengthened[3] by the
following lines that tell how, when Sedley takes to
hymn-writing, "pretty Similes sprinkled here and
there" will "Quicken our flagging zeal like Botled

[1] Brit. Mus., Add. MSS. 28, 644, p. 57*b*. The whole draft is printed
in Appendix I, p. 311.

[2] Lines and words enclosed in square brackets are crossed out in the
original.

[3] It is further strengthened by some verses in "Poems on Several
Occasions" written by Philomela (*i.e.* Mrs. Rowe), 8vo, 1696.

"To Sir Charles Sedley.

But stay, 'tis Sedley—and it were a crime
For me to grasp a subject so sublime:

Beer." In an apostrophe to the Dog and Partridge, a 1686 favourite tavern of the Wits,[1] Montague makes an interesting reference to the death of Rochester under his usual pastoral pseudonym of Strephon.[2]

["Lesse were thy joys and expectations crost
In Strephon's Death, then now when Sidley's lost."]

The subsequent lines give a short history of Sedley's return to a state of grace. The first symptoms seem to have appeared at the time of the tennis-court accident; a relapse to "prophanesse" followed, and the final conversion was sealed by a written testimony:

again

"Sidley He started once but did return [to you]   60
with his own pen
But now his ears are bored [He must be true]
When the Old Tennis Court fell on his back
Tho his soul flutter'd and the Goose cryed Quak
Devotion by Compulsion is but short
But this Relapse is of another sort."

The profane conclusion drawn by the satirist is that Sedley learned to believe in the mystery of the Trinity from "the thieving Town" of "Rumey" or New Romney which he represented in Parliament. Romney

---

Since nothing but his own Cœlestial lays
Are fit the Authour of such flights to praise,
Nor dare my thoughts make the unequal choice,
My Infant muse has yet but try'd her tender voice."

Now none of Sedley's known poems could have been called "Cœlestial" even by the most brazen flatterer. I think it is highly probable that Mrs. Rowe is referring to the religious effusion which Montague ridiculed.

[1] "I expect to see my Lord Carlingford in his way to Vienna, then you may be sure that all the remains of the Dog, & Partridge will be remembred." Etherege to Mr. Jepson, Ratisbon Letter Book, $\frac{27\ February}{8\ March}$, 1687/8, f. 170. It is one of the taverns frequented by Sparkish, the fop, in Wycherley's "The Country Wife," and Lady Vaine is invited there by Master Whiskin in Shadwell's "The Sullen Lovers." According to Mr. Montague Summers, its real name was the Setting Dog and Partridge and it was situated in Fleet Street (see notes to "The Country Wife" in the Works of Wycherley, ed. Montague Summers, 1923).

[2] See Flatman's "Pastorall" on Rochester's death, Aubrey's "Short Lives," ed. Clark, II. 305.

1686 had a great wool market, and was also notorious for smugglers. Montague suggests that Sedley came to believe in the possibility of a triune deity from watching the Romney smugglers "squeeze three fleeces into one," in order to cheat the Customs. In a squib like this something must, of course, be allowed for the exaggerations of a satirist. Sedley's conversion could hardly have been such a complete *volte-face* as Montague suggests. At any rate, it did not prevent him from writing and publishing an excellent (but by no means edifying) comedy in 1687.

"Bellamira, or the Mistress," was staged at the King's house in May 1687. It is interesting to find that 1687 King James II went to see it.[1] He was apparently unaccompanied by his Queen, who was hardly likely to attend a play written by the father of her hated rival.

The fact that this play is an adaptation (and a very clever one) of "The Eunuch" of Terence suggests that Sedley had amused himself during his convalescence by renewing his acquaintance with the classics, and especially the author whom he had cited in his conversation with Dryden in 1664.[2] The quarto edition (licensed 24 May, 1687) contains an interesting "Preface to the Reader," where the dramatist gives a short account of the genesis of the play. As he was at work upon the first act, a friend came into his chamber and "seemed to approve the design." Sedley tells us that he offered his friend to finish the play and give it to him if "he could get it Acted under his own or another's name." The "friend" was probably Thomas Shadwell, who, as Oldys tells us,[3] owed "whole scenes" to Sedley and Dorset. Shadwell did not accept the offer, probably because he was unable to produce anything under his own name because of Dryden's interference; Sedley therefore produced the piece under his own name, "or my friend would have lost

---

[1] Warrant cited in Allardyce Nicoll's "Restoration Drama," p. 313.
[2] See p. 92.
[3] Oldys's Notes to Langbaine, Note (9); see Appendix I, p. 320.

his third night." The laſt remark is an allusion to 1687 the cuſtom of giving the proceeds of the third night's performance as a benefit to the author. Had Sedley decided not to have the play ſtaged, or to give it to another dramatiſt, he would have loſt "the third night." He seems to imply that he produced it mainly in order to obtain the benefit and hand it over to Shadwell, whose finances were at a pretty low ebb at this time.[1] It is conceivable that the charaᴄter of Merryman, the fat good-natured toper, was suggeſted by that of Shadwell, and it is intereſting to compare the description of Merryman as having "drunk his Gallon every day these seven years," and as being "as true a shap'd Drunkard as heart can wish, Great Belly, double chin, thick legs," with Dryden's

> "Og from a treason-tavern rolling home,
> Round as a globe and liquor'd ev'ry chink,
> Goodly and great he sails behind his link."[2]

"Bellamira" was a great success on the ſtage, though it seems to have shocked certain ladies. Sedley twits these faſtidious "nymphs" with some juſtice in his Preface with having crowded to plays of a far more outspoken charaᴄter, and regrets that "the ice which has born so many Coaches and Carts should break with my wheel-barrow." The proteſt is, nevertheless, of some intereſt as one of the earlieſt expressions of disapproval of a comedy on moral grounds, and as showing that Jeremy Collier's famous indiᴄtment of Reſtoration drama gave voice to an opinion which had been gathering ſtrength for some time.

From "Bellamira" we find that the haunts of the fashionable world had shifted further Weſt since the date of the Mulberry Garden. In that play Coleby's Tavern and Hyde Park were the moſt weſterly points to which the sparks and their "nymphs" penetrated.

---

[1] From letters in the Sackville collection it appears that Shadwell was living chiefly on Dorset's bounty in the reign of James II.

[2] "Absalom and Achitophel," Part II. ll. 459–61.

1687 In "Bellamira" there is an assignation at a "Walk in *Kensington*" and a scene is laid at Knightsbridge.

Shadwell repaid Sedley for the "benefit" of "Bellamira" by dedicating to him "The Tenth Satyr of Juvenal, English and Latin" (published in May 1687). Although written in Shadwell's usual clumsy style, this dedication is an exceedingly interesting document, and throws important light on the careers of both authors, as well as forming a valuable commentary on Dryden's "MacFlecknoe." It testifies to the frankness of Sedley's character in words which certainly have the ring of truth.

> " . . . some [enemies] you have, though I cannot but wonder why you should have any, who are so careful in your Actions that you never injure any Gentleman, and so void of scurrilitie in your conversation, that I never heard you speak ill of anyone behind his back: a vice too often practis'd by our English Gentry."

To the charge of "obscenity" brought by "some Ladies" against "Bellamira," Shadwell retorts with that real and almost pathetic lack of decorum which was one of his chief characteristics, "that did not their thoughts lye very much that way, they could find no more obscenity in it than in any other Comedy." As though a certain amount of obscenity was essential to a comedy! There follows a tribute to Sedley's delicacy in performing the functions of a patron which is of very great value in an age when "gentlemen" often treated their literary dependents little better than their lackeys:— "The great favour you did me in giving me this play (Bellamira) I shall never forget, as I shall always be proud of an occasion to boast of so good a Patron who uses me not as some Supercilious Men would (who do good meerly out of vanity), as a troublesome hanger-on: but treats me with the civility and kindness of a Friend. And I have had the honour to have alwaies found as much of both from him, as if I had obliged him in receiving as much as he did in conferring his benefits." This passage, in spite of its clumsy grammar, does honour both to Shadwell and Sedley, and deserves to be quoted by every author who mentions the escapades of

Sir Charles's youth. The rest of the Dedication is chiefly 1687
occupied by Shadwell's well-known answer to "Mac-
Flecknoe." Incidentally, he mentions Sedley's opinion
on that "Libel" (as he calls the Laureate's satire): "I
have heard you observe the foundation of that libel is
false and unnatural, for tho' some have mistaken dulness for Wit, and commended it as such, yet no man
ever commended Dulness as dulness." If this was really
Sedley's opinion, it is valuable rather as an expression
of loyalty to his friend than as an example of his
criticism, for the "foundation" of "MacFlecknoe" is the
delightful assumption that a kingdom of dulness exists
whose standards are the reverse of those of the rest of
the world. Shadwell's parting shot at the Laureate is
the grave accusation that his plays were "taken from a
novel or stolen from a romance." Dryden might have
replied that he sinned in company with Shakespeare,
Fletcher and Corneille, and that, anyhow, such a
reproach came with a singularly bad grace from one
who had almost certainly received "whole scenes" from
Sedley, a fact which Dryden knew and mentioned in
"MacFlecknoe,"[1] and which Shadwell does not deny.

On 23 May "Gentle George," now his Britannic
Majesty's Envoy at Ratisbon, expressed his pleasure
at the success of "Bellamira."[2]

" . . . I have heard of the Success of ye Eunuch
[Bellamira]—and am very glad the Town has so good
a tast to give the same just applause to Sir Charles

---

[1] "MacFlecknoe" ll. 162–3:

> "But let no alien S-dl-y interpose,
> To lard with wit thy hungry *Epsom* prose."

[2] Apparently Etherege was originally under the impression that
Sedley had merely adapted an older play called "The Eunuch": "I saw a
play about ten years ago call'd the Eunuch, so heavy a Lump, the
Players durst not charge themselves with the dead weight. but it seems
that Sir Ch. Sidley has animated the mighty mass and now it treads the
Stage lightly he had always more wit than was enough for one man and
therefore dos well to continue his Charity to one who wants it."
Etherege to Lord Middleton: Ratisbon Letter Book, f. 105, 23 June/
3 July, 1687.

Sidley's writing, wch his friends have always done to his conversation—few of our plays can boaſt of more wit than I have heard him speak at a Supper. Some baren sparks have found fault with what he has formerly done on this occasion, onely because the fatness of the Soile has produc'd too big a Crop—I dayly drink his health, my Lord Dorsets, Mr. Jepsons, Charles Godfrys, your own & all our friends." [1]

On 19 December he mentions Sedley in language that shows that the news of the conversion of the "Apoſto-lick Bard of Mother Hewes" had reached Ratisbon: "Sir C. S. setts up for good houres, and sobriety," while on 16 January, 1688/9, in a letter to Lord Middleton, Sir George expresses the fear that his lordship has become "as temperate as Sir Ch: Sydlie."[2]

1688/89

Before Etherege's laſt letter was written, events had happened in England that put an end to the diplomatic career of that brilliant butterfly. Katherine Sedley's shrewd prophecy that the King's Catholic advisers would lose him his crown had been fulfilled. Sedley's friend Dorset, who had been dismissed by James from his lord lieutenancy, was in the inner counsels of the Whig party, and, though he did not sign the famous written invitation to William of Orange, almoſt certainly knew and approved of the projeƈted revolu-tion. Sedley, as his intimate friend, muſt have been one of the many gentlemen who kept the secret of the great conspiracy. What part he aƈtually played in the Revolution has not been recorded, but there is every reason to accept the tradition[3] that he was an aƈtive supporter of the Prince of Orange. As an intimate friend of Dorset, it is highly probable that he was one of the band of noblemen and gentlemen who formed

---

[1] Ratisbon Letter Book, f. 94 (to Mr. Will Richards, 23 May/2 June, 1687).

[2] Sir Etherege's Ratisbon Letter Book, ff. 153, 160.

[3] "At the Revolution he appeared warm on the side of King William." Defoe, (?) "Some Account," etc. prefixed to the edition of 1722.

a bodyguard for the Princess Anne in her flight from Whitehall to Nottingham. Perhaps Sedley helped his friend in the actual escape when Dorset carried off the Princess in a hackney coach on the night of 20 November, 1688.[1]

After the flight of King James, the Prince of Orange 1688 summoned "all such persons as served as knights, citizens or burgesses in any of King Charles's Parliaments to meet him at St. James's." Sir Charles, who had served in all the Parliaments of Charles II, and who was close at hand in Bloomsbury Square, must have been one of those who obeyed this summons. The body which thus assembled to meet the Prince must not be confused with the Convention which was elected later. Besides the ex-members of Parliament, it included the Lord Mayor and the Aldermen of London, and met at the Commons House, where it formed itself into a house, and elected Henry Powle Chairman. In the old St. Stephens' Chapel, looking out on the river and the green fields of Lambeth, where his mother had once petitioned the grim Puritans of the Long Parliament, and where he himself had sat in his youth among the gay sparks of the Cavalier Parliament in the 'sixties, Sir Charles Sedley probably voted with the rest for the momentous resolution, thanking the Prince of Orange for "rescuing of us all from the miseries of Popery and slavery," and calling upon him "to take over the administration of the country till the Convention could be elected."[2]

Sir Charles Sedley was not elected to the Convention, but he is said to have been present on horseback at the proclamation of King William and Queen Mary on 13 February, 1688/9. It was on this occasion that he

---

[1] Macaulay's "History of England," ed. Firth, p. 1162. When Anne was Queen, she created Sedley's illegitimate grandson a baronet (see p. 203). Perhaps this was intended to be a recompense for the assistance that Sedley may have given her in 1688.

[2] Cobbett's "Parliamentary History," V. 23, 24.

1688 made his most famous epigram. Someone had found it strange that the old courtier of Charles II should be among the most enthusiastic supporters of the Revolution. Sedley answered, "Well, I am even in point of civility with King James. For as he made my daughter a Countess, so I have helped to make his daughter a Queen."[1] According to a contemporary lampoon, Mrs. Katherine Sedley also expressed her sympathy with the Revolution in public :—

> "But Sidley has some colour for his Treason,
> A daughter Ravished without any Reason;
> Good natur'd man, He is most strangely blest,
> His Daughter's Honour is his Worship's Jest.
> And she to keep her Father's honour up,
> Drinks to the Dutch with Orange in her Cup."[2]

The fourth line places the authenticity of Sir Charles's famous jest beyond all doubt.

[1] "Some Account of the Life of Sir Charles Sedley" in the 1722 edition of the Works, I. 11. The author of the "Account" says that the jest was made "after Sir Charles had stickled hard for voting the throne vacant, as also for filling it up," and states that Sir Charles uttered it "when coming out of the Commons house." As Sedley did not sit in the Convention he could not have taken part in the debates on the Succession. The paper entitled "Reflections on our Late and Present Proceedings in England" ascribed to him by the editor of the 1722 edition (see p. 303), if it be indeed by him, shows that he was in favour of declaring the throne vacant only if the Prince of Wales was proved to be supposititious, and even then the author urges that the Princess of Orange only should succeed. As in the case of the tennis-court story, Defoe seems to have obtained an accurate account of Sedley's words but to have placed them in the wrong setting. While giving the wording of the "Account," I have followed the author of the "Life and Works of Charles Montague, Earl of Halifax" in laying the scene at the proclamation of William and Mary, at which Sedley would naturally be present. Montague's biographer absurdly ascribes the witticism not to Sedley but to Montague himself.

[2] "A Letter to my Lady Osborne" (1688, on f. 124 of a folio MS. book bound in original calf and bearing the bookplate of "the Right Honble William, Lord Craven, Baron Craven of Hampstead Marshall"). The lines quoted above were copied by Mr. G. Thorn Drury, who kindly communicated them to me.

CHAPTER VIII

"Truly, Sir, for my part, I renounce those partial measures, and if I cannot be chosen upon the account of General Service to the Nation, I will never creep into the Favour of any sort of Men and Vote against my Judgment."—Sir Charles Sedley in the House of Commons, 9 February, 1692/3.

SIR CHARLES SEDLEY'S parliamentary career is an extraordinary proof of the versatility of his character. A Wit of the Restoration usually passed his latter years idling about town and living on his reputation among the young men who gathered at Will's Coffee-house— or, if he was a Jacobite, in drinking confusion to the usurpers in Paris taverns and dancing attendance on the mock Court of St. Germain's. Unlike Wycherley and Etherege, however, Sedley, having inherited a fund of solid good sense, was capable of realising that a new England was born at the Revolution and of adapting himself to the changed conditions. He saw that the right place for a brilliant talker after 1688 was no longer the Court but the House of Commons, and, henceforward, employed the wit which had delighted Charles II and Buckingham to point a series of manly and sensible political speeches. Sedley and Rochester were, perhaps, the only two members of the fraternity of Wits who had a sense of the grim realities that formed the background of the riotous carnival of the Restoration. The Rochester who wrote that terrible (and altogether just) satire beginning

"Chaste, prudent, pious Charles the Second"

could see through the glittering tinsel of Whitehall as clearly as Andrew Marvell, and, if he had lived, might, under the guidance of Burnet, have become a great statesman. Sedley, with less genius than his friend, was incapable of leading a party, but he had the very qualities which are necessary for a brilliant parliamentary free-lance. The wit, good sense, and non-party spirit of his extant pieces call to mind the pamphlets of his great relative, George Savile, Marquis of Halifax. In those Parliaments of William III, when Sacheverell, Montague, Harley, and St. John were inaugurating the traditions of the two great political parties, it surely deserves no small praise to have helped to found that body of independent and critical opinion which has always existed since then between Whigs and Tories, and whose existence is as necessary as theirs for the well-being of the commonwealth.

When Sir Charles Sedley entered the House of Commons, it is very improbable that he had the slightest intention of playing a serious part in its debates. He was first elected as "a recruiter" (or as we say now at a by-election) for the constituency of New Romney, one of the Cinque Ports, close to the original seat of his family. The House of Commons to which he was returned was the famous Long Cavalier Parliament, which was elected in a frenzy of loyalism in 1662 **1662**, and which sat till 1679. The two members for New Romney (or "Barons" as the members for the Cinque Ports were called) at the General Election of 1662 were Norton Knatchbull and Charles Berkely. Berkely was created Lord Fitzharding (an Irish title) in 1663, and Earl of Falmouth in 1665. He was succeeded as member for New Romney by Henry Brouncker, who was expelled from the House on 1668 **21** April, 1668, for having ordered the Fleet to slacken sail while pursuing the Dutch after the battle of Southwold Bay on 3 June, 1665, and also on the more general charge of being a person of infamous character.[1]

[1] Pepys's Diary, ed. Wheatley, VII. 406 n., where it is incorrectly stated that Brouncker was succeeded as member for New Romney by Sir Charles Berkely, jun.

Sir Charles Sedley was elected to fill the vacancy thus 1668 caused in May.[1] A month later he was enjoying himself with Buckhurst and Nelly at Epsom, so it is hardly probable that his parliamentary duties weighed very heavily on him at this time. Probably he entered the House at the request of the King in order to swell the ranks of the Court party. He was certainly one of the numerous members of this "pensioners'" Parliament who received the royal bounty in exchange for supporting the King's policy in the House. This is proved by an entry in a list of "ye Parliament Pensioners in ye session of Parliament 1670" made by Sir W. Haward, where it is stated that "Sir Charles Sedley promised ye king to be absent."[2]

It is impossible to say how long Sedley remained a 1677–78 member of the Court party. By 1677 he seems to have ceased to be a "pensioner." In a list of the members who received bribes from the Court, published in that year, and probably compiled by Andrew Marvell,[3] his name does not occur, although several of the other "Barons of the Cinque Ports" are mentioned among the "Principal Labourers in the Great Design of Popery and Arbitrary Power." When the papers of the Romanist conspirator, Coleman, were seized after he had been accused by Titus Oates, Sedley was one of the gentlemen employed to translate the French documents among them. On 25 October, a letter from Coleman to the Internuncio at Brussels was read to the House of Lords in a translation by Sedley.[4] This

---

[1] "Alumni Oxonienses," IV. 1332 (Early Series).

[2] Sir William Haward's MSS. (in the possession of G. Thorn Drury, Esq., K.C.), p. 258.

[3] "A Seasonable Argument to Persuade all the Grand Juries of England to Petition for a New Parliament or a List of the Principal Labourers in the Great Design of Popery or Arbitrary Power," etc. Amsterdam, 1677, 4to (ascribed to Marvell in the British Museum Catalogue).

[4] Hist. MSS. Comm., 11th Report, Appendix, Pt. II. (MSS. of the House of Lords), p. 5. The letter was printed by Sir George Treby in

1677-78 letter, written by an agent of the Duke of York, recommends his supporters "to Distract the Parliament to that degree that they shall never agree among themselves; so that they shall be altogether useless to the King; and by that means he will be forc'd to lay them aside." Such a letter may well have convinced Sir Charles of the sinister designs of the Duke and his friends, and it is probable that he went over to the Opposition about this time. In December 1678, Bedloe, one of Oates's chief accomplices in the anti-Catholic agitation, boasted of his intimacy with "Middlesex (*i.e.* Buckhurst), Rochester and Sedley."[1] Sir Charles was also, it must be remembered, an intimate friend of Shadwell, the Whig dramatist, who was a member of the Green Ribbon Club at the King's Head Tavern in Fleet Street, the headquarters of the newly organised Whig party.[2] No complete list of the members of that society exists, and though Sedley's name occurs in none of the extant lists, it is quite possible that he may have been a member. At any rate, as Shadwell's friend, he must often have sat pipe in hand in those reeking tavern-rooms where the dangers of arbitrary power and the sinister designs of the "Papists" were discussed, and the new and heady theories of religious and civil liberty expounded. Whatever his views may have been, however, there is no record that he ever spoke in the Long Cavalier Parliament except on 8 February, 1672, when he protested against Constable Axton's invasion of his privilege.[3]

1678/79 At the General Election of March, 1678/9, Sir Charles Sedley and Paul Barret, Esq., were elected

---

his "Second Part of the Collection of Letters and Writings relating to the Horrid Popish Plot," London, 1681. The full text is given in Appendix I, pp. 310-11.

[1] Memorandum concerning Bedloe, endorsed by Ormonde, Calendar of the MSS. of the Marquis of Ormonde (Hist. MSS. Comm.), New Series, III. 273.

[2] See Sir George Sitwell's "The First Whig," pp. 197-203.

[3] See p. 131.

"Barons" for New Romney.[1] It was in this very month that the birth of Katherine Sedley's first child by the Duke of York became publicly known. Sir Charles, doubtless, availed himself of an excellent opportunity for avenging his daughter's seduction by voting for the 1679 First Exclusion Bill, introduced in May 1679. This probability is strengthened by the fact that he was re-elected both at the General Election of October 1679, when the Whigs triumphed all over the country, and again to the turbulent Parliament that met at Oxford in March 1680/81, which contained a smaller 1680–81 but still a distinct majority of Whigs.[2] The serious illness which followed the tennis-court accident in January 1679/80 must have prevented him from taking part in the debates of these Parliaments. The Oxford Parliament departed from the usual custom of those days by printing and publishing its debates. The presence of a copy of the "Debates of 1680/81" among Sir Charles's books[3] shows that, whether present or not, he followed the proceedings of the House with interest.

Sedley was not elected to King James's first and only Parliament, which met on 19 May, 1685, and this suggests that he was by now definitely regarded by the Court as an opponent. The constituent bodies had been 1685 carefully remodelled and manipulated by the agents of the Crown in order that none but Tories of the deepest dye should obtain seats, and it may be supposed that the borough of New Romney did not escape the attentions of the authorities. The two "Barons" chosen to represent this ancient constituency in 1685 were Sir Benjamin Bathurst and Sir William Goulston.[4] As Sedley was not elected for any other constituency, this

[1] Hasted's "Kent," III. 425.

[2] The dedication of Crowne's "Henry VI" definitely proves that he had joined the Whigs by the Autumn of 1681. See p. 148.

[3] See Appendix II, p. 331.

[4] "A True and Compleat List of the Lords, etc. . . . . of the Present Parliament summoned to meet the nineteenth of this inst. May, 1685" (Bodleian, Wood, 276, p. xciii *a*).

1685 evidence is sufficient to confute the often-repeated statement that he distinguished himself in this Parliament by opposing the Court on the burning question of the standing army after Sedgemoor.[1] There may, however, be a little fire behind the smoke of this story. We learn from a letter of the French Ambassador, Barillon, dated 26 November, 1685 (N.S.), that the debate of the Commons on the 12th November (O.S.) was "full of heat and disputes." The debate in question was on the Speech from the Throne, the consideration of which had been postponed for three days on the 9th November. This Speech, which demanded additions to the standing army and the retention of "Papist" officers, had, by its offensive matter and tactless wording, succeeded in creating a breach in the overwhelming Tory majority. An opposition to the Court was formed from a coalition of the few Whigs who had seats with a large body of members who, though Tories, regarded the King's arbitrary policy with just apprehensions. The difficulties of organising a solid "country party" out of such material in three days were very great, for nearly all the members of the 1685 Parliament were new-comers to the House, and utterly ignorant of Parliamentary ways. Barillon says significantly, "there was much intriguing on the eve (of the debate). Old Parliamentarians who are not in the present Parliament had coached (*avoient instruit*) the new deputies."[2] What this means is quite clear. The organisers of the new Opposition took advantage of the three days' grace to

---

[1] The author of "The Life of C. Montagu, Earl of Halifax" (in "The Works and Life of the Rt. Hon. Charles, late Earl of Halifax") writes, in atrocious English, that "the Two friends (Dorset and Sedley) violently oppos'd the Court's project of a Standing Army, one of which (Dorset) bore a great sway in the House of Peers, the other in the House of Commons, whose interest was so great in both, especially Sir Charles Sedley's," etc. The tale is repeated in the article on Sedley in "Biographia Britannica" and elsewhere.

[2] Barillon, 26 November, 1685 ("Lettres, etc., d'Angleterre," Vol. 156, f. 224).

take counsel with old Whig members of the Parlia- 1685
ments of Charles II, who had been unseated at the last
election, and who happened to be in town. Sir Charles
Sedley may well have been one of the counsellors
who breathed a spirit of revolt into the wavering
Tories. If this conjecture is well founded, there may
be some truth, after all, in the statement of the writer[1]
who tells us that Sir Charles "had a great sway" in
James II's House of Commons, and that he "violently 1688-90
oppos'd the policy of the Court in that House."

It is probable, as we have noticed above, that Sedley
was a member of the body which assembled to meet
William of Orange on 23 December, 1688, and invited
him to take over the administration till the Convention
was elected. However, in the General Election which
returned the Convention itself, he either did not stand
or was unsuccessful, for the two members for New
Romney were John Brewer and John Chadwick, and
no other constituency elected Sir Charles Sedley. In
the second Parliament of King William, elected in
March 1690, Sir Charles Sedley and John Brewer
were elected at New Romney, and it is in this Parliament that Sir Charles Sedley's political career really
begins. Hitherto he had probably never spoken on
public business, and, like the majority of members, had 1690
confined his parliamentary activities to voting. He now
became an important and influential speaker.

The General Election of 1690 was, perhaps, the first
fought on something like modern party lines, and the
utmost acrimony was displayed by both sides. The
Whigs published lists of members of the Convention
who had voted against declaring the throne vacant, and
stigmatised them as Jacobites, while the Tories set
forth the names of the supporters of the Corporation
Bill,[2] and warned the electors that they were Repub-

---

[1] The author of "The Life of Charles Montagu, Earl of Halifax."

[2] A measure designed to restore the rights of Corporations, which
had been forfeited by James II, to which Sacheverell, the Whig leader,

1690 licans, Fanatics, and Latitudinarians. Many seats were lost and gained by both sides, and when the Houses met, the Tories, together with a considerable body of Whigs, who were discontented with the policy of the Government, had a small but decisive majority.[1] Sedley's political position seems to have been close to that of the discontented Whigs, though he was, apparently, prepared to support the Ministry on certain occasions.

On 31 March,[2] eleven days after the meeting of Parliament, the Commons went into Committee on the question of Supply. They had already voted the revenue of the King and Queen, and were asked by the Government for large sums for the Army, Navy, and Civil List. The last item, a disgracefully long list of pensions for placemen and courtiers, was attacked by Sedley in a witty and manly speech; which made his reputation as a parliamentary orator. Contrasting the ease with which "the Courtiers and Great Officers," helped by their salaries, paid the heavy taxes, with the difficulties of the country gentlemen, he used a vivid image, representing the former as "charging in armour" so that "they do not feel the taxes," while the country gentleman, unaided by a salary from the State, was "shot through and through." He made the very rational suggestion that "we (the Commons) should tell him (the King) what pensions are too great, what places are to be extinguished during the time of War and Public Calamity." In language that recalls a letter which he wrote some years later to Sir Richard Newdigate, he complained that the King "sees nothing but coaches and six and great tables," and "cannot imagine the want

---

had added a clause to prevent any person who had been concerned in the surrendering of the Corporation privileges to James in any way from holding any municipal office for seven years. This clause would have kept nearly all the Tory party out of municipal offices for seven years.

[1] Macaulay, "History of England," ed. Firth, p. 1794. Trevelyan, "England under the Stuarts," p. 452.

[2] Cobbett's "Parliamentary History," V. 562; Sedley's "Miscellaneous Works," 1702 (Speeches, etc.), p. 1. Many MS. copies of this speech exist, and also a printed broadside.

and misery of the rest of his subjects." He concluded in 1690 a sensible and manly strain: "We must save the King money wherever we can, for I am afraid the War is too great for our purses, if things are not managed with all imaginable thrift. When the people of England see all things saved that can be saved, that there are no exorbitant pensions or unnecessary salaries, we shall give and they shall pay whatever his Majesty shall want, to secure the Protestant religion and keep out the King of France, and King James too, whom"—the speaker added, and we can imagine the roar of laughter which greeted this hit at the numerous Jacobites on the Tory benches—"whom, by the way, I have not heard mentioned this Session, but whether out of Fear, Discretion, or Respect I cannot tell."

Although this speech, unfortunately, had no immediate effect on the Government's policy, it had an immense success not only in the House of Commons but all over the country. Indeed, it must have been one of the earliest parliamentary speeches to exercise a considerable influence outside the capital. It was printed and probably hawked as a broadside, and many MS. copies were also circulated. Anthony à Wood, Sedley's old friend at Oxford, received a copy,[1] and, according to a letter dated 5 April, 1690, it caused quite a stir at Worcester, where the local gentry crowded to the coffee-house to read it.[2] It was answered by an anonymous defender of the Government in a broadside entitled "Remarques upon a Late Printed Speech under the Name of Sir Charles Sidley."[3] It may be supposed

---

[1] "The Life and Times of Anthony à Wood," III. 348. Wood states that "it (the speech) was spoken at the beginning of December." He must have blundered, for Cobbett's statement that it was spoken in the debate of 31 March is confirmed by the letter from Worcester quoted below, which is dated 5 April.

[2] Bodleian, Ballard MS., Vol. 35, fol. 59, Letter 34.

[3] "Remarques upon a Late Printed Speech under the Name of Sir Charles Sidley. . . . London. Printed by *W. Bonny*, 1691." See Bibliography.

1690 that the author of this production was paid by the Ministry to put up some kind of a defence against Sedley's widely-read attack. After sneering at Sir Charles's speech as something on which "it would be very silly to throw away ink and paper . . . were it not that there is nothing so absurd, but there are a great many who will readily swallow it," he proceeds to pay it the compliment of answering it in detail. His replies to Sedley's attacks, however, amount to little more than an expression of blind trust in the King and his ministers. The high salaries of the courtiers are defended on the ground that, if the King "means his affairs to prosper, he must provide Encouragement Suitable to the Places he prefers any to." The writer does not, however, attempt to answer Sedley's complaint concerning the difficulty of the country gentlemen in paying the heavy taxes, and he concludes with a curious innuendo to the effect that the real object of the member for New Romney was to promote a republican movement. On Sedley's jest that he had not heard King James mentioned during the Session, "whether out of Fear, Respect or Discretion," his adversary makes the totally unwarranted comment, "Would he have King *James* Voted in again, or made a Pretence to raise such a Confusion, as thereout may spring a Commonwealth ?"

On 3 April the House was again in Committee of Supply, and Sir Charles Sedley called on the Government to adopt a firm policy towards the Irish Jacobites, and retaliate on the administration at Dublin for its confiscations by seizing the estates of its adherents in England in order to prevent their going to Ireland "to support the War."[1] On the 30th a Regency Bill[2] to provide for the administration during King William's

[1] Debates of the House of Commons from . . . 1667 . . . to . . . 1694. Collected by the Hon. Anchitell Grey, 8vo, 1769, X. 40. Cobbett, V. 574.
[2] Cobbett, V. 611.

absence in Ireland had been brought down from the 1690
Lords. This Bill made it lawful for Queen Mary to
"adminiſtrate the government of the kingdom in his
(William's) name and her own," but enaĉted that at
the same time the King should retain all his authority.[1]
Objeĉtion was at once raised on the ground that the
Bill set up two separate powers in the State, and that a
funĉtionary might receive diametrically opposite orders
from the King and Queen; it was also ſtated that the
wording of the Bill would, if it passed into law, cause all
commissions to determine. The debate was, therefore,
poſtponed in order to give members time to hear legal
advice. When it was brought up again on 5 May,
Sedley remarked, sensibly enough, in reply to the
quibbles of the Opposition, that "he could not see any
hurt for so short a time by the authority of the King
and the consent of Parliament."[2] When amendments
were discussed on the next day, he went to the root of
the queſtion by observing that the King could not go
to Ireland (where his presence was urgently needed)
until the Bill was passed. "His foot is in the ſtirrup and
you catch him upon the shoulder and say 'he shall not go.'
Whether the King go or ſtay, leave it to his choice. If
you do not pass the Bill it is impossible for him to go."[3]

On 13 May, Sir Edward Seymour, the Tory leader,
moved that the House should go into Committee "to
consider how to preserve the Peace of the Nation in the
King's absence." Sedley, who had supported the Government on the queſtion of the Regency, now spoke in
favour of Seymour's motion on the ground that Queen
Mary, "though a wise woman," was yet a woman, and
that she would be advised by "some of his own
(William's) Council and some of King *James's* Council,
a mixed Council." This reasoning with its sly allusion
to Tory members of the Council as "King James's

---

[1] Macaulay's "History of England," ed. Firth, IV. 1830.
[2] Anchitell Grey, X. 114; Cobbett, V. 6.
[3] *Ibid.*, X. 131; Cobbett, V. 634.

1690 Council" could hardly have been welcome to Seymour.[1] On the 14th there was a debate on the motion that "the House should go into Committee to consider the Ways and Means to preserve the Peace and Safety of the Kingdom in the King's absence." The Opposition members raised objections to the powers given to the new inner Council[2] or "Cabinet" appointed by William to advise his Queen in his absence. These powers were stated to constitute a suspension of Habeas Corpus.[3] Sedley insinuated, probably with some justice, that the members who were "out" of the Queen's Council were raising difficulties out of jealousy of those who were "in." "I have been cooking this dish many a time,"[4] he said, implying that it was not the first time he had heard such interested complaints. Sir John Guise, one of the Opposition members who spoke later, twitted Sir Charles for his use of this homely metaphor as follows: "I do not doubt of Sedley's cooking and eating well." It may be imagined that Sir Charles joined heartily in the merriment provoked by this allusion to his well-known epicurean tastes. Some members tried to turn the debate into a discussion of the merits of the Marquis of Caermarthen, one of the members of the new Council, who had never been loved by the Commons, and who, under the style of the Earl of Danby, had been impeached by them in the reign of Charles II. Sedley pointed out the irrelevancy of the attacks on this nobleman, and, incidentally, stated that he "had received no disobligation nor any favour from him."[5]

The next Session opened on 22 October, after the King's return from his victorious campaign in Ireland. The Speech from the Throne emphasised the necessity (which was indeed pressing) for maintaining a strong

---

[1] Anchitell Grey, X. 138; Cobbett, V. 639.

[2] This Council consisted of Devonshire, Dorset, Monmouth and Edward Russell (Whigs); Caermarthen, Pembroke, Nottingham, Marlborough and Lowther (Tories).

[3] Cobbett, V. 642.

[4] Anchitell Grey, X. 142; Cobbett, V.   [5] *Ibid.*

fleet and army. On 9 November the Estimates were dis- 1690
cussed in a Committee of Supply. The Opposition
raised cries of protest against what was then considered
the enormous sum of four millions. All that survives
of Sedley's remarks on this occasion is the following
cryptic sentence: "If one member sits in the House in
his buff coat, and another in his shirt, one will be
sweltered while the other's teeth chatter in his head."[1]
Without the context, which seems to be missing, it is
difficult to divine the meaning of this fragment. Perhaps it is again a reference to the fact that the courtiers
could bear the cost of the Estimates more easily than
the country gentlemen.

On 18 November a Bill to amend the barbarous procedure for trials in cases of High Treason was read for
the third time.   It provided that henceforth persons
accused of High Treason should have Counsel, should
be allowed to summon witnesses for the defence, should
be given a copy of the indictment, and that no overt act
should be given in evidence excepting those which were
contained in the indictment. Sedley spoke forcibly in
favour of the Bill, which he defended with the pithy
remark that "good kings, good lawyers and good judges
are perishable commodities,"[2] the obvious inference
being that, instead of trusting to heaven to send them,
it was better to erect barriers against the encroach-
ments of bad ones. He quoted effectively the judicial
murder of Cornish, the London alderman who was
convicted and hanged in the reign of James II on the
evidence of one man with whom he had a private
quarrel. Sedley may very likely have seen the mock trial
of Cornish by the infamous Jeffreys, and his subsequent
execution, and may have remembered the ghastly
cruelty with which the Government of James II pur-
sued their victim, even after his death, by impaling his
head on the Guildhall. On 3 December there was a
debate on the money demanded by the Government for

[1] Anchitell Grey, X. 142; Cobbett, V. 170.   [2] *Ibid.*, 171.

1690 "secret service"—in those days mainly employed in bribery. Sedley made a speech of which probably only a fragment survives. The substance of it seems to have been an ironical defence of the prevailing system of organised parliamentary corruption. "We give great sums," he said, referring to the large supplies voted by the Commons, "but must not receive," and "for secret service no Parliament man ought to be ashamed." The remark that he was "an old Parliament man but a young speaker," confirms the supposition that he had rarely, if ever, spoken on public business before in any previous Parliament. He told the following anecdote to illustrate the principle on which members received bribes:—"One in my company when I was young would needs give the fiddlers two or three pieces though he loved music as little as I; but he went shares with the fiddlers." He concluded by appealing for an inquiry, on the ground that the suspicions cast on the Secret Service accounts were "a Reflection upon every member."[1]

The Bill for regulating trials for High Treason[2] came back from the Lords with an important amendment. Peers indicted of High Treason were formerly tried by the whole House of Lords, if the trial took place while Parliament was sitting; but, if it took place during a recess, they were tried by twelve peers chosen at will by the Lord Steward and called Triers. The Lords pointed out that under this arrangement a Lord High Steward could pack his little court with personal enemies of the accused, if the latter was unfortunate enough to be tried during a recess. They desired that a peer accused of High Treason should always be tried by the whole peerage, whether the Parliament were sitting or not. The Whigs in the Commons, though they could not oppose the Bill itself without denying their fundamental principles, had not supported it with the ardour which they probably would have shown if

[1] Anchitell Grey, X. 198–9; Cobbett, V. 671.
[2] Macaulay, "History of England," ed. Firth, V. 2111–17.

it had been introduced in the reigns of Charles or 1690
James. The present King was in a sense their leader
and the champion of Protestantism and liberty. Acts of
High Treason were likely to be committed, not by
Roundheads or Republicans, but by High Church-
men and Jacobites. They were therefore glad enough
of the occasion which the Lords' amendment offered to
wreck the Bill. Through their brilliant spokesman,
Charles Montague, they represented the Lords as
anxious to extend their already great privileges. A trial
by the whole peerage, they contended, meant a certain
acquittal, as so many peers were related by blood to
each other, and, as attendance was voluntary, the court
would be filled with relatives of the accused. No argument was ever listened to so eagerly by seventeenth-
century Houses of Commons as those which were
directed against an extension of the privileges of the
Lords. Sedley was one of the members who refused to
listen to Montague's appeal to class sentiment. He
urged the Commons to give the Lords "the little shed"
which they demanded to protect their order, and hinted
that, as "some strangers are now made lords,"[1] while
other peers had pensions from the Government, a Lord
Steward's court instituted on the old plan might be as
unjust as those which had sat in former reigns. The reference to the "stranger" Lords glances, of course, at the
Dutch favourites of the King, such as Bentinck,
Zulestein and Keppel.

The next occasion on which Sedley is recorded to
have spoken was when William Fuller, the apostate
Jacobite agent and imitator of Oates and Dangerfield,
was brought at his own request to the Bar of the House
on 9 December, 1691. He had formerly disclosed to 1691
the King some important letters with which he had been
entrusted by Mary of Modena. After living extra-
vagantly on the credit gained by this infamous deed, he
had run through all his own money and much of his

[1] Anchitell Grey, X. 219.

1691 patron's, and had found himself in a debtors' prison. In order to regain his former position he concocted a Jacobite "plot" on the model of Oates's famous performance. He first tried to gain the confidence of Tillotson, Archbishop of Canterbury, and William Bentinck, Lord Portland, the King's favourite adviser. When rebuffed by these dignitaries, he asked permission to tell his tale to the Commons. The substance of it was that a huge Jacobite conspiracy existed in England. Many noblemen were named, and among them the great Marquis of Halifax, who was said to be the ringleader. In the debate that followed these "disclosures," Sedley shrewdly remarked that "this young man has accused so many that were he an angel from heaven, I should not believe him."[1] Later in the debate, however, his scepticism seems to have been shaken, and he pointed to the fact that the Queen had formerly trusted Fuller as evidence that his tale might be true. He suggested that the House should take him under their protection and address the King to reward him, provided that he produced "original papers with hands and seals"—which, of course, was beyond the power of the wretched Fuller. On 4 January Fuller attended the Bar again and told a long story about two persons (apparently in France) who were afraid to come over to England, but who could give important information to the Government. Sedley suggested that "the fellow" (Fuller) should be offered a yacht or messengers[2] "to bring over his informers." The upshot of the matter was that the House, after bearing with Fuller's evasions remarkably patiently, voted him "a Notorious Impostor, a Cheat and false Accuser," and addressed the King to direct the Attorney-General to prosecute him. He ended his career of plot-monger in the pillory.[3]

1691/92 On 11 January 1691/2, various ways of raising money were discussed. Sir Robert Cotton proposed a

---

[1] Cobbett, V. 672.   [2] Anchitell Grey, X. 225.
[3] Macaulay, "History of England," ed. Firth, V. 2136.

subscription among the members. Sedley suggested 1691/92
that the amount should be £500, on the ground that
those who had "good estates" could spare it "out of
their pensions," while for those who had not it was
enough. Sir Edward Seymour's far more acceptable
project of a poll-tax was adopted.[1]

The Fourth Session opened on 4 November, 1692. 1692
The Battle of La Hogue had been fought and won on
19 May, and all danger of a French invasion was for the
time being removed. The Commons, after voting
thanks to Admiral Russell, listened to his narrative of
the victory. A debate followed on the conduct of the
fleet, and the question whether the victory had been
sufficiently followed up was discussed. Sir John Ashby,
Admiral of the Blue, was accused of allowing twenty-six
French ships to escape into St. Malo. The fire-eaters
of the House of Commons were indignant, and Sir
Robert Howard (Sedley's old friend of the days of the
"Essay of Dramatic Poesy") was absurd enough to
quote, as an example for contemporary admirals, the
attack on St. Malo in Cromwell's time, when the Protector sent Blake to batter that town until a priest who
had "abused an Englishman" was delivered up. The
chief evidence against Ashby was the "Rélation" of the
French admiral, Tourville, which had transpired.
Sedley, acknowledging that Tourville's "Rélation"
reflected on Ashley, made the sensible and eminently
just proposal that the Admiral of the Blue should be
allowed to come to the Bar of the House and speak in
his own defence. The House assented to this suggestion
and the Admiral appeared before them on the 19th and
easily cleared himself.

On the 18th November a fresh Bill for Regulating
Trials in cases of Treason was discussed, and Sir
William Whitlock moved its commitment. Sedley
supported the motion on the ground that he did not wish
"to endanger the King's safety," and added—probably

[1] Anchitell Grey, X. 226; Cobbett, V. 692.

1692 in jeſt—as an additional reason, that, if the Bill were committed, "we who cannot make long speeches can speak to parts of it."[1]

The English hatred of the King's Dutch friends, which so frequently manifeſted itself during the reign of William III, found a particularly ignoble expression on the 22nd of this month in the Commons. A motion to address the King to dismiss the foreign general officers in the English service had been proposed. Sedley raised a proteſt which does him credit:—"I think it is the higheſt ingratitude to turn out these Generals. These Gentlemen have been the King's Companions of his Arms: 'twill be hard upon the King to turn them out."[2]

Occasions for Sedley to speak on one of his favourite topics were produced by the famous Place Bills of 1692–4. These measures were direct̄ed againſt the hordes of "placemen," or salaried Government officials, who lived on the public revenue. They were the result of that indignation againſt prodigal public expenditure which Sedley himself had helped to rouse by his celebrated speech in 1690. The objec̄t of the promoters of the "Bill for Free and Impartial Proceedings," as the firſt "Place Bill" was called, was to exclude from the House of Commons all persons receiving salaries from the State. This measure was introduced into the House of Commons on 22 December, 1692. Had it become law, it would, as Macaulay points out,[3] have had a very different effec̄t from that which its promoters designed. For it would have excluded not only the numerous minor officials who were merely paid supporters of the Government, but also the great officers of ſtate, whom we now call Cabinet Miniſters, from the Lower House. The inevitable result would have been that miniſters would have found seats in the Lords, and that the centre of gravity of the conſtitution would have been shifted to the Upper House. After passing the Commons the

---

[1] Anchitell Grey, X. 251. [2] *Ibid.*, p. 255.
[3] Macaulay's "History of England," ed. Firth, V. 2292–4.

Bill was rejected by three votes in the Lords. The second 1692
Place Bill, substantially the same as the first, was
introduced about a year later, in December 1692. In
its original form it had provided that no member of the
House of Commons elected after 1 January, 1694,
should accept any place of profit under the Crown
under pain of forfeiting his seat, and being declared
incapable of sitting again in the same Parliament.
Having passed the Commons, it went up to the Lords,
who made an important amendment by adding to the
clause cited above the following words: "unless he be
afterwards again chosen to serve in the same Parliament." This amendment would have made the law
substantially what it is at the present day. The King,
however, took the view that the Bill was merely an
attempt to encroach upon his prerogative, and refused
the royal assent. On 20 February, 1694/5, a third Place
Bill was introduced. It was rejected by the Commons by
thirty-three votes on the third reading, and, as no copy
has survived, it is impossible to say whether it differed
from its two ill-starred predecessors.

Sir Charles Sedley made two speeches in con- 1692–
nection with these Bills, but no record of the dates of 1694/95
their delivery has survived. Cobbett, in his "Parliamentary History," places them both in the debates on
the first Place Bill, but there is no reason why they
should not have been spoken on the occasion of the
second or third. The earlier of the two seems to have
been delivered before one of the measures was introduced, for its opening words contain a suggestion that
such a Bill should be introduced forthwith: "We shall,
I hope, Mr. Speaker, return to our Vote and make provision by Bill that no member may be concerned in the
Revenue."[1] The second speech seems to have been
delivered soon after, for it contains references to certain
events mentioned in the first. In both Sir Charles

---

[1] "Miscellaneous Works," 1702 (Speeches, etc.), p. 13.

O

1692–
1694/95 alludes ironically to an offer (not elsewhere recorded) made by the placemen to abandon all their profits exceeding £800 a year—if they were allowed to retain their seats in the Commons. Sedley was not inclined to take this offer seriously. He compares it to a similar proposal made by Sir Harry Vane in Cromwell's time, and ironically describes "the raptures of kindness" into which he broke when he heard of the magnanimity of "these worthy gentlemen." The most forcible part of the first speech is a passage which drives home the sound axiom that the real interests of the King and the people under the English constitution alike favoured economy, while those of the placemen were opposed to any reduction in the expenditure. He cites, as a proof, the fact that Charles II, who had landed estates worth £360,000 a year at the Restoration, by yielding to the importunities of courtiers, alienated the whole of the property, and thus injured both himself and the people, who had to pay more taxes to make up the loss. Sedley's old master, "Rowley," would probably have taken a different view of the matter, and Sir Charles does not mention that a large part of the Crown lands was granted, not to courtiers, but to the King's mistresses and natural children.

The second speech suggests that, not only should the salaries of placemen be limited, but also their numbers. It contains a very shrewd criticism of the Cabinet system: "Members of Parliament, though well principled, have no privileges to be fit for anything without practice, study, or application."

1692/93 A Bill providing for Triennial Parliaments passed the Lords without a division in January 1692/3. When it came down to the Commons it was hotly opposed by the Tories and the Opposition Whigs. Sedley spoke against it several times. On 28 January he suggested that another Parliament might not be so "affectionate" as the present one "to oppose the French," and also that an act which dissolved Parliament automatically

was a serious invasion of the King's prerogative.[1] A 1692/93
second and much longer speech, delivered apparently
on the first reading,[2] made an appeal to the deep-
rooted suspicion that the Commons entertained towards
any measure coming from the Lords which was likely to
curtail their privileges. The speaker also argued
against the idea that such a Bill could provide a
security against a bad king. Such a king, he pointed out,
could use Triennial Parliaments, as well as those chosen
in the old manner, to invade the liberties of the nation,
if such were his will, and could exercise his prerogative
of choosing "the Time and Place" of the Session in
order to overawe or cajole the majority (as Charles II
had done at Oxford in 1681). A third speech on the
same subject, delivered on 9 February, makes an appeal
to Cavalier prejudice by warning members that, if the
present House passed an Act dissolving itself, it might
be compared to the Long Parliament of Charles I.
The argument that follows, however, could not have
been appreciated much by the Tories, with whom on
this occasion Sedley found himself in alliance. It is a
plea that the present measure was unnecessary under so
good a king, so staunch a Protestant and such an
indomitable foe to France as William III, and is
enforced by a comparison between that monarch and
his predecessors, Charles II and James II, the latter
a "papist" and the former "suspected for that religion."
Later in this speech, Sedley seems to imply that, if the
Bill had come from the Commons, he might have supported it, but was opposed to "a surprise upon us from
the Lords." Finally, he warns the House that to vote
for this Bill will have the appearance of truckling to the
constituencies in order to obtain re-election. His last
words have a fine manly ring and might be quoted by
honest politicians in all ages.

  "Truly, Sir, for my part I renounce these partial

[1] Anchitell Grey, X. 299.
[2] "Miscellaneous Works," 1702 (Speeches, etc.), pp. 5–9.

1692/93 measures, and if I cannot be chosen on account of general service to the Nation, I will never creep into favour of any sort of men and vote against my judgment."[1]

Sir Charles spoke once more against the Triennial Bill on the 10th. He warned the House that the Commitment of the Bill would be "the best news the Jacobites could possibly have," for it was "putting to an ingenious death a Parliament which served the King and nation well." He disavowed any personal apprehensions of a General Election, and, after recalling his thirty years' service in Parliament, wittily quoted St. Paul's *"Cupio dissolvi."*[2]

1692/93– In spite of Sir Charles's eloquence, the Bill was
1693 carried with a slight amendment lengthening the life of the actual Parliament. The upshot of the matter is curiously linked with literary history. William III, uncertain whether he should veto the Bill or not, sought the advice of the veteran statesman, Sir William Temple. The latter, too infirm to leave his retirement at Moor Park, sent young Jonathan Swift, his secretary, to Kensington with directions to use his talents to persuade the King to acquiesce in the decision of Parliament. Swift's arguments, though doubtless expressed in admirable prose, were of no avail, and William, convinced that the Bill was merely an attempt to encroach on his prerogative, exercised his right of veto. On 5
1693 December, 1693, Sedley warned the House against yielding to the popular prejudice against standing armies. The army was now the nation's defence against "France and Popery." "If Holland is to be destroyed, it is our turn next. . . ." He told members that there was "a great and terrible sum to be raised," and "We cannot be safe without an Army, neither safe at Home nor considerable abroad."[3] Nothing could have been truer or more seasonable that these arguments in the winter of
1693/94 1693/4, but it may be wondered whether the patriotism which seems to inspire them was not mingled with a

---

[1] Cobbett, V. 764.   [2] Anchitell Grey, X. 304.   [3] *Ibid.*, 341.

desire to gain the favour of William III, whose heart 1693/94
was set on the maintenance of a strong English army.

In a Grand Committee held on 26 January to consider the King's rejection of the Bill for Triennial
Parliaments, Sir Charles seems to have attempted to
speak towards the end of the debate, but "was not
heard."[1] On 1 February, in a debate on King William's
answer to the Address in which the Commons protested against his rejection of the Bill for Triennial
Parliaments, Sedley defended the King's attitude as
follows:—"I know not how a crowned Head can descend to other Answer. But an offender at the Bar may
be expected to say he will do so no more." He seems
to have been interrupted by the Opposition, as the rest
of his remarks were inaudible.[2]

At the General Election of November 1695, the 1695
Whigs gained many seats. There was a sharp contest
at New Romney. John Brewer retained his seat, but
Sir Charles Sedley lost his by a single vote to Sir
William Twisden, a Tory who had sat in James II's
Parliament. This isolated Tory victory, in an election
where the tide ran generally in favour of the Whigs,
may be attributed to the Jacobite tendencies of the
inhabitants of New Romney, whose prosperity depended
very largely on the illicit trade which they carried on
with France. Sedley, however, regained the seat, for
Twisden was also elected for Appleby, and so vacated
the Kentish constituency in favour of his adversary.[3]

The only recorded speech delivered by Sedley in the
new Parliament is one which does him great honour.
It is an eloquent and witty plea for a new "Bill for
regulating Tryals for Treason." As we have seen, he
had already laboured to persuade the Commons to pass
several previous Bills designed to remove the scandal
of the old procedure in cases of High Treason. All these
measures had been rejected or dropped. The present

[1] Anchitell Grey, X. 379.   [2] *Ibid.*, 383.
[3] Hasted's "Kent" (ed. 1790), III. 425 (note *y*).

1695/96 Bill passed the Commons in January 1695/6. The Lords, as on former occasions, added a clause providing that the Lord Steward's court for trying peers accused of treason should be constituted in the same manner during a recess as during session: *i.e.* that it should consist of the whole House of Lords. The Commons' refusal to agree to this clause had wrecked all former Bills for reforming Procedure in Cases of Treason. Sedley urged them on this occasion to accept it, arguing very justly that to compel a peer accused of High Treason to be tried by a court which would, in fact, be nominated by the Crown was to treat him worse than "the meanest commoner," who at any rate had the right of challenging his jury. Against the reasoning that nearly all the peers were connected with each other by blood-ties or affinities, and would so be biased in favour of a noble culprit, he pointed out humorously that the peerage were now accustomed to seek alliances in the City rather than among patrician families, and also that there was less to fear from the power of the nobility than formerly, because many of its members were "artificial" or landless lords—"like the Catholick Bishops *in partibus infidelium.*" He recalled very appositely the Declaration of the Prince of Orange at the Revolution, "where nothing is more complained of and abhorred than the Injustice and Corruption of Tryals in King James's Reign." The conclusion of the speech proves that it was delivered at the beginning of the winter Session of 1695/6, for the speaker argues that the present House had hitherto passed nothing but money Bills, and that it was time for them "to do something like a Parliament of England."[1] These words would be seasonable in January 1695/6, when the High Treason Bill was the first piece of legislation unconcerned with finance that passed the House. The Bill, with the disputed clause, was carried in the Commons by a majority of forty-two, and received the Royal Assent on 21 January.

[1] "Miscellaneous Works," 1702 (Speeches, etc.), p. 21.

The General Election of December 1698 resulted in 1698
a kind of stalemate. Neither the ministerial Whigs nor
the Tories gained many seats, but the body of independent Whigs who did not support the Ministry
consistently came back to Westminster in considerable
force. Sedley, who would probably have reckoned himself among the last-named group, was returned for New
Romney with his old colleague, John Brewer.

One of the first questions to be discussed was that
of the reduction of the land forces. The long struggle
with France had come to an end with the Peace of
Ryswick in September 1697, and the nation, with its
profound mistrust of standing armies, was anxious to
reduce the large war establishment as soon as possible.
The King, on the other hand, who knew more about
European politics than any of his subjects, could see
that the peace was likely to be little more than a truce,
and, in his opinion, a strong English army was necessary in order to maintain the position of equality with
France which he had won for his adopted country.
The Whig ministers, Somers and Montague, explained
to their master the fanatical antipathy of the Commons
to the idea of a large standing army. The King, who
never understood the temper of the English Parliament,
refused to heed their warning that, if a large military
establishment were demanded of the Commons by the
Ministry, there would be such an outburst of indignation that the House would probably vote the disband-
ing of the whole existing force. When the Commons
went into Committee on the Army Vote, the ministers,
having been unable to come to an agreement with the
King, remained silent, and Harley, the Tory leader,
moved the reduction of the land forces to 7000 men.
Sir Charles Sedley made a remarkable speech in the
debate that followed.[1] It was a succinct and temperate
piece of reasoning, urging upon the House a com-

[1] "Miscellaneous Works," 1702 (Speeches, etc.), pp. 4–5. Macaulay's
"History of England," ed. Firth, VI. 2864.

1698 promise between the King's view and that of the Opposition. He began by recalling the fact that he had always supported the Government during the long struggle with France, but proceeded to point out that the difference between those days and the present was a material one: "that was War, this is Peace." He then argued against the view of "those"—there is little doubt that he refers to the King and his advisers—who "think that England cannot be safe without a standing army of 30,000 men because France has 20,000." Against this reasoning, which he admitted would be unanswerable if England were a continental power, he asked the House to consider that, while we maintained a naval supremacy, no army could be very formidable to us, and demonstrated the difficulty of landing large forces in a hostile country by the examples of the Armada, the recent English attempts on Brest, and William's own landing in England at the Revolution, which, he said, could only have been permitted "by an infatuated prince." Finally, he suggested 10,000 men as a reasonable establishment, and the concluding sentence of his speech was an admirable expression of the spirit of the most sensible part of the nation.

"If we are true to our selves, 10000 Men are enough; if not, 100000 are too few." Unfortunately, the Government was too timid to consent to Sedley's proposal and Harley's vote for 7000 men was carried. The result was a long and painful struggle between King and Parliament, which might have been avoided if the King and his ministers had accepted Sedley's figure; for there is little doubt that the Commons would also have accepted it, if it had been supported by the ministers.

There is no record that Sedley spoke again in this Parliament. He kept his seat till his death in August 1701, 1701, and was succeeded by Edward Goulston, probably a relative of the Sir William Goulston who had sat for New Romney in James II's Parliament. Goulston

was returned with Sedley's old colleague, John Brewer, 1701
at the General Election of December 1701.[1]

Sedley may be classed as one of the Old Whigs,
who frequently voted with the Tories in the parliaments of William III. The following extract from
Dr. Charles Davenant's "The True Picture of an
Old Whig" describes his position fairly accurately.
It is spoken by one of the "New Whigs," with whom
such men as Sedley had little in common:—

"As for the Old Whigs in King Charles's time
many of them are dead, some of them are retired,
being ashamed to see their party play the knave as
soon as ever they got into power. Many of those
that still remain on the stage . . . vote every day
with Seymour, Musgrave and Jack How. What have
we in us that resembles the Old Whigs? They hated
arbitrary government, we have all along been for a
standing army: they desired triennial parliaments,
and that trials for treason might be better regulated;
and it is notorious that we opposed both those bills.
They were for calling corrupt ministers to account;
we have ever countenanced and protected corruption
to the utmost of our power. They were frugal for
the nation, and careful how they loaded the people
with taxes; we have squandered away their money as
though there could be no end of England's treasure."[2]

The chief glories of Sedley's parliamentary career
are his campaign against the scandalous army of
"placemen," and his long fight for the reform of the
old inhuman procedure in trials for treason. He
deserves an honourable place beside Edmund Waller
and Andrew Marvell, the other two distinguished
poets who sat and spoke in seventeenth century
parliaments.

[1] Hasted's "Kent," I. 425.
[2] Dr. Charles Davenant, "Political and Commercial Works," ed.
Whitworth, 1771. IV. 152.

CHAPTER IX

THE SEDLEYS AFTER THE REVOLUTION

"Sir Charles lived many years after the Revolution in full possession of his wit and humour and was an agreeable companion till his death."—"Biographia Britannica," s.a. Sir Charles Sedley.

"Au plaisir, maladroitement proscrit par le puritanisme, et déshonoré par les gens de la Restauration, il faut rendre sa place dans la vie sociale; en dépit de ses ennemis, en dépit surtout des ses amis, il faut le réhabiliter. Dans le plaisir, bien et largement compris, dans le plaisir délicat et intelligent, la raideur puritaine trouvera une détente nécessaire, et le soi-disant beau monde un dérivatif salutaire et durable à ses amusements grossiers et abjects."—Beljame: "Le Public et les Hommes de Lettres . . .," ed. 1897, p. 306, 7.

IT is not easy for a rake to grow old gracefully; in fact, if he remains a rake, it is nearly impossible. The vices of youth can look almost charming through a glittering veil of freshness and laughter. Those of old age stand out in all their hideous nakedness. Even the minor sins of idleness and selfishness, which are often attractive or excusable in the young, appear hateful when they are found in company with grey hairs. Wycherley was far from being the satyr of Macaulay's caricature, but the spectacle of the old beau trying to maintain the same position among the wits of the new generation as that which he had held among his contemporaries thirty years before—and devoting all his time to that task—is not a pretty one. Sedley was saved from this fate, partly no doubt by his own good sense, and partly, perhaps, by the influence of Ann Ayscough. In 1688 he was forty-nine. During the remaining thirteen years of his life he continued to be a wit, a poet, and a good companion, but he also assumed two new characters which were far more appropriate to his years: those of an active and useful politician and an excellent father.

On 12 March, 1688/9,[1] shortly after King William's 1688/89 coronation, the son of Ann Ayscough, known as Charles Sedley, was knighted by the King. He is said to have been a minor when he received this honour, and, if born in 1672, would now be seventeen. It may be supposed that his father, as one of King William's earliest supporters, hastened to present his son at Court, and to obtain for him a knighthood, which, in those days, was usually conferred on the legitimate heirs of baronets, and might be considered to remove to some extent the stain of illegitimacy.

Sir Charles Sedley appears to have proved his loyalty to the new Government by giving it some financial support, to judge from a receipt signed by him for £4618 0s. 8d., paid by Francis Villiers and the Tellers of Receipt of their Majesties' Exchequer, apparently in respect of a loan and interest.[2] Sedley may have lent this sum to the Prince of Orange when the Provisional Government was hard pressed for money before the assembly of the Convention. There is no date on the receipt, but it is written on the back of a scrap of a printed official document bearing the date of 6 November, 1689, so it is probable that the 1689 money was paid in the late autumn of that year.

[1] "Le Neve's Knights" (Harl. Soc.), p. 419.
[2] The exact wording of the receipt is as follows:—"Recd by me Charles Sedley of Francis Villiers Esq and of ye Tellers of their Ma^{ts} Recpt of Excheq^r £4618:0:8 ye sum of four thousand and Six hundred eighteen Pound eight Pence in full of Principall & interest of ye wth in written [Orders?] (word cut through) Charles Sedley." This document is in the possession of Mr. G. Thorn Drury, who has kindly allowed me to see and copy it.

*c.*1688/89   It is at the Court of William III that we are able
to catch our one glimpse of Sir Charles at divine
service. Lloyd, Bishop of St. Asaph, one of the
famous Seven who resisted James II, was Lord High
Almoner after the Revolution and preached frequently
at Court. He spent much of his time in elaborate and
mystical speculations on biblical chronology, and his
sermons were usually discourses on that subject,
which did not lend itself to brevity. One Easter
Day, Lloyd "being got into his chronology, which he
had begun from the Creation," Sir Charles was slip-
ping quietly out when he met Mulgrave coming in.
"Well," said Mulgrave, "has he almost done?" "No,"
replied Sedley, "not by 1600 years, for he has got
but to the Nativity yet."[1]

1690–   The measure of favour which Sir Charles enjoyed
1690/91 at Court does not seem to have lasted long. A coolness may well have arisen on account of his speech
against the Government on the question of the "placemen" delivered on 31 March, 1690, which was
printed and circulated widely.[2] Although the reference to the King himself in this speech is complimentary, the picture of him as the dupe of "crafty
courtiers" could hardly have been pleasing to William.
Soon afterwards Sedley fell under the suspicion of
Jacobitism. In January 1690/91, his house in Bloomsbury Square was searched "upon an information that
the Bishop of Ely was harboured there."[3] This Bishop
of Ely was the well-known non-juror, Francis Turner.
After the Revolution he had refused to take the oaths
to the new Government, and, later, entered into a
treasonable correspondence with the Court of St.
Germains. He was associated with Lords Preston,
Dartmouth and Clarendon, and William Penn, the

---

[1] This anecdote is preserved in Bishop Hough's "Table-Talk,"
s.d. 19 January, 1742, printed in "Collectanea," Second Series, ed.
Montagu Burrows, Oxford, 1890.
[2] See pp. 182–84.   [3] Luttrell's "Brief Relation," II. 158.

Quaker, in the secret league of Protestant Jacobites, 1690 who sent a collection of messages to James in the Autumn of 1690, exhorting him to rely for his restoration on his Protestant subjects, and to abandon the idea of imposing Romanism on England by means of a French army. These papers, together with others containing useful information for the exiled Court, had been seized by Lord Danby, son of the Lord President, Caermarthen, on 31 December, 1690. One of the messengers who carried them, and who was arrested by Danby, was Lord Preston, brother of Colonel James Grahame of Kendal, James's confidant and Katherine Sedley's friend. Among the papers was a letter from the Countess of Dorchester to her royal lover, containing a desperate appeal for money for herself and her daughter.[1] From this circumstance it may be supposed that Katherine was to some extent associated with the conspiracy.[2] It is possible that her father took pity on her destitute condition, and that she went to stay with him at Bloomsbury Square, where she may have received the Bishop of Ely and other Jacobite conspirators.

William was not the man to take vengeance on a woman who was, after all, only demanding what was due to her from her lover, and Lady Dorchester, whom nothing could abash, appeared boldly at the new Court. Observing that Queen Mary "looked coldly upon her," she remarked that "if it was upon her father's account, she hoped she would remember that,

---

[1] Macaulay, "History," ed. Firth, IV. 694.

[2] It is possible that she joined the conspiracy as a spy in the interests of King William. According to a letter of Nottingham to William dated 15 July, 1690 (printed in Dalrymple's "Memoirs of Great Britain and Ireland," 4to, 1773, Vol. III., Appendix, Pt. II. p. 108), information concerning the plans of the Jacobite party had been given to Nottingham by the Countess of Dorchester and Mr. James Grahame; shortly before the letter was written the latter had taken the oaths to King William. See also Finch MSS. (Hist. MSS. Comm., 1922), pp. 360, 391, 392.

1690 as she had broke one commandment with him, her Majesty made no scruple of breaking another; therefore (she) thought they were even on that score."[1]

c. 1691 The Countess also attended the Court of the Princess Anne of Denmark, the Queen's sister, in "grate splendor," covered with diamonds, and no doubt the "shocking creature"[2] glared at her old rival, Sarah Jennings, now Lady Churchill and bosom friend of the Princess. She seems to have found some favour in the eyes of King William, and, by the help of the Duke of Shrewsbury, succeeded in obtaining from him a private audience. A contemporary[3] considered that he was not "in love with her," but that he "feared the lash of her tounge, soe chooses not to anger her." Whatever the politic Dutchman's reasons may have been for conciliating the Countess, there is no doubt that he ordered that she should receive a pension of £1500 a year.[4] Possibly he took the view that she was, in her way, a sufferer for the Protestant cause. Katherine's comment was that "she knew not well, very well what shee would wish might happen, for both the queenes us'd her badly, and both kinges, she said, were civil to her."

[1] Lord Dartmouth's note to Burnet's "History of his Own Times," III. 13, 14, ed. 1824. The Countess obviously intends the seventh and fifth commandments.   [2] See p. 136, note 2.

[3] The contemporary in question is a lady (otherwise unknown) who seems to have been a mistress of James II and rival to Lady Dorchester. All the information in this paragraph is derived from a most interesting letter written by this lady to the exiled King and printed in the *Gentleman's Magazine* in October 1802. It was sent to Mr. Urban by a writer signing himself "Historicus," who claimed to have found it among "some papers of Dr. Stukely." The text is followed by the words: [This is a true coppy of a letter found in a shoe heele in my shopp at Grantham. Phillip Cooke.] The letter is dated "May the 29th." I conjecture that the year is 1691, for the public, apparently, learned that Katherine was to receive a pension from William III on 1 May, 1691. See note 4 below.

[4] Luttrell's "Brief Relation," II. 220, s.d. 1 May, 1691. A receipt for £400 "being one quarter's allowance for her daughter Katherine Darnley" dated 27 May, 1691, is extant (Bodl., Rawl. A. 306, 268).

Proof of Sir Charles Sedley's temporary disgrace, 1691
and also of his desire to regain the King's favour, is
to be found in a letter from him to the Earl of Dorset,
now Lord Chamberlain. This letter, which is undated,
is preserved among the Sackville family papers,[1] and
must have been written towards the end of October
1691, as it refers to the imminent death of Major-
General Kirke (the Kirke of Tangiers and the Western
Rebellion), who died on 31 October, 1691.[2]

"MY LORD,
        I am told that Major General Kirke is
either dead or very neare it: soe the office of
house keeper at Whitehall will soddainly bee in
the dispose either of the king or your lordship.
The vallew of it is Six hundred a year, which
will helpe me to pay the taxes wee must give
this Sessions and I am afrayd for many Yeares
more yet: I am neither ambitious nor covetous,
and only desire to put myselfe by his Maj[esties]
favor in the Condition I was before these extraordinary tho I confess most necessary payments.
the place is under your lordship, whom I shall
find noe difficulty to obey. I [h]ope you will be
soe kind to show my request to his Majesty
before he bee otherwise engaged, my lord Sydney
will second you as also lord Devonshire: if you
espouse my cause warmly I doubt not but I shall
prevayle, these are things that other men obtane
for their friends and I cannot see why your
lordships mediation should not be as effectuall
as any mans for one of yours, especially the place
being under you if not in your dispose: I thought

---

[1] This letter is calendared in the Hist. MSS. Comm., Appendix
to 4th Report, p. 281. I have been allowed to read, copy and reproduce the original by the kindness of its present owner, Lord Sackville
of Knole Park, Kent.
[2] D. N. B., s.a. Kirke, Major-General.

1691

to have spoken to you last night but you slipt off to bed ere I was aware. Tho I am an old friend and servant I will be ready to make any present where your lordship shall direct, for I am not ignorant at what [ra]te these favours are sought after.

Your Most humble and faithful
servant
CHAR[LES] SEDLEY."[1]

There is something pathetic in the mixture of flattery and earnestness in this appeal to an old friend and playmate. It is a melancholy fact that Dorset—in spite of his famous "good nature"—does not seem to have troubled to exert himself on Sedley's behalf. Kirke was succeeded by his son, who held the post of House-keeper at Whitehall till that palace was burnt in 1697/8.

1691/92   In May 1692, Sir Charles seems to have made an attempt to regain the royal favour by writing a pretty Ode for Queen Mary's birthday. It was set to music by the greatest contemporary English musician, and probably sung to the Queen on her birthday morning. Peter Motteux printed it in his "Gentleman's Journal, or the New Monthly Miscellany," for May 1692. This periodical, first issued in January 1691/2, was one of the earliest English literary journals. Sedley was a frequent contributor, and was probably acquainted with Motteux, a literary free-lance of the period, still remembered for his excellent translation of "Don Quixote."

On 19 November, 1692, Sedley's old friend, Thomas Shadwell, died at his house at Chelsea.[2] Through Dorset's influence he had been appointed Poet Laureate after the Revolution, when Dryden as

---

[1] Letters enclosed in square brackets are partially or wholly effaced in the original.

[2] D. N. B., s.a. Thomas Shadwell.

a Catholic and a Jacobite lost his official position. 1691/92
This great merry tun of a man, who continued to
write jolly, racy comedies to the end, seems to have
had a real affection for Sedley, who had probably
helped him materially in the hard times (for a Whig
poet) before the Revolution. He mentions Sir Charles
in touching language in his will, appointing him
trustee for his widow and leaving him a gold ring
"weighing twenty shillings," with the motto "memor
esto tui."[1]

Sir Charles must have regained King William's 1694
favour by the spring of 1694. There was probably
some connection between this reconciliation and his
speech in the Commons on 5 December, 1693, when
he urged on the House the necessity of maintaining
a standing army.[2] There was no surer way to William's
friendship than to aid him in any conceivable manner
in his lifelong struggle with the power of France.
On 8 May it was rumoured in London that Sir Charles
Sedley was going to be created an English Viscount.[3]
This rumour probably represents the intention of the
Government. Why it was never carried into effect
remains a mystery. Perhaps Sedley again threw away
his chances by some plain speaking in the Commons.
It is worthy of notice that on 10 May the Earl of
Mulgrave, Sir Charles's old enemy, was created
Marquis of Normanby.

During these years Sir Charles Sedley was probably
occupied a good deal with the education of his son by
Ann Ayscough. This young man, though he seems
to have had no literary ambitions, was intelligent and
affectionate. Old Tom D'Urfey, writer of innumerable
songs and plays, and a sort of privileged jester among
the Wits, had known Sedley from his youth, and was

---

[1] MS. Notes formerly in the possession of Col. Prideaux, now in
the collection of Mr. G. Thorn Drury.

[2] See p. 197.

[3] Luttrell's "Brief Relation," III. 307, s.d. 8 May, 1694.

P

1695 probably a frequent visitor at the house in Bloomsbury Square. Writing some years later he describes
the relationship between the elder and the younger
Sedley as one which might serve as a model to all
sons and fathers: "there being more between you
than the Ordinary Duty and Love Incumbent between
Father and Son, an entire, free and easie Friendship—
Submission and Satisfaction on your [the son's] side—
and Contentment with Pleasure on his [the father's]."[1]
These words call up a very charming picture of the
elder Sir Charles walking and reading with a young
man who had replaced the conventional awe of seventeenth-century children towards their parents by a
frank and affectionate comradeship. No doubt the lad
was taken by his father to Will's Coffee House, and
there presented to the great Mr. Dryden as he sat in
his armchair in the sunshine on the balcony, taking
snuff and laying down the law to a hushed circle of
powdered and periwigged admirers. As there is no
record that the younger Sir Charles entered either of
the Universities, it is probable that he was educated
by a tutor at home under his father's supervision.
This tutor may have been the Rev. Laurence Echard,
who dedicated an excellent translation of three comedies
of Plautus to Sir Charles Sedley senior in 1694.

If the younger Sir Charles did not inherit his
father's literary talent, he seems to have had a full
share of his audacity and hot blood. He fell in love
with Frances Newdigate, a girl of eighteen, third
daughter of Sir Richard Newdigate, a Warwickshire
baronet, and married her without the knowledge
either of his father or Sir Richard, at the lady's
home at Arbury in Warwickshire, on 8 May, 1695.[2]
Sir Richard was a man of an arbitrary disposition

---

[1] Epistle Dedicatory to "The Intrigues of Versailles, or a Jilt in
All Humours" (4to, 1697).

[2] Lady A. E. Newdegate-Newdigate's "Cavalier and Puritan,"
p. 191.

and a fiery temper, and his daughter probably feared 1695
that he would refuse his consent to a marriage
with a young man of illegitimate birth who was
entirely dependent on his father's bounty. The younger
Sir Charles came to London after the marriage, and
took the wise course of asking his father's old friend,
the Earl of Dorset, now Lord Chamberlain, to break
the news to Sir Charles Sedley senior, and help him
to make his peace with his father. Dorset seems to
have consented, and probably won Sir Charles's forgiveness easily. The latter was not likely to be harsh
on the escapades of a high-spirited young man. The
real difficulty was to approach Sir Richard Newdigate, from whom the young couple naturally expected
a dowry. The elder Sir Charles resolved to make use
of a common friend, and chose a certain Sir Thomas
Rowe for the purpose. His letter to that gentleman
(written in July 1695) is a model of diplomatic
caution:[1]

> "Sʳ
>
>   Since I saw you my Lord Chamberlain
> came to me and truly surprized me with the
> news of my son's being actually married to Mrs.
> Frances Newdigate. It is a matter that ought to
> be more considered off and not thus transacted
> without the privity or consent of parents. I was
> very angry with my son for his proceeding in
> this matter with such precipitation—not that I
> have not all the value imaginable for the young
> lady and for the Character all the world gives
> Sʳ Richard Newdigate of a very honorable,
> worthy and judicious person. But I think (as

[1] It is preserved among the Newdigate family papers, and has
been printed by Lady A. E. Newdegate-Newdigate in her "Cavalier
and Puritan," p. 191. It was probably given by Sir T. Rowe to Sir
R. Newdigate and was endorsed by him "18 July 1695 Sr C. S. senior
to Sr Thomas Rowe about his sons marrying Frank (*i.e.* Frances)
without his or my consent."

1695   perhaps he may) that the young couple ought not to have gone so far, but have waited for our Consent, upon which their well being so much depends. After his many submissions I have forgiven my Son, and shall do all I can to make the young couple easy. I hope S^r you will do them both good offices with Sr Richard and make the discovery to him with all alleviating circumſtances so rash an aċtion will admit of. I know this is too much trouble to impose on you upon so slender an acquaintance, but necessity muſt be my excuse, having not the good fortune to know anyone who is like to see Sr Richard Newdigate but yourself.

Y^r moſt faithful humble servant

CHARLES SEDLEY."

The mediation of Sir Thomas seems to have been successful, and soon after,[1] Sir Charles Sedley wrote direċtly to Sir Richard Newdigate as follows:—

  "S^r
   I am sorry your Daughter continues so ill, having a nearer concern in her now then I expeċted so suddenly. Since my laſt to you My Lord Chamberlain told me my son and the young lady were aċtually married. I confess it surprised me, and I was very angry that he did not wait for yours as well as my consent in a matter of so much importance to us all. I believe he chose to break it to me by my Lord rather than tell it to me himself, concluding that the great Value I have for my Lord could not but much abate my resentment, especially when he became his advocate. As soon after as possible I writ to Sir Thomas Rowe to entreat him to represent the whole matter to you in the beſt

[1] This letter is undated. It is printed in "Cavalier and Puritan," p. 193.

circumstances so rash an action would admit of. 1695 I had not curiosity enough to enquire into my son's motives, nor can I dwell with pleasure on the arguments till I receive your Judgment and apprehensions of it, which I hope will be the same with mine: which are since it is now past remedy, that we should transact together for the ease and comfort of the young couple, and mutually endeavour to satisfy each other as well as their reasonable expectations. If the young lady's condition of health will bear such a Journey, we think here that change of air, together with the help of our London doctors, might further her recovery. But you, S^r, are the best and properest Judge.

Your most faithful and humble servant
CHARLES SEDLEY.

Give my blessing to my Daughter and service to all the rest of your Good Family, if you think fit."

Sir Charles's affection for his son, mingled with a determination to mollify Sir Richard, can be read in every line of this letter. It is impossible to believe that his "resentment" can have been very formidable, and the closing sentences are doubtless an artful plea to obtain for the bridegroom the presence of his beloved. The bride had certainly fallen ill after the wedding and her husband also seems to have been ailing. The following letter is the only extant composition by that young man. It is addressed to Sir Richard Newdigate and docketed by the Warwickshire baronet "Sir C. S. junior, his excuse for marrying Frank without my Consent."

"S^r

Had not my illness prevented my writing I had before presented my humble duty and

1695

thanks for your great kindness to me, and begged your pardon for my presumption in marrying your daughter without acquainting you with it. I hope I shall always carry myself with that great Submission and duty, you will easily pardon a fault my infinite passion for your daughter made me Commit. I shall be at Banbury next Friday night and there Sr Thomas Rowe will do me the favour to meet me, and he will wait on you with

Yr moſt dutiful and obedient Son,

CHARLES SEDLEY.

Tuesday 16th July, 1695."

Sir Richard, softened no doubt by the illness of the bride and bridegroom, seems to have forgiven them at length, and to have recognised the younger Sedley as his son-in-law, though complications between the two families were to follow later.

The summer in which the younger Sir Charles Sedley won his bride saw one of the moſt ſtirring incidents in the gigantic ſtruggle between William III and Louis XIV. In July 1692 the French armies, with their King at their head and the great Vauban as their Chief Engineer, had taken the fortress of Namur, hitherto considered impregnable, and Boileau had celebrated the feat in lyric ſtrains. In 1695 the tide which had flowed so ſteadily againſt William all his life began to turn. Luxembourg, the greateſt of French Marshals, was dead, and the generalissimo of Louis's forces in Flanders was Villeroy, a Court favourite with hardly a single qualification for high command. His lieutenants, Boufflers and Catinat, were able generals, but were hampered by the feeble leadership of the commander-in-chief. William had set his heart on retaking Namur, which he rightly regarded as the key to Flanders, and spent

the opening of the campaigning season of 1695 in 1695
feinting in order to conceal his true objective from
Villeroy. So well did he succeed that, at the beginning
of July, while his lieutenant, the Prince de Vaude-
mont, was holding the French commander in check,
he succeeded in driving Boufflers with a large force
into Namur, and opened the siege of that city on
2 July. Numerous and heavy bets were laid on the
issue of this siege in London.[1] The occasion was
probably one of the first of many similar ones when
the sporting instincts of the English people expressed
themselves in this way. Sir Charles Sedley, whose
expenses must have been considerably increased by
the necessity of having to maintain a grown-up son,
was not averse from the idea of gaining a sum of ready
money in a gentlemanly way. He laid a wager which
must have been one of the earliest connected with
the siege, for it seems to have turned on the question
whether Namur was actually invested or not. That
he was not above using his friendship with the Earl
of Dorset to obtain information in a way that would
not now be considered strictly honourable is, unfortunately, proved by a note in his handwriting,
preserved among the Sackville papers.[2] This scrap
of paper, which has survived by pure accident, may
have been handed to Dorset by a servant as he sat
among his friends one evening at Knole, and thrown
carelessly by the Earl into a drawer. It may be dated
perhaps in the first week of July 1695:—

> "If I did not misunderstand your Lordship
> you told us at dinner that the king had beseigd
> Namur pray doe me the favour to let me receive
> a line or tow whither or noe it bee beseigd, for

[1] L'Hermitage, agent of the States General in England, quoted
by Macaulay, "History of England," ed. Firth, V. 2530.
[2] At the Public Record Office. I am allowed to copy and reproduce
it by the kindness of Lord Sackville.

1695   I have layd a small wager: which I may get off
from, or add to, ackording to your answer: I
will not show your lordships hand to any one.
Your moſt humbl
Servant

CHARLES SEDLEY."

Both the writer and the recipient would probably
have been amazed had they known that this note was
going to keep alive the memory of a small mean deed
for two hundred years.

The Countess of Dorcheſter, having obtained her
pension from King William, was determined to defend
her rights to the utmoſt. A Bill was introduced into
the Commons in January 1695 to reward the popular
admiral, the Earl of Torrington, with large grants of
lands. Among the lands that it was proposed to give
to the successful sailor were some of the domains
that had been assigned to the Countess by James II.
Katherine appeared at the bar of the House in person
on 18 January,[1] to lodge her proteſt, and gave a
long account of her wrongs. The House, probably
moved by her wit and courage, added a clause to the
Bill in March granting her £4000 arrears and an
1696–99 annuity of £600.[2] On 20 Auguſt, 1696, she took a
further ſtep towards consolidating her position in
respeᴄtable society by marrying Sir David Colyear,[3]
a Scottish baronet, "very much a man of honour,"
who had served with diſtinᴄtion under William III
in Flanders. The capture of this hardened veteran
was Dorinda's crowning achievement. Dorset cele-

---

[1] Luttrell's "Brief Relation," 18 January, 1695, IV. 6.

[2] *Ibid.*, IV. 29.

[3] Luttrell's "Brief Relation," IV. 99, s.d. 20 August, 1696. Macky
in his "Characters" (quoted in D. N. B., s.a. Colyear, Sir David)
gives the following description of Colyear "towards fifty years old":
"he is one of the best foot officers in the world; is very brave and
bold; hath a great deal of wit; very much a man of honour and nice
in that way, yet married the Countess of Dorchester and had by her
a very good estate; pretty well shaped, dresses clean, has but one
eye."

brated the feat in the laſt of his cycle of squibs on the 1696–99
Countess:

> "Proud with the Spoils of Royal Cully,
>   With false pretence to Wit and Parts,
> She swaggers like a batter'd Bully,
>   To try the tempers of Men's Hearts.
>
> Tho she appear as glitt'ring fine,
>   As Gems, and Jests, and Paint can make her;
> She ne'er can win a Breast like mine,
>   The Devil and Sir David take her."[1]

---

[1] "Poems on Affairs of State," Vol. III., "printed in the year 1704,"
p. 440. The following is a MS. version of this poem and the verses on
Lady Dorchester already quoted, which is preserved in the Bodleian
(Bodl., Add. MS. A. 301, f. 194). It contains an additional stanza
which, I believe, has never been printed:—

> "Dorsett on Dorchest^r.
>
> I
>
> Dorinda's Sparkling witt & eyes,
>   United caste too feirie a light;
> W^ch Blazes high but quickly dyes,
>   Warmes not ye Heart, but hurts ye sight.
>
> 2
>
> Love is a calme and tender Joy
>   Kind are his lookes and soaft his pace,
> Her Cupid is a Black-Guard Boy,
>   Who runs his Linke into yor face.
>
> 3
>
> Proud of ye spoyles of Roy^ll Cully,
>   W^th false p^rtence to witt and parts,
> She swaggers like a Batterd Bully;
>   To trye ye temper of o^r Hearts.
>
> 4
>
> Tho she appears as Gay, & fine
>   As Jests, and Gems & Paint can make her;
> She ne're shall win a heart like mine,
>   The Devill, or Sr Davy take her.
>
> 5
>
> Her Bed is like ye Scripture feast,
>   Where none whoe were invited came,
> Soe disappoynted of her Guest,
>   She took up wth ye Blind and Lame."

1696-99 Another contemporary lampoon gives a vivid if malicious picture of the Countess in 1698, and was probably written by someone who had come under the lash of her wit:—

> "A wither'd Countess next, who rails aloud
> At the reigning Vices of the Croud (*sic*),
> And with the product of that ill turn'd Brain,
> Does all her guests at Visits Entertain;
> Thinks it a crime for any one to be
> Either ill-Natur'd or as lewd as she.
> A Sovereign Judge over her Sex does sit,
> Giving full Scope to her injurious Wit.
> Too old for Lust and proof against all Shame,
> Her only business now is to defame;
> She hath done well the one ey'd Knight to chuse,
> For one, who's two wou'd ne're endure the noose."[1]

On 1 June, 1699, Sir David was created Earl of Portmore. He had two sons by Lady Dorchester, the elder of whom became the second Earl of Portmore. When they were sent to school, the mother is said to have given them the following characteristic piece of advice:—"If any body call either of you the son of a . . . . ., you must bear it; for you are so: but if they call you bastards, fight till you die; for you are an honest man's sons."[2]

1696   In the spring of 1696 the mysterious suspicion of Jacobitism cast upon Sir Charles seems to have been revived. If it had any foundation in fact, he was only doing the same as hundreds of other prudent, if unheroic, persons in corresponding with the Court of St. Germains. Everybody knew that a restoration of

---

[1] From a poem entitled "Answer to J. Pulteney's Letter, Why I do not let my Wife keep some sort of Company, 1698," which occurs on f. 198 of a folio MS. formerly the property of Sir William Augustus Frazer. It was copied by Mr. Thorn Drury, who kindly communicated it to me. The second line is probably defective and, perhaps, the original reading was "At all the reigning Vices," etc.

[2] Jesse's "Memoirs of the Courts of England under the Stuarts," III. 507-8. Jesse quotes no authority for this anecdote. It must be genuine: no one but Katherine could have made such a remark.

King James II was possible, and that such a restora- 1696 tion would probably be followed by a campaign of confiscation and proscription far more terrible even than that which followed Sedgemoor. Whatever the truth of the matter may be, Sedley's name certainly occurs in notes on persons suspected of Jacobitism, dated "March to June, 1696," compiled by the great Whig leader, the Duke of Shrewsbury,[1] who himself, in a moment of weakness, trafficked with agents of King James. It should, of course, be remembered that Jacobite informers in the reign of William III frequently accused entirely innocent persons in order to divert suspicion from the real conspirators.

In spite of these suspicions, Sedley seems to have been on good terms with King William in 1696. Before the King left England for Holland on 7 May, 1696, he told Sir Charles that he "would let him know to whom he should apply as to a promise formerly made."[2] In a letter dated 23 June in the same year, the Duke of Shrewsbury, at Sedley's request, reminded the King of this promise. What the promise was can only be guessed. If it referred to the title of Viscount (as the words "formerly made" may imply), Sir Charles was destined to be disappointed, for he died a commoner.

A good deal of dispute seems to have arisen in the autumn of 1696 between the Sedleys and the Newdigates concerning the knotty question of "settlements." An extract from Sir Richard Newdigate's Diary, dated November 1696, throws some light on the quarrel:

> "Paid my daughter Sedley's maid £1. Sir Charles Sedley refuses to pay her upon pretence that I will not pay my Daughter's Portion, whereas the true case is this; young Sir Chas. married my daughter Frank without my consent,

[1] Hist. MSS. Comm., Report on MSS. of Duke of Buccleuch & Shrewsbury, Vol. II. Pt. I. p. 320.
[2] Cal. State Papers, 1696, p. 239.

1696 as was acknowledged both by his Father and
him (see their letters in Walnut Scritoire drawer
F for Frank). Yet I am willing to pay £5000
and assign him a £1000 Debt, if he will make
a settlement, viz. Stand to his Word, for he
said he would not give sixpence away from his
Son. Now I desire to have two thirds of his
estate settled viz. £2000 per ann., but he will
settle only one. The Base usage I have had
makes me resolve not to pay the Portion this two
years; viz. the Father threatening me, the Mother
and Son slandering me and my children, and the
son threatening to put a spoke in Phill's (Amphillis,
Sir Richard's eldest daughter) cart and accordingly
traducing us all."[1]

It is interesting to learn from this private outburst
of Sir Richard that the estate of the elder Sir Charles
in 1696 was about £3000 a year. Father Bede's
estimate about 1670, it will be remembered, was
£4000. The mention of Ann Ayscough by Sir Richard
Newdigate shows that she was a firm upholder of
her son's interests.

1697 About February 1697, old Tom D'Urfey's rollicking
farce, "The Intrigues of Versailles, or a Jilt in All
Humours," was staged at the Lincoln's Inn Fields
Theatre. As it was dedicated to Sir Charles Sedley
and his son, it may be supposed that the Sedleys
attended the first performance, accompanied, it is to
be hoped, by "Frank." On such occasions the elder
Sir Charles must have entertained his son and daughter-
in-law with reminiscences of the great days of the
Restoration theatre, and told them of the glories of
Hart, Mohun, Nell Gwynne, Mary Knipp and other
stars of his youth.

The negotiations concerning the financial future
of the younger Sir Charles Sedley and his wife appar-

---

[1] "Cavalier and Puritan," p. 195.

ently came to a head in June 1697.[1] On the 29th of that 1697
month a marriage settlement between the two families
was signed. In legal language it was between "Sir
Charles Sedley Bart. of Southfleet, of first part, the
Earl of Scarborough and Sir Richard Newdigate of
second part, Sir Charles Sedley the younger knt son
of the said Sir Charles and Dame Frances, the wife
of the said Sir Charles S the younger and one of the
daughters of Sir Richard Newdigate of third part
and Richard Newdigate, Joseph Ayloffe and Stoughton
Bird of fourth part." The details of this settlement
have not been recorded. The inclusion of Joseph
Ayloffe of Gray's Inn among the signatories is significant. He was the husband of Frances Ayscough,
daughter of Henry Ayscough of Yorkshire, and
sister to Ann Ayscough. His son, William, was at
this time a young lieutenant of foot, who had published some pretty lyrics, and appears to have become
a great favourite of Sir Charles on his return to England
at the Peace of Ryswick.[2]

In January of the following year, Whitehall Palace 1698
was burned to the ground. The great rambling mass
of buildings had now for some time been deserted
by the Court, which was transferred by William III
to his beloved Kensington, but its demolition must
have been a melancholy sight for those who had seen
it in the brilliant days when its halls and galleries
were trodden by Castlemaine, Portsmouth, Rochester
and Buckingham. Scarcely less striking as a sign of
the changed times was the presentation in the same
year by Sir Charles Sedley (who had once "abused

---

[1] "Fly Leaves, No. IV.," by "Eu. Hood," *Gentleman's Magazine*,
October 1822.

[2] He was probably the poet's literary executor. In his preface to
the 1702 edition of Sedley's Miscellaneous Poems, he says, "The
Affinity between Sir *Charles Sedley* and me, gave me the first Honour
of his Acquaintance; and his own Candour and Indulgence continued
me in it during that Interval of Peace we have since enjoy'd" (*i.e.*
after the Peace of Ryswick in September 1697).

1698 the scriptures") and John Brewer, Esquire, of a gift of plate to the church of New Romney, the town which they represented in Parliament. The gift consisted of "A Pair of tall gilt flagons (with shaped lids and spreading circular feet) and a rudely-fashioned deep cup without knop on the stem."[1]

By January of the next year the Sedleys and Newdigates appear to have become completely reconciled, to judge from a letter written by Sir Charles in that month to Sir Richard Newdigate:[2]—

Endorsed

1698/99   "Sir Ch. Sedley Father of S^r Ch. Sedley who married Frances Daughter of Sr Rich Newdigate 2d Bt.

12 Jan: 169$\frac{8}{9}$ S^r Ch. Sedley a Letter of Freindship

S^r

The country beeing as busy and delightfull a scene to you, as the towne to me, I doubt wee shall not meet soe often as I could wish, this consideration obliges me to trouble you with a letter. Frindship beares sometimes bitter fruit, but it has not a more aggreable flower than an amicable Correspondence: which I shall ever preserve with you, as a person whoe in a nice and difficult emergency, have behavd your selfe to mine and the satisfaction of all persons unprejudisd My sonne was sisd upon by the Gout as hee was going to bring your dauter up to London, of which hee is still lame, but shee is expected by the next Coach which comes from

---

[1] "Archæologica Cantiana," 13. 479.
[2] This and the subsequent letters are among the family papers of Sir Francis Newdigate, Bart., of Arbury, Warwickshire, who has kindly allowed me to copy and publish them.

those parts: you have the votes of the house 1698/99 but what passes at Committees may bee news to you, this day we went into a Committee of the whole house upon a bill presented by Sr John Philips, entitled an act to prevent debauchery and profanes: after some pains and penátys aggreed to against persons keeping or frequenting bawdy houses: wee came to a clause concerning such women as should bee convicted of adultery it was provided that they should pay such cases the summ of 100 l or be publikely whipt: Some gentlemen tooke exception at the fine, which could not but light upon the husband: whoe was not only the Injured but an innocent person: and perhaps willing enough to put his horns in his pocket therefore to make him pay for his own disgrace was thought very hard: the Committee thought the clause deservd a further Consideration: it beeing about 3 a clocke they adjorned to a farther day: I wish wee had you amongst us for there seems to bee a spirit in this parlament which if well directed might bee serviceable to the nation. Doctor Daveñat hath obligd the world with an other booke but I fear disobligd some of our great men, hee is going agent to Fort St George, for the Old East India company: for 3 yeares if you have any comands for me in towne you shall find me S^r

Your most faithfull and humble
Servant

Сн. Sedley.

All here present their most humble
Service to you and your family."

It is rather surprising to find the hero of the Cock Tavern affair and the friend of Rochester discussing a Bill to prevent debauchery and profaneness. This

1698/99 measure was part of the new Puritanism of the reign of William III, which formed Vigilance Societies and prosecuted actors for using profane words on the stage. It was passed on 26 February and was one of several attempts of the so-called "Reformers of Manners" to make the nation moral by legislation.[1] The Dr. Davenant to whom Sedley refers is Dr. Charles Davenant (1656–1714), a son of Sir William Davenant, the poet, and himself a distinguished writer on economics. The book with which he had recently "obliged the world" was his "Discourses on the Public Revenues and Trade of England," in which he explains the reforms which he had introduced while Commissioner of the Excise from 1678–89, and animadverts on the conduct of his successors after the Revolution. He was answered in "Remarks on Some Wrong Confutations and Conclusions" (1698).[2]

1699 In 1699 Sir Charles the elder must have felt that he had not many years of life before him, for, in this year, in accordance with the prudent traditions of his family, he made a final settlement of his estate. The deed in which this settlement was embodied was dated 13 September, 1699, and it gives a striking proof of Sir Charles's affection for his son by Ann Ayscough. The bulk of the estate was made over to this young man, with the reservation of life estates for Sir Charles the elder and the faithful Ann Ayscough.[3] The rest of the document consisted of limitations of the reversion of the whole estate in case of the death of Sir Charles or his son. The reversion was limited firstly to Sir Charles himself; secondly, to Ann Ayscough, "one of the daurs. of Henry Ayscough

---

[1] Luttrell's "Brief Relation," IV. 606, and Krutch's "Comedy and Conscience after the Restoration" (Chap. VII.), where a good account of the "Reformation of Manners" will be found.

[2] D. N. B., s.a. Davenant, Dr. Charles.

[3] Fly-leaves, No. IV.

Esquire late of Grays Inn Gent decd."; thirdly, to 1699 "Sir Charles S of the par. of St. Giles-in-the-Fields Middx. Knt."; fourthly, "to issue of Sir C. S. knt"; fifthly, "to the use of the Rt. honorble Katherine Countess of Dorchester for life"; sixthly (this is unkind to poor Dorinda!), "to her issue *lawfully begotten*"; seventhly, "to Sir Charles Sedley of St. Clere in the Co. of Kent"; eighthly, "to his issue."[1] The real object of the settlement is disclosed by a final proviso, that "if the Countess of Dorchester or any present or future husband or their issue attempt to avoid, annul, impeach, etc. that settlement, all the uses limited to them should determine and be void."[2] Sir Charles doubtless feared that if he merely left his fortune to his son by will, Lady Dorchester or her husband would attempt to contest the validity of such a will before the courts, where juries would be likely to look with disfavour on the disinheritance of a legitimate in favour of an illegitimate child, and would be inclined to listen to the suggestion that the Ayscoughs had used undue influence in procuring a will in their favour. A settlement made while the poet was in good health, putting his son into possession of the greater part of the property, would be far more difficult to upset, and the final proviso removed any possibility of legal action against it. It is dangerous to read too much into legal documents, but surely we can clearly perceive here the results of a bitter feud between the daughter of the unfortunate Lady Sedley and the son of the woman who took her mother's place.

The younger Charles Sedley had three children by his wife Frances. They were named Charles, Richard and Anne. I can find no record of the

---

[1] Haslewood's Notes to Jacob, No. 11: see Appendix I. The italics are mine. Sir Charles Sedley of St. Clere was the poet's third cousin and son of Sir John Sedley of Ightam St. Cleers; see pp. 22–23 and pedigree.   [2] Haslewood's Notes, No. (11), Appendix I.

Q

1699 dates of their births. One of the elder Sedley's last business transactions before he made over his estate to his son seems to have been the sale of Harefield Park in Middlesex to Sir Richard Newdigate, the father of his daughter-in-law. Harefield had belonged to the Newdigates about a century before, and had been exchanged by them for Arbury in Warwickshire. It probably came to Sir Charles from his sister-in-law, Lady Chandos. It will be remembered that long before, in the year of the Restoration, Harefield House is said to have been burned by Sir Charles's carelessness while he was staying with Lady Chandos. On Saturday, 1 July, 1699, Sir Richard was in London and called on Sir Charles, and on that day and on Monday, 3rd, the details of the sale seem to have been arranged between the two baronets.[1] Richard Sedley, the younger son of the younger Sir Charles, accompanied his grandfather to the sea-coast when the latter set out on a tour in France in July 1699. The old gentleman notes in his Diary that he "tipped" little Dick Sedley a quarter of a Carolus (about five shillings) before embarking.

Our last glimpse of Sedley in a convivial society and in connection with the stage belongs to the year 1699. The famous comic actor Penkethman published in this year an "Epistle Dedicatory" to a play called "Love without Interest or the Man too Hard for the Master" (4to London 1699). In this curious document he gives a list of the names of the Gentlemen with whom he associated, or, in his own words, among whom he "thrust in his Comick Phyz" and it is pleasant to find "Sir Charles Sidley" among them.[2]

1699/ 1700 At the beginning of the following year we find Sedley again writing to inform his friend Sir Richard Newdigate of the news of the town:—

[1] "Cavalier and Puritan" (Sir R. Newdigate's Diary), p. 314.
[2] I am indebted to Mr. Thorn Drury for this interesting reference.

Endorsed "27 Jan: 1 $\frac{699}{700}$ S^r Ch. ⟨1699/1700⟩

       Sedley y^t ye Lds had
       reversed ye Judgmt
       Ag^t ye Bankers

For The Honorable S^r
Richard Newdigate at
Arbury Warwickshire
     Charles Sedley
     Free

        from the Speakers Chamber Case
        paper Jan the 28

S^r

    I have often beene obligd to write to you upon occasions diſtaſtful to us both. I am now well pleased with an Opportunity of informing you of something that may bee agreable—which is that the house of lords on tuesday laſt: in favor of tho[s]e concernd in the Bankers debt reverse my lord Chancellors decree againſt them: by a great majority: and tis the general opinion that King Charles The 2^d had (by the words of the aċt that gave him the Excise on beer and ale) a power to dispose of that revenue for ever. soe as to have sold it or given it away. if soe the Engagment hee made stands good. and thee debt muſt one time or other bee satisfyd out of the revenue: I hope we shall cutt off one sh: in the pownd from the land tax by reason the Irish resumptions will assiſt us to pay our debt: and that 2 shills will answer the current Service of this year 7000 thousand men beeing our complement as well for service at land as sea

       Your moſt humble servant

          CHARLES SEDLEY."

  The judgment of the House of Lords "in favor of those concernd in the Bankers debt" mentioned in this letter was a remote sequel of Charles II's famous ⟨1699/1700⟩

1699/
1700
   "closing of the Exchequer" in 1672. By that act the King had appropriated about a million and a half of money which should have been applied for the repayment of loans granted by the bankers. Instead of repaying the money Charles paid the bankers interest at the rate of 6 per cent. and certain annuities, which were charged on the revenue. These payments were made up till the end of Charles's reign, but James II and William III both refused to recognise the obligation. The bankers petitioned the Barons of the Exchequer for arrears in the reign of William III and the Attorney-General demurred. The Court of the Exchequer upheld the bankers' contention and directed that the arrears should be paid. The Attorney-General appealed by means of a Writ of Error to a court called the Court of Exchequer Chamber, the functions of which were to review the judgments of the Barons of the Exchequer, and almost all the judges in this Court adhered to the judgment already given in favour of the bankers. Chief Justice Treby, however, opposed it on the ground that the remedy by petition was inapplicable. His opinion was upheld by Somers, then Lord Chancellor, who reversed the decision of the Barons of the Exchequer, much to the dismay, no doubt, of persons like Sir Richard Newdigate, who probably had money on deposit with the bankers and would naturally await the repayment with some anxiety. Sedley refers to the last stage of the proceedings, when a Writ of Error on Somers's reversal was brought before the House of Lords, which reversed the reversal and upheld the original decision. The news of this final judgment must have been a great relief to many country squires, like Sir Richard, who were faced with the loss of their deposits if the Lord Chancellor's reversal held good.[1] The

---

[1] See the Life of Lord Somers in Campbell's "Lives of the Lord Chancellors" (4th ed., 1857), V. 99–101; also Luttrell's "Brief Relation," IV. 606.

hope that the seizure of the lands of the Irish Jacobites, 1699/
which Sedley had pressed in the House of Commons,[1] 1700
would enable the land tax to be reduced, would be
heartily shared by a large landowner like Sir Richard.
Sedley does not mention that he spoke in favour of a
larger military establishment in the House;[2] Sir
Richard Newdigate would hardly sympathise with a
policy that would mean a higher land tax. The following letter from Sir Charles Sedley to Sir Richard Newdigate is the latest extant example of his correspondence.
It is only headed "January 2d," but from the contents
it is clear that the year is 1700/01. The question of 1700/
the Spanish Succession, which had been troubling the 1701
minds of European statesmen for years, had come to
a head with the death of Charles II of Spain in
November 1700. The Duke of Anjou to whom
Sedley refers is the grandson of Louis XIV, who was
proclaimed King of Spain by the French on the death
of Charles II. William III had long sought to prevent
such a consummation, which he perceived would
turn the whole vast Spanish empire into an appanage
of the French monarchy. The French King, thinking
that the English Parliament was far too engaged in
party quarrels to come to their rescue, "began with the
Dutch," by seizing the "Barrier Towns" of Spanish
Flanders which Holland had been allowed to garrison
as a safeguard against French aggression. The embassy
from the Emperor which is mentioned was an attempt
to gain English support for the German candidate for
the Spanish throne, the Archduke Charles of Austria.

> "January 2d
>
> S^r
>
> If your last was writ under a great weight
> of busnes, mine is not less for the election at
> Romny is now in agitation soe that I am always
> reading or writing letters about it. beeing of

[1] See p. 185.　　　　[2] See p. 199.

Caesar mind, as exprest by Lucan, Nill actum reputans dum quid Superesset Agendum. Our news is soe uncertane that I dare write litle for truth—wee are already divided into factions about war or peace: we have had noe advice from the Duke of Anjou of his accession to the Crowne of Spain soe that we are not prest for an imediate declaration either way. The King of France has begun with the Dutch to whom hee has given a month time before hee expects Their resolution: the Emperor has sent as An Embass. who offers no great matters if wee enter into his quarrel tis a difficult conjuncture, wee hope for some light in it fron thee free debates of parlament. I wish wee had you amongst us the Nation might bee as much beholding to your Ability there, as your owne family is like to bee to your Industry where you are: the King keeps his Christmas at Hampton court where hee is out of the reach of all whose places doe not afford them Six horses to follow him with My Sonn is not yet recoverd of his gout: your dauter and the little one are in good health wee all present our most humble service to your selfe and the rest of your family I am going to dine with the french Embassador who goes away in a few weekes and will be succeeded by a man of greater quality

Yours
CH. SEDLEY."

The complaint that William III kept his Court at a distance from the town is natural enough from one who could remember the glories of Whitehall under the easy-going rule of Charles II. The French Ambassador with whom Sedley was going to dine was Poussin, who was well known for his intrigues with members of the English Parliament. Some months

later the Tory party incurred great unpopularity 1700/
because some of their members were found dining 1701
with him at a Jacobite tavern.[1] It is to be feared that
the passage referring to him in this letter points to
the probability that Sedley may have received the
bounty of Louis XIV in exchange for his vote in the
Commons. Even if the member for New Romney
was perfectly innocent of such dealings with the agent
of a foreign Power, he was certainly unwise to advertise
his intimacy with the French envoy.

The spirit of the Baronet's youth was not altogether 1700
extinguished by business and politics. It seems to
have flared up for the last time in 1700, when Sir
Richard Blackmore, the physician poet, author of
various epic poems, and the Quack Maurus of Dryden's
satire, flung down a challenge to the survivors of the
outspoken age of Charles II, by publishing "A
Satyr against Wit."[2] In this somewhat rambling
effusion the physician attacks wit in general as the
cause of the decline of English courage, virtue and
learning. Somewhat inconsistently, he proposes the
setting up of a Bank of Wit in order that true wit
may be encouraged to circulate, and that the false
article may be suppressed. The wit of Dorset, Blackmore's patron, and of his friends, is excluded from
the general condemnation. Sedley's name is not
mentioned. A little group of the maligned Wits
answered this attack in a collection of epigrams called
"Commendatory Verses on the Author of the Satyr
of the Two Arthurs and the Satyr against Wit."[3]
The contributors included Sir Charles Sedley, Captain
Richard Steele, the third Earl of Anglesey (who had
married Lady Katherine Darnley, daughter of the
Countess of Dorchester by James II), and others.

---

[1] Macaulay, "History of England," ed. Firth, VI. 2992.
[2] "A Satyr against Wit," fol. 1700.
[3] "Commendatory Verses," etc., fol. 1700, p. 2.

1700 Sedley's contribution is an amusing little lampoon ending with the telling couplet,

> "Thy Satyr's harmless: 'tis thy Prose that kills,
> When thou prescrib'st thy Potions and thy Pills."

Blackmore was defended by some of his admirers in a further volume of "Discommendatory Verses on those which are truly Commendatory on the Author of the two Arthurs and the Satyrs against Wit."[1] One of the authors of this production breaks a lance with Sir Charles in an epigram which incorrectly calls him a knight and suggests that he was so diseased that

> "both of Rhimes and Physick H'had his fill,
> And swallow'd more than ev'ry Verse a Pill."

Sir Charles's pen seems to have been as active at the opening of the eighteenth century as at any time in his life. Besides composing a long poem on Matrimony (a subject which would have surprised his old playmates at the Court of Charles II), and perhaps translating a lively French farce,[2] he contributed several pieces to a miscellany published by Charles Gildon in 1701, among which was an exquisite version of an Ode of Horace, thus showing that his appreciation of the Latin poets remained as fresh as in his youth. It is improbable that he would have lived long into the eighteenth century under the most favourable conditions. Seventy was an age attained by few men in that intemperate and insanitary period. His life was, however, almost certainly shortened by 1701 a terrible blow which fell on him at the end of May 1701, when his only son, Sir Charles Sedley, knight, died at the age of about twenty-nine. The younger Sir Charles probably died in Bloomsbury Square, for he was buried at St. Giles-in-the-Fields on 29 May.[3] His father did not survive him long.

---

[1] "Discommendatory Verses," etc., fol. 1700, p. 3.
[2] See p. 280.   [3] St. Giles-in-the-Fields Burial Register.

He fell seriously ill, and was attended by two 1701 of the most distinguished physicians of the day, Sir Hans Sloane and Dr. Edmund King. From some letters which passed between the two doctors,[1] it seems that Sedley had somewhat recovered by 3 August, and by the advice of Sir Hans resolved to seek a change of air. For this purpose he took a cottage at Hampstead,[2] a thatched building on the gentle well-wooded slope between London and the village of Hampstead. After three weeks in this pleasant place, where the ringing of distant church bells must have come faintly through the windows, mingled with the humming of bees and the lowing of cattle, Sir Charles Sedley died towards the end of August 1701. Ann Ayscough, Frances, Lady

[1] Brit. Mus., Sloane MSS. 4708, ff. 92, 96.

[2] This cottage afterwards belonged to Sir Richard Steele. He wrote to Pope on 1 June, 1712:—

"I am at a solitude, a house between Hampstead and London, wherein Sir Charles Sedley died. This circumstance set me a thinking and ruminating upon the employments in which men of wit exercise themselves. It was said of Sir Charles, who breathed his last in this room,

> Sedley has that prevailing gentle art,
> Which can with a resistless charm impart
> The loosest wishes to the chastest heart;
> Raise such a tumult, kindle such a fire
> Between declining virtue and desire,
> Till the poor vanquished maid dissolves away
> In dreams all night, in sighs and tears all day.

This was a happy talent to a man of the town; but I dare say, without presuming to make uncharitable conjectures on the author's present condition, he would rather have had it said of him that he had prayed

> O thou my lips inspire,
> Who touched Isaiah's hallowed lips with fire!"

("Works of Pope," ed. Elwin and Courthope, VI. 396.) According to Howitt ("Northern Heights of London," p. 214) this cottage was pulled down in 1867. There are engravings of it in Howitt's book and in Parke's, "Topography and Natural History of Hampstead."

1701 Sedley and her children were, doubtless, by his bed-side, and with them was a certain young Harry Davenant, grandson of old Sir William, the dramatist. Perhaps it amused Sir Charles to exchange with this young man reminiscences of his grandfather, whom he must have known well in his youth. Four years later, when Davenant was English envoy at Frank-furt, he told the young Duke of Shrewsbury that he was "with Sir Ch. Sedley in his last hours, and that he died like a philosopher without fear or supersti-tion."[1] The poet was buried on 26 August in the family vault at Southfleet Church. His executors omitted, or were unable, to certify that he had been buried in wool according to the ancient statute for the encouragement of the wool trade, and were com-pelled to pay a fine of fifty shillings to the Poor of the Parish.[2] His will,[3] proved on 30 August, con-firmed all former settlements, and appointed Sir Charles Sedley, knight, Edward Bedingfield of Gray's Inn, and Stoughton Bird executors. As the younger Sir Charles was dead, Bedingfield and Bird must have acted alone on behalf of the legatees. Five pounds apiece for mourning were left to Sir Charles's servants, and the will contained directions that the house in Bloomsbury Square was to be kept together "for one callander month," the executors to defray "all the charge of such house keeping."

1707-08 Ann Ayscough lived on until the end of February or beginning of March 1707/8. She was buried on 2 March at Southfleet Church, where the tactful scribe of the register describes her as "Ann ye Relict of Sir Charles Sedley of ye Parish of St. Giles in ye

[1] Hist. MSS. Comm., Report on the MSS. of the Duke of Buccleuch, II. 793 (Journal of His Grace, Charles, Duke of Shrewsbury, 1 November, 1700, 7 January, 1706, s.d. 1 October, 1705).

[2] Photograph of entry in Southfleet Burial Register in the possession of Mr. G. Thorn Drury.

[3] See full text of will in Appendix I.

fields in ye County of Middlesex Barrt."[1] Her 1707–08
daughter-in-law, Frances, Lady Sedley, seems to have
shone for a few seasons at Bath, to judge from a
MS. epigram by W. Taylor written about 1702,
"On Mr Jervois refusing Lady Sidley a breakfaſt at
Bath," where the poet conjeĉtures that if Adam had
been as insensible to beauty as Mr. Jervois,

"He by Stupidity had saved his race."[2]

"Frank" left the world of hoops, powdered hair,
and compliments in heroic couplets in 1711.[3]

Her eldeſt child, Charles, was created a baronet 1702–78
by Queen Anne on 1 July, 1702, with the ſtyle of
Sir Charles Sedley of Oxton, in Nottinghamshire,
where he seems to have inherited, or purchased, an
eſtate. He married an heiress of that county, Elizabeth Frith of Nuthall, and died on 18 February,
1729/30. He appears to have been a prudent young
man, for he put the eſtate in order by obtaining in
July 1721 permission from the Court of Chancery
to sell part of the lands in order to pay off the en-
cumbrances with which they were ſtill burdened. By
this means he paid off the mortgage of £4120 raised
by Sir Charles Sedley, the poet, in 1675.[4] The son
of this Sir Charles Sedley of Oxton and his wife
Elizabeth was also called Charles, and inherited the
baronetcy.[5] This Sir Charles, the second baronet of
the new creation, resided at Nuthall Temple, and is
said to have been a jovial person, somewhat resembling
his great-grandfather. He sat in three Parliaments
and was present at the opening of the Radcliffe Camera
at Oxford, in 1789, when he received the honorary
degree of D.C.L. He died, unmarried, on 23 Auguſt,

[1] Southfield Burial Register.
[2] Brit. Mus., Add. MS. 37,684, p. 4.
[3] Southfleet Burial Register.
[4] Haslewood's notes to Jacob, Nos. 4 and 10: see Appendix I.
[5] He also had a daughter named Elizabeth who married Sir R.
Burdett, and was mother of Sir F. Burdett, the well-known politician.

1702–78 1778, leaving an illegitimate daughter, Elizabeth Rebecca Ann Sedley, the wife of Henry Vernon, who ultimately succeeded to the title of Baron Vernon on the death of his elder brother. She was the ancestress in direct line of the present Baron Vernon of Kinderton.

The Countess of Dorchester, a survival of the wicked and witty days of the Stuarts, lived on well into the eighteenth century. Like her father, she seems to have been a patient of the great Sir Hans Sloane. A couple of short notes to the great physician in her handwriting survive among the Sloane Papers,[1] and show that she was rather intimate with Sir Hans. He was not her only favourite in the medical profession. She is recorded by the fourth Earl of Chesterfield to have paid a great compliment to another great doctor by comparing his skill to her wit, saying "that she and Dr. Radcliffe together could cure a fever."[2]

1703–11 On 30 October, 1703, the Commons of Ireland voted to Lady Dorchester the pension of £5000 granted to her by James II,[3] and thus, no doubt, enabled her to maintain her family in the splendour that was so dear to her heart.

In 1711, Lord Portmore seems to have been serving in Portugal, and a Mr. Conduitt, Master of the Mint, who married Sir Isaac Newton's niece, Catherine Barton, wrote a copy of verses to console the Countess in the absence of her "Hero," who, "beside the Guadiana,"

> "with unweary'd care
> Labours to animate the lazy war."

The poet pictures Lady Dorchester seeking distraction in the care of her children :—

---

[1] See Appendix III, "Some Documents Illustrative of the Life of K. Sedley, Countess of Dorchester."

[2] Chesterfield's "Letters to His Son," ed. G. Strachey (Methuen, 1901), I. 300.

[3] Luttrell's "Brief Relation," V. 353.

"There you watch o'er your darling's tender years
With painful pleasures and incessant cares,
Beguil'd awhile your absent lord enjoy
In the dear image of the smiling boy,
Cornelia-like direct their infant feet,
And show them to be good and teach them to be great—"[1]

Besides "directing the infant feet" of her children, she appears to have kept a sharp watch over her financial and political interests. In April 1711,[2] a Bill was carried in the House of Commons to appoint Commissioners "to examine the value of all lands and other interests granted by the Crown since the 13th February, 1688/9, and upon what considerations such grants were made, in order to resume the same and apply them to the use of the public." An extant letter of the Countess shows that she had well-grounded fears that her grants of land and her pension, which had been confirmed by William III, would be resumed. The letter is addressed to somebody with considerable political power, and perhaps was one of the factors which helped to secure the rejection of the Resumptions Bill by the House of Lords on 24 April.[3] From this letter we learn that the Countess had been wise enough to transfer her pension to her husband, and could therefore plead a patriotic motive for desiring to retain it.[4]

Katherine kept her wit till the end. She was present 1711-14 at George I's coronation, and when the Archbishop went round the throne demanding the consent of the people, she remarked to Lady Cowper, who was standing by her, "Does the old Fool think that Anybody here will say no to his Question, when there are so many drawn Swords?"[5] She attended George I's

---

[1] MS. in the possession of Mr. G. Thorn Drury.
[2] Cobbett's "Parl. Hist.," VI. 1005.
[3] *Ibid.*, VI. 1013, 1014.
[4] See the text of this letter in Appendix II, pp. 350–52.
[5] Lady Cowper's Diary (John Murray), 1864, p. 5.

1711–14   Drawing Rooms, and, meeting at one of these assemblies her old friend, Louise de Kéroualle, Duchess of Portsmouth, and Elizabeth Villiers, Countess Orkney, William III's mistress, she is said to have exclaimed, "Who would have thought that we three W . . . .s should have met here."[1]

1717–43   In the autumn of 1717 the old Countess, still, doubtless, bedizened with finery, was seen tottering feebly through the gay crowds at Bath. She was taken seriously ill in that city and died on 26 October.[2] The Countess of Dorchester was, in her way, as notable a person as her father. After two centuries her frailties can be condoned as the inevitable results of her education and environment. Her wit and her courage should keep her memory green. Lord Dartmouth said that "Her wit was rather surprizing than pleasing, for there was no restraint in what she said of or to any body."[3] To us it seems rather like a clean gust of truth blowing through the dusty hypocrisies of the old Court life.

1743   Her daughter by James II (or Colonel Grahame), Lady Katherine Darnley, married James Annesley, third Earl of Anglesey, on 7 November, 1699.[4] After having been shamefully maltreated by that nobleman, she obtained a divorce,[5] and on 7 February, 1703/4, became the second wife of John Sheffield, formerly Earl of Mulgrave, now Duke of Buckinghamshire.[6] Like her husband, she was famous for her almost religious worship of her own rank and

---

[1] Quoted in G. E. C. Peerage, s.a. Dorchester, Countess of, IV. 406 n.

[2] Hist. MSS. Comm., Polwarth MSS. (I. 358, Robethon to Polwarth, 27 September, 1717). See also Jesse's "Memoirs of the Court of England."

[3] Note to Burnet's "History of his Own Times" (ed. Oxford, 1833), II. 120 note o.

[4] Luttrell's "Brief Relation," IV. 578.

[5] Hist. MSS. Comm., House of Lords MSS., Vol. IV (N.S.) *passim*.

[6] D. N. B., s.a. Sheffield, John, Duke of Buckinghamshire.

titles. "Princess Buckingham," as she was called, 1743 refused to believe her mother's outspoken assurance that she was Colonel Grahame's daughter, and clung to the idea that she was of royal descent. She lived in Buckingham House on the site of the present Buckingham Palace, and, on the anniversary of the execution of Charles I, she used to receive her guests there, sitting in a chair of state, surrounded by her ladies, and dressed in deep mourning.[1] She died on 13 March, 1743. On her death-bed she is said to have sent for "a Clergyman of whom she had heard a very good Character, in order to be satisfied as to some Doubts. The first Question she asked was, Whether in Heaven (for she made no doubt of going thither) some Respect would not be had to a Woman of such Birth and Breeding? The good Man, for such he really was, endeavoured to show her the Weakness of this Notion, and to convince her that there was where she was going no Acceptance of Persons, and much more to the same Purpose. This the poor Lady heard with much attention, and then said with a Sigh, 'Well! *if it be so, this Heaven is after all a strange Place.'* "[2] If this story is true, it shows that the Duchess inherited her mother's pride without her wit. She had a funeral which would have thoroughly satisfied her exalted opinion of herself. Her "Effigy in Wax" was dressed in her coronation robes, and drawn in a car under a canopy of state by six horses covered with black velvet. Four dukes were pall bearers, and all "the Prime Nobility" drove in the procession in coaches and six.[3]

The Countess of Dorchester's eldest legitimate son, Charles Colyear, inherited his father's title and estate. By him something of the intellectual energy of the Sedleys was transmitted to two distinguished

---

[1] Allan Fea's "James II and his Wives" (London, Methuen, 1908). Mr. Fea quotes no authority for this story.

[2] *The Champion*, 7 April, 1743.   [3] *Ibid.*

1743 families. His illegitimate daughter, Elizabeth Collier,[1] was the wife of Erasmus Darwin, the poet and scientist, and grandmother of Sir Francis Galton, the founder of the science of eugenics. His legitimate daughter and heir, Caroline, married Sir Nicholas Curzon of Kedleston, from whom the late Marquess Curzon of Kedleston was descended.

Sir Charles Sedley has, hitherto, been judged from memoirs which consisted of little more than a few anecdotes concerning the frolics of his youth. The recording and piecing together of a number of forgotten facts enables us, without whitewashing these peccadilloes, to take a more favourable view of a life which was far from wholly bad or useless. To the present writer the importance of that life seems to lie, not in the dissipation of the Restoration Court, but in the period that followed the "conversion" of 1679/80. The significance of that "conversion" was not merely the successful reconstitution of a life that was drifting to ruin, but the fact that the Baronet, while becoming a respectable member of society, succeeded in retaining something of his old gaiety and intellectual freedom. In 1687 he could still write and publish "Bellamira," and later, when Blackmore attacked Wit, could chastise the physician, not with "Black Will and a Cudgel," but with the more civilised weapon of ridicule. The seventeenth century was a witches' cauldron, boiling up with alternate hell-broths of black Puritanism and aristocratic licence and corruption. English civilisation in its fullest sense could only result from a combination of the probity and decency of the Puritan, separated from his dourness and philistinism, with the culture and gaiety of the Cavalier, divorced from his licence and brutality.

[1] For a portrait of this lady see Prof. Karl Pearson's "Life and Letters of Galton," Vol. I. Elizabeth Collier was Erasmus Darwin's second wife. She was not the grandmother of Charles Darwin, who was descended from Erasmus Darwin's first wife.

Sedley belonged to the wealthy and educated class 1743
which was chiefly responsible for the future. The task
before them (to be accomplished finally in the eighteenth
century) was no less than the civilising and human-
ising of their order.   If the debauch at the Cock
and the caning of Kynaſton were reversions to the
barbarism of a former age, it may, on the other hand,
be claimed that a real contribution to the cause of
English civilisation was made by a wealthy baronet,
who devoted a large part of his time to the acquire-
ment of a really wide and liberal culture, who could
break through the barriers of rank and prejudice
sufficiently to treat professional men of letters like
Dryden and Shadwell as friends and comrades, and,
finally, who could remain faithful for nineteen years
to a woman to whom he was bound by no strictly
legal tie, and treat her son with "an entire, free and
easie friendship" in place of the old paternal tyranny.

R

PART II

THE WORKS OF SIR CHARLES SEDLEY

CHAPTER I

THE PLAYS

"While Fathers are severe, and Servants cheat,
Till Bawds and Whores can live without deceit,
Sydley, and easy *Etheridge* shall be great."

> John Evelyn the Younger (in "Poems by
> Several Hands" . . . Collected by N.
> Tate, 8vo London, 1685, p. 92).

"She[1] strait pull'd off her Sattin cap, and Band:
Bade *Wycherly* be bold in her Defence,
With pointed Wit, and Energy of Sense:
Etherege and *Sidley* join'd him in her Cause,
And all deserved, and all received Applause."

> E. Fenton, "Poems on Several Occa-
> sions," 8vo, 1717, p. 72; "An Epistle
> to Mr. Southerne."

Some twenty years ago a critic remarked that "Sedley wrote several plays, and it is enough to say of them that they were plays suited to the taſtes of the Court of Charles II."[2] This sentence is really characteriſtic of an earlier age which believed the legend (partly invented by Macaulay) that Etherege, Wycherley and the other writers of the comedy of manners in the latter half of the seventeenth century were nothing but a gang of foul-mouthed debauchees who deliberately turned the English drama into an Augean ſtable that could only be cleansed by the fire

[1] *i.e. Comedy.*
[2] Thomas Longueville in "Rochester and Other Literary Rakes of the Court of Charles II" (Longmans, Green, London), 1902, p. 78.

of a Jeremy Collier. It is true that Wycherley, Congreve, Vanbrugh and Farquhar were always to some extent excepted from the general condemnation, partly because they had been defended by such able critics as Lamb, Hazlitt and Leigh Hunt, and partly because they were all more or less competently re-edited during the nineteenth century. By the beginning of the present century Sir George Etherege had reached a similar position through the agency of Sir Edmund Gosse's charming essay, Verity's edition and John Palmer's brilliant study. Attention had also been drawn to the merits of Shadwell's comedies by Saintsbury and Churton Collins. Sedley has not hitherto been so fortunate. The sentence quoted at the beginning of this chapter still sums up what is known of Sedley's plays even by students who have a really wide knowledge of English literature. There are probably two reasons for this neglect of Sedley's dramas. The first is the very practical one that they have not been re-edited since 1778, and therefore have been unobtainable by most students of drama, and the other that he was unfortunate enough to leave four authentic plays, of which one was a passable and a second an excellent comedy, the third an inferior tragedy, and the fourth an unfinished remodelling of the same piece.[1] As the last two pieces challenge a most unfortunate comparison with works of Shakespeare and Dryden on the same subject, it is hardly surprising that attention has been drawn to them, and that Sedley's abilities as a dramatist as far as they have been remembered at all have been judged by these unlucky works. Contemporary writers, however, ranked him beside Sir George Etherege as no mean dramatist and as one of the originators of that

---

[1] Viz. "The Mulberry Garden," "Bellamira," "Antony and Cleopatra," and "Beauty the Conquerour." As "The Grumbler" was not printed till many years after the author's death, its authenticity cannot be definitely accepted.

brilliant kind of comedy which reached its culminating point in the plays of Congreve. Professor Allardyce Nicoll in his recent book on Restoration Drama has expressed the same view in some admirable sentences,[1] and it is the object of the present detailed study to show that considered on their own merits, and apart from the disastrous experiment in tragedy, his comedies alone entitle him to a place beside Etherege and well deserve to be studied both for their intrinsic merits and as interesting and important documents in literary and social history.

"The Mulberry Garden," Sedley's first original play, produced at the King's house, Drury Lane, on 18 May, 1668, was, according to Pepys, "long expected," and the same author informs us that "all the world" did "expect great matters" from so reputed a wit.[2] Already on 11 January, 1667/8, Mrs. Knipp had told Pepys of a play shortly coming on the stage, which she thinks will be called "The Wandering Ladys, a comedy which she thinks will be most pleasant."[3] There can be no doubt that "The Wandering Ladys" was merely an earlier title for "The Mulberry Garden," and one which would have been perfectly justified by the conduct of the two madcaps, Victoria and Olivia, in the play as we know it. The long-expected comedy seems to have been something of an anti-climax, at any rate in the opinion of the critics, though it was certainly liked by the theatre-going public of the day. Pepys, it will be remembered, was very disappointed, although he admits that he was prejudiced by the badness of the music: "the play when it come, though there was here and there a pretty saying and not very much neither, yet the whole play had nothing extraordinary in it at all, neither of language nor design." Charles II, if we may believe

---

[1] Allardyce Nicoll, "Restoration Drama" (Cambridge Univ. Press, 1923), pp. 222, 223.

[2] Pepys, Diary, ed. Wheatley, VIII. 19.　　[3] *Ibid.*, VII. 277 n.

Pepys, was equally disappointed. The diarist did not "see him laugh or pleased from beginning to end, nor the company; inasmuch as I have never been so disappointed with a new play in my life I think."[1] Perhaps this was true of the King, but it is very doubtful whether it was true of "the Company," whose countenances it may be supposed Pepys saw through jaundiced eyes. On the contrary, there can be little doubt that it was a great theatrical success. This is proved by the fact that it was acted again on 20 May and 29 June, on both of which dates Pepys saw it again, and was probably revived in 1675 and 1688.[2] The quarto edition published in the year of the former revival seems to have had a very wide sale. It is by far the commonest quarto edition of any of Sedley's plays. Other writers besides Pepys testify to the bad reception of the play by a section of the public. Oldham in "A Satyr" (Works, 8vo, 1703, p. 422) probably referred to this when he wrote:

> "*Sidley* indeed may be content with Fame,
> Nor care should an ill judging Audience damn":

while Sir George Etherege, Sedley's intimate friend, writing as follows from Ratisbon on 23 May, 1687, about Sir Charles's second comedy, "Bellamira," clearly refers to the bad reception of "The Mulberry Garden" by certain critics:—"Some barren sparks have found fault with what he has formerly done on this occasion onely because the fatness of the soile has produc'd to [*sic*] big a Crop."[3] Finally, Sedley himself wrote in the Prologue to "Bellamira" (4to, 1687):

> " Our Author try'd his own and *cou'd not hit*,
> He now presents you with some Forraign Wit."

---

[1] Pepys Diary, ed. Wheatley, VIII. 20.

[2] Quarto editions were published in both these years: this was usually done when a play was revived.

[3] Ratisbon Letter Book, f. 94 (to Mr. Will. Richards $\frac{23 \text{ May}}{2 \text{ June}}$, 1687).

It is true that Shadwell, one of the most competent dramatists of the day, praised "The Mulberry Garden," but he was hardly disinterested,

It is clear from these passages that contemporary criticism was not altogether favourable to "The Mulberry Garden." The stage success of the play must therefore have been due chiefly to Sedley's popularity at Court and to his reputation as man of wit and fashion. More recent critics have generally taken the same view as Pepys, Charles II and Etherege's "barren sparks." Sir A. W. Ward goes so far as to pronounce it "worthless."[1] If the play is regarded purely from an artistic standpoint, there is some reason for the condemnation of the critics, although Sir A. W. Ward's "worthless" is a great deal too strong. Judged solely as a play, "The Mulberry Garden" fails in spite of some sprightly scenes, because of its shapelessness and incoherence. It is exactly the kind of comedy that one would expect from a gifted but inexperienced amateur. Apart from one capital fault that will be considered hereafter, its structure is loose and rambling beyond even the very lax limits of the typical Restoration comedy. The first hint for the plot seems to have been taken from Molière's "L'Escole des Maris," but it is far from true to say that Sedley's play is in any sense a translation of the French comedy. It is interesting, however, to compare the treatment of the same theme by the French and the English author. Such a comparison brings out the structural defects of "The Mulberry Garden" very clearly.

"L'Escole des Maris," produced at the Théâtre du Palais Royal on 24 June, 1661, itself owes a little to the Adelphi of Terence. The opening scene, as in Sedley's play, introduces two elderly brothers who differ in their views on the treatment of young women.

---

as it is probable that he received substantial favours from Sir Charles. Moreover, his praise is given in quite general terms: "you have in the *Mulberry-Garden* shown the true Wit, Humour, and Satyr of a Comedy." Dedication of "A True Widow."

[1] "History of English Dramatic Literature," III. 448.

They are able to test their theories in practice, as they are guardians of two sisters, who have been entrusted by their deceased father to their respective cares. Sganarelle, adopting the oriental and despotic method, keeps a tight hand over Isabelle, who, schooled by adversity, learns to deceive him so artfully that he is actually lured against his will and without his knowledge to aid and abet the young gallant, Valère, to win her heart and hand. Ariste, the elder brother, allows to his ward, Léonor, the utmost freedom, and treats her as an equal, with the result that she falls in love with him and makes him an excellent wife. The play is an exquisitely proportioned little fable in defence of the treatment of women as rational beings, and is summed up in the famous line:

"Je trouve que le cœur est ce qu'il faut gagner."

Molière never strays for an instant beyond what is necessary for his purpose, which is beautifully accomplished in three acts.

To turn from "L'Escole des Maris" to "The Mulberry Garden" is like turning from the flower-beds of Versailles to the wilderness of some neglected English country garden. Sedley starts from practically the same point as Molière, except that his two brothers disagree concerning the treatment, not of their wards, but of their daughters. But the English author complicates matters at the outset by giving his Sir Samuel Forecast and Sir John Everyoung two daughters apiece, and brings in a fresh cause for disagreement between them by laying the scene in the England of the Commonwealth and making Forecast a sober Puritan and Everyoung a jolly Cavalier. The original motif of the contrast between the results of the severity of Forecast and the easy-going treatment of Everyoung is soon forgotten in a tangle of intrigue which gives Victoria and Olivia, Everyoung's two daughters, two vain young coxcombs, Modish and Estridge, as

suitors, while their friend Jack Wildish, a younger
son but a man of wit and fashion, aspires to the hand
of Olivia. A new interest arises from the rivalry
between Wildish and Estridge and Modish, resulting
in his final success in showing them in their true
colours to the ladies. An entirely separate plot is
concerned with the separation of Althea and Diana,
Forecast's daughters, from their Cavalier lovers,
Eugenio and Philander, and the attempts of their
father to make Althea marry Horatio, a gentleman of
the Roundhead party, who has already been a suitor
to Victoria. Humorous by-play is provided by a plan
of Wildish's to score off Sir Samuel by persuading
him to court a rich "widow." He alleges that this lady
is his relative, but she is actually the widow's house-
keeper, whom he persuades to impersonate her. The
romantic adventures of Eugenio, Philander, Althea
and Diana give an opportunity for Diana to adopt
the time-honoured device of English comedy and
visit her lover in male attire. Finally, the Restoration
is used as a convenient *deus ex machinâ* to untie the
whole tangle, bring about a general reconciliation,
and marry all the lovers to their mistresses except the
unfortunate Estridge and Modish, the latter of whom
is appropriately bestowed on the mock "widow."

It seems almost as if Sedley had resolved to drag
in by hook or crook every stock situation of contemporary comedy that he could think of. Etherege
probably referred euphemistically to this overloading
of the plot when he remarked that "the fatness of the
soile produc'd to big a Crop." The fault lies less in
the complexity, which is indeed unravelled with no
little ingenuity, than in the fact that there is no single
dominant interest. Sedley might well have protested
against a comparison between his play and Molière's
on the ground that the aims of the English comedy
of manners and its French counterpart were entirely
different. Molière's aim was primarily to express a

moral truth and incidentally to paint human nature. The aim of the English author, like that of his friend Etherege, was to give a gay and witty picture of the fashionable society of his day. But this is no excuse for sinning against the only dramatic "unity" that is essential to a good play, the unity of interest. Are we most concerned with the contrast between Forecast and Everyoung, the relations between Olivia, Victoria, Wildish, Estridge and Modish, or the romantic adventures of Eugenio, Philander, Althea and Diana? Even this fault might pass, and indeed does pass in certain Restoration plays, if there were a certain uniformity of style and matter. Here indeed is the capital defect of the play already mentioned. It is apparent from the very names of the characters. Harry Modish, Ned Estridge, Jack Wildish, Sir John Everyoung, his brother and his daughters might have been met any fine day between the Strand and St. James's Park, but from what fairy-land of rococo romance have Horatio, Eugenio, Philander, Diana and Althea descended? The manner and matter of their speeches are as unreal as their names. The realistic characters speak in conversational prose, the "heroic" characters in rimed couplets. It is true that Sir George Etherege in his first play, "The Comical Revenge, or Love in a Tub," had used the same incongruous mixture, but parody of the "heroic" tragedy of Orrery and Dryden was at least hinted in the title of that piece, while Sir George had since seen the error of his ways, and in his second comedy, "She Wou'd if She Cou'd," produced only four months before "The Mulberry Garden," had entirely abandoned the "heroic" element. In Sedley's first play the incongruity, not only of ideas, but of language, is especially striking. Half the characters live in the world of Pepys and the Memoirs of De Grammont, and the other half in that of Dryden's "Almanzor" and Settle's "Cambyses." Jack Wildish speaks of love as

Etherege or Rochester might have spoken of it. . . .
"I never let the Disease run on so far, I always took it
in time, and then a Bottle of Wine or two, and a She
Friend is an approv'd remedy."

But Horatio addresses Althea like nobody outside
the pages of "heroic romance" or "heroic tragedy":

> "You shou'd with pity, not displeasure, see
> The change that your own self creates in me.
> The Roman Senate had their greatness worn
> Perhaps till now, had *Cæsar* not been born.
> *Darius'* self cou'd not his Persians blame
> Because that *Alexander* overcame.
> In Love like War some Victor still there grows
> Whose spreading Empire nothing can oppose."

In the very spirit of Almanzor or Maximin, Horatio,
when he has his rival at his mercy, refuses to take
advantage of his position and fights on Eugenio's side
against the Roundhead soldiers who have come to arrest
him. We rub our eyes and wonder if we are indeed in
the neighbourhood of St. James's Park, where Sir
Samuel Forecast was cudgelled by the orders of Sir
John Everyoung, and Kynaston, the actor, suffered at
the hands of the emissaries of Sir Charles Sedley.

Having acknowledged that "The Mulberry Garden" fails as a whole, we can give due praise to
individual passages. The intrinsic value of the play
lies entirely in the comic and realistic scenes. The
romantic passages show no merit except a facile command of the heroic couplet. Much of the verse is in
exactly the strain of Sedley's own complimentary
lyrics, and he has indeed on two occasions used almost
the same lines for both purposes.[1] This hyperbolical
vein of romantic compliment may be pleasing enough
in a short "paper of verses" of ten or twenty lines,
but it is wearisome stuff when it is bandied from one
speaker to another throughout an entire scene. At its

[1] *Mulberry Garden*, II. i.:
> "But, fair Althea, you were much to blame
> With your own breath to blow a hopeless flame."

loweſt the heroic verse with its jejune and conventional rhythm and vocabulary sinks to mere fuſtian:

> "Can this Eugenio be and so unkind?
> What strange distemper rages in thy mind?
> Cou'd once my Soul of a base thought allow,
> He that believes me false shou'd find me so."

It is a relief to escape out of this monſtrous world of literary convention and liſten to the graceful, easy dialogue of the realiſtic scenes. At their beſt these scenes have a lightness and diſtinction unequalled by any contemporary dramatiſt except Etherege. Sedley's prose, always lucid and well-bred, occasionally flowers into a really beautiful cadence, such as that which is heard in Olivia's comparison of the Mulberry Garden to the "long Walk at home":

> "for in my opinion half a score young men, and Fine Ladies well dreſt, are a greater Ornament to a Garden than a Wilderness of Sycamores, Orange and Lemmon Trees; and the ruſtling of rich Veſts and Silk Pettycoats, better Musick than the purling of Streams, Chirping of Birds, or any of our Country Entertainments."

When Pepys wrote of "here and there a pretty saying," he was probably thinking of the wit of Jack Wildish,

---

These lines are practically repeated in "A Platonick" (first printed in Kemp's Collection, 1672):

> "Fair Octavia, you are most to blame
> To blow the fire and wonder at the flame."

Mulberry Garden, V. i.:

> "Look on thyself and measure thence my love,
> Think what a flame so bright a form must move:
> That knot be confident will ever last,
> Which Passion ty'd and Reason has made faste."

Cf. "Constancy" (Kemp's Collection, I. 46):

> "Look on thy self, and measure thence my love,
> Think what a passion such a form must move;
>
> . . . . . .
>
> That knot (be confident) will ever last,
> Which Fancy ty'd and Reason has made fast."

which is exactly of the gay unmoral kind that delighted
the Court of Charles II. A few of his sentences have
the dry sparkle that Congreve was to polish later to
diamond-like brilliance. The best is perhaps his
remark that

> ". . . fine Women, like Great Tables, though
> they are maintain'd by men of Fortunes, are ever
> open to Men of Parts."

And his playful defence of Sir Samuel's attitude to
Althea is a pretty piece of mockery belied by his
own suit to Olivia:

> "Now there, Sir *Samuel*, I am on your side.
> For so the Fan be played with, the hand kist;
> in fine the passion handsomly discharg'd, tis
> no great matter who does it."

The heroic characters are the merest lay figures,[1]
but Wildish, Estridge, Modish, the brothers Everyoung and Forecast, and Everyoung's daughters,
Victoria and Olivia, are drawn with a certain liveli-
ness that deserves commendation. Forecast, the Puritan
city knight, is of course a stock character of seventeenth-century comedy, but Sedley's sketch is by no
means one of the worst of this favourite butt of the
"quick comedians" of the day, and probably provided hints for Congreve's Foresight in "Love for
Love." It is lacking in the bitterness that Wycherley
shows in his terrible picture of Alderman Gripe.
Forecast is cudgelled, but he is allowed to make his
peace on very easy terms at the end, and escapes the

---

[1] Mr. C. H. Wilkinson in his recent edition of the Poems of Lovelace,
following a suggestion of Mr. Thorn Drury, points out that Eugenio is
possibly intended to be portrait of Lovelace. Like Lovelace he is in
love with an Althea, and certain phrases used by him bear a faint
resemblance to some of Lovelace's most famous lines (see "The Poems
of Richard Lovelace," ed. C. H. Wilkinson, Oxford, 1925, I. lvii.
and Editor's Preface to "The Mulberry Garden" in my edition of
Sedley's Works).

fate of marrying the sham "widow." There is a charming frugality in his reminiscence of the widow's defunct spouse: "We have drunk many a dish of coffee together." Sir John Everyoung is clearly meant to be a foil to his Puritan brother and to represent the ideal elderly man about town. His device of cudgelling Forecast makes him seem rather brutal to modern eyes, but such a proceeding would be a perfectly justifiable frolic in the judgment of a Restoration audience. For the rest, he is a merry old gentleman and his good-natured treatment of his daughters covers a multitude of sins.

The character of Jack Wildish can only be adequately studied in connection with the historical position of "The Mulberry Garden" in the evolution of the comedy of manners, and the same may be said of that of his mistress, Olivia. At this point it is only necessary to remark that the witty duet between them is both from an artistic and historical point of view the most important thing in the play.

Victoria, the deserted mistress of Horatio, lives, if only for her delicious reply to Wildish's request that she should witness his wedding with Olivia:

> "Well, *Mr. Wildish*, I'le dance barefoot to serve you."

As for Estridge and Modish, they are convincing pictures of the fops who were the usual butts of Sedley and his friends, and are good empty rattles prefiguring the great Sir Fopling Flutter and "Turk Tattle." Wildish's ironical description of the manner in which they pass their time might come out of the Memoirs of De Grammont: "Besides, every good Man is not acquainted with this Principle among you, that you can be in love with nothing but yourselves, and may be jealous of his Wife, when indeed you come innocently to take a view of your persons from Head to feet in the great Glass; comb out your Periwig, shake

your Garnitures and be gone." "What," answers Estridge, "dost think we have no other way of Entertainment? No Discourse, Jack?" "Yes, a little now and
then," Wildish replies, "about their dress, whether their
patches be too many or too few, too great or too
small, whether her Handkerchief be *Point de Venie*
or *Rome;* and having left behind you some proof of
your ability in the Mode, return to show yourselves
at the last Act of a Play." It is impossible not to feel
rather sorry for them when Wildish deliberately lures
them into talking indiscreetly within earshot of their
mistresses, though their boasts are so outrageous that
it cannot be denied that they deserved their dis-
appointment in the affair of the "widow's" abduction.

The intrinsic merits of "The Mulberry Garden" may
thus be summed up as a certain grace and distinction
of style in its prose scenes and a genuine if immature
talent in the drawing of certain characters. It receives a
much greater interest than such merits could possibly
give it from the very important position which it holds
in the historical evolution of the comedy of manners.

The English comedy of manners may be defined
as a comedy of wit and fashion representing the life
of a small, brilliant, aristocratic society which prided
itself on regarding all the problems of life from
a purely intellectual and non-moral standpoint. It
aims at being brilliant, heartless and anti-sentimental.
The least breath of romance will immediately tarnish
the glittering mirror of its wit. In the older English
comedy the portrayal of "manners" was one element
among many others. In Shakespeare it had been overshadowed by romance and in Jonson by "humour."
The comedy of the earlier XVIIth century, chiefly
inspired by Jonson, had been at once virile and
fantastic, a comedy rather of humour (both in the old
and the modern sense) than of wit, often tending
to romance and not less frequently to the grotesque.
The stock characters were the foolish young heirs with

S

more money than sense, the riff-raff of tavern and
fair who relieved them of their superfluous coin, the
Puritans, justices, bawds and cast soldiers which
Jonson delighted to portray. It was usually a painting
of middle-class or low life in the Flemish style, rich
in colour but not remarkable for lightness of touch or
distinction of style.

Beaumont and Fletcher in such plays as "The
Wild Goose Chase" had begun to experiment in
something approaching the manner of Restoration
comedy, and the lighter and more courtly note of
their plays had been happily caught by some writers
of the period immediately preceding the Civil War,
such as Shirley, Brome and Nabbes. But even in
"Hide Park," "The Witty Fair One," "The Sparagus
Garden" and "The Bride," as in the comedies of
Beaumont and Fletcher, romance and sentiment are
part of the very weft of the plot, and these qualities
can never be harmonised with the purely intellectual
and non-moral spirit of the true comedy of manners.

The older type of Jonsonian comedy continued to
be written after the Restoration by John Wilson and
Sir Robert Howard, and was soon to be revived with
great ability by Thomas Shadwell. But the spirit of
the new age demanded a comedy which would express
it better, a comedy which would give an appropriate
form to the aspirations of the wits and fine ladies of
Whitehall. To use a metaphor from another art, it
demanded a painting less in the style of Teniers and
more in that of Watteau or Fragonard. The new
comedy must be all lightness of touch, all gaiety,
ignoring both the moral pre-occupations of the Puritan
and the grotesque whimsies of the old drama. Such an
achievement was more difficult than the Restoration
Wits supposed. Not until another generation, when
they were all either dead or "converted," was the task
fully accomplished by William Congreve, the artist who
translated their strivings at last into a perfect form.

It was clear that the centre of the new kind of comedy must be the Man of Wit and Fashion as he was conceived by the courtiers of Charles II, the ideal personage who had been to some extent embodied in the persons of such men as Rochester, Etherege, Sedley and Buckhurst. The first and obvious method of making such a person an effective stage character was to contrast him with the false "pretenders to wit," the Chesterfields, Beau Hewitts and other foolish moths who circled giddily round the lights of Whitehall. He might also be appropriately contrasted with men of an older generation, who would puritanically condemn or clumsily share his pleasures. But such conflicts or contrasts between the obviously superior and obviously inferior persons (if we accept for critical purposes the standards of the Wits) are not the stuff out of which the central theme of great comedy can be evolved, although they may provide excellent diversion in sub-plots. The perfect comedy of manners, like all good forms of drama, demands a conflict between equals—in this case equals in wit and grace and style—for these are the qualities that are the chief concern of this kind of play, as intensity of imagination and heroic magnanimity are the chief concern of poetic tragedy. To place beside the ideal Wit an equally witty and graceful woman, who could meet him on his own ground and with his own weapons, could reply to his music with an equally enchanting strain of her own, and finally, without any trace of romance or sentiment, at once conquer him and yield to him—such was the goal towards which a whole school of dramatists was half consciously groping in the reign of Charles II. To disentangle these motifs from the old elements of Jonsonian humour and boisterous horseplay and from such new attractions as "heroic" poetry was the work of a whole generation. Sir George Etherege has rightly been given the leading place among the pioneers, but

Dryden and Sedley both deserve to be ranged along-side him in this work. Already as early as 1664 Etherege had given the first sketch of the new type of fashionable hero in his Sir Frederick Frollick of "The Comical Revenge, or Love in a Tub." That play is marred both by the introduction of "heroic scenes" in verse and by a large element of horseplay of the old boisterous type. Etherege's second comedy, "She Wou'd if She Cou'd," produced in February 1667/8, marks a very great advance towards the pure comedy of manners. The heroic element is entirely absent and the whole play is in prose. Moreover, the two girls, Ariana and Gatty, have a grace and a gaiety far in advance of any female characters which the new type of comedy had hitherto produced. The weakness of the play is the comparative effacement of the two sparks, Courtal and Freeman, who ought to have responded on equal terms to Ariana and Gatty, by the two amusing old knights, Sir Oliver and Joslin.

Dryden, like Etherege, had been moving in the direction of the new form of comedy, and Loveby, the hero of his very first play, "The Wild Gallant" (1662/3), faintly foreshadows the new kind of hero. In the comic underplot of his romantic play, "The Maiden Queen" (March 1667/8), he had conceived a pair of lovers which play the amatory "Battle-Dore and Shuttlecock" of wit to perfection in certain scenes, and which are the closest approach to the new comic ideals of any characters that had hitherto appeared on the stage. Shadwell's remark on this pair is worth quoting as an acute description of the new comedy from the standpoint of one who was blindly pre-judiced in favour of the old:

> "but the two chief persons are most commonly a Swearing, Drinking, Whoring Ruffian for a Lover and an impudent, ill-bred *Tomrig* for a mistress, and these are the fine People of the

Play; and there is that Latitude in this that almost anything is proper for them to say; but their chief Subject is Bawdy and Profaneness, which they call *Brisk Writing*. . . ."[1]

"The Mulberry Garden" is thus seen to be slightly archaic in its retention of the "heroic" scenes and characters, and also in the boisterous incidents of the cudgelling of Forecast and the carrying off of the "widow." However, the characters of Wildish and Olivia mark a great advance towards the final form of the comedy of manners. Here are Dryden's witty lovers taken out of their romantic setting and placed in the appropriate environment of contemporary London. And although "The Mulberry Garden" has neither the sustained gaiety nor the skilfully managed plot of "She Wou'd if She Cou'd," these figures are something that Etherege had not yet succeeded in putting on the stage. Jack Wildish is less boisterous than Sir Frederick Frollick and wittier than Courtal and Freeman. His character is exactly of the type that was perhaps first born in the minds of the young men who haunted St. James's Park and the Mulberry Garden in the latter years of the Commonwealth, that new generation who, in Davenant's words, were "uningaged in the late differences"[2] and were as alien from the temper of the old Cavaliers as from that of the Puritans themselves. It is significant in this connection that Wildish has no political prejudices. He is on friendly terms with both Royalists and Republicans, and his attitude towards fighting is in striking contrast to that of the heroic Philander and Eugenio. It is summed up in his reply to Sir Samuel when the latter appeals to him for help against the soldiers:

"these are a Kind of Gamesters I dare not meddle with."

[1] Preface to "The Sullen Lovers" (produced May 1668. Works, 8vo, 1720, I.). [2] See p. 40.

He is a realist and a man of pleasure, but he differs
from the ill-bred sparks, Estridge and Modish, by his
perfect manners. In this contrast lies the whole philosophy of the comedy of manners. Every gentleman is
assumed to be a rake, but the elect are distinguished
by wit and "good form," while the rest are damned,
not for their deeds, but for their lack of style.

The character of Olivia is also an advance on the
women that Etherege had hitherto created. Ariana
and Gatty are delightful madcaps, but they are Olivia's
inferiors both in wit and in self-possession. If Wildish
is a foe to romantic sentiment, Olivia has an equal
dislike for "whining Love" and "a whining copy of
verses." Their final duel of wit before the lady sur-
renders is by far the best thing in the play, and is
one of the first of many similar scenes which were to
delight two generations. In Olivia's complaint:

> "If I were your Wife, I must board half a
> year with a Friend in the Country, tumble about
> the other in most villainous Hackneys, lye two
> pair of Stairs high and wear Black Farrendine,
> the whole year about; see you when you had no
> money to play; and then be kist out of a Ring
> or a Bracelet. . . ."

and Wildish's rejoinder:

> "If I make but love to a Chamber-maid, I shall
> be answer'd, you have a sweet Lady of your
> own, and why will you wrong her? If I get
> acquainted with any young woman, after the
> fourth or fifth visit, be looked upon by her
> Father and Mother Worse than the Tax Gatherers
> in a Country Village":

we can now find a pleasure unknown to the first readers
of "The Mulberry Garden," for we are thrilled by the
knowledge that we are hearing a prelude to that final

duet of Mirabel and Millamant with which the comedy of manners was to reach a triumphant culmination.

The idea of naming a comedy after a public place of entertainment, where its action chiefly passes, was an old one and goes back at least to Jonson's "Bartholomew Fair." Before the Civil War there had been a "Covent Garden" and a "Totnam Court" by Nabbes, a "Hide Park" by Shirley and a "Sparagus Garden" by Brome. After Sedley's comedy, Wycherley's "Love in a Wood or St. James's Park" was to be staged in 1671 (though according to its author it was written much earlier), and an anonymous play called "The Mall, or The Modish Lovers," was acted and printed in 1674. The real Mulberry Garden was a famous pleasure ground which occupied part of the site of Buckingham Palace and its grounds. It derived its name from a garden of mulberry trees planted in 1609 by James I, who wished to encourage the manufacture of English silks. Charles I, in the fourth year of his reign, granted by letters patent to Lord Aston "the custody and keeping of the Mulberry Garden in the County of Middlesex, and of the mulberries and silkworms there, and of all the houses and buildings to the same garden belonging. . . ." Before 1632 Sir George Goring had purchased the post from Lord Aston and given his name to the residence. Not long after the house was occupied by Speaker Lenthall, while the garden under the Commonwealth became a place of public entertainment. At the Restoration Goring returned to his house. One of the other buildings became a tavern called Mulberry Garden House, and kept by a person named Coleby. The first mention of the Garden as a public resort is in Evelyn's Diary under the date of 10 May, 1654:

> "My Lady Gerrard treated us at the Mulberry Garden, now the only place of refreshment about the town for persons of the best quality to be

exceedingly cheated at; Cromwell and his partisans having shut up and seized on Spring Garden,
which till now had been the usual rendezvous for
the ladies and gallants at this season."[1]

Ludlow in his Memoirs describes Charles II drinking
healths "at a debauch in the Mulberry Garden."[2]
Pepys, after seeing Sedley's comedy on 20 May, 1668,
for the second time, "walked over the Park to the Mulberry Garden, where I never was before; and find it a
very silly place, worse than Spring Garden and but
little company, and those a rascally, whoring, roguing
sort of people; only a wilderness here that is somewhat
pretty, but rude. Did not stay to drink."[3] Nevertheless
three months later the diarist spent 18s. on Pierce and
his wife there, and on 5 April, 1669, was again at the
garden with "a good deal of company," and "we
mighty merry."[4]

Dryden used to frequent the Mulberry Garden in his
young days if we may trust the famous writer in the
Gentleman's Magazine of February 1745, recalling the
days of "plain John Dryden": "I have eat tarts with him
and Madam *Reeve* at the Mulberry-Garden when our
author advanced to a sword and chadreux wig." In
1709, Dr. King described the changes that had taken
place in the neighbourhood in his "Art of Cookery":

> "The fate of things is always in the dark;
>   What Cavalier would know *St. James's* Park?
>   For *Locket's* stands where gardens once did spring,
>   And wild ducks quack where grasshoppers did sing;
>   A princely palace on that site does rise,
>   Where *Sedley's* noble muse found Mulberries."

The "princely palace" was Buckingham House,
erected by John Sheffield, Earl of Mulgrave, and sub-

[1] Diary, ed. Dobson, II. 71.
[2] Ludlow's Memoirs, ed. Firth, II. 275.
[3] Diary, ed. Wheatley, VIII. 23.
[4] *Ibid.*, VIII. 87, 285.

sequently Duke of Buckinghamshire, who in 1709 was living there with his haughty consort, Sir Charles Sedley's granddaughter. Probably the laſt record of the Mulberry Garden is in a Report to the Lords of the Treasury dated 25 February 1762, which describes it as "containing about four acres twenty-two perches, over which ſtands more than half of Buckingham House."

The Mulberry Garden figures in many contemporary plays as a public pleasure resort much frequented by lovers, young sparks and women of the town. Aᶜt II. sc. ii. of the Duke of Newcaſtle's "The Humorous Lovers" (produced about 30 March, 1667), is laid there, and Etherege in the sprightly firſt scene of the second aᶜt of his "She Wou'd if She Cou'd" had also anticipated Sedley by placing the Mulberry Garden on the ſtage. Wycherley followed Newcaſtle, Sedley and Etherege by laying the firſt scene of "Love in a Wood or St. James's Park," in "The Dining-Room in Mulberry Garden House." Shadwell alludes to the Mulberry Garden's bad reputation in "The Humouriſts" (4to, 1670), Act III. where Friske, a woman of the town, says to her friend, Mrs. Striker: "O me, Madam, why does not your Ladyship frequent the Mulberry Garden oftner? I vow we had the pleasanteſt Divertizement there laſt Night." To which Striker replies, "Ay, I was there, *Mrs. Friske*; and the Garden was very full, Madam, of Gentlemen and Ladies, that made love together till twelve a Clock at Night, the prettily'ſt, I vow 'twould do one's Heart good to see them."

Finally, in Betterton's "Amorous Widow" (8vo, 1706; produced *c.* 1670) Lovemore asks Lady Laycock if she walks "in the evenings into St. James's Park or into the Mulberry Garden," and praises the "wilderness" that Pepys found "somewhat pretty."

"Bellamira, or the Miſtress," Sedley's second comedy, was produced at the King's house in May 1687 and printed in the same year. The only contemporary criticism which survives is that of Sedley's old friend, Sir George Etherege, who wrote of it in the following words from Ratisbon to the Duke of Buckingham: "my witty Friend Sir C . . . . . S . . . y's 'Bellamira' gave me that intire Satisfaction that I cannot read it over too often."[1] This high commendation from such a good judge as Sir George is not undeserved, and we can agree without hesitation to Genest's emphatic statement that "this is by far the best of Sedley's plays." Beside these judgments should be placed the opinion of the author whose curt dismissal of Sedley's dramatic works has already been quoted: "It is difficult to imagine the time when such a coarse and atrocious production as the play in question could have been tolerated on the English stage."

"Bellamira" has exactly the qualities that "The Mulberry Garden" lacked: organic unity, vigour and sustained interest. The silly "heroic" element which disfigured the earlier comedy has entirely disappeared and the whole is written in admirably easy and lucid prose with a fine racy flavour. "The Mulberry Garden" is the work of a young beau, slightly effeminate and distinctly boyish. "Bellamira" is mature and masculine. Acute observation of contemporary life combined with the study of the classics and of Shakespeare, of which this play bears obvious signs, have borne fruit in a comedy of manners which is worthy to be ranked beside the best work of Wycherley and Etherege, and only falls below the dazzling achievements of the mature Congreve. The words "coarse and atrocious" seem singularly inapplicable to such a play, and can only be explained as representing the criticism of an age which was quite unable to understand or appreciate the purely intellectual and non-moral view of life which the authors of the comedies of manners expressed in

[1] Buckingham's "Miscellaneous Works," 8vo, 1704, p. 140; letter from Etherege to Buckingham dated Ratisbon, October 21, 1689.

their plays. Any lover of fine English prose should be able to enjoy the *manner* of "Bellamira." To appreciate its *matter* it is necessary to share Charles Lamb's delight at finding plays in which there is "a privation of moral light" and "a happy breathing place from the burthen of moral questioning." In the words of the same critic, the characters of "Bellamira" "break through no laws or conscious restraints. They know of none," or, to quote one of themselves, "in matter of women" they "are all in a State of Nature, every man's hand against every man."

The main features of "Bellamira" are borrowed or rather adapted directly from the "Eunuch" of Terence, which is itself an adaptation of a lost Greek comedy by Menander of the same name. A comparison with the Latin original will show how remarkably Sedley's sense of dramatic form and architecture had developed since "The Mulberry Garden," and with what consummate skill he turned the work of the Latin author into a play which breathes the very spirit of Restoration England.

In Terence's play, Phaedria, a young Athenian gentleman, elder son of old Laches, is infatuated with Thais, a beautiful courtesan. She begs her lover to go into the country for a few days in order to give place to Thraso, a braggart soldier. Her excuse is that she wishes to obtain from Thraso a slave girl called Pamphila, who was brought up as her foster sister. Pamphila is actually a freeborn Athenian, who was kidnapped as an infant by pirates and sold to Thais's parents, and Thais has a shrewd suspicion of her origin. Phaedria sends Parmeno, his adroit and humorous valet, with a eunuch and a black girl as presents to Thais. Phaedria's younger brother, Chaerea, sees Pamphila and falls violently in love with her. At Parmeno's suggestion, he dresses up as the eunuch and is delivered to Thais who is delighted with his beauty and intelligence. His object is, of course, to be left alone

with Pamphila. When this is achieved, he is overcome
by passion, ravishes her and makes good his escape.
Chremes, another young gentleman and a friend of
Chaerea, is sent for by Thais, who suspects that
Pamphila is related to him. When he arrives he finds
that Thais has gone to sup with Thraso. He joins them
and the soldier becomes drunk and quarrelsome, and
insults Thais by shouting for Pamphila. She leaves the
banquet and returns home with Chremes. Meanwhile
Phaedria has returned and learned of his brother's
escapade. Chremes receives proof from Thais that
Pamphila is his sister, and, when Thraso comes with a
ragged army of his followers to storm Thais's house,
and carry Pamphila off, he is daunted by the news that
she is a freeborn Athenian. Parmeno is frightened by
Pythias, Thais's slave, who tells him in jest that, as
Pamphila is a free citizen, Chremes is going to inflict
on Chaerea the traditional Athenian punishment for
ravishers. He goes and confesses all to old Laches,
who is very angry at first, but who becomes reconciled
to his sons when he discovers that Chaerea has arranged
with Chremes to marry Pamphila. An excellent final
touch is given by Gnatho, Thraso's parasite and flatterer. For a weighty consideration he promises the
soldier to get him readmitted into Thais's house. He
sends Thraso away and suggests to Phaedria that he
should allow Thais to receive Thraso, as the latter is
too ridiculous to be a serious rival, and is sufficiently
wealthy and foolish to keep them all in funds besides
supplying an endless source of amusement. Phaedria
consents and Thraso calls back his patron, who is over-
joyed by the cordial reception which he receives, and
which he ascribes entirely to the information concerning his rank and achievements which had been imparted
by his admiring friend.

The play is a typical production of the Athenian
New Comedy. It is neat, elegant and a little bloodless.
The discreet humour of Gnatho's ironical flatteries,

Parmeno's elaborate intrigues, the lovelorn Phaedria
and his good-humoured but business-like mistress are
all characteristic of the art of a small, highly civilised
but tired and over-refined community. The most
notable adaptation of it in a modern language before
Sedley's was "L'Eunuque" of La Fontaine, published
in 1654, but never acted. La Fontaine follows Terence
fairly closely, but departs from his original in one
important detail. Pamphila, in Terence's play, like most
virtuous women in the New Comedy, is mute, and we
only hear the story of her rape from Chaerea. La Fontaine's Pamphile is a speaking character, and for the
incident of the rape there is substituted a scene where
Chérée, disguised as the eunuch, is left alone with
Pamphile in the house of Thais and makes honourable
love to her in polished alexandrines, revealing to her his
rank and promising to marry her, and departing after
obtaining permission to kiss her hand. Although Sedley
does not follow La Fontaine in this departure from
Terence, there is at least one passage which inclines
me to think that he knew the French play.[1] But he
handled his original on the whole in a far freer manner

[1] Cf. Terence, *Eunuchus*, II. 365–368:

"*Chaer*. O fortunatum istum eunuchum qui quidem in hanc detur
domum!
  Par. Quid ita?
  Chaer. Rogitas? summa forma semper conservam domi videbit,
conloquetur, aderit una in unis ædibus;
cibum non numquam capiet cum ea; interdum propter dormiet";

with La Fontaine, *L'Eunuque* (Œuvres, Paris, 1827, IV. 58), II. iv.:

"*Chérée*. S'il est ainsi reçu, qu'il me donne d'envie !
  Parmenon. Vous préservent les dieux d'un heur pareil au sien!
Ce seroit pour Pamphile un mauvais entretien.
  Chérée. Quoi! garder une fille et si jeune et si belle!
Coucher en même chambre, et manger auprès d'elle";

and Sedley, "Bellamira," II. i. 8:

"*Lion*. Oh, happy Eunuch! that art to live in the same house with
this Divine Creature.

than the French author. His chief departure from Terence's scheme is inspired by a remarkably sound instinct. He hit on the character who is the real centre of the action in the "Eunuch" as the most essentially un-English thing in the play. By changing this character into a person who is at once thoroughly English and characteristic of Sedley's own age, he has altered the whole tone of the play and, as it were, has brought it out of the close atmosphere of Levantine intrigue into the fresh air of the Park and the Mall. The character in question is that of Parmeno, the crafty rascal of a valet and the real hero of Terence's comedy, whose versatile and adroitly unscrupulous character is typical of the popular heroes of Southern Europe. Had Molière or Beaumarchais adapted the play we can be sure that somebody very like Sganarelle, Mascarille or Figaro would have appeared in Parmeno's place. Sedley rightly felt that such a character was an exotic in England, where valets have never been popular, and has made the whole play intimately English by substituting for Parmeno a jolly old toper called Merryman, who is the boon companion of Keepwell (Phaedria's English counterpart). Merryman's name, as well as that of his rival, Cunningham, comes from Betterton's "The Amorous Widow" (acted about 1670), and the hint of a contrast between a fat and a thin suitor may, as Genest remarks, have been given by James Howard's absurdly crude farce, "All Mistaken" (acted 1667, published 1672), but his character is borrowed from neither of these plays. It is impossible that it should not have been to some extent suggested by that of Thomas Shadwell, whose connection with this play has already been

---

Merr. Why so? the nearer he is to a fine Woman the more sensible he must be of his loss.

Lion. But he'l see continually his fair fellow Servant, sit by sometimes and talk with her. . . ."

It is noticeable that Sedley has amplified Parmeno's simple "Quid ita" in a very similar way to La Fontaine.

noticed.[1] Merryman is a great jolly tun of a man like
Shadwell, and like him glories in the depth of his pota-
tions. And when Keepwell finds him in an embarrass-
ing situation he sings to him three lines of one of Shadwell's own songs.[2]

If Merryman owes something to Shadwell, he has
a still more illustrious progenitor. His speeches immediately call to mind the words of no less a person than
Sir John Falstaff. They have exactly Falstaff's relish
and gusto. What more Falstaffian words have ever been
penned than these?

> "Survey my Bulk: it was not built for hast;
> 'tis the slow Product of Tuns of Claret, Chines of
> Beef, Ven'son Pastyes, and so-forth,"

and what other character except Sir John could have
inspired such a description as this?

> "Peace, thou moving Dropsie, that wadlest
> with Fat, worse than a Goose with Egg."

Sedley's other important deviation from Terence's
work is in the treatment of the female characters. His
Bellamira is a very different person from that very
conventional hetæra, Thais. She is said[3] to be modelled
after Barbara Palmer, Countess of Castlemaine and
afterwards Duchess of Cleveland, the most beautiful
and dissolute harlot of the Court of Charles II, and there
is no reason to disbelieve the tradition. When Keepwell
is away she is unfaithful as a matter of course, and

---

[1] See above, p. 169.
[2] "Bellamira," IV. i.:

*"Her Breasts of Delight are two Bottles of White and her Eyes are
two Cups of Canary."*

The lines are from a song sung by Clodpate in "Epsom Wells,"
V. i.
[3] By Genest: "Some Account of the English Stage," I. 455.

instead of supping with her military suitor like Thais, she tells him to meet her in "the walk you know of by Kensington." When he has gone to the rendezvous she dresses in men's clothes and, in company with Merryman, waylays the braggart, thoroughly frightens him and relieves him of his medals and superfluous coin. The picture of Restoration life is made more convincing by the introduction of another female character, Thisbe, the ward of Merryman, who has no counterpart in Terence. She is courted both by her guardian and the lean rake, Cunningham, who is said to be a portrait of that Colonel Jack Churchill who nearly married Sir Charles's daughter, Katherine. Although a virtuous woman, she is on intimate terms with Bellamira, and such a connection was as natural in Restoration England as it was impossible in the Athens of Menander. One of the most brilliant passages in the play is a conversation between the two women which tells us more about the demi-monde of the reign of Charles II than all the history books:

> *This.* You are a great Politician.
> *Bell.* There goes more to our Trade, than a good Face; I have known many of these unthinking Butterflyes, Debauch'd, Pox'd, and in Gaol, the same Summer: Let's up into my Chamber; I must set myself out for *Dangerfield* he'l be here anon.
>
> .   .   .   .   .   .
>
> *This.* They say he has been Hansome.
> *Bell.* 'Twas so long ago every Body has forgot it but himself: He is a Pretender to Wit; but his is worse than none: as a Country Scraper is worse than no Musick at all.
> *This.* And yet this Fellow for a little Mony——
> *Bell.* No, for a great deal of Mony. I will make the Presents he gives me, my Baits to Catch others with: fine Cloaths and rich Furniture, are great

Provocatives to those that don't pay for 'em, which are the Men for our Turn.

This. Like the Gentlemen that live in Town, you have your pleasure in one place and receive your Rent from an other: 'tis the way to have your Tenement thrown into your Hands.

Bell. Keepwell has taken a Lease for Life, and laid out so much in Improvements, that I am secure of him; and for the Rest, they shall pay me as they are Able.

This. My Guardian and I have now and then a small Quarrel, about my keeping you so much Company.

.   .   .   .   .   .

Bell. Does he not see that we Govern the Town? Have Power and Plenty follow us? we Visit, Dance, Play at Cards, go to Hide Park, *St. James's,* and Sup together, and are a World among our Selves.

This. But like the Inhabitants of the other World, you neither Marry nor are given in Marriage; and he wou'd have me fit for a Husband.

Bell. Get Mony enough and you can never want a Husband. A Husband is a good Bit to Close ones Stomach with, when Love's Feast is over. Who wou'd begin a Meal with Cheese? Come into my Chamber, and I will instruct thee farther in these Mysteries."

The passage which illustrates best how Sedley's power in comic dialogue had increased since the "Mulberry Garden" is that in which Lionel (the English Chaerea) tells Merryman of his first glimpse of Isabella (the counterpart of Pamphila):

"*Merry.* What's the matter? you look as if you were Drunk.

T

Lion. I am worse; I am mad; I am anything; I am in Love.

Merry. How *Keepwell* will Laugh at you! But with whom?

Lion. Not with a ſtale Wench, like him; nor with any of the little Tinsel, short Liv'd Beauties of the Town, squeez'd into shape by Taylors, and ſtarv'd into it by their Mothers.

Merry. How then?

Lion. A new turn of a Face, unknown till now to Nature's self, in all her Numberless Varieties.

Merry. 'Tis wond'erous; you are Maul'd; *Cupid* has shot you with a Blunderbus.

Lion. What eyes! Teeth white . . .

Merry. As a new Tobacco-pipe.

Lion. Peace, Prophane Wretch, thou art not fit to mingle in these Miſteries. Her own Complexion; Her Body solid and full of Juice; the Nobleſt Fabrick of unſtinted Nature!

Merry. Her Age?

Lion. Seventeen.

Merry. I have drunk excellent *Hockamore* of that Age.

Lion. Damn thy dull Hockamore and thy base Jaded Pallat, that affeᶜts it; Cou'd I but get this Divine Creature into my hands by Fraud, Force, Price, Prayer, any way so that I enjoy her, I care not.

Merry. Who is She? she may be a Person of Quality, and you may bring an old house upon your head.

Lion. 'Tis but a Duel or two that way; and if her Relations be Numerous, we'l Fight Six to Six and make an end on't.

Merry. What Country Woman is she?

Lion. I know not.

Merry. Where does she live?

Lion. I can't tell.

Merry. We are upon a very cold Scent : where did you see her?

Lion. In the Street; with a Servant behind her.

Merry. How come you to lose her?

Lion. That's it I was cursing at: Nor do I think there is a Man whom all the Stars conspire against like me. What Crime have I committed to be thus Plagu'd?

Merry. The Stars are Pretty Twinkling Rogues, that light us home, when we are Drunk sometimes, but neither care for you nor me nor any man."

This is abler dialogue and finer prose than anything which had hitherto been produced by the Wits outside the best passages in "Sir Fopling Flutter" and "The Country Wife." It flows as easily as conversation, and yet, to use Synge's fine simile, "every speech is as fully flavoured as a nut or apple." The bouts of abuse between the fat drunkard, Merryman, and the lean rake, Cunningham, are obviously suggested by the similar passages at arms between Falstaff and Prince Hal. They are not unworthy of such distinguished parentage: the final "flyting" has a splendid and joyous extravagance in which we can detect what is perhaps the last embodiment of the lusty old English comedy that began with the farces of John Heywood and reached its zenith in Falstaff and Sir Toby Belch:

"*Cunn.* Every man's constitution will not run out into Fat, 'tis the Commendation of a Capon: a good Cock is alwaies lean as I am.

Merr. A good Coxcomb alwaies thinks well of himself; why, thou lean Rascal Deer, thou visible Pox, thou Common-shore of Physick, Reproach of Doctors and Ruine of Apothecari's, who Flux'st away thy Flesh as often as an Adder cast his Skin and art full as venemous.

Cunn. I am sure you look like a full Moon or a Fat Bawd swell'd with the Tooth Ach.

Merr. When I walk the Streets, men say there goes an honeſt well natur'd Fat Fellow to drink a bottle with, and a good Husband I warrant him.

Cunn. A good Cuckold perhaps: but the Ladies cry foh, there goes a greasie Sot, a Chandler's Shop in the shape of a man, a meer Lump, a Spunge full of Terse[1]: whose mouth ſtinks worse than the Bung hole of a Barrel, a Load of manifeſt impotency, Guts and Garbage for the Bear Garden.

Merr. Thou meer ſtake to hang Cloaths upon, thou Scarrow,[2] thou piece of Shrivil'd Parchment, thou walking Skelleton, that may'ſt be read upon alive, can'ſt thou think any Woman so sharp set as to pick thy rotten Bones, which are but the leaving of Pox, Mercury and Consumption?"

This passage and indeed the whole play is a perfeſt dramatic example of that quality of *guſto* that Hazlitt desiderated in all forms of art. By infusing English red blood into the shapely Terentian form, Sedley has produced a type of the comedy of manners that ſtands completely alone. It is wholly free from the satiric and moral purpose of Wycherley's fineſt work, and in spirit is akin rather to the maſterpieces of Etherege and Congreve. But whereas the comedies of these authors are concerned chiefly with the slightly affeſted atmosphere of the drawing-rooms and boudoirs of fine ladies, Sedley's play is a comedy of manners that deals rather with the bohemian world of the tavern and the demi-monde, and yet retains the fine ariſtocratic flavour which is essential to the type. It succeeds in doing what Shadwell attempted throughout a great part of his career and never quite accomplished.

---

[1] *i.e.* claret.   [2] *i.e.* scarecrow.

It is a pity that instead of producing more comedies like "Bellamira," Sedley spent a great deal of his time in trying to achieve what was entirely beyond his powers. The passion, the high seriousness and profound ethical sense necessary for the writing of great tragedy were not compatible with the qualities of the circle of Charles II and "Gentle George," and it must be admitted that Sedley's tragedy of "Antony and Cleopatra," produced at the Duke's house in 1676, deserves most of the unkind things which the critics have said of it, even though we grant that almost any play on the story is likely to seem feeble beside the masterpieces of Shakespeare and Dryden. Sedley's play has indeed found one defender[1] in Prof. R. H. Case, the editor of the Arden edition of Shakespeare's "Antony and Cleopatra," who describes it as "full of life, bustle, combat and siege," and who thinks that "the whole can appeal, if we forget Shakespeare." Prof. Case's defence is perhaps justified if we regard the play purely as a piece of stage carpentry, a libretto for Clark's music. But it must always be matter for astonishment that the author of "Phillis is my only Joy" and "Bellamira" could have produced a piece of this length with hardly a single passage of real literary excellence.

It is true that the ranting which disfigures most of the riming tragedies of the reign of Charles II is not to be found in Sedley's "Antony and Cleopatra," but the colourless, conventional diction and the unenterprising metre make us almost long for the wildest moments of Almanzor and Maximin. Imagine Antony, the Antony of Plutarch and of Shakespeare, speaking like this:

[1] I am not reckoning such uncritical estimates as those of Shadwell, who wrote, "in this Play the *Romans* are true *Romans*, and their Style is such; and I dare affirm that there is not in any Play of this Age so much of the Spirit of the Classick Authors, as in your *Antony* and *Cleopatra*" (Dedication of "A True Widow"); and Ayloffe, who in his preface to Sedley's Miscellaneous Works (1702) remarks that "*Cleopatra* dy'd not more gallantly in Alexandria than by our Author in *Drury Lane*"!

> "The timerous Deer, their female standing by,
> Each other will to Wounds and Death defie.
> Love gives short courage to the meanest soul,
> The creeping things he arms, and winged fowl.
> Yet overcharg'd with love, I lost the day,
> And in my Mistress's presence ran away."

And imagine the dying Cleopatra apostrophising the asp thus:

> "Good Asp, bite deep and deadly in my breast
> And give me sudden and eternal rest."

The only passages that have the slightest literary value are one or two cynical epigrams that are quite unsuitable to such a setting:

> "Let Fools the Fame of Loyalty divide,
> Wise men and Gods are on the strongest side."

The love of Antony and Cleopatra and the struggle in Antony's mind between love and honour, which must surely dominate the whole action in a successful play on this theme, are obscured in Sedley's piece by other motifs that are not particularly interesting in themselves, and which are quite unwarranted by history. Plutarch tells how Photinus, an Egyptian eunuch, plotted against Julius Cæsar and Cleopatra, when the former was in Egypt, and Corneille uses the story as part of the main action of his "La Mort de Pompée," which Sedley helped to translate in his youth. In his "Antony and Cleopatra" Sedley transfers the story of Photinus's plot and insurrection to the time of the final defeat of Antony by Octavius, and embroiders it by making Photinus a zealous Egyptian statesman, who aspires to the crown of Egypt and the hand of Iras, Cleopatra's favourite. And, as though this were not enough to disturb the balance of the story he has to introduce another unnecessary and unhistorical subplot by making Mæcenas the devoted but unsuccessful suitor of Octavia! The division of the

charaĉters into pairs of lovers almoɬt reduces the great
legend to the level of comic opera. However, we have
at leaɬt one reason to be thankful for "Antony and
Cleopatra." There is a tradition, preserved by Eusden,[1]
the eighteenth-century poet (1688–1730), that it
suggeɬted the theme to Dryden, and so Sedley may be
held to have an indireĉt responsibility for the fineɬt
Reɬtoration tragedy, "All for Love."

The play called "Beauty the Conquerour, or the
Death of Marc Antony," printed in the 1702 edition
of Sedley's Miscellaneous Works, is not, as Sir A. W.
Ward incorreĉtly ɬtates, in his "Hiɬtory of English
Dramatic Literature" (III. 446), a reprint of "Antony
and Cleopatra." It is an unfinished reconɬtruĉtion of
that play as a classical tragedy with a chorus that sings
lyrics between the aĉts. The charaĉter of Oĉtavia is
eliminated, and the place of Photinus is taken by
Achillas, an Egyptian captain, mentioned by Plutarch.[2]
The couplets are moɬtly taken from the earlier version,
though they are re-arranged and slightly altered, and
a few additions are made, of which the following passage
will serve as a specimen:

> "We on proud Rome shall see ourselves Reveng'd,
>   Her Laws struck dumb, and her Republick Chang'd.
>   *Romans* shall welter in each other's Blood,
>   And *Nile*-bred Monsters drink the Purple Flood."

The lyrics are obviously incomplete, but the fragments do not give the impression that Sedley was

---

[1]   "So Dryden sweetest sang, by envy fir'd,
         Thirst of Revenge, when Phœbus fail'd inspir'd;
         His Anthony did Sedley's muse o'ertake,
         And Absolom was writ for Zimri's sake."

"On a Lady who is the most beautiful and witty when she is angry."

"The Shorter Poems of the Eighteenth Century," ed. Iolo Williams,
1923, p. 140.

[2] In one obviously unfinished passage in Act V. sc. i., the abbrevia-
tion "Pho" appears before two of his speeches.

likely to succeed as a writer of the ſtatelier forms of ode.

Two other dramatic pieces are printed in the 1722 edition of Sedley's Collected Works. One is a very literal translation of the famous French farce, "Le Grondeur."[1] This piece was twice adapted for the ſtage in the eighteenth century, firſtly by Garrick in 1754,[2] and secondly by Goldsmith as a benefit for Quick, the actor, in 1773.[3] A specimen scene from Goldsmith's version is printed in his Miscellaneous Works.[4]

The presence of this piece in the edition of 1722 is no guarantee that it is Sedley's, as many of the contents of that edition are certainly spurious. There is, however, no great improbability that he may have amused himself by making such a translation in his laſt years, perhaps for a private performance. The other is entitled "The Tyrant King of Crete," and is merely a shortened version of a very poor play by Henry Killigrew called "Pallantus and Eudora," printed in folio in 1653. It had been written by Killigrew for the marriage of Lady Mary Villiers and Lord Charles Herbert as early as 1638. A printed version of it appeared in that year under the title of "The Conspiracy," which, according to Killigrew, was published without his permission from "a false and imperfect Transcript."[5] The dialogue of all three versions is in a blank verse that has reached the laſt ſtage of degeneration, and is often only diſtinguishable from prose by the fact that it is cut into lengths of approximately ten syllables. The only evidence that Sedley had anything to do with it is its inclusion in the edition of 1722 that contains pieces which are certainly not from his pen, and the only conceivable excuse for

---

[1] By Brueys and Palaprat, produced at the Théâtre Français, 1691.
[2] Genest, IV. 391.
[3] Forster's "Life and Times of Goldsmith" (ed. 1871), II. 342.
[4] Miscellaneous Works, London, 1837, 8vo, IV. 333.
[5] "Pallantus and Eudora," fol. 1653, Preface.

its appearance among his works is that Killigrew may have asked him to correct it and that a version with his corrections may have been found among his papers at his death. It is time, however, that he was freed from all responsibility for this shapeless mass, which has been falsely attributed to him for two centuries.

CHAPTER II

THE NON-DRAMATIC WORKS; AND TRANSLATIONS

"For pointed Satyrs I would *Buckhurst* chuse,
The best good Man, with the worst natur'd Muse,
For Songs and Verses, mannerly, obscene,
That then stir Nature up by Spring unseen,
And without forcing Blushes, warm the Queen.
Sidley has that prevailing gentle Art,
That can with a resistless Charm impart
The loosest Wishes to the chastest Heart,
Raise such a conflict, kindle such a Fire
Betwixt declining *Virtue* and *Desire*,
Till the poor vanquisht Maid dissolves away
In Dreams all Night, in Sighs and Tears all Day."

> "An Allusion to Harace (*sic*), the tenth
> Satyr on the First Book." Poems, etc., by the
> Right Honourable the E. of R. (Rochester),
> Antwerpen (n.d. ? 1680), pp. 41–42.

"Here gentle *Etheridge*'s and *Sidley*'s Muse
Warm the coy Maid, and melting Love infuse:
No unchaste Words with harsh offensive Sound
The tender Ears of blushing Virgins wound;
Nor Thought, which nauseous Images inspire,
And damp the glowing Heat of soft Desire:
But calm and easy the sweet Numbers move,
And every Verse is influenced by Love."

> Mr. Charles Tooke: "To a Young Lady with
> the first edition of A Collection of Poems,
> viz. The Temple of Death, etc.," third
> edition, 12mo, 1716, p. 2.

"But for the Wits of either Charles's days,
The Mob of Gentlemen who wrote with Ease;
Sprat, Carew, Sedley, and a thousand more,
(Like twinkling stars the Miscellanies o'er)
One Simile that solitary shines
In the dry desert of a thousand lines,

282

Or lengthen'd Thought that gleams through many a page
Has sanctified whole poems for an age."
> Pope, "Imitations of Horace," Bk. II. Ep. I.
> ll. 107–114.

"Sir Ch. . . . that can write and better Translate
Was likewise Deny'd it,[1] for he'd an Estate,
And from Homer to D. . . . n it never was known
That the Laureat had three Pence a Year of his own."
> Prior, "A Session of the Poets" (Poems from
> the Longleat MSS., Cambridge English
> Classics, 1907, p. 301).

POPE in conversation with Spence remarked that Sedley was "an insipid poet except in a few of his little love verses."[2] The exception is important, because the "little love verses" are the one portion of his writings which have kept his memory alive and which are ſtill appreciated by the general reader. It is true that the critic who found "Bellamira" "atrocious" has little use for Sedley as a poet: "From his amatory poems," he writes, "we will make no extraɕts. It may be a fine point whether at their worſt Sedley or Rocheſter was the coarseſt writer of the pair (*sic*)."[3] Thomas Bailey, a nineteenth-century hiſtorian of Nottinghamshire, writes that Sedley "was in his day much diſtinguished for his poetical talents . . . but his verses being chiefly devoted to loose and amorous subjeɕts, his fame perished with the voluptuous age in which he lived."[4] These critics are merely following in the footſteps of such earlier writers as the authors of the articles on Sedley in Cibber's "Lives of the Poets" (1753) and "Biographia Britannica" (1763). The former tells us that Sedley's verses are "amorous, tender and delicate, yet have not much ſtrength nor

[1] *i.e.* the laureateship.
[2] Spence's "Observations, Anecdotes and Characters," ed. Malone, 1820, p. 89.
[3] T. Longueville in "Rochester and Other Literary Rakes of the Restoration," p. 78.
[4] T. Bailey, "Annals of Nottinghamshire," IV. 62 (8vo, 1853).

do they exhibit great marks of genius," and speaks of
them as "propagating the immoralities of the times,"
while the latter writes that his "art wholly consisted of
raising loose thoughts and lewd desires without giving
any alarm and so that the poison worked slowly and
irresistibly." These criticisms may be traced to three
causes. The first is the nimbus of scandal which surrounded the poet's memory, and which interested
compilers of literary biography far more than a study
of the poems themselves. The second is Rochester's
allusion in his "Imitation[1] of the Tenth Satire of the
First Book of Horace," which is taken as a serious
criticism instead of what it obviously is, a piece of
amusing chaff which might have been written about
any writer of love lyrics by a playful friend. The third
is the fact that Sedley's works have been studied almost
wholly in a series of dishonest editions published many
years after his death, which contain a number of coarse
and inferior pieces that were never attributed to him
in his lifetime, and that in some cases can be definitely
proved to be the work of other authors.[2] Sedley's verse
has not, however, wanted defenders. His earliest
editor and "affinity," Captain Ayloffe, not inaptly
compares it to the "gallant easie wit of Horace," and
sixty-three years later Dr. J. Langhorne, in his "Effusions of Fancy and Friendship,"[3] distinguished Sedley
from "the Mob of Gentlemen who wrote with Ease,"
and ascribed to him "a good deal of wit, some genius
and a tolerable ear." This critic devotes seven pages
to an excellent analysis of Sedley's non-dramatic works,
illustrated by well-chosen quotations.

Nearly a century after Langhorne Sir Francis
Palgrave, in his notes to "The Golden Treasury,"

[1] Quoted at the head of this chapter.
[2] For a complete account of the text and canon of Sedley's work see
the Preface to my forthcoming edition of his Works.
[3] "The Effusions of Fancy and Friendship," by J. Langhorne, London,
2766, II. 157–64.

mentions "the courtly compliments" of Sedley as the latest example of "the poetry of simple passion" before its revival in the age of Burns and Cowper, and A. H. Bullen, in the introduction to his "Musa Proterva" (1889), writes: "From Sir Charles Sedley I have drawn very freely. In his own sphere Sedley is unapproachable; such songs as 'Love still has something of the sea,' or 'Phillis is my only Joy,' easily outdistance all rivals. He does not occupy an exalted place in English literature, but that place is secure." Bullen's appreciation of Sedley's best lyrics is repeated in a more critical form by Mr. Whibley in his article on the Restoration Court Poets in the "Cambridge History of English Literature," and Sir Walter Raleigh in his monograph on Milton gives high praise to "the self-abandonment and passion" of two or three of Sedley's songs.

To appreciate properly the qualities of Sedley's verse, it is necessary to understand the position of the group to which he belonged in the history of the English lyric. These authors form the last genuine school of English Court poets, and with them the tradition of Court poetry which began with the circle of Wyatt and Surrey in the reign of Henry VIII came to an end. There was, of course, Court poetry before Henry VIII and after Charles II, but neither before nor after was it considered an essential accomplishment of a courtier to write verse. However far Rochester, Sedley, Buckhurst and their friends may have fallen in their conduct below the great ideal of the Renaissance courtier as set forth by Baldassare Castiglione and even of Peacham, his English disciple, the conventions of their poetry are still to a large extent the conventions of the Renaissance Court life which placed on what Palgrave calls courtly compliments a value which it is difficult for a modern mind to understand. It is in their verse that we find almost for the last time the successful use of those pastoral names and metaphors which Virgil and the Greek romances had handed down as a sort of sacred language for courtly lovers. They are the laſt poets who can talk gracefully if not quite seriously about shepherdesses and swains and flames and darts.[1] On the other hand, they were something more than the laſt practitioners of the courtly manner. They were really important figures in the hiſtory of the great change that came over English poetry in the course of the seventeenth century. That change may be roughly described as the triumph of the intellectual and logical side of the Renaissance over the imaginative and emotional elements. All poetry worthy of the name, of course, from its very nature is to some extent imaginative and emotional as well as intellectual and logical. Even in the works of Poe or Mallarmé, the latter elements are not wholly suppressed any more than the former are in the verses of Swift or Voltaire. What has been called the "classical" or "Auguſtan" period of English poetry was a period when colour and passion and music were comparatively (but it muſt be insiſted, only comparatively) subordinated to the demands of logical thought and clarity of ſtatement. The very great eſteem in which such Latin poets as Horace, Ovid, Martial and Juvenal were held by all the leading scholars and critics muſt have had a great deal to do with the change, and this eſteem, together with the influence of social changes, would probably have brought it about without the example of contemporary France, which only helped a tendency that was already ſtrong, and that can be traced back as far as the poems of Ben Jonson.

The other ſtrain in English seventeenth-century poetry besides the Renaissance Court tradition and the "classical" tendency towards logic and clarity was

[1] I am not forgetting Pope's Pastorals. They are, however, in spite of the charm of several fine passages, merely the schoolboy exercises of the great poet of the "Rape of the Lock," the "Satires" and the "Dunciad."

the so-called "metaphysical" manner of Donne and his imitators, a curious and often splendid combination of mystical and sometimes cynical thought with far-fetched and quaint imagery, expressing itself usually in elaborate metrical patterns. This manner completely dominated the religious poetry of the first half of the century, and even the love poetry of the reign of Charles I was so strongly tinged by it that a courtier like Sir John Suckling can scarcely write a song without a strange and "curious" conceit like the following:

> "There never yet was woman made,
>   Nor shall but to be curst;
> And O, that I, fond I should first,
>   Of any Lover,
> This truth at my own charge to other fools discover!
>
> .   .   .   .
>
> All mankind are alike to them
>   And, though we iron find
> That never with a loadstone join'd,
>   'Tis not the iron's fault,
> It is because near the loadstone it was never brought."[1]

The new Court poetry of the Restoration was to aim at avoiding the "metaphysical" manner as far as possible, and by combining the clarity and logic of the "classical" tradition with the courtly conventions of the Renaissance to produce a kind of poetry which would be at once graceful and lucid and in the older sense of the word "polite." Edmund Waller had achieved this simplification of language and imagery in such a poem as the following, written before 1645:[2]

> "Chloris! what's eminent we know
>   Must for some cause be valued so;
>   Things without use, though they be good,
>   Are not by us so understood.
>   The early rose, made to display
>   Her blushes to the youthful May,

---

[1] Suckling's Works, ed. Thompson, p. 19.
[2] Waller's Poems, ed. Drury, I. 122.

> Doth yield her sweets, since he is fair,
> And courts her with a gentle air,
> Our stars do show their excellence
> Not by their light but influence;
> When brighter comets, since still known,
> Fatal to all are liked by none.
> So your admired beauty still
> Is by effects made good or ill."

It must have been from Waller, his mother's friend, that the young Sedley learned to write verses with exactly the same flowing rhythm, lucid thought and easy and rather obvious imagery:

> "*Cloris*, I cannot say your Eyes
> Did my unwary Heart surprise;
> Nor will I swear it was your Face,
> Your Shape, or any nameless Grace:
> For you are so intirely Fair,
> To love a Part, injustice were;
> No drowning Man can know which Drop
> Of Water his last Breath did stop;
> So when the Stars in Heaven appear,
> And joyn to make the Night look clear;
> The Light we no one's Bounty call,
> But the obliging Gift of all.
> He that does Lips, or Hands adore,
> Deserves them only, and no more;
> But I love All and every Part,
> And nothing less can ease my Heart.
> *Cupid*, that Lover, weakly strikes,
> Who can express what 'tis he likes."[1]

This kind of graceful, complimentary and quite unimpassioned love poetry, which unites admirably the logic and lucidity of the "classical" strain with the courtliness of the Renaissance tradition, is the first type of poetry practised by the Wits. What a relief its clearness and obvious good sense must have been to a generation surfeited with "enthusiasm" and metaphysical raptures of all kinds! Sedley is perhaps the ablest of the group in turning such pretty compliments:

[1] "Miscellaneous Works" (1702), pp. 15, 16.

> "Your Words fell on my Passion like those Showers
> Which Paint and multiply the rising Flowers;
> Like *Cupid's* self, a God and yet a Child,
> Your Looks at once were awful, and yet mild."[1]

> "As in those Nations, where they yet adore
> Marble and Cedar, and their Aid, implore:
> 'Tis not the Workman, nor the precious Wood,
> But 'tis the Worshipper that makes the God:
> So cruel Fair, though Heaven has giv'n you all
> We Mortals (Vertue or can Beauty) call,
> 'Tis we that give the Thunder to your Frowns,
> Darts to your Eyes, and to ourselves the wounds:"[2]

Buckingham was probably alluding to dainty work of this kind when he spoke of Sedley's "Witchcraft."[3] It may not be love poetry as it was understood by Shakespeare and Shelley, but it would have pleased Mrs. Millamant. Indeed she seems to have known the last lines and answered them admirably in the following words:

> "O the Vanity of these Men! *Fainall*, d'ee hear him? If they did not commend us, we were not handsome? Now you must know they could not commend one, if one was not handsome. Beauty the Lover's Gift—Lord, what is a Lover that it can give? Why, one makes Lovers as fast as one pleases, and they live as long as one pleases, and they die as soon as one pleases: And then if one pleases one makes more."[4]

Closely allied to these "courtly compliments" is a type of poetry which was practised by most of the fashionable poets of the day and which may be called

---

[1] Sedley's "Miscellaneous Works," 1702, p. 30.

[2] *Ibid.*, p. 52.

[3] "Some Account of the Life of Sir Charles Sedley," prefixed to the edition of 1722. The Author of this "Account" is the earliest authority that I can find for this criticism.

[4] "The Way of the World" (ed. Montague Summers, 1925), II. i.

U

the Dresden China dialogue. In such pieces, a conventional shepherd and shepherdess discuss such subjects as Love, Honour and Constancy in dainty lyrical verse. This kind of poem, which is probably the descendant of the estrifs and pastourelles of the Middle Ages, tinged with memories of Virgilian eclogues and Horace's famous "Donec gratus eram tibi," is the exact literary antitype of the *fêtes galantes* of Watteau and Fragonard. It must be judged purely as decoration and its success depends wholly on lightness of touch. Sedley's "Amintas and Celia" is not inferior in this respect to Rochester's charming "Strephon and Daphne":

> *"Strephon.*
>
> Women can with Pleasure feign:
> Men dissemble still with Pain.
> What Advantage will it prove,
> If I Lie, who cannot Love?
>
> *Daphne.*
>
> Tell me then the Reason why,
> Love from Hearts in Love does fly?
> Why the Bird will build a Nest
> Where he ne'er intends to rest.
>
> *Strephon.*
>
> Love, like other little Boys,
> Cries for Hearts, as they for Toys:
> Which when gain'd in Childish Play,
> Wantonly are thrown away."[1]

> *"Celia.*
>
> *Amintas*, I am come alone,
>   A silly harmless Maid,
> But whither is thy Honour flown?
>   I fear I am betray'd;
> Thy Looks are chang'd and in the Place
>   Of innocent Desires,
> Methinks I see thy Eyes and Face
>   Glow with unusual Fires.

---

[1] Rochester, "Poems on Several Occasions" (8vo, 1705), p. 2.

Amintas.

See's not my *Celia*, Nature wear
  One Countenance in the Spring,
And yet another Shape prepare
  To bring the Harvest in?

   .   .   .   .   .

Fears might my Infant Love become;
  'Twere want of vigor now
Should modesty those Hopes benum,
  The Place and You allow."[1]

The Wits are less successful when they attempt the full-length Virgilian eclogue, and I suspect that Pope was thinking of Sedley's "Pastoral Dialogue between Thirsis and Strephon" when he spoke of his insipidity:

"*Strephon*, O *Strephon*, once the jolliest Lad
That with shrill Pipe did ever Mountain glad;
Whilome the foremost at our Rural Plays:
The Pride and Glory of our Holydays:
Why dost thou now sit musing and alone,
Teaching the Turtles yet a Sadder Moan?"

This reminds us less of Arcadia than of Lady Wishfort when she longed to "retire to Desarts and Solitudes, and feed harmless Sheep by *Groves* and *purling* Streams."[2] Sedley and Rochester could, however, forget sometimes that they were courtiers and disciples of Mr. Waller. Alone among the Wits they possessed the secret of writing songs that are as simple and direct and passionate as those of Lovelace and Brome and Jonson. In Rochester's

"My dear Mistress has a Heart,
  Soft as those kind Looks she gave me;
When with Love's resistless Art,
  And her Eyes she did enslave me";

---

[1] Sedley in the "Miscellaneous Works," 1702, p. 40.
[2] "The Way of the World," V. i.

and Sedley's

> "Not *Celia*, that I juster am
>   Or better than the rest,
> For I would change each Hour like them,
>   Were not my Heart at rest,"

we hear for the last time before the age of Blake and
Burns the singing voice which is also the genuine voice
of passionate feeling. Sedley's song which is quoted
above is his masterpiece in this manner and was
written before 1672.[1] He retained his lyrical gift,
however, when he was middle-aged and respectable,
and it was probably after the Revolution that he
produced his best known and most musical song.[2]
In these lines he shows a power of metrical invention
which is quite astonishing in the reign of William III:

> "*Phillis* is my only Joy,
>   Faithless as the Winds or Seas;
> Sometimes coming, sometimes coy,
>   Yet she never fails to please;
>   If with a Frown
>   I am cast down,
>   Phillis smiling,
>   And beguiling,
> Makes me happier than before.
>
> Tho', alas, too late I find,
>   Nothing can her fancy fix,
> Yet the Moment she is kind
>   I forgive her all her Tricks;
>   Which tho' I see,
>   I can't get free;
>   She deceiving,
>   I believing;
> What need Lovers wish for more?"

The playful tone of this song is found in other poems
of Sedley and is not the least significant element in

[1] Sedley's " Miscellaneous Works," 1702, p. 11.
[2] Not printed till 1702, when it appeared in the "Miscellaneous
Works."

his work. What is interesting about the poetry of the
Wits is the fact that they came to perceive the incongruity of their own intellectual and non-moral spirit
and the old conventions of Renaissance poetry which
they continued to use. They were all conscious of the
justice of such criticisms as that of Prig in Shadwell's
play:

> "I observe you Wits are always making Songs
> of the Love of Shepherds and Shepherdesses; a
> Company of block-headed, clownish, ugly, tawny,
> Sun-burnt People; I had as lief hear songs upon
> the Love of their Sheep as their own."[1]

Their realisation of this incongruity was expressed
in different ways by the chief poets of the group according to their respective characters. Rochester's method
was that of irony, well illustrated by his song called
"Grecian Kindness":[2]

> "There, the kind Deity of Wine
>   Kiss'd the soft wanton God of Love;
> This clapp'd his Wings, that press'd his Vine;
>   And their best Pow'rs united move.
> While each brave *Greek* embrac'd his Punk,
> Lull'd her asleep and then grew drunk."

This treatment of the heroic figures of literary tradition
is not far from that of the ironical poets of the twentieth
century:

> "Often he wonders why on earth he went
>   Troyward, or why poor Paris ever came,
> Oft she weeps gummy-eyed and impotent;
>   Her dry shanks twitch at Paris' mumbled name.
> So Menelaus nagged and Helen cried;
> And Paris slept on by Scamander side."[3]

---

[1] "A True Widow," II. i. ("Collected Works," 1720, III. 147).
[2] Rochester, "Poems on Several Occasions," 1705, p. 21.
[3] Rupert Brooke, "Menelaus and Helen" ("Collected Works,"
1918, p. 93).

Buckhurst, "the best good man, with the worst natur'd Muse," found a solution of the problem in the writing of satire. His little poems on Lady Dorchester quoted in the first part of the present study are good examples of his success in that very rare and extremely difficult kind of poem, the satiric lyric. Sedley, who seems to have had a gentler character than either of his friends, expresses the gulf between the new spirit and the old conventions by using the latter in a half-playful manner:

> "*Phillis*, this mighty Zeal asswage,
>   You over-act your part;
> The Martyrs at your tender Age,
>   Gave Heaven but half their Heart.
>
> Old men (till past the Pleasure) ne're
>   Declaim against the Sin,
> 'Tis early to begin to fear
>   The Devil at Fifteen."

This is the conventional address of the courtly lover to the cruel fair one, used by a poet who no longer took it seriously but regarded it as an amusing game. The famous Knotting Song is another exquisite example:

> "The God of Love in thy bright Eyes
>   Does like a Tyrant reign;
> But in thy Heart a Child he lyes,
>   Without his Dart or Flame.
> Phillis, *without Frown or Smile*
> *Sat and knotted all the while.*"

Such lines with their mixture of playfulness, sentiment and good breeding are the first real English *vers de société*, and Sedley has the honourable if not lofty distinction of founding the charming tradition which was to be carried on by Prior, Gay, Locker Lampson and Austin Dobson. No judgment on such works as the Knotting Song could be juster or better expressed than that of Professor Lascelles Abercrombie: "A delicious moment! and is there not an

exquisitely personal distinction in it? And could anything be better as art than the precision and proportion of its rendering into language? But no one would
suggest that Sedley's version of unpropitious love
has anything of the quality we call greatness."[1]
Anyone who comes to Sedley's poetry to find "the
quality we call greatness" will be woefully disappointed. Only once does he approach what may be
called the "great" manner. It is in that marvellous
opening which has deserved the praise of countless
critics:

> " Love still has somthing of the Sea,
> From whence his Mother rose."

The rest of the poem is competent in the manner
of the Buckhursts and Mulgraves, but the first two
lines for once carry us into the sphere of Sappho, of
Catullus and of Landor.

In some late pieces Sedley abandons the last vestiges
of the courtly convention and writes verses which are
as realistic and unemotional as Swift's:

> "There was a prudent grave Physician,
> Careful of Patients as you'd wish one;
> Much good he did with Purge and Glister,
> And well he knew to raise a Blister."

The series of Court Characters, which are chiefly
clever imitations of Martial, belong to the same
category. One couplet is worthy of quotation as a
vivid picture of the society in which Sedley must have
spent much of his time:

> "Of all that starving Crew we saw to Day,
> None but has kill'd his Man, or writ his Play."

The long poem in heroic couplets called "The
Happy Pair" was probably one of its author's latest
works. Its subject must have been suggested by

---

[1] "The Idea of Great Poetry," 1925, p. 36.

Sedley's own unhappy matrimonial experience. It belongs to the new kind of reasoned and argumentative poetry first used effectively by Dryden in such pieces as "Religio Laici." A poet of the Elizabethan or the Victorian age who wished to treat the subject would certainly have used the symbolism of a classic or mediæval legend or a story of contemporary life. Had Sedley himself lived fifty years later, "The Happy Pair" would probably have been written in Thomsonian blank verse, and its argument would have been enlivened by "Episodes" like those of "The Seasons." As it is he treats his theme in general terms and describes the effect of ill-assorted marriages not upon Helen or Guinevere or Catherine of Braganza, but upon Man and Woman:

> "This must be then our issue, where our Love
> Does not together with our Nuptials move.
> Possessions can't for fickle Joy provide,
> When Love, the end of Living, is Destroy'd.
> Alas! we're all mistaken in the Kind,
> A Happy Man is measur'd by the Mind."

There is argument and example but no narrative. If the general form of Sedley's poem belongs to the age of prose and reason there is much of the seventeenth-century colour and music still in it. The lines describing the fall of man from innocence owe something to Milton, but they have ringing vigour of their own:

> "When damning PRIDE, that Architect of Hell,
> Made not, as yet, his Tempted Soul Rebel.
> When plunging Avarice no Birth had found,
> Nor tore the precious Entrails of the Ground."

And there is an emotional richness in lines like the following that was not common after Dryden:

> "Cheek clings to Cheek, and swimming Eyes to Eyes."

The dualism in the matter of the poem is equally interesting. A large part of it is obviously suggested

by the sixth Satire of Juvenal and is a description in
the true "Augustan" manner of the blighting effects
of mercenary marriages. Here are lines that follow
Juvenal as any satirist in verse from Dryden to Gifford
might have followed him:

> "Man, like the sordid Earth, from which he sprung,
>   Corrupts his Soul by a base heap of Dung:
>   Forgetting the Celestial Form he bore,
>   He values not the Woman but her Store:
>   Extends his treach'rous Pledge to golden Charms,
>   And joins his hands to none but spangled Arms."[1]

But the idealism of the "noble savage" and the praise
of a rustic and "natural" life go back to the "heroic"
plays which were popular in the poet's youth and
forward to the new naturalism of the eighteenth
century. The following passage in its tenderness, its
feeling for nature and its metrical originality is quite
extraordinary for the opening of the eighteenth
century, and is probably unparalleled for these qualities
at that date except by the remarkable works of Sedley's
younger contemporary, Anne, Countess of Winchelsea:

> "Love, like a cautious fearful Bird, ne'er builds,
>   But where the Place, Silence and Calmness yields:
>   He slily flies to Copses, where he finds
>   The snugging Woods secure from Blasts and Winds.
>   Shuns the huge Boughs of a more stately Form,
>   And Laughs at Trees tore up with ev'ry Storm.
>   The pleasant Nightingale can ne'er be won,
>   To quit a Temp'rate Shade, to scorch i' the Sun;
>   In some low Grove, he sings his Charming Note,
>   And on a Thorn tunes the sweet warbling Throat."

When Wordsworth said that "A Nocturnal Reverie"
and "Windsor Forest" were the only poems between
"Paradise Lost" and "The Seasons" which contain
new images of external Nature,[2] he had certainly

---

[1] Cf. Juvenal, Satire VI. ll. 136–41.
[2] Essay Supplementary to the Preface to the Second Edition of
"Lyrical Ballads."

forgotten Sedley's "snugging Woods." The whole passage both in form and matter (except perhaps for the epithet "Charming") suggests the age of Coleridge and Keats rather than that of Swift and Pope.

The existence of such poetry as this about the year 1700 should make us reconsider the old conception of a "romantic revival" following an "age of prose and reason," and regard the emotional and intellectual strains in English poetry as two elements which have always existed side by side, although one or the other may from time to time have assumed a special importance.

As a verse translator Sedley fully deserves the praise of Prior quoted at the head of the present chapter. Of his share in the early version of "Pompey the Great," in which he collaborated with Waller, Godolphin, Filmer and Buckhurst, it is difficult to speak with any certainty, as it is impossible to say which act was translated by him. As Waller is said to have translated the first and Buckhurst the last,[1] Sedley must be responsible for the second, third or fourth. In his own play, "Antony and Cleopatra," a few lines bear a faint resemblance to some words spoken by Cæsar in the third act of "Pompey,"[2] but this is hardly sufficient evidence on which to attribute the third act to him. As the Epilogue admits, the

[1] See pp. 80–83.
[2] The resemblance is rather in the sense than the actual words. Cæsar in his generous indignation at Pompey's death in the earlier play cries:

> "What publique Joy had our sad Warr ensu'd,
> If I and Pompey o're our former feud,
> Triumphant had in the same Chariot rid,"

and Octavius in Sedley's play expresses a very similar wish after the death of Antony:

> "O what a Godlike pleasure it had been
> With thee t' have shar'd the Empire once agen!
> And to have made a Second Sacrifice
> To friendship of each other's Enemies."

"Mounsieur is something altered" in his English dress. The translation is very free—free enough to be called a paraphrase—but this is probably due in part to the exigencies of the English audience, which would never have liſtened to the interminable tirades of Corneille's Romans.[1] In spite of some vigorous passages, the whole performance is less spirited and less faithful than the contemporary version of Mrs. Katherine Philips.[2]

Sedley's fineſt work as a translator is to be found in his version of the eighth ode of the second book of Horace. Page in his edition of Horace[3] writes, that "this Ode has the peculiar intereſt of being perhaps the only Ode of Horace of which there is an adequate English rendering—that by Sir Charles Sedley." It is certainly the only version that will compare with Dryden's superb paraphrase of the twenty-ninth Ode of the same book. Unlike Dryden's work, however, it is a very literal translation, besides being an exquisite English poem. The reason for the translator's success is doubtless due in part to the faċt that the original is written in a spirit very closely akin to that of the Reſtoration Wits. Sedley muſt have been thinking of the Clevelands and Mazarins of his own day, who, like Horace's Barine, corrupted the youth of several generations when he wrote:

> "The Nymphs and cruel *Cupid* too,
>   Sharp'ning his pointed Dart
> On an old Hone, besmear'd with Blood,
>   Forbear thy perjur'd Heart.
> Fresh Youth grows up to wear thy Chains,
> And the old Slave no Freedom gains.

---

[1] *E.g.* in Act II. sc. ii., where the long account of Pompey's death given by Achoreus is only twice interrupted in the French original, but five times in the version of the English "confederates."

[2] See p. 82.

[3] "Q. Horatii Flacci Carmina," edited by T. E. Page (Macmillan, 1909), p. 247.

> Thee, Mothers for their eldest Sons,
> Thee, wretched Misers fear,
> Lest thy prevailing Beauty should
> Seduce the hopeful Heir:
> New marry'd Virgins fear thy Charms
> Should keep their Bridegroom from their Arms."

The translation of the Fourth Georgic, printed in the "Miscellaneous Works" of 1702 as "The Fourth Book of Virgil," is also an admirable piece of work and challenges a comparison even with Dryden's noble version. It has been well said of the latter that Vergil's "silver trumpet has disappeared and a manly strain is breathed through bronze."[1] Sedley's version, on the other hand, has a gently limpid flow which is far closer to the spirit of the original. Much of his success in this instance is certainly due to his bold use of the "overflowing" couplet instead of the strictly stopped form, which was becoming increasingly popular at the end of the seventeenth century; and though he does not always keep very close to the Latin, his diction is fresher and less conventional than that of his great rival. The picture of Cyrene[2] and her sister nymphs interrupted at their spinning by the complaint of Aristæus is rendered thus by Dryden:

> "A mournful sound again the mother hears;
> Again the mournful sound invades the sisters' ears.
> Starting at once from their green seats they rise;
> Fear in their heart, amazement in their eyes.
> But Arethusa, leaping from her bed,
> First lifts above the wave her beauteous head,
> And crying from afar thus to Cyrene said:
> 'O sister, not with causeless fear possess'd!
> No stranger voice disturbs thy tender breast.
> 'Tis Aristæus, 'tis thy darling son,
> Who to his careless mother makes his moan,
> Near his paternal stream he sadly stands,
> With downcast eyes, wet cheeks, and folded hands,
> Upbraiding heav'n from whence his lineage came;
> And cruel calls the gods, and cruel thee by name.'"

---

[1] Sir C. Bowen, "Vergil in English Verse" (Preface, p. 7).
[2] "Georgics," IV. 349–56.

This is a fine exercise in the Augustan manner, but Sedley's version is much more—it is genuine poetry:

> "The Nymph hears again
> Nearer and nearer still her Son complain,
> All rise astonisht from their green Abode;
> But Arethusa first above the Flood
> Lifts her bright Head: the Crystal Waters bow'd,
> And spying him afar; 'Twas not in vain,
> Sister, she said, we heard a Voice complain;
> Sad *Aristæus*, once thy Care and Joy,
> See at thy Father's Spring the weeping Boy:
> By Name he calls thee Cruel and Unkind."

Dryden expands Vergil's eight lines to fifteen, while Sedley's version occupies only nine and a half. The epithet "bright" is an infinitely better translation of "flavom" than Dryden's very insipid "beauteous," and "thy Father's Spring" is good English and good sense, while "the paternal stream" is neither.

The translations from Martial among the "Court Characters" are admirably pointed and rank among the very best renderings of that poet's work into English verse. The following version of the forty-third Epigram of the second book is a good example of Sedley's felicitous rendering of Roman wit in terms of Restoration England:

> "*To Canidius*
>
> All Things are common among Friends, thou say'st;
> 　This is thy Morning and thy Ev'ning-song,
> Thou in Rich Point, and Indian Silk art dress'd,
> 　Six foreign Steeds to thy Calash belong,
> Whil'st by my cloaths the Ragman scarce wou'd gain,
> 　And an uneasie Hackny jolts my Sides;
> A Cloak embroider'd intercepts thy Rain,
> 　A worsted Camblet my torn Breeches hides;
> Turbots and Mullets thy large Dishes hold,
> 　In mine a solitary Whiting lies;
> Thy Train might Fire the impotent and old,
> 　Whilst my poor Hand a *Ganimede* supplies.
> For an old wanting Friend thou'lt nothing do,⎫
> Yet all is common among Friends we know; ⎬
> Nothing so common, as to use 'em so."[1] ⎭

---

[1] "Miscellaneous Works" (1702), pp. 132, 133.

There is no reason to suppose that the author of such excellent translations as these should have been responsible for the inferior versions of the Eclogues of Vergil and Cicero's Oration for M. Marcellus included in the collected edition published in 1722. If they are his, they are probably schoolboy exercises, found among his papers, which he never intended to publish.[1]

Three elegies from Ovid's "Amores," englished by Sedley, were published in Tonson's "Miscellany" of 1684.[2] For some reason or other they were never reprinted in any collected edition of his works. They are inferior in vigour and fire to Dryden's translations of Ovid in the same collection, but fully deserve the praise which Mr. Montague Summers has bestowed upon their "finish."[3]

Except for the letters and speeches already cited, Sedley's non-dramatic prose is of very slender dimensions. There is an "Essay on Entertainments," which was included by Captain Ayloffe in his edition of 1702 and is therefore almost certainly genuine. It is very archaic in structure and, like many of Bacon's essays, is a mere expansion of an apt quotation without any attempt at narrative or characterisation even in the way of anecdote. Such an essay is a good illustration of the magnitude of the revolution effected by the authors of the *Tatler* and *Spectator*. The matter of this little piece is curiously illustrative of Dryden's remarks on Sedley in the dedication of the "Assignation."[4] Sir Charles was probably thinking of the "genial nights" which Dryden praised so highly when he wrote that the conversation at a party should be "of chearful and delightful Subjects, such as Beauty,

---

[1] See Preface to my forthcoming edition of Sedley's Works.

[2] Pp. 116, 122, 144. They are the eighth Elegy of the First Book, the fifth of the Second, and the fourth of the Third. See my forthcoming edition of Sedley's Works.

[3] Introduction to Congreve's Works, Nonesuch Press, 1925, p. 61.

[4] See above, pp. 93, 94.

Painting, Musick, Poetry, the Writers of the Past
and Present Age; whereby we may at once improve
and refresh our Wits." The paper entitled "Reflections
on Our Past and Present Proceedings," published
originally in 1689 and attributed to Sedley in the
collected edition of 1722, is probably authentic, as
it is attributed to him in a manuscript copy preserved
in the Bodleian.[1] It deserves the praise given to its
moderate views and "clear and facile style" by Sir
A. W. Ward.[2] Another able and vigorous pamphlet,
entitled "A Modest Plea for Some Excises at this
Time," and dated 1694, exists in a contemporary
transcript in the Bodleian[3] and was never, apparently,
printed. In this essay the Member for New Romney
urges the Government of William III to raise money
by means of excises instead of the land-tax—which
was so bitterly resented by the squirearchy. It is
curious to find the old courtier of the Restoration
condemning the reign of Charles II as "luxurious
and effeminate." His praise of the English landed
gentry, who, he contends, were being crippled by the
land-tax, as "of a free, open and generous temper"
and "Famous for Hospitality in all ages," was certainly
justified by the record of his own family.

Sir Charles Sedley's writings were only episodes in
the crowded life of a courtier and a politician. But
"Bellamira" and the best lyrics are sufficient to give
him a place among the "little masters" of English
literature, for whom there is ample room in halls so
richly hung with works of high genius. And if literature is considered to be an interpretation of life,
they are valuable as expressions of that vision of a

[1] MS. Rawl., D. 924, 319. This transcript bears no date.
[2] D. N. B., s.a. "Sir Charles Sedley."
[3] MS. Rawl., D. 380, 227. Another copy is calendared among the
MSS. of the Marquis of Bath (Hist. MSS. Comm., Appendix to
3rd Report, p. 184).

world of wit and charm and distinction, which was as truly characteristic of the age as the sordid realities of street and tavern, and which was to find its most perfect expression in "The Way of the World" and "The Rape of the Lock."

APPENDIX I

I

LETTER OF LADY SEDLEY, MOTHER OF SIR CHARLES
SEDLEY, TO DUDLEY CARLETON, VISCOUNT DOR-
CHESTER

(State Papers Dom., Chas. I, 45, p. 22. 21 June,
1629.)

MY MOST HONORD LORD
at my laſt being in London my ill fortune
denying me the injoyment of that happiness your
Lo^p beſtowed on me in your vissitts, I was bold to
leve a sute to my Lady Barrington's delivery, who hath
upon account of it, lett me in much arreridge of
thanks for your noble inclination to give me satisfaction, and since you have seconded it by being
pleased to remember it to Mr Sedley; at his waiteing
on your Lo^p but seemed not then to know where I
ment to end in my solicitation; which gives me now

ocation to present it to your vew, my aime being
only to recomend Mr Wright to your pleasure, so
hee may be acounted by your Lo^P in the number of
your servants. This is the uttermoſt of his ambition;
and therefore of my sute, whatever more your Lo^P
shall find him capable of; and imploy him in; muſt
be your meere grace which I daresay shall be obeyed
by a faithfull harte and received with all humility and
now it becomes nessisary that I conclud with petition
for pardon, for my thus longe troubling your L^P which
I onely add the tender of my most affeſtionat service,
which muſt ever bind me

Your L^{ops} humble devoted
servant ELIZA SEDLEY.

Ailsford the 21 of June.

II

LETTER OF SIR A. WELLDON TO THE COMMITTEE FOR
    ADVANCE OF MONEY CONCERNING THE SEDLEY
    FAMILY

(State Papers Int., A. 90, f. 110. 3 July, 1645.)

NOBLE GENTLEMEN,
    I receivd yr letter wch I sent to the Lady and
shall firſt give you the answer the L^{dy} returnd to mee.
that hirself nor any of her servants evr received any
tickett nor hath she or Sr Wm Sedley, Enhabited
London or whin 20 myles since she acquitted herself
by oath in Habberdashers Hall Therfor not taking
any benifytt by dwelling in that house, wch made her
liable before (beeing long time tennanted) she humbley
conceves herself noe weye concernd by that order sent
to mee, wh you very well apprehend to be noe waye
preiudiciall to Sr Wm Sedley.
    Butt ffor the eſtate, I shall (if th wer Juſt Cause) be
ready, to make that appere, in a far worse condition

then I presented unto you. that so plentifull a ffortune brought by accident so lowe; that necessary payments swallows up; not only the wards estat and Ladyes Joynter, wh I believe is unprecedented through the kingdom. This I humbly give to your Consideration.

Yr most humble servant
ANTHONY WELLDON

Aylsford this
third of July

III

DOCUMENTS CONNECTED WITH SIR CHARLES SEDLEY'S
TRIAL AND FINE

(1) Extract from Siderfin's Reports (second edition, Mich., 15 Car. II, B.R.).

> (Les Reports des Divers Specials Cases etc. Colligées par Tho. Siderfin Esq. La Second Edition: Revue & Corrigee par Robert Dobyns Esq. . . . London MDCCXIV. I, 168.)

Le Roy *versus* Sr Charles Sidley.[1]

S^r Ch. S. fuit indict al common Ley pur several Misdemeanors encounter Le Peace del Roy et que fueront al grand Scandal de Christianity, et le cause fuit quia il monstre son nude Corps in un Balcony in *Covent Garden* al grand Multitude de people et la fist tiel choses et parle tiel parolls &c (monstrant ascun particulars de son misbehavior) et cet Indictment fuit overtment lie a luy en Court & fuit dit a luy per les Justices que coment la ne fuit a cel temps ascun *Star Chamber* que cest Court Est

(29)
Fine &c sur Indictm' pur Misdemeanors.

[1] Keb. 620.

---

[1] In the first edition (1683) "Sir Charles Sidney."

Cuſtos Morum de touts les Subjeĉts
de Roy. Et eſt ore haut temps de
Punnier tiels profane Aĉtions fait encounter tout modeſty queux sont cy
frequent sicome nient solement Christianity mes auxy morality ad eſttre
derelinquy, Et apres que il ad ee
continue in Court p recogn del
Terme de *Trin.* al Terme de St *Mich.*
Le Court luy demand daver son Triall
pur cel al Barr, Mes il aiant advise
submit luy mesme al Court et
confesse L'indiĉtment. Pur que le
Court consider quel Judgment a
doner. Et pur ceo q il fuit Gent home
de trope aunc Family (ore del pays
de *Kent*) et son Eſtate incumber
(nient intendant son Ruine mes pur
luy reforme) ils fine luy forsque
2000 Marks et que serra imprison
pur un Weeke sans Baile et del bone
porte pur 3 ans.

(Original in black letter except words here in
italics.)

(2) Extraĉt from Keble's Reports.

(Reports in the Court of the King's Bench
at Weſtminſter . . . taken by Jos Keble of
Greys Inn Esq. The Firſt Part London
MDCLXXXV 4to.)

(95) Siderf. i. 168. pl. 29. Sir Charles Sydlyes
Case ante

Peace He was Fined 2000 Mark, committed without
Bail for a week, and Bound to his good be-
haviour for a year, on his Confession of
Information againſt him, for shewing himself
naked on a Balkony, and throwing down
Bottles (piſt in) *vi et armis* among the people

in *Covent* Garden contra pacem and to the Scandal of the Government.

(Original in black letter except words here in italics.)

(3) State Papers Dom., Chas. II. Ent. Bk. 16, p. 118.

Mr
Hamilton
to have Sir
Charles
Sidley's
fine.

Whereas upon informaĉon exhibited in our Court of Kings Bench in Trinity term laſt againſt Sr Charles Sidley Bart for severall offences and misdemeanors therein expressed the sd Sr Charles was therefor ye same Terme by ye same Court fined ye sum of 1000 markes to be paid to us as by ye Record of ye sd Court may appear: our will and pleasure is that you forthwith prepare a Bill fit for Our Royall signature authorizing our truſty and well beloved Sr Thomas Fanshaw Knt Clerke of yr crowne to pay ye sd one thousand marks when ye same shall be paid to him unto our truſty and Well: George Hamilton Esq or his assign to be at his or their dispose

By his Majeſtyes &c
Command.
Henry Bennett.

To our Attorney Generall.

(4) State Papers Dom., Chas. II. Docquet 67.

July 5th, 1664.

P.L.

Grant unto George Hamilton Esqe of the sum of 1000 marks which was a fine sett upon Sir Charles Sidley Baront by the Court of Kings Bench for severall Offences and misdemeanours by him lately remitted. Subscr. by Mr. Attorney generall, by a significacon of his Maty pleasure undr his signe mannall, Procur. by Mr Secr. Bennett.

Phil. Warwick.

IV

(LETTER FOUND AMONG THE PAPERS OF EDWARD
COLEMAN)

Seized on 29 September, 1678; translated by
Sir Charles Sedley from the French and read
to the House of Lords on 25 October, 1678;
printed by Sir George Treby in "The Second
Part of the Collection of Letters and other
Writings, relating to the Horrid Popish Plott.
Printed from the Originals, etc. . . . London,
MDCLXXXI" (fol.), pp. 11 and 12.

Coleman to the Internuntio, July, 75.

SIR,

I cannot but let you know the part I take in
the Honour the *Pope* has confer'd upon the Cardinal
of *Norfolk:* for which I am sure he will ever acknowledg his obligation to the *Emperour*, and Mr *Gabriel*
the *Internuntio;* Since 'tis only by them, and their
Credit, that *England* is upheld at *Rome:* and 'tis in
them that the *Duke*, and our *Catholiques* put all their
Confidence. Therefore I think myself oblig'd to
return you a Thousand Thanks for the part you have
taken in the Affair of the Cardinal of *Norfolk:* and to
Acknowledg you the Author of a Benefit so Advan-
tagious for *England*, and to expect good success from
the Prosperous beginning. Our Affairs are at present
in a very ill posture; and that which yet makes 'um
worse, is that the *Duke's* Friends have contributed to
it in a great measure, by accident, and for want of
foreseeing that which was Visible enough: making
use of a little Courage instead of a base and servile
compliance: but by their assistance the great manager
of our money[1] is so exalted, that he is the only person
who has at this time any Credit with the King: and

[1] This probably refers to Danby, the Lord Treasurer.

being got to this height is resolved to eſtablish himself upon the Authority of Parliament, and the Credit
of the Religion of *England;* & by that means to ruine
the *Catholicks* & the *Duke:* and to play the same Game
that my Lord *Arlington* propos'd to himself, when he
had more power than he has at present. We have but
one Remedy for all these Mischiefs we foresee: which
is to Diſtraɛt the Parliament to that Degree that they
shall never agree among themselves; so that they shall
be altogether useless to the King; and by that means
he will be forc'd to lay them aside: this is the only
thing we have at present any hope in: Perhaps with
much difficulty, we may be so happy as to succeed
in it. But that we may be more capable of serving
You, we desire your holy Prayers for the *Duke,* and
for the *Catholiques:* and for him, who scarce deserves
your remembrance, being but an inconsiderable
Wretch, although he be with more Respeɛt and
Passion, than any man living,
Yours,

*I have sent every Poſt all our News by our Common
Friend.*

Translated by Sir *Charles Sedley.*

V

DRAFT OF A SATIRE ON SIR CHARLES SEDLEY IN HAND-
    WRITING OF CHARLES MONTAGUE, AFTERWARDS
    EARL OF HALIFAX.

(Brit. Mus., Add. MSS. 28, 644, p. 57*b*.)

Go let the fatted Calf a Viɛtim burn   **(1)**
            loose
For Sidley's the [loſt] Prodigals return
Sidley the Bold, the witty and the gay

Whose tongue has led
[That has seduced] so many Maids a ſtray
Has laid aside the Vices of the Lay   (5)
And in the Arms of Mother Church at laſt
More than attones for All his wandrings paſt
               Whynyard
[Rises her Champion and his Weapon draws]
     support
[In the defence of her moſt doubtfull cause]
     Knight
Prodigious *Man* that among Husks and swine   (10)
Couldſt learn the Myſterys of yᵉ sacred Trine
    Could fathom myſterys and turn Divine
2 [And in the sacred Trinitys Defence]
   [Defys at Arms Reason and Comōn sense]
1 Has drawn his Pen and thrown his Gantlet down
To his forsaken Bretheren of the Town   (16)
To all that dare the Trinity disown
        the myſtick Trinitys
And in [that Doɕtrines wonderfull] defense
Boldly defyes Reason and Comōn sense
1 Commence a Doɕtor reeking from ye ſtews   (20)
The Apoſtolick Bard of Mother Hewes
    gy
As antient Knights who has huge Giants slain
And mow'd down Sarrasens on Pagan plains
To crown the Labours of their murdering Trade
Did Offer up their spurs and truſty blade   (25)
     valiant
So our Great Sidley who has triumphed long
    us   our
Kil'd [men] wᵗʰ Satyr and [their] wives wᵗʰ Song
Hew'd down the Monſtrous Fopperys of men
On the High Altar Dedicates his Pen
Dos Club his Talent to the Churches ſtock   (30)
And in the Quire displays the Comick sock
What Anthems and wᵗ Hymns will now be heard
When Organs are inspired by such a Bard

Assume

Devotion will [receive] another Air
When Sidleys gentle muse dos pen a Prayer   (35)
pretty
And wth [sweet] smiles our spirits chear

this
2 Who doſt [a] Mission wonderfull professe
(Like Antient Prophets) in a savage dresse
3 And so Display the Compass of thy wit
Joinſt Hymns with Baudy Farce and sacred Writ   (40)
3 And pretty Similes sprinkled here and there
Wt Quicken our flagging zeal like Botled Beer

heightened by his
1 Ejaculations will become thy ſtile
will in
And pious Brethings *in such* Numbers smile
[Go on great S^r the Churches Banner raise]   (45)
[And Teach the Wits and Athieſts pious Lays]
[And make them leave their nauseus songs and plays]

Brave
Go on Great S^r w^t Hopkins could not reach
Nor Quarles attain, thy greater Muse shall teach

Railleurs
Subdue the Wits and Athieſts of the Age   (50)
And fix the Churches ſtandard on ye Stage
Oh! Dog and Partridge thou haſt cause to mourn
Thy Darling Son is from thy Bosom torn
Sidley is gone and never will return
Prophanesse cannot ſtand w out thy Aid   (55)

none can support
Withdraw thy ſtock and they muſt quit the Trade
[Lesse they affliſtion was, more mild]
[Lesse were thy joys and expeſtations croſt]
[In Strephons Death, then now when Sidleys loſt]

again
Sidley He ſtarted once and did return [to you]   (60)

with his own pen
But now his ears are bored [He muſt be true]

When the Old Tennis Court fell on his back
Tho his soul flutter'd and the Goose cryed Quak
Devotion by Compulsion is but short
But this Relapse is of another sort (65)
As to Damascus rid the Elective Knight
(In Kentish Dialect 'tis Rumey height)
He saw wth wonder in that thieving Town
How they can squeeze three fleeces into One
 To
[And] make them pass the Custom house for none (70)
This Contemplation did his soul surprise
And [thick] black scales fell from his enlightened eyes
     my dull
And w^t, said He, shall [saucy] Reason doubt
     these rogues
That in Religion, wch my friends make out
[May there not be three Persons in one God] (75)
  se w^h compound [constitute] the
As here there are three fleeces *in* a Tod
2 Are of like
Of equal weight of the same thred and wool
Three Fleeces are one Tod the Proof is full
[Can] Can Mystick Truths convincing Reasons lack
   w^ch
When Lo the fleeces [that] compound ye pack (80)
His Faith [from]
From this strange Vision [did] did proceed
Hence date the Hurika of Sidleys Creed
Who tho a Reprobate before, a very Saul
Shall after, this Conversion, be Sr Paul. (84)

N.B.—Words and whole verses crossed out in Montague's MS. are here enclosed in square brackets. The numbering of the lines is mine.

VI

SIR CHARLES SEDLEY'S WILL

PREROGATIVE COURT OF CANTERBURY

118 DYER

Tm
Dni Caroli
Sedley
Barti

I Sr Charles Sedley of Southfleete in the County of Kent Baronett being in good health of body and of perfect mind and memory doe make this my last Will and Testament as followeth Whereas after the Settlement which I formerly made of certaine of my Mannors and Lands of Inheritance upon or in consideration of the marryage of Sr Charles Sedley of the parish of St. Giles in the ffeilds in the County of Middx Knight with a Daughter of Sr Richard Newdigate I have by severall Indentures beareing date respectively the twelfth and thirteenth dayes of September in the yeare of our Lord one thousand six hundred ninety nine by certaine whereof such provision is made for the payment of my funerall charges without limitting any particular sume of money to be expended or not to be exceeded therein together with such provision for the payment of such my debts and in such manner as are for those purposes therein contained setled the rest of my Mannors and Lands of Inheritance and some Leasehold estate respectively I doe by this my will declare that I have not altered or revoked the same deeds or Settlements therein contained nor doe intend any revocation or alteration hereby to be made thereof But doe by this my Will confirme the same And I doe alsoe by this my will confirm the Settlement made by one Indenture beareing date the six and

twentyeth day of November in the yeare of
our Lord one thousand six hundred eighty
seaven of my interest in the House where I
now dwell scituate in Bloomesbury Square in
the said Parish of St. Giles in the ffeilds And
whereas by one Deed Poll beareing date the
nine and twentyeth day of Aprill in the said
yeare of our Lord one thousand six hundred
ninety nine I did assigne and dispose of
certaine Jewells Plate and Goods therein
mencõned in such manner as is therein contained And afterwards by one other Deed
Poll beareing date the eleaventh day of September in the said yeare of our Lord one
thousand six hundred ninety nine the said
Jewells and part of the said plate and goods
were soe assigned and disposed of as therein
is contained I doe by this my Will confirm
the said last menconed Deed Poll and the
said assigment [*sic*] and disposicon of the said
Jewells and part of the said plate and goods
thereby and alsoe the assigment and disposition of the residue of the said plate and goods
made by the said other Deed Poll beareing
date the said nine and twentyeth day of Aprill
in the said yeare of our Lord one thousand
six hundred ninety nine And I referr my
decent buryall to the discretion of my Executors
herein after named And I doe hereby give
and bequeath unto such of my servants as
shall have lived with me twelve moneths
imediately before my death ffive pounds
apiece for mourning And my Will is and I
order that my ffamily shall be kept together
at my dwelling house in such manner as now
it is for one callander moneth after my death
and that my Executors defray all the charge
of such house keeping during that time And

I doe hereby nominate and appoint the afore-
said Sr Charles Sedley Knt Edward Bedingfeild of Grayes Inn in the County of Middx
Esqr and Stoughton Bird of the parish of
St. Andrew Holbourne in the County of Middx
gent. Executors of this my laſt Will and
Teſtament And I give unto my said Executors
for their trouble and care in the execũcon of
this my Will ffifty pounds apiece to be paid
unto them respeɕtively as soone as con-
veniently may be after their respeɕtive proving
of this my Will and takeing upon them
respeɕtively the burthen of the execution
thereof And I give unto the said Sr Charles
Sedley Knt all the residue and overplus if
any shall be of my personall eſtate not otherwise setled or disposed of by any of the afore-
said Deeds that shall remaine after that the
reſt of this my Will shall be performed And
I revoke all former Wills whatsoever by me
heretofore made In witness whereof I the said
Sr Charles Sedley Baronett have to this my
laſt Will and Teſtament sett my hand and
seale this (blank) day of (blank) in the thirteenth yeare of the reigne of his Majeſtie
King William the Third over England &c.
Anno Domini One thousand seaven hundred
and one. Charles Sedley. Signed sealed published and declared by the above named Sr
Charles Sedley Baronett to be his laſt Will
and teſtam^t in the presence of us Mary
Townshend Ed. Leigh John Thorold.

Probatum fuit hum̃oi Teſtamentum apud
Londõn coram veñti viro Willimo Clements
Legum Doctore Surrogato ventis et egregii
viri Domini Richardi Raines Militis Legum
etiam Doɕtoris Curiae Praerogativae Can-

tuariensis Maḡri Cuſtodis sive Comissarii Ĩtime
conſtituti Tricesimo die mensis Auguſti Anno
Domini Millimo Septingenmo primo jura-
mento Stoughton Bird unius Executorum in
eodem Teſtamento nominat. Cui cõmissa fuit
Adm̃ſtraõo omnĩu et singulorum bonorum
jurium et creditorum diõti defunõti de bene et
fideliter adm̃ſtrando eadem ad Sanõta Dei
Evangelia Juraẽ Reservata poteſtate similem
Comnem faciend Edvardo Bedingfeild arm̃
alteri Executorum in eodem Teſtamento nominat cum venerit eandem petitur. Domino
Carolo Sedley Milite altero Execŭt in diõto
Teſtamento nominaẽ demortuo.

VII

MS. NOTES ON SEDLEY BY W. OLDYS AND J. HASLEWOOD
(The numbering of the notes is mine.)

1. W. Oldys's Notes on the article on "Sir Charles
Sidley" in "An Account of the English Dramatick
Poets . . . by Gerard Langbaine . . . Oxford . . .
1691" (Brit. Mus., c. 28, g. 1), pp. 485–6.

(1) Sʳ Charles was an handsome plump middle
sizd man There was a great Resemblance
in the Shape and Features between him and
Kynaſton the Aõtor who once got some
Lac'd clothes made exaõtly after a suit Sir
Charles wore who therefore got him well
can'd Sir Charles his Emissary pretending to
take Kynaſton for Sʳ Charles quareld with
him in St James's Park for some private
Misusage and beat him as Sʳ Charles.

(2) Sr Charles Sedley had a daughter named
Katharine by his wife Katherine and a

natural son named Charles Sedley alias
Ascough and two natural daughters named
L. and E. Charlot. Upon these natural
children he settled a part of his Estate in
Kent Essex etc. I have a copy of the Deed
of settlement drawn by Sr Fras Winnington
and approved by Holt and Pollexfen.

(3) Remr the sharp saying about King James his
making his Da^r a whore and he making the
King's daughter a Queen, in my vol. of
apoth:

(4) He was a man of Wit and Pleasure, but too
much given up to the extravagances and
Debaucheries wch were so fashionable among
the other Wits of Fortune and Quality in
those Times.

(5) Remembr ye shameful shitten story that Ant.
Wood has recorded of him in the silly
account he has given of his own life which
is worse written than any of the many hundreds as he had a hand in.

(6) Remr the Frolick that old Mrs Partridge told
40 years ago, of his companions when they
saw him with a very valuable lac'd neck loth
on, which by every one's toasting a Health
and leaving some part of their Apparel he
was in his turn obligd to sacrifice to the
Flames. In revenge for wch he had his Frolick
at another Meeting, and by his previous
Instructions of a Tooth drawer for that purpose made everyone of that Company not
without Tears from their Eyes and oaths
enough frõ their mouths before the Frolick
was over lose a sound Tooth, for a painful
rotten one he wanted to get rid of—Patience,
Gentlemen, Patience, you know—you promised I should have my Frolick too.

(7) 4 years after, the Mulberry garden in St.

Martins Parish was given by the King to Hen: Ld Arlington.

(8) Sr Charles Sidley's speach in the House of Commons upon the Civil Liſt, againſt exorbitant Pensions and Unnecessary Salaries— in the collection of scarce & valuable Tracts &c in 4 vols. vol. 2. 1748, p. 487.

Further note from Oldys's Langbaine opposite the article on Shadwell, p. 443.

(9) I have heard that Dorset, Sedley and others of those idle Wits would write whole Scenes for him.

2. MS. Notes by J. Haslewood on the article on "Sir Charles Sidley" in "The Poetical Regiſter or the Lives and Characters of all the English Poets [by Giles Jacob] . . . London . . . 1723" (Brit. Mus. c. 45, d. 17), pp. 242–3.

(1) Malone cites authorities for Sidley. See "Life of Dryden," Vol. I. pp. 65–7. I have seen two original autographs of the poet and several of his descendants, and they wrote their names indisputably Sedley.

(2) In all the old Deeds from the time of Charles the 1st. the name is uniformly spelt Sedley. Himself and anceſtors resided at Southfleet co: Kent and he is supposed to have died there. The family eſtates were extensive. In Kent Southfleet, Northfleet, Ridley, Hartley, Gt. Oakley, Honeychild, Triſton, Wormshill, Muttenden, Milton Mills, Alisford Mill, Boxley Woods, Impton Woods, Plushenden, Marsdens. In Leiceſt. Wymondham & Dalby. In Camb. Stretham. In Oxford Winbush.

(3) In 1718 there were mortgages of Sir C. S. the poet outſtanding for 1300£, 1000£ and

4000£ and Estates appear to have been subject to other Debts contracted by him.

(4) Sir C. S. of Oxton Co. Nottingham Bt. only son, Heir of Sir C. S. of the par. of St Giles and grandson of the poet sold under a Decree of the Court of Chan. part of the Estates in order to clear the incumbrances in July 1721.

(5) In "Some Account of the Life of Sir Charles Sedley" before his works in Octavo (1722 I copy from) is the following story: "It was at the acting of the play call'd Bellamira, that the roof of the playhouse fell down. But what was particular, was that very few were hurt but himself. His merry Friend Sir Fleetwood Shepherd told him: There was so much fire in his play that it blew up the poet, House, and all. He told him again, NO: the play was so Heavy that it broke down the House and buried the Poet in his own Rubbish." This story there can be very little doubt grew out of the accident that happened to Sir Charles in 1679/80, when he was hurt severely by the fall of the Tennis Court, and where "being at play" has no reference to the play of Bellamira which appears to have been first acted and printed in 1687.

(6) Sir John Sedley (father of the poet) by his Will dated the 5th Oct. 1637, gave his Manors in trust to his wife Lady Eliz., Sir Edw. Hales Kn^t. B^t., Sir Anthony Weldon Kn^t, Anthony Crofts and Anthony Langston 1st for Henry Sedley on attaining age of 23 and in case of death 2^d to Willm S. like limitation, 3d to the third son lawfully to be begotten, (therefore the poet was not then born) 4 to his daurs, Eliz., Marg^t on marriage

Y

or attaining 17—gave his daughter Elizabeth
5000£, William 12000£, Margaret 2500£
such child as his wife sho^d be ensient with
at the time of his death 2500£. Residue of
psonal est. to Henry.

He devised 400£ of his personal estate to
be laid out in purchase of Lands to be settled
for the maintenance of a Schoolmaster in
the par. of Wymondham, Leicest/shire, 400£
for like purposes at Southfleet in Kent.
500£ for better maintenance of scholars of
Moreton [*sic*] Coll. Ox. called postmasters.

500£ like purpose scholars of Magdalen
Coll. Ox. called Domies [*sic*] for ever.

(7) Time of death of Sir John Sedley not known,
probably immly after making his will & his
wife then encient with Charles.

(8) Henry the son appears to have died a Minor.

(9) Sir Willm was in posson in 1655 and Sir Charles
as his brother, heir at law in Jan. 1663. Sir
Willm appears to have died without issue
and probably unmarried as a deed of appointment in 1655 limits to his first and other
sons but does not name any, nor mention
any Wife.

(10) By Mortgage dated 21st June 1675 Sir Charles
raised 4120£ which was only paid off in
July 1721 when it vested in William Peer
Williams, the reporter.

(11) 1699. Sep. 13. by Settlement of this date Sir
Cha. S. limited his Estates in Kent first to
himself, 2^d to the use of Ann Ayscough one
of the daurs of Henry Ayscough late of
Gray's Inn Middx Gent decd, 3d to the use
to Sir Charles S. of the par. of S. Giles in
the Fields Middx Knt. 4th to the Issue of
Sir C. S. knt. 5th to the use of the Rt
hono^{ble} Katherine Countess of Dorchester

for life 6th to her Issue lawfully begotten for default of such Issue 7th to the use of Sir Charles of St. Clare in the Co. of Kent B^t 8th to his issue Q how related?

(12) The object of this settlement is not easily elicited by anything upon the face of the deed unless it was to give a life estate to Ann Ayscough who probably might be living with the poet and might have some claim on his generosity. She died at York 1765.[1] One provisoe in the Deed may be noticed which is that if the Countess of Dorchester or any present or future husband or their issue should attempt to avoid, annul impeach etc. that settlement all the uses limited to them should determine and be void.

(13) Sir Charles S. knt. marr. Frances and had issue Anne who had a charge created in her favour on the estates of 3000£.

(14) This Sir C. S. knt was the son of poet. His marr. settlement dated 29th June, 1697. His wife Frances probably a dau^r of Sir Richd Newdigate party to the settlement.

[1] This is a mistake, see p. 234.

APPENDIX II

A Note on Sir Charles Sedley's Library

Sir Charles Sedley's boast to the Judge that he had read more books than his Lordship is justified to some extent by a catalogue of part of his library, a copy of which survives in the British Museum. The full title of this remarkable document is as follows:—

> A/ Catalogue/ of the/ Books/ of Sir *Charles Sidley*, B^{nt} Dec./ with the Addition of part of a Library of a Late/ Eminent Divine./ To be/ Sold by Auction at Tom's/ Coffee-House adjoyning to *Ludgate*; On/ *Wednesday* the 23rd of *March* 1702/3. At/ Four of the Clock in the Afternoon./*Catalogues* are Distributed *Gratis*, at/ Mr *Hartley's* over against *Grey's Inn* in/ *Holborn*, Mr *Brown's* at the *Black Swan*/ without *Temple Bar*, Mr. Davis's over a-/ gainst the *Royal-Exchange* in *Cornhill*, Mr/ *Clement's* in *Oxon*, and Mr *Thurlburn's* in/ *Cambridge*, and at the place of Sale.   (Brit. Mus., S.C. 389(1).)

It might be supposed that the task of separating the books of the "Eminent Divine" from those of Sir Charles Sedley would not be a difficult one. As a matter of fact there are some tastes which they might well have had in common. Both would probably possess the chief Latin and perhaps some of the Greek classical authors; both might have collected works on the history and antiquities of Oxford, and both might have taken some interest in contemporary philosophy. On the other hand, we can be fairly sure that all the numerous theological works in the catalogue were not from Sedley's library (though he may have acquired some at the time of his "conversion"), and that moſt of the contemporary verse, light French and English literature and works on the theatre, was not the property of the Eminent Divine. The following liſt is a seleċtion from the catalogue containing some of the books which I consider may have been Sedley's. The numbers on the left are the numbers printed in the catalogue; the figures on the right are the prices fetched by some of the books, which are written in ink in the British Museum copy.

Libri Latini, Gr. &c. in Folio.

		£	s.	d.
89.	Livii Tit. Opera *Basil* 1543 .		3	2
90.	Virgilij Opera Joh. Ogilvy Lat. Impft. *Lond.* 1658 . .		6	0
93.	Virgilij Opera Servij notis Joh. Petit		3	0
98.	Mercatori Atlas cum Tabulis .		2	6
128.	Rerum Anglic. Scriptores poſt Bedam editi ab H. Savilio *Lon.* 1596	1	1	0
135.	Marmora Oxoniensia cum Com. H. Prideaux & fig. *Oxon.* 1676 .		14	0
136.	Hiſtoria et Antiquitates Universitatis Oxoniensis *Oxon.* 1674 .		12	6
149.	Juvenalis D. Satyrae *Loover* 1644			
150.	Terentij Comediae *Paris Typog.* Regia 1642			
151.	Homeri Caſtalio *Bas.* 1567			
152.	Plutarchi quae Extant Omnia, Gr. Lat. 2 Vol. *Frances.* 1650 .	1	2	6
159.	Gassendus de Vita, Morib. Placitisq; Epicuri *Lugd.* 1675 .		5	0
160.	Epicuri Philosophia par Pet. Gassendum, 3 vols. . . .		6	0

		£	s.	d.
161.	Catalogus Bibliothecae Bodleianae à Tho Hyde. *Oxon.* 1674 .		5	2
162.	Senecae L. An. Opera cum scholij Fed. Morelli *Paris* 1613 .		7	6
174.	Gratulatio Academ. Cantabrig. de Reditu R. Guil. III. 1697 *Cantab.*			
175.	Pietas Universit. Oxoniensis in Obitum Reginae Mariae 1695.			

Libri Latini, Quarto.

48.	Lucret. T. Car. cum Dion. Lambini Com. apud *Benenat* 1570 .		13	6
58.	Spinozae Opera Posthuma 1677 .			
59.	—— Tractatus Theologico Politicus *Ham.* 1670		7	4
63.	Oxford Catalogue *Oxon.* 1620			
73.	Des Cartes Ren. Principia Philosophiae *Amst.* 1664 . .		3	0
84.	Sinibaldi Jo. Den. Geneanthropia sive de Hominis Generat. *Franc.*		2	6
99.	Juvenalis D. Jun. Satyrae *Paris* 1635			
103.	Suetonius cum Notis Casauboni 1611		1	6
104.	Stephani Car. Dict. Hist. Geog. & Poet. *Gen.* 1660 . . .		9	6
225	Socratis &c. Epistolae Gr. Lat. Not. L. Allatij *Paris* 1637 . .		3	6
226	Adagia Graecorum Gr. Lat. cum Schol. And. Schotti *Ant.* 1612 .		4	4
227.	Pindarus Gr. & Lat. cum Notis J. Benedicti *Salm.* 1620 . .		6	10
228.	Sophoclis Tragediae cum. Scol. Gr. & Not. Camerarij *H. Steph.* 1565			

Libri   Latini   in   Octavo.

		£	s.	d.
3.	Plutarch de Audientis Poetis Gr. Lat. &c. cum. Not. Jo. Potter *Oxon.*		1	3
46.	Lucretius T. cum notis Tho. Creech *Oxon.* 1695 . . .		3	2
53.	Plauti Comediae cum Notis J. Phil. Parei *Franc.* 1610 . .			8
58.	Luciani Pseudo Sophista Gr. Lat. cum Nots. J. Geo. Graevij *Amst.* 1668		3	0
81.	Terentij P. Comediae Anglo a G. Heel London 1676 . .		1	8
119.	Heliodori Aethiopica Gr. Lat. cum. H. Commelini Notis *Lugd.* 1612			
135.	Theophrasti Eth. Charactere Gr. Lat. Notis Is. Casauboni *Lugd.* 1612			
142.	Luciani Opera Gr. Lat. cum Varier Notis Alex. Tollij Tom 1 *Amst.* 1670			
144.	Gassendi Pet. Institutio Astronomica *Lond.* 1675			
146.	Nebulo Nebulonum L. E. Jocoseria modernae censura cum figur. & carm. à Jo. Flitnero *Franc.* 1620			
148.	Aristotelis Ethica Gr. Lat. à D. Lambino 1596			
149.	Horatius Q. cum. Interpret et Not. in usum Delph. *Lond.* 1675			
150.	Apuleij Opera 2 vol. *Bas.*			
167.	Breviarum Romanum			
170.	Camdeni Britannia			
177.	Erasmi Adag. Epitap.			
191.	Horatius Stephanus			
193.	Horatius			
235.	Terentius Donatus			
236.	Plutarchi Morales 3 vol.			
237.	—— Vitae 2 vol.			

120 &c. in Gr. & Lat. &c.

		£	s.	d.
2.	Erasmi Desid. Apothegma . .			6
17.	Miltonij pro Populo Angl. Def. .			7
22.	Literae Cromwellij &c. Scripta a Jo. Miltono. . . .			4
34.	Epistolae Obscuror. Virorum .	1		6
38.	Terentij Comaed. sine Tit ap. Elz.			8
49.	Terentius cum not. J. Farnabij. .			8
54.	Oweni Epigrammata			
66.	Thesaurus Poeticus			
67.	Statuta Oxonienses			
68.	Sheltoni Tachy-Graphia			
70.	Roma Illustrata			
87.	Homeri Odyssea 2 vol.			
90.	Des Cartes Ethices.			
115.	Erasmi Epit.			
116.	Erasmi Enconium.			
120.	Machiaveli. Hist. Forent.			
121.	Mori Utopia			
122.	Luciani Dialogi			
125.	Martialis Epigram.			
129.	Mantuan			
130.	Plautus			
140.	Tullij Orat.			
142.	Tullij Sentent.			
142.	Virgilij Opera			
155.	Plautus			
158.	Martial Farnabij			
161.	Luciani Dialog.			
163.	Ciceron M.T. Opera edit. à Jac. Gronovio 11 vol. . . .	1	6	6
166.	Adagior Erasmi Epitome . .			10
171.	Lucani Pharsalia . . .			4

English Books in Folio.

45. Sir Tho. More's Works 2 vols.
46. Heylin's Cosmography with Maps, 1669.
47. Burnet's Theory of the Earth, 1684.
50. Raleigh's Hist. of the World with his Life and Tryal. 1687.
55. Ogilby's Virgil. 1668
56. —— Homer's Iliads. 1669
57. —— Homer's Odysses 1669
58. Dugdale's Baronage of *England* 2 vol. 1675
59. Mille's Catalogue of Honour. 1610
60. Bacon Of the Laws and Government of *England* 1689.
61. Davila's Hist. of the Civil Wars of France, 1678.
62. Dodington's Hist. of the Civil Wars of France, 1657.
64. Nero Caesar. 1623.
67. History of Portugal, 1700.
69. Guiccardini's Hist. of Italy, 1579.
70. Athenae Oxonienses 2 vols. 1691.
71. Bacon's Advancement of Learning *Ox.* 1640.
74. Chardin's Travels into Persia and East-Indies with Fig. 1691.
75. Pembrok's Arcadia 1627.
78. Bochas's Tragedies, Black Letter.
79. Exemplary Novels by Mic. Cervantes Saavedra. 1640.
81. Stafford's Pacata Hibernia with maps *Lond.* 1633.
82. Military Inst. for the Cavalry *Camb.* 1632.
83. Corn. Tacitus Annals 1622.
86. Dryden's Juvenal Lond. 1693.
91. Devotions of his Majesty in his Solitudes, in Verse. 1657.
97. Works of Joh. Taylor the Water Poet (wants the Title).

98. Torriano's Ital. and English Dictionary, etc. *Lond.* 1698.
99. The Young Student's Library 1692.
101. Sidney concerning Government, *Lond.* 1698.
102. Stowe's Survey of London, 1633.
103. Burton's Anatomy of Melancholy, 1676.
104. Morery's Historic. Geographic. and Poetic. History 1694.
105. The Grand Cyrus 5 vols. 1655.

English Quartos.

1. Milton's Eiconoclastes *Lond.* 1649.
5. Lock's 3 Letters of Toleration 1690.
10. Whole Art of the Stage, 1684.
18. Terence in English and Latin 1629.
38. Earl of Clarendon's Survey of Hobb's Leviathan *Ox.* 1676.
45. Tryal of the Regicides, 1660.
85. Raleigh of the Prerogative of Parliaments, 1628.
97. Swinburn of Testaments and last Wills, 1590.
99. Donn's Poems, 1633.

English Octavos.

1. Glanvil of Witches and Apparitions *Lond.* 1681.
2. Sharp's Voyages and Adventures into the South Sea 1684.
4. Gildon's Miscellany Letters and Essays, 1694.
5. Theocritus's Idylliums by Tho. Creech *Oxf.* 1684.
7. Poems and Translations by Oxford Hands. 1685.
11. Kennet's Lives of the Ancient Greek Poets, 1697.
13. Dryden's 3d part of Miscellany Poems, 1693.
14. Sir Rob. Cotton's Posthuma, 1672.

19. Essay on Ways and Means of Supplying the War, 1695.
20. Debates of the House of Commons in 1680.
21. Debates 1680.
23. Casaubon of Enthusiasm *Lond.* 1656.
29. Playford's Introduction to Musick, 1697.
30. Evremont's Miscellaneous Essays, 1692.
31. Debates, 1680.
33. Donn's Poeme.
57. Godolphin of the Admiralty.
82. Rolle's Burning of London.
83. Wilkins of Prayer.
90. Dr. Bentley against Boyle, *Lond.* 1699.
91. Wilkin's Beauty of Providence.
92. Answer to Rehearsal transpos'd.
97. Lock's Letter to the B^p of Worcester, *Lond.* 1697.
98. —— Reply to B^p of Worcester's Answer, 1697.
99. —— Reply to the B^p of Worcester's Ans. to his 2nd Letter, 1699.
101. Vind. Reasonableness of Christianity, 1695.
102. —— 2nd Vindicat. of the Reasonabl. of Christianity, 1696.
103. Kath. Philip's Poems, 1664.
104. Boyle against Bently's Dissertat. on the Epist. of Phalaris. 1698.
105. Sir R. Filmer's Natural Power of Kings, 1680.
107. Bond's Guide for Justices of the Peace, *Lond.* 1685.
110. Hobb's State of Nature consider'd by J. Eachard 1672.
112. Milton's Paradise Lost, 1678.
113. Smith's Fr. Ital. Span. and Eng. Grammar, 1674.
115. Collier's Defence of his View of the Stage, 1699.
122. Culpepper's Directory for Midwives, with Cuts *Lond.* 1681.

124. Sir W. Dugdale's usage in bearing Arms *Oxf.* 1682.
134. Montaigne's Essays, by Cotton. Vol. 3d. 1685.
136. Gildon's new Collections of Poems *Lond.* 1701.
137. Capt. Dampier's Voyages and Descript. Voll. 2d. 1699.
138. Sir Jo. Denham's Poem of Old Age, 1689.
139. Lucretius with Notes by Thomas Creech. *Lond.* 1683.

English Twelves.

1. Walker's English and Latin Idioms. *Lond.* 1690.
2. Lilly's Royal Grammer, made plain 1678.
3. The Refin'd Courtier, 1679.
4. Reflect. on the Secret Hist. of K. Ch. II and K. James 2d. 1691.
7. The Lady's New-Year's Gift, 1688.

Livres Francois en Folio.

3. Histoire Universelle du Sr. D'Aubigne. 3 vols. en 2 Tom *à Maille.* 1616.
4. Dictionaire Etymologique de la Langue Francoise par M. Menage *Par.* 1694.
6. Les Metamorphoses D'Ovide enrichies de Figures *Par.* 1622.
7. James Howell's French and English Dictionary *Lond.* 1673.

L. Francois en Quarto.

3. Les Recherches de la *France* d'Est. Pasquier. 1607.
4. Les Voyages du Sr. de la Bovelle-le-Gouz. avec fig. *Troyes.* 1657.

7. Antiquitez de Paris Par Jacques du Brevi. *Par.* 1639.
11. Voyage de Franc. Pyrard Delaval. *Par.* 1679.
12. Traitez conclus entre les Potentats de l'Europe 1683.
13. Recueil de Edits &c. du Roy. *Par.* 1673.
14. Ordonnonance de Louis XIV Roy de *France* touchant la Marine. *Par.* 1681.
15. Confernces des Nouvelles Ordonances de Louis XIV avec des Annot. par Phil Bernier. 2 vols. *Par.* 1694.
16. Tachart Dict. Nov. Lat. Latine-Gall. et Gall. Lat. 2 vols. *Par.* 1698.

L. Francois en 8°.

2. Les 6 Comedies de Terence en Lat. & Franc. par M. de Marolles avec des Remarques *Par.* 1660.
3. De la Sagesse par P. Charron, *Par.* 1607.
4. Claude Mauger's French Grammer *Lond.* 1688.
5. Nouvelle Grammaire Francoise par P. Festeau, *Lond.* 1679.
8. Du Royaume de Siam par M. de la Loubere— Tom 1, *Amst.* 1691.
9. Parallele des Anciens & de Modernes par M. Perault Tom 2d. *Par.* 1693.
11. Les Characteres de Theophraste traduits par M. de la Bruiere Bruxel. 1693.
12. Histoires de Indes Occidentales, *Par.* 1569.
14. La Galatee & les Adventures du Prince Astiages, *Par.* 1626.
15. Crispin bel Esprit Comedie, *Par.* 1682.
16. Grammaire pour Scavoir la prononciation de Langue Espagnole. *Rouen,* 1636.
17. Cronique du Roy Loys II &c. par Ph. de Comines.
18. Mauger's French Grammar, *Lond.* 1682.

L. Francois en 12°.

1. Hiſtoire du Gouvernement de Venise Par le Sr. Am. de la Houssaie avec des Figures, 3 Vols. *Amſt.* 1695.

2. —— des Anabatiſtes avec des Figures *Par.* 1695.

3. —— de la Medecine *Gen.* 1696.

4. —— de P. d'Aubusson Grand-Maiſtre de Rhodes, 2 vol. *Par.* 1676.

5. —— Poetique entres les Anciens & Modernes, *Amſt.* 1688.

6. —— de France par le Sr. de Bonair, *Par.* 1682.

8. —— des 12 Cesars par Suetone et traduite par M. de Teil. *Lion.* 1685.

9. Les Oeuvres de Lucrece avec de Remarques Par M. le Barn de Coutures. 2 vols. *Par.* 1692.

10. —— D'Horace en Lat. et Franc. Tom 1, 2; 4 *Par.* 1681.

11. Melange D'Hiſtorie & de Litterature Par. M. de Vigreu Marville. Tom 1. *Rouen.* 1700.

12. Sentiments de Clearte sur les Entetret. d'Ariſte et Eugene, Partie 2d. *Par.* 1672.

13. Comedie de Terence en Lat. & Franc. avec des Notes *Par.* 1672.

14. Traduites par Madam D. Tom 1, *Amſt.* 1691.

18. Ouvres de Racine Tom 2. 1682.

20. Le Poetique D'Ariſtote avec des Remarques par Mrs. Dacier, *Par.* 1692.

22. Du Poeme Epique par le P. Bossu, *Par.* 1683.

24. Valesiane ou les Pensees Critiques de M. de Valois, *Par.* 1694.

27. Plutarque de la Superſtition par M. le Flore *Saum.* 1666.

30. Voyage d'Espagne *Col.* 1688.

31. Lettres Nouvelles de M. Boursault. 1698.

32. Memoirs des Contraventions faites par la France (il manque le Titre) 1649.

33. L'Alcaran de Mahomet par le Sr. de Ryez. 1649.

34. Remarques Critiques, Morales et Historiques. *Par.* 1692.

35. Memoires de M. Le P. Bourdeille Sr. de Brantome. Tom 2. *Leyd.* 1666.

37. Nouvelle de la Repub, des Lettres pour Mois de Mars, Aout, May, Juin, Juillet. *Amst.* 1684.

38. Boralde Prince de Savoye, parte I. *Leyd.* 1672.

39. Les Comedies de Pierre de d'Arivey. *Rouen.* 1600.

40. Entretiens de Philandre et d'Euariste *Gen.* 1683.

41. Sorberiana, ou Bons Mots de M. Sorbiere. *Par.* 1694.

42. Histoires Tragiques tom. 2, 3, & 7. *Lyon.* 1591.

47. Les Entretiens d'Ariste & d'Eugene. *Amst.* 1671.

Libri Italiani Folio.

1. Palazzi di Roma de piu celebri Architetti disegnati da Pietro Ferreterio Pittore & Architetti. Roma.

Libri Italiani &c. Hispan.

2. Tesoro de las 3 Lengues Espanola, Francesc. & Italiani. *Gen.* 1648.

3. Prima & 2 parte de Don Quixot de la Mancha, *Madr.* 1655.

Libri Italiani 4°.

1. Historia d'Italia de France Guiccardini. *Ven.* 1599.

3. Rime d'Isabelle Andreini, *Par.* 1603.
9. Le Vite de gli Imperadori & Pontef. Romani da Fr. Petrarcha. 1625.
26. Vite di Plutarch tradotte, per Lod. Domeniche. *Ven.* 1620.

L. *Italiani* 8°.

1. Del Cortegiano del Conte Baldes. Caſtligione. *Ven.* 1559.
4. Le Metamorfosi di Ovidio ridotte da Gio. Andrea con. annot. et Fig. *Ven.* 1661.
5. Dittionario Italiano et Francese par Nath. Duez. 2 vols. *Gen.* 1678.
11. Ritratto di Roma antica di Bart Marliani con Fig. *Rom.* 1638.
12. —— di Roma Moderna con Fig. *Rom.* 1638.

L. *Italiani* 12°.

3. Il Putanismo Romano, *Colon.* 1668.
5. L'Anacreonte Drame per Musica *Livern.* 1700.
6. La Magia d'Amore del Sig. Guido Casoni. *Ven.* 1622.
12. Dell'Arte Hiſtroica d'Agoſt. Mascardi. *Ven.* 1662.
14. Le Rete di Vulcano. *Ven.* 1641.

L. *Italiani* 12°.

Il Paſtor Fido del S. Bart. Guarini. *Amſt.*

A brief analysis of this liſt may help us to a closer underſtanding of our author's mind.

There is no Shakespeare and no Molière, though it is certain that Sedley muſt have possessed the works of both. It may be supposed that they were retained by his heirs.

The classical section is very comprehensive, but, as I have suggested, the Eminent Divine may have been a classical scholar. We can be fairly sure, however, that most of the numerous editions of Terence —there are no less than eight—belonged to the author of "Bellamira." The Latin texts include the superbly printed folio, published by the Royal Press in Paris in 1642. The two English translations are the fifth edition (1629) of R. Bernard's fine Elizabethan version, originally published in 1598, which may well have belonged to the poet's father, and Charles Hoole's very bald word for word "crib" "for the use of young scholars" (1676). The three French translations include that of the famous Madame Dacier. The Latin and Italian versions of Plutarch's Lives were probably used for "Antony and Cleopatra," and some of the Virgils, Horaces and Martials must have been Sedley's, for he translated from all three poets, while the appeal that would have been made to him by such ancient and modern wits as Plautus, Lucian, and Erasmus, is obvious. "Rerum Anglic. post Bedam Scriptores editi a H. Savilio" and "Oweni Epigrammata" must have been heirlooms. The former is the monumental edition by Sir Charles's maternal grandfather, Sir Henry Savile, of the early English historians after Bede, and the latter is one of the numerous editions of the Latin poems of John Owen, who, it will be remembered, addressed panegyrics to Sir William Sedley and his son, Sir John. The philosophical works are remarkable. They include books by the most advanced thinkers of the day. Among them are Spinoza, the great Jewish pantheist (represented by his most daring work, "Tractatus Theologico-Politicus"), Gassendi (Pierre Gassend), the French defender of Epicurus and teacher of Molière, and the famous René Descartes. The presence of Milton's "Pro Populo Anglicano Defensus," his Latin letters written for Cromwell, and "Eiconoclastes," if

z

they were Sedley's, is a further proof of the broadness of his culture. "Nebulo Nebulonum" is a series of burlesque Latin poems by a German scholar, Flittner, with amusing woodcuts, illustrating popular proverbs concerning fools, and "Sheltoni Tachygraphia" is the work of Thomas Shelton (1601–50?), the inventor of the system of shorthand used by Pepys for his Diary.

The English books are an interesting collection. Fiction is represented by "Pembrok's Arcadia" (*i.e.* Sir Philip Sidney's "The Countess of Pembroke's Arcadia"), a translation of Cervantes' "Exemplary Novels" and, as we should expect, "The Grand Cyrus," Madeleine de Scudéry's "Artamène ou le Grand Cyrus," englished by F. G. and published in five massive folios in 1653–5.

There is a fair selection of English verse, and the presence of "Paradise Lost" and two editions of Donne's poems does credit to Sir Charles's taste. "Bochas's Tragedies Black Letter" is probably Lydgate's "Fall of Princes," translated from Boccaccio's "De Casibus Virorum et Fœminarum Illustrium," originally printed by Pynson in 1494. This may well have come down from old John Sedley of Southfleet, Henry VIII's Auditor of Exchequer. "Dryden's Juvenal" of 1693 is the original folio edition of the English Juvenal edited and partly translated by Dryden. It contains a reference to Sedley on p. 87, where, in his introduction to the sixth Satire, Dryden informs us that he requested "Sir C. S." to undertake this satire "because he could have done more right to the Author," but that after a long delay "he absolutely refus'd so ungrateful an employment." "The Devotions of his Majesty in his Solitudes in Verse 1657" is a folio pamphlet entitled "Psalterium Carolinum, the Devotions of his Sacred Majesty Charles II in his Solitudes and Sufferings Rendred into Verse . . . Set to musick for 3 voices,

and an Organ or Theorbo, By *John Wilson* Dr. and
Musick Professor of *Oxford* ... London ... 1657."
It may be conjectured that this book was once the property of the loyal Elizabeth, Lady Sedley, the poet's
mother. "Works of Joh. Taylor, the Water Poet" is
probably the collected folio edition (1630) of the
voluminous doggerel of that literary bargee. The
"Poems and Translations by Oxford Hands 1685" is
a miscellany of verses by Oxford men printed by
Anthony Stephens, an Oxford bookseller. It contains
on p. 165 a copy of verses "Upon the Slighting of his
Friend's Love," signed "C. S." and attributed in the
Table to "Mr. C. S. of Wadham." It is not impossible
that this may have been an early piece by Sedley, which
somehow drifted into Stephens' hands.[1] "Dryden's
3d part of Miscellany Poems 1693" is a volume of
the famous miscellany of contemporary verse published by Tonson, to an earlier part of which Sedley
himself contributed some translations of Ovid. The
1664 edition of Katherine Philips's poems contains
most of her lyrics and shorter pieces, but not her
versions of Corneille. "Gildon's new Collections of
Poems *Lond.* 1701" is "A New Miscellany of Original
Poems on Several Occasions," edited by Gildon, and
containing several poems by Sedley, including his fine
version of Horace's Eighth Ode of the Second Book,
as well as some of Dorset's witty lines on Katherine
Sedley. "Sir Joh. Denham's Poem of Old Age" is
"Cato Major of Old Age," a version in heroic couplets
of Cicero's "De Senectute": the date should be 1669.

The presence of works by Bacon, Burton, Montaigne
(in Cotton's excellent translation) and Locke bears
witness to an excellent taste in English prose, and
there is a very interesting collection of contemporary
literary criticisms, including Gildon's "Miscellany
Letters and Essays of 1694," with their "Vindication"

---

[1] See my forthcoming edition of the "Works of Sir Charles Sedley,"
where the full text is given.

of Shakespeare against Rymer's attack, the "Miscellany
Essays" of St. Évrémond, the famous French critic
who lived at the Court of Charles II and was one of
the earliest Frenchmen to write intelligently about the
English drama, Basil Kennet's "Lives of the Ancient
Greek Poets" of 1697, a very uncritical work, and
"The Whole Art of the Stage" translated from the
French of the Abbé François Hédelin and published
in 1684. The latter is less remarkable for its dramatic
criticism proper, which is of the stiffest pseudo-
classical brand, than for its excellent arguments and
proposals in favour of improving the dignity and
status of the theatre, actors and dramatists. Along with
these we may notice Jeremy Collier's Defence of his
"Short View of the Stage," which indicates that Sir
Charles was interested in the controversy provoked by
the non-juror's famous onslaught, and the two works
of the protagonists in the dispute concerning the
authenticity of the Letters of Phalaris, which was
linked with the wider controversy concerning the rival
merits of the Ancients and the Moderns. The political
works were doubtless purchased at different stages of
Sir Charles's parliamentary career. Among them may
be noted Dr. Davenant's "Essay on Ways and Means
of Supplying the War," which recalls the reference to
his writings in Sedley's letter to Sir R. Newdigate of
12 January, 1698/9. The "Military Instruction for
the Cavalry," "Bond's Guide for Justices of the Peace"
and "Swinburn of Testaments and Last Wills" reflect
the needs of the militia officer, the lord of the manor,
and the owner of an extensive property. "Glanvil of
Witches and Apparitions 1681" is the first edition of
"Saducismus Triumphatus," in which Joseph Glanvil
conclusively demonstrates (with awe-inspiring illustra-
tions) the "Possibility" and "Real Existence" of witches
and witchcraft. The numerous books of travel and
historical and geographical works both in English and
French are interesting testimonies to the increasing

curiosity concerning the nature and history of the world that was characteristic of the age. "The Refin'd Courtier 1679" is a curious little work on etiquette and deportment by a certain N. W., who dedicates it to the Duke of Monmouth. Some of the things that N. W. advises the Duke to avoid throw considerable light on Restoration manners. For instance, there is an alarming glimpse of persons "who more like so many *swine* than men, put their Noses into a mess of Broth, and never lift up their Faces or Hands from the Dish, and that with their Cheeks distended and swoln (as if they were sounding a Trumpet or blowing a Fire) don't so properly *eat* as devour their Meat." "The Lady's New-Year's Gift" is another book on behaviour, being the advice of George Savile, Marquis of Halifax, the famous "Trimmer," to his daughter, published anonymously in 1688. It is rather curious that Sir George Etherege also possessed a copy of this work according to the list of his books made by his secretary at Ratisbon on his departure in 1689.[1] "Reflect. on the Secret History of K. Charles II and K. James 2d" must be a reply to a very scurrilous little book called "The Secret History of K. Charles II and K. James II," published in 1690. We may suppose that the theological works by Bishop Wilkins, formerly Warden of Sedley's college, were the property of his old pupil. "Wilkins of Prayer" is "A Discourse concerning the Gift of Prayer " (1653), and "Wilkins Beauty of Providence" is "A Discourse concerning the Beauty of Providence in all the Rugged Passages of It" (1649).

The French section displays, as we should expect, a wide acquaintance with French literature. The drama is represented by an early collected edition of Racine, "Crispin bel Esprit," a comedy by Juvenon de La Thuillerie, a minor dramatist of the school of Molière, and the plays of Pierre de L'Arivey (1540–1611?), one

---

[1] Ratisbon Letter Book, f. 192: "A Catalogue of Sr Georges Bookes."

of the earliest writers of French comedy, who, it may be noticed, was, like Sedley, an adapter of Terence.

There is a good selection of French prose, beginning with Philippe de Comines's famous Chronicle of Louis XI (wrongly catalogued as Loys II). "Memoires de M. le P. Bourdeille Sr. de Brantôme Tom 2. *Leyd.* 1666" is Brantôme's "Memoires contenant Les Vies des Hommes Illustres François de son temps." It may be confidently surmised that the writings of the author of "Les Vies des Femmes Galantes" appealed strongly to Sir Charles. "Histoires Tragiques tom. 2, 3 and 7. *Lyon.* 1591" is an early edition of François Belleforest's well-known collection, which contains the story of Hamlet. There is also an early edition of one of the greatest French prose classics of Sedley's own day, La Bruyère's "Caractères," which was published as a modest appendix to his translation of Theophrastus. There is much French literary criticism as we should expect in the library of Lisideius. Aristotle's Poetics in Madame Dacier's translation, with her commentary, and Bossu's "Du Poème Epique," are two of the chief expositions of the principles of the French classical school, and Sedley's interest in the controversy between the "Ancients" and the "Moderns" is again shown by the presence of Charles Perrault's "Parralèle des Anciens et Modernes," in which he upholds the claims of the "Siècle de Louis XIV" against the "Ancients." Besides these well-known works, there are a number of those miscellaneous books of literary criticism, compliment, gallantry and anecdote which were so numerous and popular in the reign of Louis XIV. They were probably the source of much of Sedley's admired conversation. "Valesiana ou les Pensées Critiques, Historiques, et Morales de Monsieur de Valois...à Paris...1693" contains the literary remains of Adrien de Valois, historiographer royal to Louis XIV (1607–93), a curious collection of odd learning and anecdote, with a long discussion of the coiffure of ladies of the ancient world, illuſtrated by an engraving of Cleopatra, which may have inter-eſted Sedley. "Lettres Nouvelles de M. Boursault. 1698" is an amusing collеction of letters by Edme Boursault, a well-known writer of comedies (1638–1701). The "Lettres Nouvelles" contain a great many excellent ſtories which probably furnished material for Sir Charles's after-dinner conversation. "Sorberiana ou les bons Mots de M. Sorbière" is the table-talk of Samuel de Sorbière, a French writer, who trans-lated Hobbes and wrote a moſt intereſting account of his travels in England. "Les Entretiens d'Ariſte et Eugène" is a series of polished dialogues by the Jesuit Père Bouhours. The two dialogues on "Le Bel Esprit" and "Le Je ne sais quoi" muſt have been very con-genial reading for a man of Sedley's taſtes. Such passages as the following furnish an intereſting parallel to the new ideals of good writing which he and his friends were imposing on English literature. "Au reſte, il ne suffit pas, pour avoir l'esprit beau, de l'avoir solide, pénétrant, délicat, fertile, juſte, universel; il faut encore y avoir *une certaine clarté* que tous les grands génies n'ont pas. Car il y en a qui sont naturelle-ment obscurs, et qui affeсtent même de l'être."

"Cependant il ne doit y avoir ni obscurité ni embarras dans tout ce qui part d'un bel esprit: ses pensées, ses expressions doivent être si nobles et si *nettes* que les intelligents l'admirent et que les plus simples l'entendent."[1] These sentences express the reaсtion of Dryden and his friends againſt the "meta-physicals," as well as that of Racine and Boileau againſt the Hôtel de Rambouillet.

Among the Spanish and Italian books we may notice "Don Quixote," Guarini's immensely popular "Il Paſtor Fido" and Caſtiglione's "Il Cortegiano."

---

[1] "Entretiens d'Ariste et Eugène," ed. René Radouant (collection des Chefs-d'œuvres Méconnus) . . . 1920, pp. 160, 161. [The italics are mine.]

Some of the other Italian works have titles which are hardly likely to have been found in the library of an Eminent Divine. The presence of dictionaries and books of engravings of Rome suggests that Sedley may have visited Italy.

If this list represents fairly accurately the contents of Sedley's library, it is in itself a sufficient answer to the theory that the Restoration Wits were mere idlers with a thin veneer of meretricious culture. It is the library of a man of wide and genuine learning, who appears to have been in touch with most of the important currents of the European thought of his day.

APPENDIX III

I

SOME LETTERS OF KATHERINE SEDLEY

THE following note, which bears no date or superscription, is preserved among the Sackville family papers at the Public Record Office. I have been allowed to copy and print it by kind permission of Lord Sackville. It is the earlieſt specimen of Katherine's correspondence that I have been able to find. It was probably written soon after she was granted the title, and seems to refer to the house in St. James's Square in which she was to be inſtalled. This house (No. 21, according to Dasent's " St. James's Square," pp. 181, 244) was formerly the property of another miſtress of James II, Arabella Churchill, who married a Colonel Godfrey. Sir Edward Seymour was the well-known Tory politician, and Lord Godolphin is the firſt Earl, who was Chamberlain to Mary of Modena, and would naturally be consulted in an affair of this kind.

I

Madam   I am grown A moſt hardend teaser which you are like to suffer by, the busines of my lodgins not being over, Sʳ Edward Seymour

345

tells me the Queen spoke to y^r Brother before him to geve me A warrant for them Ld Godolphin who is a friend of the Noble race of the Churchills desierd hee might fir$t$ geve notis to Mis Godfry but that being some time sence and my Ld Godolphens busines haveing taken it upon him I hope y^r brother will make his, helping me I shall leave a man in town to reseave these Keas dear Madam get this matter off my hands, for this solissiting makes me fit for Beaddlam

y^r most humble

servant

DORCHESTER.

The following two letters were formerly in the Morrison Colle&tion of Autograph Letters (2nd Series, iii. 128). They were transcribed by Mr. G. Thorn Drury, who has kindly allowed me to copy his transcripts. They are addressed to a "Mr Nelson" and appear to have been written when the Countess was in exile in Ireland. The fir$t$ is dated "March the 16" (?1686) and mu$t$ have been written soon after the Countess reached Dublin.

2

I was never negglegent off my owne fault, but it will make me yet more carefull toe find people of your merett concerned for me, soe I thank you for the assurance you geve me. You will hear, by a letter I wret Lady Thea, that I am got to Dubblin without any ill acsident. The English have generally a humour I doe not aprove off, which is afe&ting toe like nothing but thare owne country, soe ware it possible I would commend this place, but tis intollerable. I find them not only senceless, but a mallincolly sort of people and speak all in the tone off the

cripples off London, yet I doe not find my Lord
Clarrindon takes much amongſt them, but one
may perceave thare feare of Lord Torconnell
makes them speake less ill than otherways they
would doe.

Mr Fergus Grahms tells me you say my
lodgings are gone. I had nott heard off itt before
but 'tis very probable, because 'tis so very
gentealy done. Pray writ tow me and send me
all the news. Adieu. My humble service toe yʳ
lady.

The second letter is dated "12th May," probably
in the same year.

3

I wish I had better news to send you off
myself, but I have bin and am ſtill, very ill; and
now that I disspaire of having any helth in this
place, the Queen's pious mind is in sume dangeur
off being discomposed, iff my return will doe itt.
I confess I wonder itt should, for she knows the
respeᶜt the King has for the preſts; and they say
to him as toe my persecutour, as God did toe
Adam, "Off every tree in the Garding thou
mayeſt freely eate, but off this tree thou shalt
not eate off itt, for in the day that thou eatiſt
thou shalt surely dye." Iff such a declaration
as this will not sever the King from me in the
Queen's openioun, she thinks much better off
me then I deserve. Pray give my humble service
to my Lord Bartle, and thanke him for me. I
have reseaved three potts more of lampress that
ware extreme good, and as good company as
this place afords drunck his helth.

The match you writ off concerning the Lord
Arron I beleve true, for some people love to

propagaite ffools. I doupt the pretty little widdow will come in at that toe, for her choyse is not very good. I thought she would have bin true toe love, and have marryed Tolmedge; sure she has Royall blood in her, she is soe fickle. Pray write toe me offen, for letters from England are the only thinges that make this place suportable. Send the news true or false, I care not. I love an English lye, I am sure tis non to tell you I am your moſt humble servante."

I am unable to identify "Lady Thea." "Clarrindon" is the second Earl of Clarendon, Lord Lieutenant of Ireland and brother of Lawrence Hyde, Earl of Rocheſter, Katherine's old ally. "Torconnell" is Richard Talbot, Earl of Tyrconnel, the beſt hated of James's Roman Catholic advisers, at this time in command of the English army in Ireland. "Mr Fergus Grahms" is probably a relative of Colonel James Grahme, Katherine's old admirer. "My Lord Bartle" may be the Countess's spelling of "Lord Berkely," firſt Earl, who formerly entertained her father at the Durdans. "The Lord Arron" is the second Earl of Arran, eldeſt son of the Duke of Hamilton, who married Ann Spencer, daughter of the second Earl of Sunderland on 12 January, 1677–8. This muſt be the match to which the Countess refers so tartly. She muſt have borne Sunderland a grudge because of the part he played in persuading James II to dismiss her. I cannot identify "the pretty little widdow," but "Tolmedge" muſt be Thomas Tollemache or Talmash, the well-known soldier, later distinguished for his service in William III's wars with France. He was created a lieutenant-colonel of Fusiliers by James II, but threw up his commission because of his disagreement with the King's policy.

Another letter, probably written in Dublin, survives in the British Museum among the Clarendon papers, and shows that, with all her faults, Katherine had a good heart. It seems to convey her thanks to the Earl of Clarendon, then Lord Lieutenant of Ireland, for his influence exercised on behalf of a needy gentleman at her request. "Mr Grahme" is probably the Mr. Fergus Grahme mentioned in the second letter to Mr. Nelson.

4

The bearer of this my Lord is the Gentleman I desierd Mr Grahme to recomend to Your lordship and tho he tells me you have bin so oblidging toe grant my request for which I return my humble thanks yet I cannot but be ashaimed that he made it in my name for having so smale an acquaintance with you my lord your lordship may jeustly look upon it as an impertinence in me to ask you anything but the party is in want, and when you consider how much we wemen are inclined to do Good natur'd things and how seldom they do proper ones, you will not wonder at this proseeing off

My Lord,
Yʳ Lordships
humble servante
K. SEDLEY." [1]

Among the Sloane MSS. in the British Museum are the following brief notes from Lady Dorchester to Sir Hans Sloane. They are undated, but the reference to "my Lord" shows that they were written after her marriage.[2]

5

Sr
Pray be with me at teen to morrow morning or before five in the Evening my Lord has

[1] Brit. Mus., Add. MSS. 15,892, f. 259.
[2] Sloane MSS. 4060, ff. 64, 66.

had a present of white wine from Gebraltaire I
have sent you by the porter three dozen of it
thinking it very good I hope wee shall be alone
for I cannot underſtand that theres safety in
multitude of Councillers tho Solomon himself
sayes it

Your moſt humble servant
DORCHESTER.

Saterday
  night
    to Sr Hans Sloane.

6

Sir

    Pray let me know if I am to drink the Bath
waters with my wine at meales for I never drink
but then being of a hott dry Conſtitution (so)
I have been told; and pray tell me what sort of
wine I may drink besides sack that being a wine
dos not help apetite.

Your
humble servant
DORCHESTER.

To Sir Hans Sloane.

The Counteſs's lateſt extant letter almoſt certainly
refers to the Resumptions Bill of April 1711, when
she ran a grave risk of losing the eſtates granted to
her by her royal lover (see p. 237).

7
Brit. Mus., Add. MSS. 28,569, f. 38.

S^{ir}

    The vote that has bin carryd In the Parle-
ment of the land againſt my pention, geves you
this trouble tho Sir our acquantance is not enough
to exspeĉt on every occation your assiſtance as a

zealous friend, yet your carricture in the world
being such as to assure me of your good sense,
and good Nature, and mine being a matter in
which you may shew at a time both these qualities.
I dare depend upon your utmoſt Indeavers to
shelter my lord and me from this rash neſt of
our Enimys, not to geve it the term which between
You and me it deserves, of Mallice. It is sure
a great egnorance, if not worse to term a grant
five thousand per an that is but three, and but
for life as Baron Worth can perticulourly Inform
you and of which I beg you to Inſtruct others, I
have so worthyly beſtood this pention in the
persone of my Lord Portmore, that I cant but
wonder it should be attackt, at leaſt in a Country
where he has aɾted so honnorably and if I may
put them in mind of it, so deferantly in that
from what many other offecers did In the troubles
waire lately amongſt them, I hope the Irish
Nobelity and Gentry will not geve us reason here
to think: useing them well or ill is all one, when
a return is exspeɾted, now Sⁱʳ, if a Lady be not
thought too pretending in geveing her opinoun
in these high matters I would say, tis a little
unpolitick In them so grossely to spare one
anoether of which I could geve several inſtance
and onely fly at the English; and a Part of the
Clargey that is not taken to be quite so frendless
as thay may supose. but as thay have repented
of their cruelty to them as some letters inform
us, I hope they will turn more favorable in what
relates to me and my lord I muſt beg you to
use your intereſt in bringing that about, for tho
I can never think the Queen will be brought to
overturn a grant of her fathers or ruing my lord
at home while hee is imployed in so dangerous
service abraud yet, I muſt oone to you I should
be sorry to be obledged to the Queen for not

takeing from me what I have, I hope to have occasion toe thank her for whats to come; therefore onse more, I intreate you to apeer in my enterest, I am sure it will be acknowledged with a sincere gratitude to my lord and you & ever engage

S^{ir}

Your most humble
Servant
Dorchester.

My lord geves you
his most humble service
hee hopes my letter will be as efectual
with you as his hee has not a moments time to
him self.

II

Extracts from "Correspondance d'Angleterre"

(Archives of French Foreign Office, Quai D'Orsai.)
Bonrepaux a Londres ce 3 Jan^{er} 1686.

tom. 157, ff. 47, 48.

Il y a une nouvelle icy Mgr qui occupe et qui partage toute la Cour. Le Roy d'Ang^{le} a declaré *M^{le} Chidley Comtesse* elle estoit fille d'honneur de la Reine lorsqu'elle estoit duchesse d'York. Sa M.B. en devint amoureux, et en a eu deux enfans dont l'on vit encore. A son avénement a la Couronne ce Roy declara qu'il ne la verroit plus et rompit, publiquement avec elle. Je scay bien certainement que cette rupture estoit de bonne foy en cetems la, quoyque aujourdhuy le public ne le croye point, mais une personne qui est la confidente et l'intime amie de la D^e et qui ne me cache rien me dit il y a un mois qu'il estoit vray que le Roy d'Ang^{le} avoit esté trois mois sans la voir apres cette declaration, mais que depuis quelque

tems il la voyoit en cachette a Witheall ou elle a toujours
logé dans l'appartement que Me Bocky, qu'on appele
icy presentement Mad^e Sophie, luy a cedé, et ce que
me confirme dans la pensés que le Roy d'Angl^re a
toujours entrenu un commerce avec elle, c'est que je
scay par un de ses confidens qu'il luy a acheté une
maison dans la ville de 30°° escus, et que les meilleurs
peintres et les meilleurs sculpteurs de Londres travail-
lent a l'orner. Je scay aussi qu'on luy a augmenté sa
pension qui n'estoit que de deux mil livres sterlin, et
qu'outre cela le garde de la privé bours qui est le
confident de cette intrigue luy fournit tout l'argent
dont elle a besoin pour ses meubles, et pour ses menus
plaisirs, cette fille est forte laide, aigre et hautaine,
mais elle a beaucoup d'esprit, la plus part des courtisans
pensent que c'est Milord Rochester et sa femme qui
ont renoué cette aff^re, mais assurement il ny a que
l'inclination que le Roy d'Angl^e a pour elle qui a
fait cela, n'ayant point d'autre confident pour ce qui la
regarde que M. Grimps garde de la privé bourse et
frere de Milord Preston, une Irlandoise qui a esté
femme de Chambre de Mad^e de Portsmouth mariée
avec Oglethorp colonel d'un regiment, et une au-
[tr]e personne dont j'ay eu l'honneur de vous parler.
Le Reine d'Ang^re a eu un chagrin extreme de cette
declaration qu'elle na pû dissimuler au public je scay
mesme que le Roy d'Ang^re pour la contenter a escrit
un billet au Chan^cr pour luy ordonner de surceoir
l'expedition des lettres. Ce n'est cependant qu'un
retardement car il est bien assuré que Mlle Cidley
sera Countesse.

Londres le 4 Février 1686, f. 53.

Depuis que j'ay escrit cecy j'ay eu occasion d'entretenir Milord Sunderland sur l'eloygnement de M^le
Cidley a present Comtesse de Dorchester dont j'auray
l'honneur de vous parler. . . .

f. 54, 55.

La Reine d'Ang^e a repris le dessus et a eu toute
sorte de satisfaction au sujet de la nouvelle Comtesse
d'Orchester [*sic*] elle a consenti que les lettres fussent
expediées a condition que le Roy d'Ang^re ne la verra
plus et qu'elle sortira de Wethall, elle en sortit effective-
ment hier au soir et coucha dans sa maison de la ville,
on croit a la Cour qu'elle ira en Hollande, La Reyne
s'en flatte et elle se dit a une de ses confidentes qu'il
n'avoit tenu qu'a elle d'empescher l'expedition des
lettres que le Roy son mary en usoit si bien sur cela
qu'elle s'en fioit a sa parole. Il est certain que la
Reine d'Ang^re a temoigné beaucoup de conduite et
de fermeté dans cette occassion.

Barillon to Louis XIV 31 Jan. 1686.

tom. 158, ff. 74, 75.

Mad^lle Sidelay a le titre de Comtesse de Dorchester.
On a sceu que le Roy d'Ang^re la voyoit assez souvent,
et qu'elle venoit chez Chifins, mais on ne s'attendoit
pas quil luy donnast un titre. Le bruit de la Cour
est que dans la suite, Elle aura les logemens de Mad^e
de Portsmouth. Je ne scais point que cela doive
estre, et je croirois plustost que le Roy d'Ang^re ne la
verra, que comme il faisoit.

Cette nouvelle fait un grant bruit a Londres, et
cause une grande agitation dans le dedans de la Cour.
Les Catholiques en sont affligés et alarmés, croyons
que cela ne s'est fait que par une cabale dans laquelle
quelqu'un des ministres est entré.

Barillon 4 fév. 1686. tom. 158, f. 82.

L'Affaire de Mad^lle de Sidelay a receu un grand
changement. Elle a la patente de Comtesse de Dorchester, mais le Roy d'Ang^re a declaré qu'il ne la
verroit plus. Il s'est engagé de parole formelle a la

faire sortir de Londres et mesme d'Angleterre. Elle
a desja pris le party de sortir de la Cour. Ce Prince
a reconnu de quelle consequence il estoit pour luy de
contenter en cela non seulement le Reyne Sa femme,
mais mesme les plus zélés de ses serviteurs Catholiques
et protestans. Cette affaire a causé un mouvement
fort grand dans le dedans de la Cour pendent plusieurs
jours.

Il y a encore des gens qui s'imaginent que l'eloigne-
ment de cette nouvelle Comtesse ne sera que pour peu
de temps mais je crois scavoir le contraire, et que le
Roy d'Ang^re a pris sur cela de engagemens trop forts
pour y manquer.

Barillon 7 fév. 1686. f. 84–92.

Le Roy d'Ang^re temoigna ouvertement a son avénement a la Couronne qu'il ne vouloit pas voir Mlle
Sideley. Il le promit aux Cat^ques et le monde crût en
ce temps la que cette declaration avoit produit un fort
bon effet pour luy.

Mad^lle Sidelay est demeurée dans un petit logement
en vue des cours de Withehall qu'elle avoit acheté
pendant la vie du feu Roy. Elle venoit souvent chez
Mad^e de Portsmouth, et étoit fort ben traitté du feu
Roy, qui prenoit plaisir à l'entretenir.

Elle a beaucoup d'esprit et de vivacité mais elle
n'a plus aucune beauté, et est d'une extresme maigreur.
Elle se comporta fort hardiment a la mort du feu Roy,
et declara qu'elle ne sortiroit point, de Withehall.
Elle y est demeurée, quoyqu'elle eust une maison fort
bien meublée dans la place de St. Gemes qui luy avoit
esté achetée par le Duc d'York.

Le confident de l'intrigue avec Mademoiselle
Sideley est le S^r. Cremme, qui a la bourse privée du
Roy d'Anglet^re. C'est le frere de Milord Preston. Il
n'est pas mal avec son maistre et est fort uny avec
Milord d'Artmouth [*sic*] grand Escuyer. Il y a quel-
ques mois que le Roy d'Angleterre a recommencé a

voir Mad^{lle} Sideley. Elle venoit le plus souvent chez Chiffins ; c'est un appartement au dessous l'appartement ou tout le monde entre. On a sceu que le grand Tresorier avoit des mesnagements pour Mad^{lle} Sideley et qu'il la voyoit quelquefois mais on ne croyoit pars que cela devoit avoir d'autre suites que de demeurer, comme elle estoit à Withal et de tirer beaucoup de presents et d'argent.

Mlle de Sideley s'est trouvée grosse. Elle avoit eu un fils qui est mort. Il luy reste une fille ses amis ont crû qu'elle devoit avoir une titre et que le Roy d'Ang^{re} ne pouvoit le luy refuser. Il se sont bien attend^{us} que la Reyne d'Ang^{re} temoigneroit d'abord quelque chagrin mais ils ont crû que sa resistance se termineroit a refuser au plus de la voir, et de la traitter, comme une Comtesse.

On pretend que Milord Rochester et sa femme ont assuré le Roy qu'il luy seroit aisé d'appaiser la Reyne, et qu'ainsy il s'estoit determiné a donner le titre de Comtesse a sa Maitresse.

En mesme temps on croit que Mad^e de Rochester avoit insinué à la Reyne que la veritable inclination du Roy estoit pour Mademoiselle de Grafton, Et on a remarqué que la Reyne la traistoit moins bien que l'ordre. Tout cela se faisoit dans de dessein de faire penser a la Reyne que l'Affaire de Mad^{lle} de Sideley n'etoit rien de consequence, et que le Roy vouloit seulement donner un titre à une personne qu'il avoit aymée et dont il ne se soucioit plus.

Mais quand il a esté publié que Mad^{lle} Sideley seroit Comtesse et qu'elle pretendoit paroistre à la Cour, la Reyne a esté dans une affliction desmesuré.

Elle ayme de bonne foy le Roy son Mary. Elle est Italienne et fort glorieuse. Sa douleur a esclaté vivement. Je crois que sous main on l'a fortifiée et encouragée. Elle a declaré nettement qu'Elle ne souffriroit point le Scandale public qu'on pretendoit etablir, qu'elle ne verroit point la nouvelle Comtesse et que si le Roy ne s'en separoit elle se retireroit dans une Couvent en quelque pays que ce fuſt. Le Roy d'Ang^re a eſté fort surpris d'abord de cette resiſtance, qu'il a attribuée a la passion que la Reyne a pour luy. Il a cru qu'il pourroit l'appaiser mais il a trouvé une fermeté qui l'a etonné.

Les Catholiques et Milord Sonderland a leur teſte sont venus au secours de la Reynè. On a fait parler le père Petirs et tous ceux qui ont du credit et en qui sa Majeſté Britannique a confiance. Ils luy ont representé quel scandale ce seroit a Rome et dans toute la Chreſtienté qu'un Prince qui a tout hazardé pour la Religion Cath^que vouluſt paroiſtre dans un dereglement tel que celuy là. On luy a insinué que s'eſtoit l'effet d'une Cabale de gens qui vouloient le decrier au dedans et au dehors de son Royaume et le detournir des bonnes resolutions qu'il semble avoir prises. Le Chancelier s'eſt joint a Milord Sonderland. Le Roy d'Angleterre a trouvé du fondement a ce qu'on luy disoit. Il ne se soucie pas beaucoup dans le fond de Mlle Sideley. Enfin il s'eſt determiné a faire ce que la Reyne vouloit et a croire le conseil de ses plus confidens serviteurs.

Ils n'ont pas jugé de voir s'opposer a ce que le titre de Comtesse fuſt donné a Mad^lle Sideley parceque l'affaire avoit eclaté et n'eſt en soy d'aucune consequence.

Mais on s'eſt renfermé a demander qu'Elle sorte de la Cour et de Londres. Le Roy d'Angl^re a promis l'une et l'autre positivement a la Reyne sa femme, et l'a declare aux Milords Cat^ques et aux Miniſtres qui luy en ont parlé.

Il eſt a remarqué que le grand Trésorier n'a point paru en tout cela et n'a fait aucun pas en faveur de la Reyne. Il a eſté mesme quatre ou cinq jours sans la voir. On n'a pas manqué de faire connoiſtre, qu'Elle a eſte trahie et abandonnée par ceux en qui Elle avoit plus de confiance. Elle a eſté honteuse de n'avoir rien

sceu du commerce que le Roy d'Ang^re avoit depuis
quelque temps avec Mad^lle Sideley.

Milord Tresorier et sa femme ont voulu se justifier
aupres de la Reyne, Elle le fait semblant d'admettre
leur excuses mais ils sont perdus en son esprit et
l'autre Cabale pretend mesme faire connoistre au Roy
d'Angleterre qu'on l'a embarqué dans une affaire qui
blessait sa reputation et qui ruinoit son repos domes-
tique. Tout cela a causé une grande agitation dans le
dedans de la Cour et est devenu une affaire de party.
Tous les Catholiques ont paru d'abord consternés et
affligés mais les protestans Zelés tout affligés a leur
tour.

On dit mesme que la Comtesse de Dorchester publie
qu'Elle est la victime de la Religion Protestante et
qu'Elle est opprimée par la faction des Catholiques.

Elle ne se pas [*sic*] d'avoir souvent dit au Roy
d'Angleterre que Milord Arundel et Milord Tirconel
luy feroient perdre sa Couronne. Le Comte d'Adda a
joué son personnage, quoyqu'il n'ait pas paru, et a
dit son avis qui a esté rapporté au Roy d'Angleterre
et a produit son effet.

Cela paroist presentement comme une victoire
remportée par le Party de Catholiques et de ceux qui
sont joint a eux.

Le Roy d'Angleterre temoigne estre fort content
de ce qu'il a fait et se scait bon gré d'avoir suivy les
conseils de ses veritables serviteurs.

Il a intention qu'on croye que son dessein n'a point
esté d'establir a la Cour la Comtesse de Dorchester
mais seulement de luy donner une titre et de l'éloigner;
Il est vray cependant que l'affaire s'est passée comme
j'ay honneur de la mander a V.M.

Milord Sonderland m'a informé a mesure de tout
le detail qu'il arrivoit quelque incident. Je me suis
tenu une grande retenue sans paroistre me mesler de
rien, mais j'ay redoublée mon assiduité à la Cour, et

la Reyne a étée bien assurée que je suis dans ses intereſts par la connoissance qui j'ay de l'amitié et de l'eſtime que V. M. a pour elle. Peuteſtre me serat-il necessaire que je dise quelque chose de la part de V. M. car cette Princesse regarde cette affaire comme la plus importante qu'elle aura de la vie. Je le feray sans me commettre, quand V. M. m'en aura donné l'Ordre.

Milord Sonderland croit tirer de grands avantages pour luy, et pour son party d'avoir si bien servy la Reyne. Il croit le grand Tresorier fort affoibly, et que c'eſt une marque de son peu de credit d'avoit formé ou Souſtenue le projet de l'etablissement d'une maitresse a la Cour, et de n'avoir pas reussy en ce projet.

Les amis de la Comtesse de Dorcheſter luy ont conseillé de point consentir a son éloignement, et de s'opiniaſtrer a demeurer dans sa maison Cela donna encore hier quelque inquietude a la Reyne, mais le Roy luy a promis positivement de ne se point relascher. Il consulta sur le champ avec Milord Chancelier, Milord Sonderland, et Milord Godolfin. Il fut resolu que Milord Midelton secretaire d'Eſtat iroit declarer a Made la Comtesse de Dorcheſter de la part du Roy d'Angre qu'ayant dit d'abord que son dessein eſtoit d'aller en Hollande, il y avoit un yacht preſt pour l'y conduire, et que si elle ne prenoit pas le party de s'embarquer incessament, elle seroit conduite et menée ailleurs, selon qu'il seroit trouvée plus a propos.

On a fait une raillerie pendant tout hier, que la Comtesse de Dorcheſter se tenoit aux priviliges de *Magna Carta*, et pretendoit qu'on ne pouvoit pas obliger a sorter d'Angleterre.

Cette pretention eſt fort mal fondée en une affaire de cette nature, mais il y a des gens qui croient que la Comtesse de Dorcheſter eſt fortifiée sous main et que le Roy d'Angre mesme n'eſt pas fasché de la resistance qu'elle y apporte. Peuteſtre cela se terminera

par une retraite a la campagne. Les amis du grand
Tresorier disent qu'il n'a aucune part a ce que se
passe et qu'il ne s'eſt meslé ny de l'elevation de la
Comtesse de Dorcheſter ny de sa grace, qui dans le
poſte ou il eſt, son devoir l'engage a vouloir tout ce
qui plaiſt a son maiſtre, et qu'il n'appartient a personne
d'entrer dans de telles affaires pour les traverser ou
pour les favoriser sans y eſtre appelé. Il eſt vray
cependant que Milord Rocheſter et sa femme parois-
sent abattus et fort chagrin on ne croit pas que la
Reyne leur pardonne, ny que le Roy luy mesme soit
content d'avoir eſté engagé a une chose dont il a eſté
obligé de se dédire, et dont il reconnoiſt a present tout
les inconveniens.

f. 98 [same date].

J'ay sceu ce soir que la Comtesse de Dorcheſter
fait semblant d'eſtre malade pour ne point partir.
Elle a fait proposer d'aller en Irlande pour ne point
sortir des Eſtats de Sa Maj^te Britannique. Elle demande
aussy qu'en cas qu'elle aille en hollande il luy soit
permis de voir Madlle la Princesse d'Orange, et
qu'elle soit bien traittee. Cette negociation et les delais
deplaisent fort la Reyne qui ne sera point enrepos
qu'elle ne soit pas partie. Cela peut aller encore a
quelques jours, mais il n'a a guere d'apparence que
le Roy d'Ang^re change de resolution, ny qu'il se
relasche apres s'eſtre declaré aussy positivement qu'il
a fait.

Barillon 21 fév. 1686. f. 106-7.

La Comtesse de Dorcheſter pretend s'eſtre blessée
et avoir fait une fausse couche. Elle declare—pourtant
qu'elle partira dans peu de jours et se retirera ou il
plaira a sa M^te Britannique. On ne scait encore si
ce sera en Irlande ou dans une province d'Angleterre
eloignée de Londres. Les amis de cette Comtesse
disent qu'Elle n'a jamais refusé de se retirer de la
Cour, mais qu'Elle n'a pu se resoudre d'aller en

flandres ou en france comme on le luy a proposé
craignant qu'on ne la miſt dans un Couvent ce qu'elle
apprehende plus que la mort. Un discours si peu
raisonnable se tient pour nourrir toujours dans les
esprits une aigreur contre la Religion Catholique. La
Reyne d'Ang^re paroit fort contente et cette affaire qui
a causé beaucoup d'agitation dans le dedans de la
Cour paroiſt finie, mais l'aigreur et les conteſtations
qu'Elle a formées ne finiront pas si toſt. Le Grand
Tresorier pretend n'avoir eu aucune part a tout ce
qui s'eſt passe, et que ce qu'on a dit sur ce sujet eſt
une artifice de ses ennemis qui l'ont voulu mettre mal
avec la Reyne.

Barillon 14 fév. 1686. f. 111.

L'affaire de la Comtesse de Dorcheſter paroiſt
entierement terminée. Elle doit partir dans trois jours
pour d'Irlande ou Elle a des terres qui luy ont eſte
données par le Roy d'Angleterre.

Barillon 18 fév. 1686. f. 119.

La Comtesse de Dorcheſter doit partir tous les
jours pour l'Irlande mais elle differe le plus qu'Elle
peut et le Roy d'Ang^re a de la peine a user contrainte
a son egard de quelque jours plus ou moins. Cependant
on luy represente que ce retardement fait tenir de
discours opposes en ce qu'il desire et que sa reputation souffre de ne pas finir entierement cette affairs.
Je crois que luy mesme a fort envie d'eſtre hors de
cet embaras et qu'il voudroit que la Comtesse de
Dorcheſter fuſt partie.

Toutes les apparences sont que le dessein eſtoit
formé de se servir d'Elle pour avoir dans le Cour un
party qui s'opposaſt a tout ce qui se fait en faveur de
la Religion Catholique—et qui puſt mesme tourner en
ridicules ceux qui ont le plus de part aux resolution
qui se prennent, a quoy la Comtesse reſté fort propre.
On prend beaucoup de soin d'ouvrir entierement les

yeux de la Reyne d'Angleterre sur cela et de luy faire comprendre que ne pouvant esperer qu'Elle voulust entrer dans les mesures opposées aux veritables interests et aux desseins du Roy son mary on vouloit avoir dans le Cour un appuy qui put au moins retarder l'execution des bonnes resolutions et soutenir le party des Protestans Zelés.

23 fév. 1686. f. 133.

On croit que la Comtesse de Dorchester doit partir incessament pour l'Irlande. La Reyne d'Angleterre paroist contente. Je ne m'avanceray trop en luy parlant sur une matiere si delicate. Elle voit bien que les amis de la Comtesse de Dorchester ne sont pas partisans de la France ni de la Religion Catholique. . . .

APPENDIX IV

I. Principal Manuscript Sources

Correspondance d'Angleterre: Louis XIV.
> (Letters of French Ambassadors in England: Quai d'Orsai.)

Etherege, Sir George. Ratisbon Letter Book.
> (Transcript of Letters, etc. written by Sir George Etherege while English Envoy at Ratisbon in MS. of Secretary: Brit. Mus., Add. MS. 11,513.)

Haward, Sir William. MS. Diary.
> (Collection of Mr. G. Thorn Drury.)

Le Neve, Peter. MS. Diary.
> (Collection of Mr. G. Thorn Drury.)

Newdigate Family Papers: Letters of Sir Charles Sedley, etc.
> (By kind permission of Sir Francis Newdigate, Bart., of Arbury, Warwickshire.)

Prideaux, Col. W. F., MS. notes, etc. on the Sedley genealogy, formerly in the possession of Col. W. F. Prideaux.
> (Kindly lent to the author by Mr. G. Thorn Drury.)

Rugge's Diurnall.
> (Brit. Mus., Add. MSS. 10,116; 10,117.)

Sackville Family Papers: Letters of Sir Charles Sedley, etc. (Public Record Office.)
> (By kind permission of Baron Sackville of Knole.)

Stanhope, Philip, second Earl of Chesterfield. Letter Book.
> (MS. of Secretary. Brit. Mus., Add. MS. 19,253.)

State Papers, Domestic: Charles I, Interregnum, Charles II, William III. (Public Record Office: *see* references to "State Papers Dom." in footnotes.)
State Papers, France, Charles II.
(Public Record Office: see references to " State Papers, France " in footnotes.)

II. Bibliography

(Only short titles are given.

In the case of rare works, shelf numbers in the British Museum, Bibliothèque Nationale, etc. are quoted.

For a detailed Bibliography of Works by or attributed to Sir Charles Sedley, see my forthcoming edition of the Works.

Works dedicated to members of the Sedley family are preceded by an asterisk.)

ABERCROMBIE, Lascelles.
The Idea of Great Poetry. London, 1925. 8vo.
AIRY, Osmund.
Charles II. London, Paris and Edinburgh, 1901. Fol.
AITKEN, George A.
Life of Richard Steele. London, 1889. 2 vols. in 8vo.
ANNESLEY, Arthur, first Earl of Anglesey.
A Letter from a Person of Honour in the Countrey written to the Earl of Castlehaven. London, 1681. 8vo. (Brit. Mus. 601, d. 10.)
ARBER, E.
The Term Catalogues 1668–1709. Privately Printed, London, 1903. 3 vols. in fol.
ARCHÆOLOGIA CANTIANA, being Transactions of the Kent Archæological Society. London, 1860. 18 vols. in 8vo.
ARMSTRONG, G. F.
The Ancient and Noble Family of the Savages of the Ards . . . by G. F. A. London, 1888. 4to.

AUBREY, John.
Brief Lives chiefly of Contemporaries set down
. . . between the years 1669 and 1696. Edited
from the author's MSS. by Andrew Clark.
Oxford, 1898. 2 vols. in 8vo.

BAILEY, Thomas.
Annals of Nottinghamshire, 1853. 8vo.

BAILLON, Comte Henri de.
Henriette Anne d'Angleterre. Paris, 1886. 8vo.

BAKER, David Erskine.
A Companion to the Playhouse, 1764. 2 vols. in
8vo. (Brit. Mus. 239. d. 5.) *See also* Biographia
Dramatica.

BARRET, William.
*Heliodorus his Ethiopian History: Done out of
Greeke, London, 1622. 4to. (Brit. Mus. 1074,
l. 10.)
(Underdown's translation, edited by William
Barret, dedicated to Sir John Sedley of South-
fleet.)

BEHN, Aphra.
Poems upon Several Occasions . . . London, 8vo,
1684. (Brit. Mus. 1078, l. 8.)
The Works . . . edited by Montague Summers,
Stratford-on-Avon, 1915. 6 vols. in 8vo.

BELJAME, Alexandre.
Le Public et les Hommes de Lettres en Angleterre dans le Dix-huitième Siècle, 1660–1744.
Paris, 1881 (1st edition); Paris, 1897 (2nd
edition, enlarged). 8vo.

BETTERTON, Thomas.
The Amorous Widow; or the Wanton Wife, a
comedy, London, 1729. 12mo. (Brit. Mus.
11,775, b. 53.) *See also* Lowe, Robert W.

BIOGRAPHIA BRITANNICA, or the lives of the most
eminent Persons who have flourished in Great
Britain and Ireland. London, 1747–66. 6 vols.
in fol.

BIOGRAPHIA DRAMATICA, or a Companion to the Playhouse (by David Erskine Baker). London, 1782. 2 vols. in 8vo.

Second edition, " with additions and improvements," London, 1812. 3 vols. in 8vo.

Biographie Générale, Nouvelle . . . publiée par MM. Firmin Didot Frères . . . sous la direction de M. le Dr. Hoefer. Paris, 1855.

Biography, Dictionary of National.

Ed. Leslie Stephen and Sidney Lee. London, 1908.

Birrell, Augustine.

Andrew Marvell (English Men of Letters). London, 1905. 8vo.

Bouhours, Le Père.

Entretiens d'Ariste et d'Eugène. Introduction et Notes de René Radouant. Paris, 1920. 8vo. (Collection des Chefs-d'Œuvres Méconnus.)

Brewer, J. S.

Letters and Papers Foreign and Domestic of the Reign of Henry VIII, Second Edition, revised and greatly enlarged by R. H. Brodie. London, 1920. 12 vols. in 8vo.

Brown, Thomas, of Shifnal (Tom Brown).

The Works of Mr. *Thomas Brown*. Serious and Comical in Verse and Prose. In Four Volumes. London, 1720. 4 vols. in 12mo. (Brit. Mus. 12,271, a.15.)

Brueys, David Augustin de, et Palaprat, Jean.

Le Grondeur, comedie . . . Paris . . . 1693. 12mo. (Bibl. Nat. Yf. 3664.)

Buckingham, second Duke of. *See* George Villiers.

Buckinghamshire, first Duke of. *See* Sheffield, John.

Bullen, A. H.

Musa Proterva. London. Privately Printed, 1889. 8vo.

Burghclere, Baroness.

George Villiers, Second Duke of Buckingham. London, 1903. 8vo.

Burke, John and John Bernard.

A Genealogical History of Extinct and Dormant

Baronetages of England, Scotland and Ireland. Second Edition. London, 1844. 8vo.

BURKE, Sir Bernard.

A Genealogical History of the Dormant, Abeyant, Forfeited, and Extinct Peerages of the British Empire. London, 1883. 8vo.

BURNET, Gilbert.

History of His Own Time, with the suppressed passages . . . notes of the Earls of Dartmouth, Hardwick and Speaker Onslow . . . cursory remarks of Swift. Oxford, 1823. 6 vols. in 8vo.

History of My Own Time, Part I, The Reign of Charles II. Edited by Osmund Airy. Oxford, 1897. 2 vols. in 8vo.

A Supplement to Burnet's History of My Own Time derived from his Original Memoirs, etc. . . . all hitherto unpublished. Edited by H. C. Foxcroft. Oxford, 1902. 8vo.

Some Passages of the Life and Death of the Right Honourable John Earl of Rochester . . . the Sixth edition. London, 1724. 8vo.

CALENDAR OF STATE PAPERS, Domestic Series.

Ed. Mary Everett Green. (See references in footnotes.)

CALENDAR OF STATE PAPERS: Treasury Books.

Prepared by W. A. Shaw. (See references in footnotes.)

CALENDAR OF THE PROCEEDINGS OF THE COMMITTEE FOR ADVANCE OF MONEY.

Ed. Mary Everett Green. London, 1888. 3 vols. in 8vo.

CALENDAR OF THE PROCEEDINGS OF THE COMMITTEE FOR COMPOUNDING, ETC., 1645–60.

Ed. Mary Everett Green. London, 1889. 5 vols. in 8vo.

CAMBRIDGE HISTORY OF ENGLISH LITERATURE. *See* Whibley, Charles H.

Modern History. *See* Firth, Sir C. H.

CAMBRIDGE UNIVERSITY.

Moeſtissimae ac Laetissimae Cantabrigiensis affeĉtus decedente Carolo II succedente Jacobo II ... Cantabrigial 1684/5. 4to. (Brit. Mus. 161, n. 13.)

CAMDEN, William.

Britain ... written firſt in Latin by William Camden ... Translated newly into English by P. Holland ... Amended and enlarged. London, 1610. Fol. (Brit. Mus. 456, l. 16.)

CAMPBELL, John, Baron Campbell.

The Lives of the Lord Chancellors and Keepers of the Great Seal from the Earlieſt Times to the Reign of King George IV. Fourth edition. London, 1856/7. 10 vols. in 8vo.

CARLELL, Lodowick.

Heraclius Emperour Of the East. A Tragedy ... Englished by Lodowick Carlell, Esq.; London, 1664, 4to. (Brit. Mus. 643, c. 64.)

CHANCELLOR, Edwin Beresford.

The Lives of the Rakes. London, 1924.
   Vol. I. Old Rowley.
   Vol. II. The Reſtoration Rakes: Buckingham, Rocheſter, Sedley, Etherege, Wycherley. 2 vols. in 8vo.

CHARACTER OF A TAVERN, The.

With a brief draught of a Drawer. London, 1675. 4to. (Brit. Mus. 12,352, c. 8.)

CHARACTER OF A TOWN GALLANT, The, exposing the extravagant fopperies of some vain, self conceited pretenders to Gentility and Good Breeding. London, 1675. 4to. (Brit. Mus. 12,352, d. 10(1).)

CHARACTER OF A TOWN MISSE, The. London, 1675. 4to. (Brit. Mus. 12,352, d. 7(1).)
   The Town Misse's Declaration and Apology; or an Answer to the Charaĉter of a Town-Misse. 4to. (Brit. Mus. 12,352, d. 9.)

CHARLANNE, Louis.
L'Influence Française en Angleterre au XVIIe siècle. Paris, 1906. 8vo.

CHASE, Nathaniel Lewis.
The English Heroic Play. New York, 1890. 8vo.

CHESTERFIELD, second Earl of. *See* Stanhope, Phillip.

CHESTERFIELD, fourth Earl of. *See* Stanhope, Philip Dormer.

CIBBER, Colley.
An Apology for the Life of Mr. . . . Second edition, London, 1740. 8vo.

An Apology for the Life of Mr. . . . A new edition with Notes and Supplement by R. W. Lowe. London, 1889. 8vo.

CIBBER, Theophilus.
The lives of the poets of Great Britain and Ireland by Mr. Cibber and other Hands. London, 1753. 5 vols. in 12mo. (Really by Robert Shiels and others.) (Brit. Mus. 1066, f. 22.)

CLARK, Ruth.
Life of Anthony Hamilton. London, 1921. 8vo.

COBBETT, William.
Cobbett's Parliamentary History of England. London, 1808. 8vo. Vols. IV and V.

COKAYNE, G. E. (G. E. C.)
Complete Peerage. London, 1895–98. 7 vols. in 8vo.

The Complete Peerage, edited by the Hon. Vicary Gibbs, Vols. I to V. London, 1910–1921. 5 vols. in 4to.

Complete Baronetage. London, 1900–1909. 5 vols. in 8vo.

COLLECTANEA. Second Series.
Edited by Montague Burrows. Oxford, 1885. 8vo. (Oxford Historical Society's Series.)

COLLINS, Arthur.
The Baronetage of England. London, 1720. 2 vols. in 8vo. (Brit. Mus. 607, f. 8.)

B B

The Peerage of England, the third edition. London, 1715. 2 vols. in 8vo. (Brit. Mus. 607, h. 12.)

COMMENDATORY VERSES on the Author of the Two Arthurs and the Satyr against Wit. London, 1700. Fol. (Brit. Mus. 163, n. 12.)

CONGREVE, William.

The Complete Works. Ed. Montague Summers. London, 1923. 4 vols. in 4to.

CORNEILLE, Pierre.

Théâtre. Prefaces et Notes de M. Mornet. Paris, 1914. 4 vols. in 8vo.

COURTHOPE, William John.

History of English Poetry. London, 1895–1910. 6 vols. in 8vo.

COWPER, Lady.

The Diary of Mary, Lady Cowper, 1714–1720. London, 1864. 4to.

CROWNE, John.

*Henry the Sixth, the First Part with the Murder of Humphrey, Duke of Gloucester. As it is acted at the Duke's Theatre. Written by Mr. Crown, London, 1681. (Brit. Mus. 81, d. 22.) (Dedicated to Sir Charles Sedley.)

CUNNINGHAM, Peter.

The Story of Nell Gwyn and the Sayings of Charles II. Edited by H. B. Wheatley. London, 1892. 8vo. *See also* Wheatley, Henry B.

DALRYMPLE, Sir John.

Memoirs of Great Britain and Ireland. Edinburgh, 1771. 3 vols. in 8vo.

DANGEAU, P. de Courcillon, Marquis de.

Journal. Paris, 1854–60. 19 vols. in 8vo.

DASENT, Arthur Irwen.

The History of St. James's Square and the Foundation of the West End of London. London, 1895. 8vo.

Nell Gwynne, 1650–1687. London, 1924. 8vo.

DAVENANT, Charles.

An Essay upon Ways and Means of Supplying

the War. London, 1695. 8vo. (Brit. Mus. 1028, h. 1(1).)

Discourses on the Publick Revenues of England. London, 1698. 8vo. (Brit. Mus. 1028, f. 1.)

DAVENANT, Sir William.

The Dramatic Works, with prefatory Memoir and Notes. Edinburgh, 1872. 8vo. 5 vols. in 8vo. *See also* Firth, Sir Charles H.

DENNIS, John.

The Comical Gallant . . . To which is added an Account of the Taste in Poetry by J. D. London, 1702. 4to.

Original Letters, familiar, moral and critical. London, 1721. 2 vols. in 8vo.

DISCOMMENDATORY VERSES on those . . . on the author of the Two Arthurs. 1700. fol. (Brit. Mus. 643, l. 24(16).)

DOBREE, Bonamy.

Restoration Comedy. Oxford, 1924. 8vo.

DORSET, sixth Earl of. *See* Sackville, Charles.

DOWNES, John.

Roscius Anglicanus, Or an Historical Review of the Stage . . . from 1660 to 1706, London, 1708. 8vo. (Brit. Mus. 641 f. 15 (1).)

DROLLERY.

Merry Drollery Compleat. Edited with a special introduction by J. W. E[bsworth]. Boston, 1875. 8vo.

Choyce Drollery, Songs and Sonnets. Edited with a special introduction by J. W. E[bsworth]. Boston, 1876. 8vo.

DRYDEN, John.

*The Assignation or Love in a Nunnery . . . (Herringman). London, 1673. 4to. (Brit. Mus. 11,774, d. 1 (1).) (Dedicated to Sir Charles Sedley.)

Of Dramatick Poesie, An Essay. By John Dryden, Esq. London, 1668. 4to. (Brit. Mus. C. 59, ff. 19.)

The Satires of Decimus Juvenalis Translated by Mr. Dryden and Several Other Eminent Hands. London, 1693. Fol. (Brit. Mus. 75, h. 10.)

Mack Flecknoe, or a Satyr upon the true-blew-protestant poet T.S. London, 1682. 4to. (Brit. Mus. C. 71, e. 8.)

The Works of John Dryden edited by Sir Walter Scott, with a Life of the Author, 1821. Edinburgh and London. 18 vols. in 8vo.

The Poetical Works, ed. G. R. Noyes. Cambridge, U.S.A., 1909. 8vo.

The Critical and Miscellaneous Works of John Dryden. With an ... Account of the Life and Writings of the Author ... by Edmond Malone, Esq. London, 1800. 3 vols. in 8vo.

Essays selected and edited by W. P. Ker. Oxford, 1900. 2 vols. in 8vo.

See also Saintsbury, George, and Van Doren, Mark.

D'URFEY, Thomas.

*The Intrigues at Versailles: or a Jilt in all Humours. London, 1697. 4to. (Dedicated to Sir Charles Sedley and his son.) (Brit. Mus. 644, h. 24.)

EACHARD, Laurence.

*Plautus's Comedies, Amphitryon, Epidicus, and Rudens, made English: ... by L. E. London, 1694. 8vo. (Dedicated to Sir Charles Sedley.) (Brit. Mus. 11,707, bbb. 8.)

EBSWORTH, J. *See* Drollery.

ELLIS CORRESPONDENCE. The Letters written during the Years 1686, 1687, 1688, addressed to J. Ellis, Esq. Edited by the Hon. G. A. E. London, 1829. 8vo. (Brit. Mus. 1086, g. 23.)

ETHEREGE, Sir George.

The Man of Mode, or Sr Fopling Flutter, A Comedy ... London, 1676. 4to. (Brit. Mus. 644, h. 35.)

The Works of Sir *George Etherege*, containing his Plays and Poems. London, 1704. 8vo.

The Works of Sir George Etherege. Plays and Poems. Edited, with critical notes, by A. W. Verity. London, 1888. 8vo.

EVELYN, John.

A Character of England. As it was lately presented in a Letter to a Noble Man of France. By J. E[velyn]. London, 1659. 12mo. (Brit. Mus. 292, a. 43.)

The Diary. Edited with an Introduction by Austin Dobson. London, 1906. 3 vols. in 8vo.

FAITHORNE, W. *See* Newcourt and Faithorne.

FEA, Allan.

James II and his Wives. Methuen: London, 1908. 8vo. *See also* Hamilton, Anthony.

FELL-SMITH, Charlotte.

Mary Rich, Countess of Warwick. London, 1901.

FELTON, Henry.

A Dissertation on reading the Classics and forming a just style. London, 1713. (Brit. Mus. 1088, d. 27.)

FENTON, Elijah.

Poems on Several Occasions. London, 1717. 8vo. (Brit. Mus. 993, k. 8.)

FIRTH, Sir Charles H.

Cambridge History of English Literature, Vol. V. ch. v.: "The Stewart Restoration."

English Historical Review, Vol. XVIII, p. 319: "Some Observations concerning the People of England." Printed from Sir William Davenant's MS.

FORGUES, E. D.

John Wilmot, Comte de Rochester: *Revue des Deux Mondes*, August, September, 1857.

FOSTER, Joseph.

Alumni Oxonienses, Early series. The Members of the University of Oxford, 1500–1714. London, 1891. 4 vols. in 4to.

GARDINER, Rev. R. B.
> The Regiſters of Wadham College, 1613–1719.
> London, 1889. 8vo.

GENEST, Rev. John.
> Some Account of the English Stage, etc. London,
> 1832. 10 vols. in 8vo.

GENTLEMAN'S JOURNAL, The; or The Monthly Mis-
> cellany. London, 1691/2–1694. (Brit. Mus.
> PP. 5255 (1) and (2).)

GENTLEMAN'S MAGAZINE, The; or Monthly Intelli-
> gence. (See references in footnotes.)

GILDON, Charles: edited by.
> A New Miscellany of Original Poems on Several
> Occasions. London, 1701. 8vo. (Brit. Mus. 1077,
> l. 12.)

GOODWIN, Gordon.
> Letter in Notes and Queries. S. IX. I, 32. *See
> also* Hamilton, Anthony.

GOSSE, Sir Edmund.
> Seventeenth-Century Studies. Third edition.
> London, 1897. 8vo.

GRANGER, Rev. James.
> A Biographical Hiſtory of England. London,
> 1769–74. 3 vols. in 8vo. Edited M. Noble.
> London, 1806. 3 vols. in 8vo.

GREY, Hon. Anchitell.
> Debates of the House of Commons from 1667
> to 1694, colleĉted by A. G. London, 1769. 10
> vols. in 8vo.

HALIFAX, firſt Marquis and firſt Earl of. *See* Savile,
> George, and Montague, Charles.

HAMILTON, Anthony.
> Memoirs du Chevalier De Grammont ... avec
> introduĉtion, commentaire, etc. par M. G.
> Brunet. Paris, 1859. 8vo.
>> Memoirs of Count Gramont, ed. Gordon
> Goodwin. London, 1903. 2 vols. in 8vo.
>> Memoirs of De Gramont, ed. Allan Fea.
> London, 1906. 8vo.

HASLEWOOD, Joseph. *See* Jacob, Giles.

HASTED, Edward.
> The History and Topographical Survey of Kent.
> ... Canterbury, 1778. 4 vols. in fol.

HATTON, Correspondence of the Family of ... A.D.
> 1601–1704. Printed for the Camden Society,
> Westminster, 1878. 2 vols. in 4to.

HISTORICAL MANUSCRIPTS, Royal Commission on,
> Reports of. (See references in footnotes.)

HOLLAND, Philemon. *See* Camden, William.

HOWARD, Hon. James.
> All mistaken or the Mad Couple ... A Comedy.
> London, 1672. 4to. (Brit. Mus. 11,774, g. 28.)

HUNT, James Henry Leigh.
> The Town: Its Memorable Characters and
> Events. London, 1906. 8vo.

HYDE, Edward, first Earl of Clarendon.
> The Life of, etc. . . . Written by himself.
> Oxford. 1857. 3 vols. in 8vo.
> History of the Great Rebellion. Oxford, 1705.
> 7 vols. in 8vo.

HYDE, Henry, second Earl of Clarendon.
> Correspondence of. Ed. S. W. Singer. London,
> 1828. 2 vols. in 4to.

JACOB, Giles.
> The Poetical Register or the Lives and Characters
> of the English Dramatick Poets. London, 1719.
> 3 vols. in 8vo. (Brit. Mus. C. 45, d. This copy
> contains the important MS. notes of Joseph
> Haslewood.)

JESSE, John Heneage.
> Memoirs of the Court of England during the
> Reign of Stuarts, including the Protectorate.
> New edition, revised, in three volumes. London,
> 1855. 3 vols. in 8vo.

JOHNSON, Samuel.
> The Works of ... a new edition with an Essay
> on his Life and Genius by Arthur Murphy.
> London, 1792. 12 vols. in 8vo.

The Lives of the English Poets, ed. G. B.
Hill. Oxford. 1905. 3 vols. in 8vo.

JOURNALS OF THE HOUSE OF COMMONS.

JOURNALS OF THE HOUSE OF LORDS.

JOYNER, Sir William.

*The Roman Empress, A Tragedy. London, 1671.
4to. (Dedicated to Sir Charles Sedley.) (Brit.
Mus. 644, h. 43.)

KEMP, Hobart.

A Collection of Poems ... by several Persons
never before in print. London, 1672. 8vo. (Containing earliest versions of many of Sedley's best
lyrics.) (Brit. Mus. c. 57, k. 20.)

KILLIGREW, Henry.

The Conspiracy, a tragedy. London, 1638. 4to.
(Brit. Mus. 644, c. 57.)

Pallantus and Eudora, a Tragoedie. London,
1653. 4to. (Brit. Mus. 162, i. 37.)

KING, Dr. William.

The Art of Cookery. London, 1708. fol. (Brit.
Mus. 11,633. h. 7.)

KRUTCH, Joseph Wood.

Comedy and Conscience after the Restoration.
New York, 1924. 8vo.

LANGBAINE, Gerard.

An Account of the English Dramatic Poets.
Oxford, 1691. 8vo. (Brit. Mus. C. 28, g. 1.
This copy contains the important MS. notes of
W. Oldys.)

LANGHORNE, John.

The Effusions of Friendship and Fancy; in
several letters. 1763. 8vo. Second edition, 1766.
8vo.

LAWRENCE, W. J.

The Elizabethan Playhouse and other Studies.
Stratford on Avon, 1912. 2 vols. in 8vo.

LE NEVE, Peter.

Catalogue of Knights (Harl. Soc.). 8vo. 1869.

LINCOLN'S INN, Records of. 1897. 3 vols. in 8vo.

LISSNER, Max.
> Sir Charles Sedley's Leben und Werke. Halle,
> 1905. 8vo.

LL.D.
> "Memoirs of Sir Charles Sedley," *London Maga-*
> *zine*, September 1822.

LODGE, Sir Richard.
> The History of England from the Restoration
> to the Death of William III, 1660–1702. London.
> 1905. 8vo.

LONGE, Julia C.
> Martha Giffard, her Life and Correspondence
> (1664–1722). London, 1911. 8vo.

LONGUEVILLE, Thomas.
> Rochester and other Literary Rakes of the
> Restoration. London, 1902. 8vo.

*LOVE WITHOUT INTEREST OR THE MAN TOO HARD
> FOR THE MASTER. A Comedy . . . Printed for
> Arthur Bettesworth. . . . London, 1699. 4to.
> (Collection of Mr. G. Thorn Drury.) (Dedicated
> to Sir Charles Sedley and others.)

LOVELACE, Richard.
> The Poems of Richard Lovelace. Edited by
> C. H. Wilkinson. Oxford, 1925. (2 vols. in 8vo.)

LOWE, Robert W.
> Thomas Betterton. London, 1891. 8vo.
> Bibliographical Account of English Theatrical
> Literature. London, 1888. 8vo.

LUTTRELL, Narcissus.
> A Brief Historical Relation of State Affairs from
> September 1678 to April 1711. Oxford, 1857.
> 6 vols. in 8vo.

LYSONS, Rev. Daniel.
> An Historical Account of those Parishes . . .
> which are not described in the Environs of
> London. London, 1800. 4to.

MACAULAY, Lord.
> History of England. Ed. C. H. Firth (with
> Illustrations). London, 1913–15. 6 vols. in 8vo.

MALLET, Sir Charles Edward.
> A History of the University of Oxford. . . .
> London, 1924. 2 vols. in 8vo.

MANNINGHAM, John.
> The Diary of. Printed for the Camden Society,
> Westminster, 1868. 4to.

MARVELL, Andrew.
> Poems and Satires. Ed. G. A. Aitken (The Muses
> Library). London, 1891. 2 vols. in 8vo.
>
> (?) A Seasonable Argument to Persuade All
> the Grand Juries of England to Petition for a
> New Parliament or a List of the Principal
> Labourers in the Great Design of Popery or
> Arbitrary Power. Amsterdam, 1677. 4to (Brit.
> Mus. 100, g. 75.)
> *See also* Birrell, Augustine.

MASSON, David.
> The Life of John Milton. Cambridge, 1859–80.
> (Index, 1894.) 6 vols. in 8vo.

MIDDLE TEMPLE RECORDS.
> Ed. C. H. Hopwood, K.C. London, 1905. 3 vols.
> in 8vo.

MILES, Dudley Howe.
> The Influence of Molière on Restoration Comedy.
> New York, 1910. 8vo.

MISSON, Henry de Valbourg.
> Memoires et Observation Faites par Un Voya-
> geur en Angleterre (H. M. de V., *i.e.* Henry
> Misson de Valbourg). 1698. 8vo. (Brit. Mus.
> 980, b. 3.)

MOLIÈRE, Jean Baptiste Poquelin de.
> Les Oeuvres de . . . accompagnées d'une vie de
> Molière . . . par Anatole France. Paris, 1876–
> 1906. 7 vols. in 8vo.

MONTAGUE, Charles, first Earl of Halifax.
> The Works and Life of the Rt. Honourable
> Charles, late Earl of Halifax. London, 1715. 8vo.

MONTAGUE SUMMERS, The Rev. *See* Behn, Aphra;
> Congreve, William; Wycherley, William.

MORANT, P.
History of Essex, London, 1768. Fol.
MUSGRAVE, Sir William, Bart.
Obituary. (Harl. Soc.) London, 1899–1901. 6 vols. in 8vo.
N. W.
The Refin'd Courtier, or a Correction of several Indecencies crept into Civil Conversation. London, 1679. 12mo. (Brit. Mus. G. 530.)
NEWCOURT and FAITHORNE.
An Exact Delineation of the Cities of London and Westminster by Richard Newcourt, W. Faithorne sculpsit, 1658, engraved from the Original by G. Larman. London, 1857. (Brit. Mus. Maps 348 (149).)
NEWDIGATE NEWDEGATE, Lady A. E.
Cavalier and Puritan in the Days of the Stuarts, compiled from the private papers and diary of Sir Richard Newdigate, second Baronet. London, 1901. 8vo.
NICOLL, Allardyce.
Restoration Drama. Cambridge, 1923. 8vo.
OLDHAM, John.
The Works of Mr. . . . Sixth edition. London, 1703. 8vo. (Brit. Mus. 1076, m. 8.)
The Compositions in Verse and Prose, to which are added Memoirs of his life. London, 1770. 2 vols. in 8vo. (Brit. Mus. 11,609, a. 26–28.)
OLDYS, William. *See* Langbaine, Gerard.
OSBORNE, Dorothy, afterwards Lady Temple.
Letters from . . . to Sir William Temple. Ed. E. A. Parry (Everyman's Library). London, 1906. 8vo.
OWEN, John.
Epigrammatum Joannis Owen . . . Editio Secunda Londini, 1618. 8vo. (Brit. Mus. 11,048, a. 46 (1).)
J. Owen's Latine Epigrams Englished by

Harvey. London, 1677. 8vo. (Brit. Mus. 1213, b. 36.)

PALAPRAT, Jean.

See Brueys, D. A. de.

PALMER, John.

The Comedy of Manners. London, 1913. 8vo.

PARRY, E. A.

What the Judge Thought. London, 1922. 8vo.

PAUL, Harry Gilbert.

John Dennis, his Life and Criticism. New York. 1911. 8vo.

PEACHAM, Henry.

The Compleat Gentleman, third impression much enlarged. London, 1661. 4to. (Brit. Mus. E. 1088 (1).)

Peacham's Compleat Gentleman, 1634, with an introduction by G. S. Gordon. Oxford, 1906. 8vo.

PEARSON, Karl.

The Life and Letters of Sir Francis Galton, Vol. I. Cambridge, 1914. 4to.

PEPYS, Samuel.

The Diary of . . . with Lord Braybrooke's Notes. Ed. Henry B. Wheatley. London, 1893–9. With Index and Pepysiana. 8 vols. in 8vo.

PERRY, H. Ten Eyck.

The First Duchess of Newcastle. Boston, 1918. 8vo.

PERWICH, William.

The Despatches of . . . English Agent in Paris, 1669. Edited for the Royal Historical Society, London, 1903. 4to.

PHILIPOT, S. and T.

Villare Cantianum or Kent Surveyed. London, 1659. Fol. (Brit. Mus. 678, i. 21.)

PHILIPS, Katharine.

Pompey a Tragedy. 1663. 4to. (Brit. Mus. 11,737, d. 8.)

Poems by the incomparable Mrs. K[atharine] P[hillips]. 1664. 4to.

Letters from Orinda to Poliarchus. 1705, 8vo.
(Brit. Mus. 1086, b. 9.)

PLÜCKHAHN, Edmund.

Die Bearbeitung ausländischer Stoffe in englischen Drama am Ende des 17 Jahrhunderts
dargelegt an Sir Charles Sedley's The Mulberry
Garden und Bellamira or the Mistress. Hamburg,
1904. 8vo.

POEMS. The Fourth (and Last) Collection of Poems,
Satyrs, Songs, &c. . . . London, Printed *Anno
Dom.* 1689. 4to (Brit. Mus. 1077, h. 32.)

POEMS ON AFFAIRS OF STATE, from the Time of Oliver
Cromwell to the abdication of K. James the
Second. London, 1697. 2 vols. in 8vo. (Brit.
Mus. 11,603, bbb. 25, 6.)

POEMS ON AFFAIRS OF STATE, from Oliver Cromwell
to this Present Day by the Greatest Wits of
the Age. 1698. 8vo.

POEMS ON AFFAIRS OF STATE, from 1640 to this present
Year 1704. Written by the Greatest Wits of the
Age. Vol. III. Printed in the Year 1704. 8vo.

POMPEY THE GREAT, A Tragedy . . . Translated out of
the French by Certain Persons of Honour.
London, 1664. 4to. (Brit. Mus. 643, d. 50.)
("La Mort de Pompée," translated from the
French of P. Corneille by Waller, Sedley,
Godolphin, Filmer and Buckhurst; see pp.
82, 83.)

POPE, Alexander.

The Works of. Ed. W. Elwin and W. J. Courthope. London, 1871–89. 10 vols. in 8vo.

POPE, Walter.

The Old Man's Wish. Broadside ?1685. (Brit.
Mus. Rox. ii. 386.)
The Life of Seth, Lord Bishop of Salisbury.
London, 1697. (Brit. Mus. 1124, b. 10 (1).)

PRIDEAUX, Lieut.-Col. W. F.

Letters in *Notes and Queries,* Ser. 7, X. 286, 505;
Ser. 8, III. 388, XII. 485; Ser. 9, VIII. 157.

PRIOR, Matthew.

The Writings of. Ed. A. R. Waller. Cambridge, 1905–7. 2 vols. in 8vo. (Cambridge English Classics.)

RALEIGH, Sir Walter.

Milton. London, 1900. 8vo. *See also* Savile, Sir George.

REMARQUES upon the late Printed Speech under the name of Sir Charles Sidley. London, 1691. (Brit. Mus. 1876, f. 119 (9).)

RERESBY, Sir John.

The Memoirs and Travels of. Ed. A. Ivatt. London, 1904. 8vo.

RICHARDSON, Jonathan.

Explanatory Notes and Remarks on Milton's Paradise Loſt, by J. Richardson, Father and Son. With the Life of the Author and a Discourse on the Poem. By J. R. Sen. London. MDCCXXXIV. 8vo. (Copy with author's MS. annotations in the London Library.)

ROCHESTER, second Earl of. *See* Wilmot, John.

SACKVILLE, Charles, Lord Buckhurſt, afterwards fifth Earl of Dorset and Middlesex.

The Works of the Earl of Dorset in the Works of the moſt Celebrated Minor Poets. 1749. 2 vols. in 8vo. (Brit. Mus. 238, c. 1.)

SACKVILLE-WEST, Hon. Victoria Mary.

Knole and the Sackvilles. London, 1922. 8vo.

SAINTSBURY, George.

Dryden. London, 1902. (English Men of Letters Series.) 8vo.

SATYR TO HIS MUSE. By the Author of Absalom & Achitophel. London. Printed for T. W. 1682.

SAVILE, Sir George, Marquess of Halifax.

The Complete Works of. Ed. with an Introduction by W. Raleigh. Oxford, 1912. 8vo.

SAVILE CORRESPONDENCE.

Letters to and from Henry Savile, etc., 1661–

1689. Ed. Camden Society, Weſtminſter, 1858.
4to.

SEDLEY, Sir Charles.

The Mulberry Garden, a Comedy. London,
1668. 4to. (Brit. Mus. 841, c. 1.) (Reprinted
1675 and 1688; also included in Collected Works
of 1722, 1776 and 1778.)

Antony and Cleopatra, a Tragedy. London,
1677. 4to. (Reprinted in 1690 and 1696 and in
Collected Works of 1722, 1776 and 1778.)
(Brit. Mus. 11,778, g. 39.)

Bellamira, or the Miſtress. A Comedy. London,
1687. 4to. (Reprinted in Collected Works of
1772, 1776 and 1778.) (Brit. Mus. 644, h. 34.)

Reflections upon our late and present proceedings . . . in England. London, 1689. 4to.
(Brit. Mus. T. 1675 (15).) (Reprinted, Edinburgh, 1689. 4to.) (Brit. Mus. 8138, bb. 20.)

The Speech of Sir Charles Sidley in the
House of Commons. London, 1691. Broadside.

The Miscellaneous Works. Published from
the Original Manuscripts by Capt. Ayloffe.
London, 1702. 8vo. (Not in Brit. Mus.)

The Happy Pair: or a Poem on Matrimony.
London, 1702. Fol. (Brit. Mus. 1347, m. 30.)

The Poetical Works . . . With *Large Additions
never before made* Publick. Published from the
Original MS. by Capt. Ayloffe. With a New
Miscellany of Poems. (etc.). London, 1707. 8vo.
(Brit. Mus. 11,623, e. 11.)

The Poetical Works . . . with *Large Additions*
never before made Publick. To which is prefix'd
[*sic*] The Earl of Rocheſter's Mountebank
Speech on Tower Hill . . . The Second Edition.
London, 1710. 8vo. (Not in Brit. Mus.)

The Works . . . in Two Volumes containing
his Poems, Plays, &c. with Memoirs of the
Author's Life by an Eminent Hand. London,
1722. 2 vols. in 12 mo. (Brit. Mus. 644, a. 33.)

The Works ... In Prose and Verse ... With
Memoirs of the Author's Life, Written by an
Eminent Hand. London, 1776. 2 vols. in 8vo.
(A reprint with slight variations of the fore-
going.) (Brit. Mus. 12,268 aaaa. 6.)

The Works ... In Prose and Verse ... the
greatest Part never Printed before ... With
Memoirs of the Author's Life, Written by an
Eminent Hand. London, 1778. 2 vols. in 8vo.
(Not in Brit. Mus.)

See also Commendatory Verses, Tonson's
Miscellany, Kemp's Collection, and Pompey the
Great.

SHADWELL, Thomas.

Epsom Wells, A Comedy. London. 1673. 4to.
(Prologue by Sir C[harles] S[edley].) (Brit. Mus.
644, i. 24.)

*A True Widow, A Comedy. London, 1679.
(Brit. Mus. 644, i. 34.) (Dedicated to Sir
Charles Sedley.)

*The Tenth Satyr of Juvenal, Latin and
English. London, 1687. 4to. (Brit. Mus.
11,388, cc. 8.) (Dedicated to Sir Charles
Sedley.)

The Dramatic Works of. London, 1720. 4
vols. in 8vo. (Brit. Mus. 644, a. 35-8.)

SHEFFIELD, John, Earl of Malgrave, afterwards
Marquis of Normanby and Duke of Buckinghamshire.

The Works of. London, 1723. 2 vols. in 4to.
(Brit. Mus. 641, l. 11.)

SHIELS, Robert. *See* Cibber, Theophilus.

SITWELL, Sir George.

The First Whig, An Account of the Parliamentary Career of William Sacheverell. Scarborough, 1894. (Privately Printed.) 8vo.

SMYTH, Richard.

The Obituary of ... being a catalogue of such

persons as he knew in their life. Westminster, 1849. 4to. (Camden Society.)

SORBIÈRE, Samuel de.

Relation d'un Voyage en Angleterre. Paris, 1664. (Bibl. Nat. N. 30.)

Sorberiana ou bons mots . . . de M. Sorbière. Paris, 1691. 12mo. (Brit. Mus. 1088, a. 30.)

SPENCE, Joseph.

Observations, Anecdotes, and Characters of Books and Men. Ed. E. Malone. London, 1820. 8vo.

STANHOPE, Phillip, second Earl of Chesterfield.

The Letters of. London, 1829. 8vo.

STANHOPE, Philip Dormer, fourth Earl of Chesterfield.

Letters of . . . to his Son. Ed. C. Strachey, London, 1901. 2 vols. in 8vo.

STEPHENS, Anthony.

Miscellany Poems and Translations by Oxford Hands . . . Printed for Anthony Stephens. Oxford, 1685. 8vo. (See p. 339.) (Brit. Mus. 11,641, bbb. 38.)

SUTTON, Rev. C. N.

Historical Notes of Withyham, Hartfield and Ashdown Forest, together with the History of the Sackville Family. Tunbridge Wells, 1902. 8vo.

TATHAM, John.

*The Distracted State; a Tragedy. London, 1651. 4to. (Brit. Mus. 644, c. 73.) (Dedicated to Sir William Sedley.)

The Dramatic Works. Edinburgh, 1872. 8vo.

TERENTIUS AFER, P.

Terence. With an English translation by John Sergeaunt. 1912. (The Loeb Classical Library.) 8vo.

THOROTON, Robert.

History of Nottinghamshire, Republished with Large Additions by John Throsby, Nottingham, 1790. 3 vols. in 4to. (Brit. Mus. 192, b. 15–17.)

C C

TONSON, Jacob.
> Miscellany Poems Containing a New Trans-
> lation of Virgill's Eclogues, Ovid's Love Elegies
> . . . Printed for Jacob Tonson. London, 1684.
> 8vo. (Contains three elegies translated by Sedley
> from Ovid's "Amores.") (Brit. Mus. 995,
> b. 23.)

TREBY, Sir George.
> The Second Part of the Collection of Letters
> relating to the Horrid Popish Plot. London, 1681.
> Fol. (Brit. Mus. 8122, i. 2/12.)

TREVELYAN, G. M.
> England under the Stewarts. London, 1904. 8vo.

VAN DOREN, Mark.
> John Dryden. New York, 1920. 8vo.

VILLIERS, George, second Duke of Buckingham.
> The Miscellaneous Works; written by . . . col-
> lected in one Volume from the Original Papers.
> London, 1704. 8vo.

WALLER, Edmund.
> Poems, etc., the Sixth Edition. London, 1693.
> (2nd Part with title-page dated 1690.) 8vo. (Brit.
> Mus. 11,623, b. 33.)
> Poems. Ed. G. Thorn Drury (The Muses
> Library). 1891. 8vo.

WARD, Sir A. W.
> A History of English Dramatic Literature to the
> Death of Queen Anne. London, 1899. 3 vols.
> in 8vo.

WELDON, Sir Anthony.
> *The Court and Character of King James. London,
> 1651. Reprinted Edinburgh, 1811. 8vo. (Brit.
> Mus. 2394, d. 13.) (Dedicated to Lady Elizabeth
> Sedley of Southfleet.)

WHEATLEY, Henry B.
> London, Past and Present. Based upon the Hand-
> book of London by the late Peter Cunningham.
> London, 1891. 3 vols. in 8vo.

WHIBLEY, Charles H.
> In the Cambridge History of English Literature, Vol. VIII, chap. viii.: "The Court Poets."

WHIPPING TOM; the Second Part of, or a Road for a Proud Lady. London, 1722. 8vo. (Collection of Mr. G. Thorn Drury.)

WILLIAMS, H. Noel.
> Five Fair Sisters. London, 1906. 8vo.

WILMOT, John, second Earl of Rochester.
> Poems on several occasions: by the E. of R. Antwerpen. n. d. (?1680). 8vo. (Dyce Collection, South Kensington Museum, 8281.)
>
> Poems on several occasions written by a late Person of Honour. London, 1685. 12mo. (Brit. Mus. 11,623, a. 37.)
>
> Poems on Several Occasions, with Valentinian, A Tragedy. London, 1705. 8vo.
>
> Familiar Letters. London, 1697. 8vo. (Brit. Mus. 11,632, a. 43.)
>
> The Works of John, Earl of Rochester, containing Poems, letters, etc. London, 1714. (Brit. Mus. 11,632, a. 43.)

WILSON, John.
> The Cheats, A Comedy Written in the Year MDCLXII. London, 1664. 4to. (Brit. Mus. Huth, 159.)

WOLSELEY, Viscount.
> The Life of John Churchill, Duke of Marlborough, London, 1894. 2 vols. in 8vo.

WOOD, Anthony à.
> Athenae Oxonienses. Ed. P. Bliss. London, 1813–20. 4 vols. in fol.
>
> Life and Times, collected from his Diaries by A. Clarke. Oxford, 1891. 5 vols. in 8vo. (Oxford Historical Society's Series.)

WYCHERLEY, William.
> Plays. Ed. W. C. Ward. London and New York, 1903. (Mermaid Series.)

The Complete Works. Ed. Montague Summers. London, 1924. 4 vols. in 4to.

ZIMMERMAN, B.

Carmel in England, A History of the English Mission of the Discalced Carmelites, 1615–1849. London, 1899. 8vo.

INDEX

(I owe this Index to the skill and industry of my wife.)

389